Genders and Sexualities in History

Series Editors: John H. Arnold, Joanna Bourke and Sean Brady

Palgrave Macmillan's series, Genders and Sexualities in History, aims to accommodate and foster new approaches to historical research in the fields of genders and sexualities. The series promotes world-class scholarship that concentrates upon the interconnected themes of genders, sexualities, religions/religiosity, civil society, class formations, politics and war.

Historical studies of gender and sexuality have often been treated as disconnected fields, while in recent years historical analyses in these two areas have synthesised, creating new departures in historiography. By linking genders and sexualities with questions of religion, civil society, politics and the contexts of war and conflict, this series will reflect recent developments in scholarship, moving away from the previously dominant and narrow histories of science, scientific thought, and legal processes. The result brings together scholarship from contemporary, modern, early modern, medieval, classical and non-Western history to provide a diachronic forum for scholarship that incorporates new approaches to genders and sexualities in history

Unemployment, Welfare, and Masculine Citizenship: 'So Much Honest Poverty' in Britain, 1870–1930 is a groundbreaking study of the politics of unemployment, welfare and masculinities in late nineteenth and early twentieth century Britain. This fascinating and highly original book explores how concepts of 'honest poverty' developed in the contexts of chronic and mass unemployment, and the ways in which these were applied to men. Through the lens of 'honest poverty', Marjorie Levine-Clark examines political and social expectations of working-class masculine status, with its emphases upon the work imperative, independence, self-sufficiency, and support of families. Men who failed or refused to uphold their responsibilities shaped the boundaries of what it meant to be a citizen in Britain. The 'honest poverty' work-welfare system, in which men remained 'men' in spite of dependence upon welfare, has shaped the rhetoric of welfare in Britain ever since. In common with all volumes in the Genders and Sexualities in History series, *Unemployment, Welfare, and Masculine Citizenship* presents a multifaceted and meticulously researched scholarly study, and is a sophisticated contribution to our understanding of the past.

Titles include:

John H. Arnold and Sean Brady (*editors*)
WHAT IS MASCULINITY?
Historical Dynamics from Antiquity to the Contemporary World

Heike Bauer and Matthew Cook (*editors*)
QUEER 1950s

Cordelia Beattie and Kirsten A. Fenton (*editors*)
INTERSECTIONS OF GENDER, RELIGION AND ETHNICITY IN THE MIDDLE AGES

Valeria Babini, Chiara Beccalossi and Lucy Riall (*editors*)
ITALIAN SEXUALITIES UNCOVERED, 1789–1914

Chiara Beccalossi
FEMALE SEXUAL INVERSION
Same-Sex Desires in Italian and British Sexology, c. 1870–1920

Roberto Bizzocchi
A LADY'S MAN
The Cicisbei, Private Morals and National Identity in Italy

Raphaëlle Branche and Fabrice Virgili (*editors*)
RAPE IN WARTIME

Matt Cook
QUEER DOMESTICITIES
Homosexuality and Home Life in Twentieth-Century London

Peter Cryle and Alison Moore
FRIGIDITY
An Intellectual History

Lucy Delap and Sue Morgan
MEN, MASCULINITIES AND RELIGIOUS CHANGE IN TWENTIETH CENTURY BRITAIN

Jennifer V. Evans
LIFE AMONG THE RUINS
Cityscape and Sexuality in Cold War Berlin

Kate Fisher and Sarah Toulalan (editors)
BODIES, SEX AND DESIRE FROM THE RENAISSANCE TO THE PRESENT

Christopher E. Forth and Elinor Accampo (editors)
CONFRONTING MODERNITY IN FIN-DE-SIÈCLE FRANCE
Bodies, Minds and Gender

Rebecca Fraser
GENDER, RACE AND FAMILY IN NINETEENTH CENTURY AMERICA
From Northern Woman to Plantation Mistress

Alana Harris and Timothy Jones (editors)
LOVE AND ROMANCE IN BRITAIN, 1918–1970

Dagmar Herzog (editor)
BRUTALITY AND DESIRE
War and Sexuality in Europe's Twentieth Century

Josephine Hoegaerts
MASCULINITY AND NATIONHOOD, 1830–1910
Constructions of Identity and Citizenship in Belgium

Robert Hogg
MEN AND MANLINESS ON THE FRONTIER
Queensland and British Columbia in the Mid-Nineteenth Century

Julia Laite
COMMON PROSTITUTES AND ORDINARY CITIZENS
Commercial Sex in London, 1885–1960

Marjorie Levine-Clark
UNEMPLOYMENT, WELFARE, AND MASCULINE CITIZENSHIP
"So Much Honest Poverty" in Britain, 1870–1930

Andrea Mansker
SEX, HONOR AND CITIZENSHIP IN EARLY THIRD REPUBLIC FRANCE

Jessica Meyer
MEN OF WAR
Masculinity and the First World War in Britain

Meredith Nash
MAKING 'POSTMODERN' MOTHERS
Pregnant Embodiment, Baby Bumps and Body Image

Jennifer D. Thibodeaux (editor)
NEGOTIATING CLERICAL IDENTITIES
Priests, Monks and Masculinity in the Middle Ages

Kristin Fjelde Tjelle
MISSIONARY MASCULINITY, 1870–1930
The Norwegian Missionaries in South-East Africa

Hester Vaizey
SURVIVING HITLER'S WAR
Family Life in Germany, 1939–48

Clayton J. Whisnant
MALE HOMOSEXUALITY IN WEST GERMANY
Between Persecution and Freedom, 1945–69

Tim Reinke-Williams
WOMEN, WORK AND SOCIABILITY IN EARLY MODERN LONDON

Midori Yamaguchi
DAUGHTERS OF THE ANGLICAN CLERGY
Religion, Gender and Identity in Victorian England

Forthcoming titles:

Melissa Hollander
SEX IN TWO CITIES
The Negotiation of Sexual Relationships in Early Modern England and Scotland

---

Genders and Sexualities in History Series
Series Standing Order 978–0–230–55185–5 Hardback
978–0–230–55186–2 Paperback
(*outside North America only*)

You can receive future titles in this series as they are published by placing a standing order.
Please contact your bookseller or, in case of difficulty, write to us at the address below with
your name and address, the title of the series and the ISBN quoted above.

Customer Services Department, Macmillan Distribution Ltd, Houndmills, Basingstoke,
Hampshire RG21 6XS, England

Unemployment, Welfare, and Masculine Citizenship

"So Much Honest Poverty" in Britain, 1870–1930

Marjorie Levine-Clark
University of Colorado Denver, USA

palgrave
macmillan

First published 2015 by
PALGRAVE MACMILLAN

Palgrave Macmillan in the UK is an imprint of Macmillan Publishers Limited, registered in England, company number 785998, of Houndsmills, Basingstoke, Hampshire, RG21 6XS

Palgrave Macmillan in the US is a division of St Martin's Press LLC, 175 Fifth Avenue, New York, NY 10010.

Palgrave is the global academic imprint of the above companies and has companies and representatives throughout the world.

Palgrave® and Macmillan® are registered trademarks in the United States, the United Kingdom, Europe and other countries.

ISBN 978–1–137–39320–3

This book is printed on paper suitable for recycling and made from fully managed and sustained forest sources. Logging, pulping and manufacturing processes are expected to conform to the environmental regulations of the country of origin.

A catalogue record for this book is available from the British Library.

A catalog record for this book is available from the Library of Congress.

Typeset by MPS Limited, Chennai, India.

*For my mom, Ann Friedman, and
my dad, Robert Levine. Thanks.*

Contents

List of Figures, Tables, and Maps

Figures

Tables

Maps

Preface

When I began the research for this book, I was not living in a moment when unemployment was a "problem." Political and public attention were not focused on people without jobs, the provision of state benefits, or poverty in general, even if these issues were pressing for those experiencing them. As historians well know, a lot can change in a decade. The global financial crisis beginning in 2007 lingered through the writing of this book and contributed to a significant "problem of unemployment," although a problem fundamentally different from the one I discuss here. Today, "jobseekers" include young people who have never secured stable employment, middle-aged men and women powerless to compete with new technologies, and middle-class professionals unable to reenter the labor force after being laid off in the recession; in the late nineteenth and early twentieth centuries, concerns about joblessness focused almost exclusively on working-class men. While I wrote about the first uses of the term "unemployment" in the late nineteenth century, I listened to a constant media loop playing sound-bites about the long-term unemployed. Both Britain and the United States engaged in debates about the extension of unemployment benefits in which strong voices insisted that unemployed people themselves were responsible for being out of work. Hearing these debates develop as I read about government approaches to unemployment from a century ago was both fascinating and discouraging.

I had for the first time printed out a complete draft of this book manuscript as Barack Obama's second presidential inauguration approached. The U.S. President was battling an aggressive attack on government programs directed toward helping the poor and unemployed. He appealed to a communitarian vision of the U.S. founding to promote an understanding of a state that actively supports its citizens through social and economic crises:

> We, the people, still believe that every citizen deserves a basic measure of security and dignity. . . . . We recognize that no matter how responsibly we live our lives, any one of us, at any time, may face a job loss, or a sudden illness, or a home swept away in a terrible storm. The commitments we make to each other – through Medicare, and Medicaid, and Social Security – these things do not sap our initiative;

they strengthen us. They do not make us a nation of takers; they free us to take the risks that make this country great.[1]

President Obama gave this address on Martin Luther King, Jr. Day in 2013. He emphasized the fragility of our lives, the uncertainty surrounding job stability and good health, which can lead even the most "responsible" to need welfare assistance. The President used the language of the American dream to challenge politicians and the public to uphold, not cast off, a government that works to bolster its citizens' economic, political, social, and civic possibilities.

Yet even while articulating the promise of welfare to enhance citizenship, President Obama's stance was defensive: he was responding to a prevalent discourse that blamed poverty on poor people, that labeled those who claimed state assistance as undeserving. This discourse was current in Britain as well as the United States. At the Conservative Conference in October 2013, Iain Duncan Smith, the British Secretary of State for Work and Pensions, very clearly expressed the position that people without work were moral failures. Referring to Britain's "something-for-nothing culture," Duncan Smith maintained that those applying for benefit should have to prove an active search for work, preferably "under supervision," emphasizing the suspicion that those without jobs "cheat the system."[2] In both Britain and the United States, increasing cuts to benefits demonstrate resistance to the argument that structural changes have altered the employment landscape in ways that mean jobs actually are not available to those looking for them. From the perspective that unemployment results from individual choices rather than economic developments, government support is a hindrance rather than a help to solving the "problem of unemployment."

In many ways, the struggle between the promise of "the commitments we make to each other" and the criticism of "the something-for-nothing culture" is the struggle at the heart of this book. The centrality of work to Anglo-American conceptions of identity and worth mean that this struggle over the state's welfare role has been particularly clear in relationship to histories of unemployment. These are histories full of blame and demonization, but also of possibility.

Marjorie Levine-Clark

Acknowledgments

When a book gestates for as long as this one did, the list of people and institutions that nourished the process is long and meaningful. An American Council of Learned Societies Fellowship; numerous Faculty Development Grants from the University of Colorado Denver; a College of Liberal Arts and Sciences Dissemination Grant; and generous support from CU Denver's History Department, especially funds established for faculty research by Mark Foster (history professor emeritus) and the Walter S. Rosenberry III Charitable Trust, furnished travel and time. In the most material of ways, I could not have completed this book without these resources.

This funding also supported a superb team of student research assistants. For their work finding and organizing newspaper articles, searching through parliamentary papers, and reading poor law guardians' minutes for obscure details, I heartily thank Noelle Bailey, Kendra Black, Judith Davies, Mary Lester, Dani Newsum, and Jenny Taylor. For database and spreadsheet building, data input, and super-duper analytical skills, I am indebted to Lisa Boyd, Susan Gustin, Chris Hubble, Tracey Limbaugh, Jennifer Purcell, Rivka Weisberg, and Jarett Zuboy. To Chris, I owe huge thanks for the hours spent explaining how to read my data in Excel spreadsheets. Jarett became my partner in pulling the book together, creating tables and figures, cleaning up citations, and reading and editing the whole manuscript. I am enormously appreciative of his careful attention to this project. Keith Moore did great work securing image permissions and turning endnotes into a bibliography.

When I started this research, I imagined a book on health care and the poor law. The Stourbridge Poor Law Union collection at the Staffordshire Record Office sent me in a new direction. The archivists at the SRO provided excellent assistance and suggestions, and it was a delight to work in Stafford. From the well-funded SRO, I made my way to the Dudley Archives and Local History Service in Coseley, which struggled to keep the doors open when I was doing my research. The DALHS staff was extremely helpful, and I thank them for their expertise. I am thrilled that the DALHS recently moved to a purpose-built home in the center of Dudley. I also owe thanks to the highly efficient staff at the National Archives, where it is an absolute pleasure to do research. I cannot overstate the spousal privileges that come with being married to an

Associate Dean of the University of Denver Libraries. Their digital collections, thanks in large part to the collection development proficiency of Michael Levine-Clark, gave me access to many important resources as questions arose.

My time in the Midlands enriched my sense of place and expanded my appreciation for the diversity of England. Rob and Judy Hodge, friends of a friend, graciously spent a day walking me around Black Country canals, from Netherton to Stourbridge, where I saw the last remaining glass cone chimney in the region and what was the Wordsley workhouse, and heard the sound of a forge. Alison Evans and her family led me and mine on explorations of the region, from the Clent Hills to the Black Country Living Museum. I spent a sabbatical term affiliated with the University of Birmingham, arranged by Hugh McLeod, and learned from discussions with the wonderful faculty of the History Department. I especially owe thanks to Francesca Carnevali, who invited me to join her students on a fascinating excursion to the Iron Bridge Gorge sites, where I discovered what actually happened at an iron foundry. Francesca's death in 2013 came as a shock, and I thought of her often as I was finishing this manuscript.

From the first point of contact, the Palgrave Macmillan team was positive and enthusiastic. Sean Brady, co-editor of the Genders and Sexualities in History series, has been an amazing advocate for this project and great fun to work with. Clare Mence, Palgrave Macmillan's history commissioning editor, her editorial assistants Emily Russell and Angharad Bishop, and my project manager K. Nithya were consistently ready to answer questions, and I thank them for their attention to my work. The anonymous reviewers for the press provided insightful suggestions and queries that helped me clarify my arguments.

My support system at CU Denver has been extraordinary. Thank you, thank you, thank you to Chris Agee, Pam Laird, Myra Rich, and Bill Wagner: fabulous history colleagues and friends who read and commented – sometimes over and over again – on the book from beginning to end. Two overlapping groups of amazing women (a feminist writing/reading group and a humanities writing group) gave invaluable feedback over the years. Hearty thanks to Michelle Comstock, Jana Everett, Marylynne Lawson, Gillian Silverman, Sarah Tyson, Cate Wiley, and Margaret Woodhull. Dan Howard and Laura Argys, who at different times served as Deans of the College of Liberal Arts and Sciences, helped me stick to the Wednesday research days that "master mentor" Brenda J. Allen encouraged me to take in the first place. All three offered much needed support and friendship, as did associate deans Rich Allen,

Jeff Franklin, and John Wyckoff. Tabitha Fitzpatrick, History Department program assistant, and Karen Fennell, Executive Assistant to the Dean, helped keep my life in order and provided open office doors when I needed somewhere to take a deep breath. Student assistants in the History Department and the Dean's Office aided me with a variety of tasks. Special thanks to John Leech and Kendall Smith for struggling through drawing maps with me.

The North American Conference on British Studies and the Western Conference on British Studies have given me terrific colleagues and dear friends, many of whom have commented on my work. I thank especially Andy August (who generously read the whole manuscript), Sascha Auerbach, Lynn Botelho, Jamie Bronstein, Anna Clark, Paul Deslandes, Chris Frank, Stephen Heathorn, Karl Ittmann, Dane Kennedy, Lara Kriegel, Philippa Levine, Andy Muldoon, Erika Rappaport, Jim Rosenheim, Greg Smith, Ellen Ross, Susie Steinbach, and Janet Watson. I presented parts of this project at many other conferences over the years and received excellent suggestions from commentators Eileen Boris, Janet Fink, and Colin Gordon, among others, as well as audience participants. Jeff Cox and Linda Kerber encouraged the direction I was taking from the very early days of this project; I have been so fortunate to have their friendship and mentoring. Sonya Rose helped fuel my energy to finish up, and I thank her warmly for her support and feedback.

In Denver, I leaned heavily on a community of wonderful people who nurtured me with food, drink, conversation, laughter, music, childcare, and child-schlepping. Deepest thanks to Chris Agee, Beth Allen, Rich Allen, Elissa Auther, Kendra Black, Michelle Comstock, Jill Cooper, Todd Cooper, Jan Ediger, Jason Gilman, Patricia Gilman, Stephen Hartnett, David Hildebrand, Tess Jones, Philip Joseph, Yvonne Kellar-Guenther, Lisa Keranen, Pam Laird, Kelly Palmer, Myra Rich, Susan Robertson, Bridget Rosenberg, Natalie Schaefer, Gillian Silverman, Maren Stephenson, Richard Stephenson, Bill Wagner, Cathy Walker, Margaret Woodhull, and Ye Wanton Singers. From afar, Emma Gardner, Denis Provencher, Amy Randall, Catherine Rymph, and Facebook friends from many parts of my life carried the highs and lows of the starts and stops of this project. I needed it all.

I was three months pregnant with my daughter Isabel when I took that first research trip to Stafford. This project has grown with Isabel, who now understands why I ask the questions I do and has a keen sense of social justice, of which her mom is deeply proud. Isabel and her dad, Michael, make the everyday more than routine, and their extraordinary contributions to my life surely have entered the pages of this book.

My wider family has cheered me along, picking up the pieces when I lost three months of writing and steadying my resolve when I became chair of my department and then associate dean before finishing the manuscript. My mom, Ann Friedman, and my dad, Robert Levine, inspire me every day, as, on their separate paths, they work to make the world a better place. This book is for them.

I adapted portions of Chapter 6 from my article, "The Politics of Preference: Masculinity, Marital Status, and Unemployment Relief in Post-First World War Britain," *Cultural and Social History* 7, no. 2 (2010): 233–52, © The Social History Society, Bloomsbury/Berg publishing; portions of Chapter 8 from my article, "The Gendered Economy of Family Liability: Intergenerational Relationships and Poor Law Relief in England's Black Country, 1871–1911," *Journal of British Studies* 45 (January 2006): 72–89, © North American Conference on British Studies, University of Chicago Press; and portions of Chapter 9 from my article, "From 'Relief' to 'Justice and Protection': The Maintenance of Deserted Wives, British Masculinity, and Imperial Citizenship, 1870–1920," *Gender and History* 22, no. 2 (2010): 302–21, John Wiley and Sons Ltd.

1
"So Much Honest Poverty": Introduction

"A large muster of unemployed" assembled in the Vegetable Market in the West Midlands town of Dudley in mid-September 1921. Many of the men present had been out of work for long stretches and had used up their eligibility for national unemployment benefits. They met to discuss strategies for approaching local government bodies for assistance. The featured speaker of the gathering was James Wilson, the Labour Member of Parliament for Dudley. He rallied the crowd, insisting that

> the unemployed of Dudley did not want doles, and they had not met there that afternoon to ask for doles. What they wanted was genuine employment. (Hear, hear.) They were not loafers, but were men who protested against unemployment and were entitled to approach their local authorities ... and ask them to do all they could to remove unemployment and provide useful and productive schemes which would find them work.

Wilson recognized the limitations of existing national unemployment policies, so he urged unemployed men to exercise their right to demand relief at the local level from the Board of Guardians, who administered the long-stigmatized Poor Law:

> There were men who felt their manhood would be affected by going to the Guardians ... but he told them that to cherish those feelings they would be worse than cowards if they allowed women and children to starve as a result. They were entitled to go to the Guardians and claim, when the right to work was not met, such sustenance as would enable them to keep their women-folk and their kiddies healthy.

Wilson concluded by exhorting the crowd "to continue to protest against the conditions and enforce their ideals; to continue to make approaches to their local Councils and Boards of Guardians and compel them to do their duty; and also in every way to bring pressure upon the central Government to do its duty."[1]

Wilson's powerful speech captures fundamental themes in the politics of unemployment and welfare in late nineteenth- and early twentieth-century Britain. While Wilson addressed his gathering in the early 1920s, his themes would have resonated in the late nineteenth century, when the "problem of unemployment" first became part of people's vocabularies and experiences. Wilson identified the unemployed as men who desperately wanted to work – "They were not loafers, but men" – equating being a man with the desire to work. By admonishing the men in the crowd for putting their own feelings above the survival of their wives and children, Wilson also associated "men" with those who were responsible for families, whose "manhood" was contingent upon providing for "their women-folk and their kiddies." According to Wilson, a man's dependence on public funds did not threaten his manhood if his aim was to support his wife and children. In fact, "men" were entitled to ask for welfare in the name of their families when there was no work available for them. That right extended from local to national resources.

The men that Wilson addressed were members of the "honest poor." From the last quarter of the nineteenth century, Britons confronted the modern realities of chronic and mass unemployment and commonly referred to "honest poverty" and the "honest poor" to bemoan the extent of suffering among "deserving" people. In 1919, for example, the *Dudley Herald* editor lamented that the region was experiencing "so much honest poverty" that the increased expenditures of poor law boards of guardians were justified.[2] I take up the phrase "honest poverty" as an analytical tool to examine relationships among unemployment, welfare, and citizenship. From this perspective, honest poverty was a category applying to *men* ("honest" when referring to women had predominantly sexual rather than class connotations). Honest poverty describes a model of working-class masculine status built on the pillars of the male breadwinner ideal: the *work imperative*, which required men to demonstrate that they were willing to work, and *family liability*, which required men to support their families responsibly. A man who performed these roles signified his respectability – he could be poor and still fulfill the expectations of what it meant to be a man – but many working-class men faced regular challenges to their abilities to work and maintain families. Many found themselves needing help from the state. I introduce "honest poverty" as a way to think about a working-class masculine citizenship status tied explicitly to welfare.

This book asks two big questions: 1) what happened when working-class men, who were expected to fulfill the male breadwinner ideal by working and maintaining dependants, either were unable or unwilling to take on these responsibilities? and 2) how did attempts by the British government and local officials to address that inability or unwillingness – and poor men's interactions with these attempts – shape new boundaries around what it meant to be a citizen? I argue that, from the late nineteenth century, the visibility of unemployment and demands from new voters pushed policymakers, welfare providers, and unemployed men to reconceptualize relationships among unemployment, welfare, and citizenship. This reconceptualization incorporated dependence on the state into constructions of respectable working-class masculinity and citizenship. This was "honest poverty." The work-welfare system associated with the male breadwinner ideal insisted on self-sufficiency and independence.[3] The honest poverty work-welfare system opened a space for working-class men to remain "men" even when they depended on public welfare.

Unemployment and welfare

Sociologist Mike Savage has argued that "structural insecurity" has been the "distinctive feature of working-class life," forcing workers "to find strategies for dealing with the chronic insecurity of everyday life."[4] One of those strategies has been to turn to public welfare provisions. For the purposes of this study, I use the term "welfare" to mean social policies and practices intended to contribute to (but not necessarily meet) basic living needs. I focus on welfare in relationship to unemployment, so many of the programs I discuss relate specifically to providing poor law relief or government benefits to men out of work. Because unemployment insurance was never untangled from non-contributory benefits in the period I cover, I talk broadly about unemployment benefits as welfare. I also include other forms of assistance, such as court-ordered "maintenance payments" for elderly parents and neglected wives and children, as part of the welfare system of the time. Men and women moved among different forms of welfare, sometimes concurrently, sometimes serially, seeking survival from the district poor law authorities, national benefit providers, and local courts. They also drew on private charity and their friends and families to help them through hard times. Scholars have stressed the significance of this "mixed economy of welfare."[5] While my focus in this book is on public forms of assistance, the contributions of friendly societies, voluntary relief committees, charities, trade unions, and other non-government forms of relief were significant. Indeed, central and local government actors for much of the period expected the poor to cobble together a subsistence income from a combination of public and private resources. And, until after the First World War, the central government expected local bodies to take on the bulk of the welfare burden. Most of that burden fell on the Poor Law.

The only system of state assistance available to the poor before the 1911 Unemployment Insurance Act came through the Poor Law, originally Elizabethan, but which took its nineteenth-century form from the Poor Law Amendment Act of 1834 (the "New" Poor Law). The Poor Law Amendment Act transformed a system of relief being criticized for its cost to local ratepayers, its supposed encouragement of dependence on public funds as opposed to independent initiative, and its outdated administrative machinery. Collecting small parishes into larger unions overseen by the newly-created Boards of Guardians, the New Poor Law was funded by local taxes (rates), but the central government took on more responsibility with a Poor Law Commission to establish national policy and monitor practice. The Commission was replaced by the Poor Law Board in 1847, which in its turn was replaced by the Local Government Board in 1871, which oversaw all local government bodies, including the Poor Law Guardians. Finally, the new Ministry of Health took over management of the Poor Law in 1919.[6]

The ideology of the New Poor Law helped enforce economic independence as the masculine norm.[7] It insisted that able-bodied men without gainful employment were blameworthy agents of their jobless status; they were not innocent victims of economic forces. While they could be viewed as the unfortunate sufferers of temporary slumps, they were supposed to have anticipated and saved for this possibility to maintain their self-sufficiency. The New Poor Law mandated that, in order to obtain assistance, able-bodied men prove their desperate circumstances by accepting indoor workhouse relief. If a man was married and had children, his family had to follow him into the workhouse, reinforcing both assumptions about the husband/father's responsibility for his family and his failure to fulfill those breadwinner obligations. Life in the workhouse meant families separated into different wards, regimented days of task work such as picking oakum and breaking stone, wearing uniforms, and eating barely nutritious food. The intention was to create a humiliating test of people's claims of destitution, and the poor universally hated the workhouse.[8]

The poor law bureaucracy closely investigated poor law operations and produced volumes of reports that reflect an attempt to refine policies to better control local conditions.[9] Practice was often far different from policy, however, and many poor law unions continued to award outrelief, relief in cash or in kind outside the workhouse, especially when the economic environment made it impossible to offer the workhouse to all who needed help. The early 1870s saw a reassertion of the principles of 1834, the "crusade against outrelief," an effort to clamp down on poor law unions that inspectors identified as being too generous with outdoor assistance.[10] All poor law relief, however, was designed to stigmatize, and when working men were politically enfranchised in the late nineteenth century, becoming a "pauper" by accepting relief meant relinquishing the vote. A man who depended on public assistance was not a full citizen. Or was he?

In the last third of the nineteenth century, poor law authorities faced new types of applicants: men they regarded as honest even though they were unemployed. These seemingly honest jobless men challenged poor law assumptions, for they were not the unskilled and casual laborers that officials expected to become paupers. They were not the "residuum," whose "vices, drunkenness, improvidence, mendicancy, bad language, filthy habits, gambling, low amusements, and ignorance," according to Gareth Stedman Jones, authorities essentially equated with pauperism.[11] In this context, policymakers introduced the idea of "unemployment" to try to capture the structural rather than the individual causes of joblessness.[12] The problem of unemployment in the late nineteenth century came to be framed above all by the social survey literature of Charles Booth and Seebohm Rowntree.[13] Yet even before the publication of *Life and Labour of the People of London* (1889–1903) and *Poverty: A Study of Town Life* (1901), "unemployment" was conceptually taking shape. Economic analyses of industrial capitalism combined with demonstrations by unemployed men, argues Matt Perry, to force a recognition that unemployment could exist even when a man was aggressively searching for work.[14] Indeed, unemployment was a "problem" precisely because men who clearly were looking for work could not find any. The development and increasing use of the term "unemployment" in the 1880s acknowledged a problem beyond individual fault.[15]

If people could understand joblessness as more of an economic than a moral problem (or at least consider a combination of structural and individual factors), then able-bodied, unemployed men could be "honest," which meant the state could legitimately assist them in non-stigmatizing ways outside the poor law framework, and unemployed men could continue to vote. "New liberal" thinkers emphasized a positive role for the state that focused on facilitating civic and economic agency for honest poor men.[16] While these ideas began circulating in the 1880s, it was with the Liberal "landslide" of 1906 that the national government actively began to legislate new welfare provisions informed by this thinking.[17] William Beveridge's 1909 publication of *Unemployment: A Problem of Industry* explicitly framed the problem of unemployment as economic in nature and beyond the control of individual unemployed people, which contributed to government approaches.[18] The Unemployment Insurance Act of 1911 introduced the first national system of unemployment insurance, designed for honest poor men, which Parliament expanded and revised throughout the 1920s. Yet the limitations of national insurance meant the unemployed continued to rely on the Poor Law and also on the non-contributory benefits system the government developed in the 1920s. National policy and local practice intersected and diverged, constructing the boundaries of the honest poverty work-welfare regime.

My work draws on the complex analyses that scholars of gender and welfare have provided of, in Ann Orloff's words, "the mutually constitutive relationship between systems of social provision and regulation and gender."[19] Most studies of gender and welfare have focused on the ways developing welfare arrangements in the United States and Western Europe, premised on male breadwinner norms, disadvantaged women. Jane Lewis writes that welfare systems "have deployed models of individual 'survival' based on relatively firm assumptions about family organization and gender relations" that propped up the male breadwinner.[20] These welfare systems circumscribed (married) women's citizenship, mediating women's access to the state through their husbands.[21] Yet men's dependence on state welfare presented a fundamental challenge to independent breadwinner masculinity and working-class men's citizenship claims as well. These issues are the central concern of this book.[22]

Masculine citizenship

Historically, poverty and unemployment have restricted men's abilities to act out dominant models of masculinity, even while men were acutely aware of the cultural expectations. As historian John Tosh has put it with reference to manhood in the nineteenth century, "The injunction 'Be a man!' implied that there were only certain ways in which one *could* be a man."[23] The male breadwinner ideal was certainly the norm when Britons confronted the problem of unemployment in the late nineteenth century. Men who earned a regular income that allowed them to support wives and children who remained outside the labor market sat atop the hierarchy of patriarchal privilege. Scholars of British labor, gender, and welfare history, however, have illustrated the wide gap between the male breadwinner ideal and material realities; most working men could not earn a family wage, many women were forced to earn out of economic necessity, and many women had to survive on their own.[24] The discourse of honest poverty recognized this structural insecurity of working-class life and created an acceptable category of dependent able-bodied masculine status that tried to solve the problem of the failed working-class male breadwinner. The process through which this discourse took shape and the social practices it engendered opened new possibilities for citizenship for working-class men that promised political, economic, and social rights.[25]

Citizenship, as Kathleen Canning and Sonya Rose argue in *Gender, Citizenship, and Subjectivities*, "can be understood as a political status assigned to individuals by states, as a relation of belonging to specific communities, or as a set of social practices that define the relationships between peoples and states and among peoples within communities."[26] My analysis weaves these various understandings together, considering formal political status but more importantly the cultural meanings associated with that status and the ways that "peoples and states" struggled to define relationships of belonging through social practices. These relationships were in flux in the period I examine with a changing franchise, a transformation of the state's role with regard to social provision, and the growing politicization of the poor. Canning and Rose also stress the ways that "citizenship provides the languages, rhetorics, and even the formal categories for claims-making, sometimes in the name of national belonging or on behalf of specific rights, duties, or protections, or visions of political participation."[27] Unemployed men unquestionably drew on the categories of honest poverty to claim their rights to work and welfare, to make claims based on an understanding of citizenship that valued their experiences as workers and family men.

Citizenship, in this view, expresses a community's values and norms, as well as conferring rights and requiring obligations.[28] In the words of the much-cited sociologist T.H. Marshall, "citizenship is a status bestowed on those who are full members of a community. All those who possess the status are equal with regard to the rights and duties with which the status is endowed."[29] For Marshall, citizenship status was tied to rights, and he envisioned a progression from civil rights in the eighteenth century, to political rights in the nineteenth century, to social rights in the twentieth century. While his theory of progressive citizenship has been rightly criticized, I adopt his "social citizenship" to express the idea that, in order for citizens to fully enjoy civil and political (and economic) rights, they have to have a basic minimum standard of living, and the state has an obligation to provide that minimum. As Marshall declares, social citizenship signifies "the right to share to the full in the social heritage and to live the life of a civilized being according to the standards prevailing in the society."[30] While not dictated through law or formal policy, only married men in the honest poverty work-welfare system could experience the full benefits of social citizenship that signified their place as "full members of a community."[31] As this book will show, citizenship status was circumscribed by both gender and marital status, which positioned women and unmarried men outside the welfare (and other) advantages conferred on married men.

While the discourse of honest poverty held out the promise of more inclusive citizenship relationships, women did not experience citizenship (formal or otherwise) in the same ways that men did, and men's experiences of citizenship depended on their social locations relative to work and family.[32] All men (and women, too, in theory) could meet the first qualification of honest poverty: adhering to the work imperative. Even if jobs were unavailable, a person could prove his or her deservedness by showing a good faith effort to find employment. Yet the second qualification – assuming family liability – required a person to be a head of household with a wife (and children) to maintain. Because women and unmarried men could not meet the qualification of family liability in the honest poverty work-welfare regime, they were marked as less worthy of assistance and, indeed, as less than full citizens.

Citizenship, then, can be understood as a status that, while creating the potential for equality, has been "bestowed" unevenly depending on the cultural meanings invested in it and the historical circumstances. Tosh has argued that masculinity also needs to be recognized as a "social status, demonstrated in specific social contexts."[33] Scholars following R.W. Connell have used the concept of "hegemonic masculinity" to argue that masculinity not only takes shape in opposition to femininity as an expression of patriarchal power, but that dominant (or hegemonic) masculinity also produces subordinate masculinities.[34] A fundamental tension between the hegemonic breadwinner and the honest poor man existed around the dichotomy of independence/dependence. The breadwinner was always independent, while the honest poor man was dependent. In terms of sociological theories of welfare, honest poverty helped frame welfare as a right of citizenship (rather than a need), the only way dependence could be reconciled with masculinity.[35] With unemployment increasingly understood to be structural, unemployed men and welfare providers established honest poverty masculinity as a social status to bolster deserving honest men's abilities to act like independent breadwinners, downplaying their failures to find work and provide for families. In a specific social context, welfare assistance became a sign of masculinity, a sign of membership in the community. Many voices at the local and national levels demanded an understanding of masculinity where welfare and citizenship could coexist, but other voices retorted that men who could not succeed independently were indeed failures as men. Honest poverty, therefore, was not an easy or a comfortable masculine citizenship status, even for the men it benefited.

Additionally, honest poverty could only work as a masculine citizenship status if it was temporary. At both the national and local levels, officials saw both poor law unemployment relief and national unemployment insurance as solving acute rather than chronic problems. In this way, unemployed honest men were different from "regular paupers" or "unemployables," who were socially constructed as permanently and irresponsibly in need.[36] If a man became dependent for the long haul, his dependence eventually overrode his presentation as a potential breadwinner. The honest poor were basically independent men who needed some assistance to resume their lives of self-sufficiency. When men remained chronically out of work, policymakers and welfare providers reverted to blaming the unemployed, revealing the fragility of rights claims within the honest poverty work-welfare system. State assistance could be a sign of incorporation into the nation, a sign of citizenship, but only if it was short term. Honest poverty had to be transitional – a means to get deserving men back on their feet so they could wear the full mantle of masculine citizenship as independent breadwinners.

If economic independence through work was one fundamental component of hegemonic masculinity, marriage was the other, meaning that unmarried men occupied a subordinate position across the board.[37] Historians of the family have emphasized the centrality of marriage to "being a man" in the nineteenth century. Marriage and fatherhood, according to Joanne Bailey, were "part of achieving 'full' or 'patriarchal' manhood,"[38] and John Gillis has referred to the period after 1850 as "the era of mandatory marriage" for both men and women.[39] Scholars of Victorian working-class politics have illustrated that many organizations increasingly adopted an ethos of "respectability" focused on a masculinity grounded in the home, with the independent ability to support a wife and children signifying that men had earned the right to be incorporated into the nation.[40] Men who remained unmarried failed to live up to patriarchal expectations and simultaneously signaled gender nonconformity regardless of their sexual identities or practices.

While my focus is not sexuality, I intend this study to contribute to understandings of what I call "welfare heteronormativity," exploring not just the ways patriarchal welfare policies and practices privileged men over women but also privileged certain men over other men by insisting men demonstrate their masculine status through (heterosexual) marriage. Margot Canaday's work on the United States in the twentieth century has influenced how scholars conceptualize "the straight state,"[41] arguing, among other things, that welfare schemes served to shape and reinforce heterosexual arrangements and institutions. In her introduction to the collection *Thinking Straight*, Chrys Ingraham also emphasizes the ways that individuals "embrac[e] a sense of entitlement, social and economic, just by virtue of participating in married heterosexual life regardless of the ways that entitlement denies those who do not have access to equal opportunity and citizenship."[42] While policymakers and relief providers sought ways to help honest unemployed married men claim their rights to assistance, they continued to blame most single men for their poverty or simply ignored single men's circumstances. They also punished married men who gave up their entitlements: men who, for example, refused to work or abandoned their families, men who refused to live "a normal way of life."[43]

Black Country contexts

As historians have been asserting for several decades now, the poor law story is a local one, and, while the national trend by the late nineteenth century might have been a turn away from the Poor Law, this was not the case for inhabitants across all poor law unions. Historians generally have not had a lot to say about the role of the Poor Law in reference to unemployed men of the honest poor. José Harris, for example, in her now-classic study of unemployment, contends that the Poor Law was essentially irrelevant to the problem of unemployment, "that, at least since 1870, the Poor Law had never been a major source of relief to the unemployed."[44] Similarly, poor law historian Lynn Hollen Lees argues that in the late nineteenth century fewer people used the Poor Law, and "being a pauper became a much less familiar status," which led to increasing antagonism towards poor law relief.[45] Honest poor men created "alternatives" to the Poor Law in "friendly societies, benefit clubs, and trade unions ... diminishing the likelihood that they would need poor relief if their incomes declined."[46] Scholars have been more interested in these new forms of working-class self-help than in the ways the draconian Poor Law continued to matter. An exception is Elizabeth Hurren who, in a study of the rural Brixworth Poor Law Union, argues that poor people in the period after 1870 reasserted their entitlement to relief in the face of the crusade against outrelief. Rather than leading to reluctance to rely on the Poor Law, enfranchisement encouraged poor men to demand what they saw as their right to relief.[47]

Part of my project in this book is to demonstrate the Poor Law's continuing relevance to dealing with the problem of unemployment. To do so, I use the Black Country region of the West Midlands to put flesh on the policy skeleton (Map 1.1). The region provides an excellent case study of honest poverty, as chronic un- and underemployment eroded men's ability to support their families and led them to seek help from local and national government resources. The Black Country got its name from its coal and iron production, whose close-to-the-surface coal seams and blast furnaces blackened land and sky (Figure 1.1). As a Birmingham journalist wrote in 1884, "Blue skies change to a reeking canopy of black and grey smoke. The earth is one vast unsightly heap of dead ashes and dingy refuse. Canals of diluted coal dust teach how filthy water may be and yet retain fluidity. Tumbledown houses, tumbledown works, tottering black chimneys, fire belching furnaces, squalid and blackened people."[48] This evocative passage speaks to the industrial decline, environmental degradation, and endemic poverty that the region suffered by the last quarter of the nineteenth century.[49]

I examine the experiences of the Black Country poor by focusing on records from the Dudley and Stourbridge Poor Law Unions, which contained parishes in southwestern Staffordshire and northern Worcestershire (Map 1.2). In addition to Dudley and Stourbridge, towns like Rowley Regis, Tipton, Cradley Heath, Brierley Hill, Halesowen, Quarry Bank, and Lye struggled with the economic changes of the late nineteenth and early twentieth centuries. The region had come to prominence in the eighteenth and early nineteenth centuries through specialization in coal and iron production centered around the district's ten-yard coal seam and rich deposits of ironstone and limestone.[50] The Black Country was also known for chain- and nailmaking, and for glass, bricks, tools, and other industries tied to iron, such as "hollow ware" (metal table items like sugar bowls, creamers, and teapots). The extractive coal and iron industries went into serious decline in the 1870s

Map 1.1   Map locating Black Country

from flooding and overworking, while the staple domestic wrought nailmaking collapsed from factory competition to the point where the Nailmakers' Union folded in 1895. Domestic nailmaking employed about 20,000 people in the region in the mid-1870s, but this was down to a few hundred at the start of the First World War.[51]

Perhaps because of the nature of the economy, at least until the turn of the century, the region saw men outnumber women at a time when the general census of England and Wales revealed a large imbalance towards women.[52] Interestingly, Black Country scholar George Barnsby

Figure 1.1 The "Black Country" round Wolverhampton, Staffordshire, 1866
Source: © Illustrated London News Ltd/Mary Evans.

argues that "the Black Country was not an area of early marriage," and many people stayed unmarried. His study of the 1861 census indicates that "no less than one third of the population of marriageable age remain[ed] single," and "that the proportion of people remaining single was considerably higher than for the rest of the country."[53] Barnsby also emphasizes that many more men than women remained unmarried.[54] While he is cautious about comparing the numbers from the 1901 census to 1861 because of differences in the registration districts counted, Barnsby concludes that the numbers of unmarried adults actually rose about five per cent to 38 per cent of the Black Country population. Likewise, late marriage continued to be the pattern.[55]

Men predominated in the physical work of the iron and coal industries (Figure 1.2) and in the making of the heavy chains and anchors that were a pride of the region (Figure 1.3). Many a miner had a wife who worked making nails or small chains, as these were occupations considered simple to learn, whose skills were passed down within families, and that were most often conducted on the basis of domestic production in sheds annexed to workers' houses (Figure 1.4). When mines flooded and blast furnaces shut down, displaced men often turned to the domestic sector of chain- and nailmaking, accelerating wage declines by further

Map 1.2 Dudley and Stourbridge Poor Law Unions

overcrowding.[56] According to Barnsby, the area saw little rise in the standard of living over the course of the nineteenth century and had about 20 per cent of its population "almost perpetually below the minimum level necessary to maintain life," with over half "above subsistence but below the minimum standard of comfort all their lives."[57]

What contemporaries came to understand as the "Great Depression" of the late nineteenth century hit the Dudley and Stourbridge districts of the Black Country particularly hard, and many of the old trades surrounding coal and iron production never rebounded from the effects of the economic downturn. While the Black Country region as a whole was eventually able to recover through the development of new industries associated with transport and engineering, the people whose

Figure 1.2 Miners working underground, c.1900
Source: © Dudley Archives and Local History Service, ref. p/1862.

livings depended on coal and iron production and nailmaking did not. Chainmakers, who maintained more economic stability for a while, struggled with overcrowding and wage reductions from the entrance of nailmakers, miners, and iron workers into their industry. Other skilled trades associated with wrought iron – like hollow ware work and edge tool making – also eventually declined with mechanization. The brick and glass industries realized the same fate. Un- and underemployment in the Dudley and Stourbridge Unions became endemic.[58] Between 1870 and 1930, the region generally battled a combination of the exhaustion of local resources, mechanized challenges to local industries, and poor demand for local products.

The area experienced a temporary boom during the First World War, as its infrastructure transitioned smoothly to munitions production, but the old industries continued their decline in the postwar period. Writing in 1929, G.C. Allen concluded his study on *The Industrial Development of Birmingham and the Black Country* by noting that, while the Black Country did not fare as badly in the 1920s economic crisis as did other

Figure 1.3 Titanic Anchor, forged by Hingley and Sons, Netherton, being pulled through the streets, 1911
Source: © Dudley Archives and Local History Service, ref. p/92.

Figure 1.4 Dudley cottage, with nail shed attached to the back, c.1900
Source: © Dudley Archives and Local History Service, ref. p/59.

older industrial districts, towns with specialization in the traditional staple industries had high unemployment, suffering "severely" from declines in iron and coal.[59] In his study of Staffordshire, D.M. Palliser notes that, by the mid-twentieth century, the Black Country landscape had changed: "gone are the pitheads, most of the glasshouses, nailers' and chain-makers' workshops, the tilery chimneys, the taller factory chimneys, and the proud facades of the major Victorian manufactories."[60] These economic developments and their impact on the inhabitants of the Dudley and Stourbridge Poor Law Unions illuminate the tensions between ideology and practice, the challenges of a work-welfare system premised on male breadwinning in the face of economic realities.

Structure and sources

My chronology is a poor law historian's chronology: beginning with the "crusade against outrelief" in the early 1870s and ending with the abolition of a nineteenth-century institution, the Boards of Guardians, in 1929. Some of my chapters cover themes that cross the entire period; the continuities are informed by the stretch of the Poor Law across the decades. The remaining chapters deal more explicitly with the changes brought about by new policies and economic conditions. My themes and chronologies overlap and pull apart, creating stories that cannot neatly fit into a single narrative.

I have arranged the book in three parts, interweaving local and national stories. Part I, "Unemployment and the Continuities of Honest Poverty," traces the pressures that the "problem of unemployment" put on the Poor Law, which brought into sharp relief the inability of many poor men to achieve masculine breadwinner status. Chapter 2 introduces the work imperative, an ideology that required men who were unemployed to prove their desire for work. When local Boards of Guardians were faced with increasing numbers of honest unemployed men demanding relief, they searched for ways to separate these men from "regular paupers." Task work became the predominant means through which honest poor men could demonstrate their welfare deservedness, although they experienced it as demeaning. I examine the ways the work imperative evolved under the Poor Law and through local work relief schemes, showing the limitations of relief efforts that depended solely on local resources.

Chapter 3 argues that, while adhering to the work imperative was a universal sign of masculine status, only by being married – and preferably having children as well – could a man achieve full masculine status and welfare deservedness. Married men had family liability, responsibility for maintaining wives and children, which placed them at the top of the hierarchy of welfare deservedness. Unemployed married men used their marital status to argue for their right to assistance, helping to construct unemployment as a problem of married men.

Chapter 4 explores the ways the assumptions of honest poverty became foundational to the system of national unemployment benefits. National politicians and government bureaucrats used the same languages of the work imperative and family liability as local authorities and institutionalized the heteronormative framework of honest poverty as the basis of national unemployment schemes. While policies in the postwar period increasingly expected women as well as men to adhere to the work imperative, men's family liability remained constant so that women and single men could not make the same rights claims as married men with reference to unemployment benefits.

In Part II, "Honest Poverty in National Crisis," I work through the ways that the First World War and major industrial actions of the 1920s revealed the privilege of family liability in determining welfare deservedness. Chapter 5 explores how the First World War opened up the possibility of a new path to masculine citizenship for men: military service. Yet military service was experienced differently for married and single men. Married men did not need war to prove their masculine citizenship, because they had already achieved that status through work and marriage. Single men, by contrast, could use military service as a path to citizenship, and the British public, simultaneously, demanded single men's sacrifice to protect married men and their families.

Chapter 6 argues that, in the postwar period, the welfare of veterans was measured against already-existing assumptions about the state's role in supporting married men and their families. As unemployment reached unprecedented numbers in the early 1920s, the government found it more and more difficult to hold to the promises it had made to ex-servicemen regarding welfare preferences connected to service. Indeed the principles of welfare preferences for veterans and welfare preferences for married men often conflicted, creating policy and practical problems at both the national and local levels. In the end, family liability continued to garner the most masculine credit.

Chapter 7 focuses on the massive coal strikes of 1921 and 1926. I argue that these strikes were contests over the willingness to work, with striking men claiming that their status as citizens allowed them to refuse to work under unacceptable conditions and terms. Authorities, however, saw striking men as giving up the privileges of honest poverty by refusing to work. These strikes were also contests over the relationships between striking men and their families vis-à-vis the state, since authorities wanted to punish men on strike as no longer blamelessly unemployed, but they did not want married men's dependent wives and children to suffer. This created major policy headaches, as the government tried to assist wives and children without benefiting striking husbands.

Part III, "Honest Poverty and the Intimacies of Policy," investigates family relationships under the framework of honest poverty, showing that family members used the language of honest poverty against each other to pursue welfare benefits. Chapter 8 examines the ways age played a large role in officials' determinations concerning men's welfare. As men grew older, they were increasingly unable to meet the terms of honest poverty: age and poor health contributed to an inability to work to provide for a family. They were therefore blameless in their need and deserving of welfare. The Old Age Pensions Act of 1908 codified this assumption by providing automatic state assistance to elderly men (and women) who could prove histories of honest poverty. Yet the state still expected that adult children would assist their older parents. Officials held unmarried sons primarily accountable to maintain their parents, since married sons already had family liability for wives and children, and the state did not consider daughters full economic agents.

The final chapter examines marital separation and maintenance cases as welfare struggles, fought over husbands' adherence to the work imperative and family liability. Men who neglected their wives gave up the privileges of honest poverty masculinity, and estranged wives and poor law officers highlighted husbands' failures as men, summoning them to magistrates' courts for maintenance orders. Authorities tracked down men who deserted their families, especially when those families became dependent on poor law relief. The politics of honest poverty played out on an imperial stage when heads of state argued for legal changes to facilitate finding and punishing men throughout the British Empire who failed to uphold their family responsibilities.

This book has ended up quite a distance from the project I started. I began my research asking questions about gender, health, and the late nineteenth-century Poor Law. The collections I found in the Staffordshire Record Office pushed me in a new direction, and a story about masculinity and unemployment pulled this one-time Victorian historian into the unfamiliar territory of the twentieth century. Most challenging to my conceptualization and writing of this book was that very different types of materials and diverse levels of coverage exist for the different periods that I include in the study. In particular, I came up against the scholar's dilemma of access. Some of the documents I worked with on my first research trip, before I knew what this book was going to become, were on subsequent trips "closed" by new data privacy provisions. This means that I incorporate some materials that I was unable to study as deeply as I would have liked or through the lens I came to use on the rest of my sources.

The documents that changed the path of this project are applications for poor law relief from the Stourbridge Poor Law Union. The applications come in two forms. The first is a set of serial ledgers of Relieving Officers' Application and Report Books that exist in ten-year intervals from 1871 to 1911. These are enormous registers in which relieving officers recorded applications by date, including demographic data, the reasons for the application, the applicant's request, and the outcome of the application. I assume that at some point a decision was made to archive these books only for the census years and a few others. While the coverage is not exhaustive (and is uneven across the years), I created a database (Dataset 1, DS1) that contains more than 7,700 applications from about 4,500 separate applicants in the parishes of the Stourbridge Union.[61]

The second set of applications reflects changes in recordkeeping: relieving officers moved from serial ledgers to case files. Each applicant had a separate file, which could include only a single request for aid on one day or many applications that stretched over the decades. I have a much smaller dataset for these records (Dataset 2, DS2) that encompasses the 221 extant case files from 1912 to 1929.[62] I only viewed this collection once, and, painfully, I did not examine the part of the collection containing unemployment insurance materials for the same period. I simply did not know I would be writing about unemployment before my access was restricted. Because of the privacy issues that emerged during my research, I use first names and last initials in reference to these poor law applications. Where names were used in public documents, such as in newspapers or open archives, I use the full names.

In addition to the relieving officers' records, for the local context I draw heavily on three newspapers – the *Dudley Herald*, the *County Express*, and the *County Advertiser* – all of which were published once a week throughout the period. These newspapers reported regularly on Boards of Guardians' and local government meetings, committees of unemployed men, police matters, the impact of national events like the First World War on local people, and many other items of tremendous use in understanding what life might have been like in the Stourbridge and Dudley Unions. The Stourbridge and Dudley Guardians' Minutes and Committee Books vary in terms of their detail but provide a good sense of the struggles facing these local welfare providers as they confronted increasing demands on their scant resources.

To understand national policies and their development, I rely on parliamentary debates and the reports of various parliamentary commissions and committees as well as archives of government correspondence, memoranda, meetings, and other relevant papers. The files of appeals brought to the Crown-appointed Umpire by men and women who were denied unemployment benefits in the 1920s illuminate the implementation of national welfare policies, which in turn influenced subsequent practices. Most of these materials are housed at the National Archives in London, in the documents of the Ministries of Labour, Health, and Pensions and in the Treasury and War Office papers.

Unemployment, Welfare, and Masculine Citizenship does not tell an easy tale of the replacement of the poor law system with a "better," more modern system of welfare, a smooth transition from needs- to rights-based welfare. Rather, in some ways, the Poor Law in the 1920s became more practically expansive, while national unemployment benefits became more ideologically restrictive. Although those deemed worthy to receive national benefits experienced fairly generous state assistance, the terms on which they were eligible for assistance drew upon the same expectations of honest poverty that were central to the administration of the Poor Law. And, as poor law authorities at the local level became increasingly unwilling to leave applicants to starve, national policymakers were more and more willing to force those they perceived as undeserving of national assistance back on local resources. The tensions between central government policy and local discretion in practice created an unpredictable context for the ways men and women negotiated their welfare.

Part I
Unemployment and the Continuities of Honest Poverty

2
Not "Weary Willies" or "Tired Tims": The Work Imperative in the Poor Law World

The *Dudley Herald* frightened its readers with the "The Demon of Unemployment" in November 1908, describing a depressed region where workers struggled for survival. Worst of all, the "full extent [of] the sufferings of a large proportion of the people" in the district would be difficult to ascertain, because they were "unwilling to parade their poverty, and would rather put up with a pinch than apply for pauper relief." The "people" about whom the writer was concerned were "honest, decent, hard-working men" who were unable to find employment: "many of them being encumbered with large families, their cases deserve the utmost commiseration and timely assistance."[1]

The reporter went on to describe "one of the saddest sights," which he had witnessed at the Stourbridge Union Workhouse the previous Friday:

A band of over 20 men were waiting to appear before the Guardians to appeal for temporary work. Not one of them belonged to that class which could by any stretch of imagination be designated 'Weary Willies' or 'Tired Tims.' They were in every case men willing to labour, but, owing to the exigencies of trade circumstances, were debarred from pursuing honest toil, in fact they were clamouring for work, however menial it might be, in order that they might keep the bodies and souls of their progeny intact.[2]

This language highlights a tension between old understandings of joblessness and new economic realities. Traditional explanations of joblessness characterized the lack of work as personal failure. "Weary Willy" and "Tired Tim," tramps featured in Tom Browne's popular comics published in *Illustrated Chips* from 1896 through 1953 (Figure 2.1),

25

Figure 2.1 Weary Willy and Tired Tim recruit the "merry Out-of-Work Brigade" to fight in the South African War by promising "Free drinks, mind you!" *Illustrated Chips*, 1899

Source: Lambiek Comiclopedia, http://www.lambiek.net/artists/b/browne_tom.htm.

exemplified this personal failure: they were out of work because they were lazy, and so it was appropriate to mock them.[3] Here, the tramps provided a foil for real men, those who were "willing to labour." The Stourbridge unemployed did not fit into the traditional narrative of poverty; they were poor but looking for work and, therefore, from the reporter's perspective, were deserving of "the utmost commiseration and timely assistance."

As increasing numbers of honest poor men came to rely on the Poor Law, becoming "paupers" and losing their votes after so recently becoming enfranchised, they challenged the punitive assumptions of pauperism, arguing that the stigma of relief should not be applied to their situations. Policymakers and poor law officials attempted to construct new methods of assistance for which men out of work "through no fault of their own" would not be ashamed to apply.[4] For attitudes toward poverty and welfare to change, unemployed men had to establish that their joblessness was a structural problem rather than a result of individual moral failing. Policymakers worked with the new category of "unemployment" to address the underlying realities of industrial capitalism, but they could not fully let go of personal responsibility as a cause of being out of work.[5]

The discourse surrounding honest poverty masculinity became the means through which both unemployed men and welfare officials managed the tension between seeing unemployment as an inherent element of capitalism that hurt skilled men and seeing it as the result of individual behavior. An unemployed man who could prove that he met the key expectations of masculine personal responsibility – desiring work and taking care of a family – would benefit from new state programs that tried to solve the structural problem of unemployment. He was not a "Weary Willy" or "Tired Tim" whose laziness led him to the Poor Law. This chapter examines the ways the "work imperative," and the tests associated with proving a man's commitment to work, expanded as unemployment spiked in the late nineteenth century.

The Poor Law and the Labour Test

For the poor, the obligation to work was nothing new: the plight of the poor man was to toil, which historically separated him from his betters. The English state built this assumption into the Elizabethan Poor Laws of 1597 and 1601, the first legislation specifically to grant the destitute an entitlement to public assistance. The 1601 Act insisted that paupers work for relief, giving overseers of the poor the responsibility for "setting to work all such persons married or unmarried, having no means to maintain them, or no ordinary and daily trade of life to get their living by."[6] Adherence to the work imperative was also a major component of the Vagrancy Act of 1824, which allowed authorities to imprison those perceived to be idling without respectable employment or failing to maintain themselves and their families.[7] Both the Poor Laws and the Vagrancy Act judged unfit the man who was not engaged in honest work and who could not provide for his family.[8] By the mid-nineteenth century, this work imperative was a cross-class norm, applying to any man without an independent income. In working to support a family, a man aimed to meet the breadwinner ideal, the hegemonic form of masculinity for working- and middle-class men.[9]

The Poor Law Amendment Act of 1834 strengthened these assumptions and offered guiding principles for addressing poverty in the nineteenth century. According to José Harris in her study of unemployment policy, the New Poor Law of 1834 "had been specifically devised to deal with the 'able-bodied' pauper, by driving him into the open labour market and forcing him to retain his independence when out of work."[10] The ideology behind the New Poor Law stressed that lack of work was a moral failing, and it was therefore perfectly reasonable to humiliate unemployed men with the workhouse. In practice, however, Boards of Guardians continued to administer "outrelief" of cash or in-kind assistance much more liberally than was hoped by the central authorities, in many cases because the local boards were overwhelmed by the extent of poverty in their districts and could not possibly house all able-bodied applicants in their workhouses.[11]

To try to rein in local discretion, the Poor Law Board instituted the Outdoor Labour Test in 1842, which made outrelief to able-bodied men contingent upon the performance of task work, usually breaking stones at the workhouse itself.[12] The Labour Test was constructed on the premise that only the truly honest poor would perform demeaning task work for assistance; idlers would be put off by the work itself. Distinguishing between "men" and "idlers" or "loafers" framed discussions of unemployment relief for the entire period from 1870 to 1930. From its creation, the Outdoor Labour Test applied only to able-bodied men. While women were put to work inside workhouses, they were not subject to the same work test for outrelief, since women's contributions to the state were not grounded in a need to prove womanhood through employment. While men were identified as men through their productive labor, by the 1840s women's value was predominantly measured through reproductive labor.[13]

The Outdoor Labour Test came to play an increasingly important role in the administration of outrelief as the numbers of unemployed "honest" men applying to the poor law authorities grew in the last quarter of the nineteenth century. The Local Government Board, the central government unit overseeing the Poor Law and other local government bodies, sent out a circular upon its foundation in 1871 reasserting the strictures of 1834, urging local Boards of Guardians to abide more closely by the letter of the law. The Charity Organization Society and the Local Government Board worked together to push a "crusade against outrelief," which sought to limit relief to the able-bodied outside the workhouse even further.[14] "Ironically," Lynn Hollen Lees points out in her study of the Poor Law, "just as the wider society was softening its views of the destitute and incorporating workers more extensively in political structures, the poor law was tightening the screws on the poor."[15] Historian Keith McClelland sees it as "perhaps no accident that, within a few years of admitting 'independent artisans' to the franchise in 1867," the poor law became "even more punitive."[16] Working-class men would lose their fragile right to vote if they received any poor law assistance. What were local guardians to do?

The crusade against outrelief framed poor law policy when the Black Country staple industries began their precipitous decline in the 1870s. As historian Richard Trainor has argued,

> In the last three decades of the century Black Country guardians had to formulate policies for outdoor relief in the face of increased need, rising sympathy, and increased working-class pressure, on the one hand, balanced by strained resources, residual hostility to the destitute, and the Local Government Board's energetic though not formally coercive crusade to cut out-relief, on the other.[17]

At a time when pauperism overall was decreasing, in 1884–85, for example, Worcestershire, the county home of the Dudley and Stourbridge Unions at the time, saw the third-largest percentage increase in England and Wales, and the West Midlands as a whole had poor law expenditures second only to London.[18]

The Dudley and Stourbridge Boards of Guardians encountered a crisis that would continue with little respite until the abolition of the existing poor law system in 1929. By the end of 1878, Black Country coal and iron industries were suffering from a "prevalent depression," according to Francis Longe, the Local Government Board inspector for the region.[19] Longe identified both the Dudley and Stourbridge Unions as having high demands on poor law resources and Dudley as one of three unions in especially bad shape. The five unions, including Dudley and Stourbridge, which Longe grouped in his district as having in common a large number of "labouring classes," saw an increase of nearly 90 per cent in the numbers of people being relieved by the Poor Law in two years. He attributed this increase "to the gradual impoverishment of the working classes of this district by the depression in the Iron Trade."[20] Trade union unemployment nationally in 1879 registered over ten per cent after averaging below three per cent for the 1870s.[21]

The winter of 1878–79 created particular anxieties for the Dudley Board of Guardians related to their administration of the work imperative through the Labour Test. According to the local newspapers and poor law records, skilled Dudley men who never before had turned to the Poor Law were compelled to do so in the hard winter of 1878–79. The quality of men applying for relief was taken to be sure evidence of the desperate times. For example, at a December 1878 meeting convened by the mayor of Dudley to establish a soup kitchen for the district, William Challingsworth, a Dudley guardian, argued that "it was appalling to see the number of distressed persons who presented themselves at the Board of Guardians' meeting each Friday morning . . . At the meetings of the Guardians they saw men who were good mechanics craving to obtain work at a shilling a day."[22] This identification of the "craving" of "good mechanics" was seen as so important by the editor of the *Herald* that he repeated it in the leader "Christmas": "It is a pitiful sight to attend the meetings of the Boards of Guardians and see the number of able-bodied men, skilled mechanics, craving for work at the Workhouse in order to eke out a miserable existence."[23] Even while bemoaning the fact that men had to beg for menial work, guardians and commentators nevertheless insisted on this very "craving" as signifying honest poverty. Men's desperation for work implied that their joblessness was not their fault. Although the idea of blameless unemployment was not normative in the late 1870s, it was more believable for "skilled mechanics" than it was for the unskilled men poor law authorities usually confronted.

The Dudley Board of Guardians strictly adhered to the Labour Test, which in their union (as in most others) meant assigning men to break stone at the workhouse, in a space designated for that purpose. By January 1879, the Dudley Union had almost 500 men breaking stone, but the numbers asking for assistance overwhelmed the stoneyard resources, which certainly were not meant to accommodate hundreds of men. The stoneyard master reported that "in the labour yard the men were as thick as bees, and could scarcely strike for fear of hurting each other." While the Board of Guardians' chairman George Bagott, a chemist, insisted on the necessary continuation of the Labour Test, he indicated that the men could expand out of the stoneyard to workhouse land as a means of dealing with the overcrowding.[24]

The Board of Guardians, however, expressed ambivalence about the value of task work as a proof of deservedness, even while they demanded it. The effort the men put into their tasks became a point of contention for the Dudley Board as early as February 1879, and the newspaper reports on the board's meetings suggest the members' skepticism about whether breaking stone could be read transparently as a sign of men's willingness to work. Bagott argued that "if there were 500 men at work at the Union, 500 tons of stone should be broken per day," but the amount of broken stone was far less than that. He demanded that "if the work was not done properly then the workmen must be stopped."

The board worried that the men they had seen as honestly craving work were in reality loafers. The guardian John Hughes, a maltster, said "he was informed that many of the men, instead of being at work, were in the hovels surrounding the Workhouse. He also believed that many of those who were now running for relief had never done a day's work in their lives," suggesting that undeserving, unskilled applicants were taking advantage of relief efforts meant only for the honest unemployed.[25] While the work was brutal, it was a "privilege," because through it an unemployed man could earn relief outside the workhouse and sleep in his own home.

The Dudley guardians faced conflicts among ideological pressures to conform to the work imperative, diverse opinions regarding the blamelessness of unemployed men, and local conditions that threatened to defeat their ability to adhere to poor law rules. It fell to the stoneyard master to assess men's commitment to the work imperative. He reported at the same early February meeting that "some of the men worked well, others only moderately well, and others were habitually idle, but he would single out the idle ones and set them to work by themselves, so that he would be able to give an account of their work." Because of the crowding, it was hard to differentiate those willing to work from loafers. Guardian William Smith, a hotel owner, pointed out that "it was impossible for 500 or 600 men to break stones together." Bagott, however, persisted that "any man who would not work should be ordered from the yard."[26] Even when it was realistically unmanageable to monitor individual men, the Dudley guardians held fast to the principles of the Labour Test.

As they continued to struggle with resources to keep the work test functioning correctly, the guardians disagreed over how unemployed men should express their faithfulness to the work imperative. In March, Guardian Challingsworth, a licensed victualler who consistently advocated for the Dudley unemployed, called his colleagues to task, saying they focused too much on the quantity of broken stone. He argued that stone breaking "was merely a test to see whether [the unemployed] wanted labour or not." If they expressed a willingness to work by showing up at the workhouse, that should be sign enough of their honesty, since they sacrificed their vote by receiving poor law relief. Challingsworth commented that "he had visited the Workhouse, and [had] found it anything but pleasant to be up in that bleak spot where the stoneyard was situated. He protested against the men being compelled to break a given amount of stone."[27] Guardians should trust the declarations of honest men as to their adherence to the work imperative. Yet the quantity of broken stone remained the measure of willingness to work.

The winter of 1878–79, with its combination of severe weather and already existing unemployment, brought home to Dudley's guardians the challenges of implementing the tests of the work imperative in the face of significant local unemployment. The outcome of the board's debates was an increasing emphasis on men's performance of menial task work for relief. Honest men had to demonstrate their deservedness actively, since most officials were unwilling to accept a man's self-representation as willing to work. Discussions of the challenges, however, offered others an opportunity to argue that the Poor Law was unsuitable for honest poor men. The work imperative had to get beyond stone breaking at the workhouse, with its obvious limitations and punitive associations, and provide deserving men with a more meaningful test of their willingness to work.

Task work versus work relief

The national registers of trade union unemployment of the early 1880s returned to less than five per cent, although the numbers began to climb as early as 1884, reaching almost ten per cent again in 1886.[28] The increasing number of "respectable" unemployed men strained poor law resources further and created additional impetus to interpret unemployment outside the framework of personal responsibility. Historians have identified 1886 as a watershed year regarding the social awareness of unemployment as a structural problem of capitalism and the politicization of the unemployed, who increasingly inserted themselves into the debates. As John Burnett has noted in his history of unemployment, while meetings of the unemployed had been occurring regularly from the early 1870s, "the events of 1886–87 were different in scale and character from anything before. For the first time, unemployment became a political issue, perceived as a problem distinct from poverty, caused by factors other than moral failings, deserving of public sympathy and remedial action by the state."[29] Unemployed men held massive demonstrations in London, creating fears among government officials that the honest unemployed would be influenced by the unskilled "mob."[30]

Workers' politicization of unemployment created a new knowledge among Black Country men of the need to assert their right to assistance. Deputations applied collectively to the Boards of Guardians, claiming their right to relief as honest poor men. They pressured their boards to recognize that local conditions did not always fit into the poor law framework, but they came up against the tests of the work imperative. In March 1886, for example, members of the Stourbridge Board received a deputation of 15 men from a local ironworks. Discussing the workers' petition as the men waited outside the room, the board's chairman articulated his recognition that matters were very grave, but he also "was informed that one of the men had not been in the habit of working. (Oh!)." This doubt about a man's honesty created an obvious problem for the guardians, who were only prepared to provide outrelief to men willing to work. The chairman indicated, "The applications placed the Board in a very awkward position," as they did not want to relieve a "loafer." Yet, even with doubts about one of the men's honesty, "to offer them a note for the [work]house would be too much."[31] Although policy dictated that all relief to the undeserving able-bodied must be through the workhouse, guardians did not want to lump men suffering from unemployment with regular paupers.

While authorities expressed concerns about idlers taking advantage of the work test, the depression of the late nineteenth century made it increasingly clear that most men applying for assistance were in fact doing so "through no fault of their own." In a context when many of these men, skilled workers, had recently gained the franchise in 1867 and 1884, questions about citizenship became central to discussions of poor relief. According to Lees, "as workers asserted their rights to political citizenship, they adopted a broader conception of social citizenship that made welfare in the form of 'poor' laws unacceptable."[32] Since many of the newly unemployed had been deemed responsible enough for the franchise, Boards of Guardians worried about pauperizing these respectable men, who would lose their vote even if they received the more "respectable" outrelief.[33]

Unemployed men themselves were aware of the threat to their franchise from poor relief. The *Advertiser* reported in January 1891, "Some of those who are the worst off show the most independence of spirit. Says one man: – Do you think I would apply to the Guardians for relief and lose my vote? Why I'd sooner lie down on the snow in the gutter there." The article went on to comment, "It is owing to this spirit of sturdy independence that some of the hardest cases do not come to light."[34] While serving as a prescription for the proper attitude about poor relief and citizenship, this item also points to the struggle facing men needing income support. Given the dire circumstances of 1886, both local and central government officials sought strategies through which the unemployed could be relieved while retaining their political citizenship.

One way this could be accomplished was by finding the unemployed non-pauperizing work outside the framework of the Poor Law: work relief as opposed to task work. A March 1886 circular from Joseph Chamberlain, then president of the Local Government Board, emphasized this strategy by urging local authorities to support public works projects in periods of hardship. Work relief for the public good was far different from the monotonous, unproductive task work required by the Poor Law and offered a means to separate the honest poor from regular paupers. While the strategy itself remained part of the toolbox of unemployment relief throughout the entire period of this study, it was, according to Harris, a failure, primarily because the national government did not fund the mandate.[35]

The Chamberlain circular encouraged an alternative to poor law relief, seeing unemployed men through the lens of honest poverty. According to Chamberlain, "The spirit of independence which leads so many of the working classes to make great personal sacrifices rather than incur the stigma of pauperism, is one which deserves the greatest sympathy and regret, and which it is the duty and interest of the community to maintain by all means at its disposal."[36] The increase in the unemployment of this imagined class of men, the honest poor who avoided the Poor Law at all costs, pressured the Local Government Board to find some substitute for poor relief. Yet Chamberlain was not willing to sanction any relaxation of the work imperative, fearing it would normalize relief and damage working men's sense of independence.

Chamberlain noted that the Labour Test, in its usual form of stone breaking, was not suitable to men of the artisan class whose skills might be damaged by this degrading work. The circular thus set up the possibility that the honest poor could sink to the level of the pauper if their circumstances were not distinguished from "the classes who usually seek" poor law relief.[37] Chamberlain recommended that Boards of Guardians and local authorities work together to provide non-pauperizing employment for the honest men who were out of work in their communities. Work such as paving roads, creating parks and cemeteries, and helping lay sewer and water systems "is work which is in no way degrading, and need not interfere with existing employment."[38] The Boards of Guardians should recommend for this type of employment men whose histories made them unsuitable to be "treat[ed] as subjects for pauper relief."[39] Chamberlain's emphasis on an individual's work history as a sign of welfare deservedness was echoed in discussions of unemployment relief as programs expanded during the twentieth century. The honest unemployed, especially skilled men, were granted an occupational identity, a work history, while "subjects for pauper relief" – Weary Willies and Tired Tims – were not.

The local authorities in the Stourbridge and Dudley areas became engaged with Chamberlain's project of trying to find work relief for the honest unemployed. Yet while part of the intention of work relief was to get away from employment that was "degrading," the assigned projects were often no better than those provided by Boards of Guardians. This was certainly the case in Tipton in March 1886, when town officials resolved "to find employment for the unemployed in stonebreaking and clearing away the rubbish from the streets," as a response to the "exceptionally acute" distress in the parish.[40] The Coseley local authorities had also been employing men breaking stones, and by April 1886 a Mr. Cornfield "complained of the manner the stones were broken in many cases, and said the Board had been grossly imposed upon ... The Road Foreman stated that 'great tricks' had been played by the relief men in breaking stones, many of them never being broken at all and hid in the great heaps."[41] While town work relief supposedly did not contain the stigma or disenfranchisement of poor law relief, the assumptions of those administering the schemes were not so different from those in charge of the Poor Law. Welfare providers continued to require honest poor men to perform their deservedness in often demeaning ways.

The growing honest poor/pauper dichotomy

The economic crisis of 1886 led the British government to its first meaningful questioning of the Poor Law's power to address the problem of unemployment. The next serious economic downturn in the mid-1890s revealed that work-relief schemes were clearly insufficient, both in terms of the numbers of men they could assist and in the funding available to support them.[42] In response to increasing anxieties about unemployment and the uncertainty regarding how best to assist the unemployed, the government constituted a Select Committee in 1895 to investigate "Distress from Want of Employment." This committee was reappointed in February 1896 and issued reports in both 1895 and 1896.

To gather information about local conditions for the committee, the Local Government Board sent letters asking local authorities to comment on the distress in their districts. The replies from the Stourbridge and Dudley regions uniformly described very grave circumstances resulting from a combination of harsh winter weather that was preventing work outdoors, the decline of staple trades, and the closing of large ironworks in the area. Most of the replies, written by the chairmen or clerks of the urban or rural district councils, indicated that much of the relief was being handled by voluntary groups and private donations, with the local authorities unable to help in any significant way. According to G.M. Waring, clerk to the Tipton Urban District Council, "The District Council is not in a position to make any suggestions for the relief of distress beyond what is already being done, unless a grant was made by the Government to poor districts from the Consolidated Fund. The public authorities are powerless to give employment as suggested in your recent Circular, in consequence of the long-continued and severe frost practically stopping all out-door work."[43] Local authorities recognized the gap between what they were able to do to assist the unemployed and what was expected by the central government. More and more frequently, local officials asked for national solutions and resources.

Yet while they stressed acute structural economic and environmental causes of unemployment, local authorities continued to worry that public work relief was itself pauperizing, revealing the fluid boundaries between blameless honest poverty and blameworthy pauperism. For example, several replies mentioned the "chronic distress" that existed outside the immediate problem of unemployment. W. Jones, chairman of the Stourbridge Urban District Council, argued that work-relief schemes led men to rely on local authorities to provide work for them instead of independently seeking it themselves. N. Bassano of the Rowley Regis Urban District Council remarked, "There is of course the regular substratum of poverty due to the idle, improvident, drunken, badly made, unhealthy, vicious, the mistakes of humanity, but these are dealt with by the ordinary machinery, and will apparently always be with us."[44] The "ordinary machinery" referred to the Poor Law, clearly suggesting that the honest poor should be dealt with in another way. The committee's questions seemingly gave Bassano the opportunity to vent his frustration with regard to the undeserving poor, incorporating prevalent theories regarding the connections between pauperism, heredity, and degeneration.[45]

The 1896 Select Committee's charge included explicitly differentiating these "mistakes of humanity" from the honest poor, by considering "the means of discriminating in cases of exceptional distress between 'the deserving man forced to become dependent upon public aid' and the ordinary claimants for parish relief."[46] The committee argued that, while Boards of Guardians were empowered to assist the honest unemployed and their families, "the respectable 'unemployed' not only do not desire poor law relief, but . . . they have positive objections to accept the same on account of the stigma it involves." Additionally, welfare providers worried about the honest unemployed becoming habitual paupers: "fears are sometimes expressed lest the better class of unemployed brought into contact with poor law relief might be taught to rely more or less permanently upon receiving assistance from this source, and that in this way their independence might be gradually undermined." As a result of these issues "it is urged that a distinction should be made between the ordinary applicants for parochial relief and the deserving unemployed, that the needs of the former should be met in the ordinary way, and that other means, which are regarded as involving neither degradation nor reproach, should be devised to aid the deserving poor when suffering from want of employment."[47] No clearer articulation of the lines between the honest poor and "Weary Willies" or "Tired Tims" could be made. Figure 2.2 visually captures this repeatedly emphasized distinction between the deserving and undeserving, illustrating the physical and moral degeneration of those who did not desire work.

These concerns about relationships between the honest poor and "loafers" raised new questions about how and where to draw the boundaries of political citizenship. While the 1895 Select Committee had suggested discriminating between "the deserving man" and "the ordinary claimant

Figure 2.2 The Unemployed and the Workhouse, postcard c.1907. Mary Evans/ Peter Higginbotham Collection

for parish relief" in order to maintain the franchise for the former,[48] the 1896 report concluded that, in practice, it would be very difficult to distinguish who should lose their vote and who should not. "At present," they wrote, "no well-defined meaning attaches to the expressions 'exceptional distress,' 'deserving man,' and 'ordinary claimant for parish relief,' and even if it were possible to give a legislative interpretation to the same, large reliance would have to be placed upon the judgment of those investigating the cases. Such judgment would necessarily be imperfect and wanting in uniformity."[49] This extremely telling analysis of the lack of definitional clarity for the key terms in determinations of deservedness suggests the practical difficulties facing local boards and even more so the men applying to them, who would be subjected to individualized readings of their circumstances. In the event, no changes regarding the Poor Law and the franchise were carried out until the Representation of the People Act of 1918, when receipt of poor law assistance was no longer grounds for a man to be disenfranchised.[50]

Even with their very specific concerns regarding the efficacy of stoneyards and the problems with the franchise, the 1896 committee concluded that "there is no alternative but a labour test." They stressed the need to have good oversight in stoneyards to assure the work was getting done and the importance of having a scale of relief that was not competitive with independent labor: "The conditions under which out-relief is given should be such that the recipients would have inducements to seek independent employment or to return to their ordinary occupations when opportunity offered."[51] Still, the committee felt that Boards of Guardians had to do something to prevent the "deserving poor [from suffering] by being brought into contact with the loafing class in the stoneyard."[52] They feared that the honest unemployed could degenerate through exposure to men who had no desire to work. No one participating in discussions of the work imperative presented the alternative possibility: that "Weary Willies" and "Tired Tims" might have their manhood restored by the example of the honest poor.

The nation in the poor law world

Drawing on new liberal and Labour ideas about the positive role of state intervention, local councils and Boards of Guardians, as well as unemployed men themselves, expressed higher expectations of national solutions to the problem of unemployment. In 1905, the Conservative government brought in the Unemployed Workmen's Act, which facilitated the employment of men by local Distress Committees and certain

Figure 2.3 Labour Exchange in South London
Source: © Illustrated London News Ltd/Mary Evans.

businesses by providing grants to help with the costs of work-relief projects. The hope was that this would remove some of the burden from local bodies while simultaneously providing the honest poor with an alternative to the Poor Law. The Labour Exchanges Act of 1909, promoted by William Beveridge, set up exchanges (Figure 2.3) where men seeking work could find listings of available jobs.[53]

In pressing the need to develop alternatives to the Poor Law, like the Unemployed Workmen's Act and Labour Exchanges, the Bishop of Southwark argued to the House of Lords in August 1905 that the threat to the nation's manhood was not public relief but economic uncertainty:

He thought nothing damaged manhood more than for a man to feel himself in the power of forces which he was unable to control . . . [H]e was perfectly certain that the great economic forces had a character very similar to the appalling and intractable strength of the forces of nature itself, and he ventured to say that it did crush and weaken the manhood in men if they felt themselves to be the playthings of forces like that. . . . [T]he Poor Law did not deal with a man until he had become at least temporarily a wreck, and it went far to make him a wreck. Surely they would not think that that was the limit of what the intelligence and the sympathy of the community could do for its citizens, who were singly, and even in bodies and organisations, so weak and so powerless in the presence of the great economic forces.[54]

National government had a positive role in preventing honest poor men, victimized by economic forces, from becoming "wrecks." At issue was the relationship between welfare and masculine status, and the bishop directly connected honest men's citizenship with assistance from the state. In a context when concerns about national efficiency were paramount, anything that served to strengthen the nation's manhood was a positive step. The bishop clearly believed that poor men were more endangered by blameless destitution than they were by state assistance. Public welfare, indeed, could enhance working-class masculine citizenship and help strengthen the state. Here was a crack in the independent breadwinner ideal.

As the national government became more involved in the relief of unemployment, local authorities used the language of honest poverty to challenge the state to provide aid, both to augment local resources and to emphasize the deservedness of their local communities. The Dudley Distress Committee, a body constituted under the 1905 Unemployed Workmen's Act to apply for grants to support applicants for work relief, for example, castigated the national government in October 1909 for ignoring the honest poverty of the Dudley unemployed. The chairman, complaining that Dudley was not receiving the government attention it warranted, stressed that "he thought the unanimous opinion of the committee had been that Dudley stood as high as any town with regard to the character of the men with whom they had to deal."[55] The committee insisted that the town's men deserved state assistance because of their honest poverty. The Dudley Council also pressed for government consideration by appealing to local men's honesty. Councilor Taylor argued that there were more registered "honest unemployed in Dudley" than there had ever been before, and many of those were "on the books" for the first time. They were men "who had been employed in the town for more than thirty or forty years."[56] Seemingly, local officials saw the government's neglect of Dudley men's welfare as marking the local unemployed as dishonest or not deserving. Public assistance itself, in this framework, served as a sign of masculine status. This was new.

Addressing many of the questions arising from the perceived inadequacy of existing welfare and unemployment provisions, the 1909 Royal Commission on the Poor Laws and the Relief of Distress was the first major investigation of the Poor Law since the 1830s.[57] The commission noted that the conditions in the early twentieth century were very different from those of the 1830s that had brought in the New Poor Law, predominantly due to the extent of unemployment among honest poor men. In 1834, officials regarded public assistance and masculine status as essentially incompatible for able-bodied men. By the first decade of the twentieth century, this incompatibility was being questioned. The poor law system, they argued, was "degrading to the honest man who is anxious to reinstate himself in independence. The workhouse does not afford any abiding help to the class of distressed unemployed who are willing and anxious to work."[58] The work test administered through workhouse stoneyards had been conceptualized as an exception, yet it had become the rule and tended to "demoralise even the best workman."[59] Honest men's performance of their willingness to work in the context of the Poor Law was not a fair test of their deservedness. The Minority Report of the Poor Law Commission went even further, arguing for the abolition of the entire poor law system.[60]

The commission also criticized existing work-relief schemes, which were organized to "tide over" men who were seen as temporarily unemployed.[61] This strategy did not address the fact that many men were out of work for long periods. Additionally, while work relief was designed to help the honest unemployed, it wound up benefiting the "lower class" of worker.[62] The report condemned municipal relief works laid out in the Chamberlain circular as having a "demoralising effect on the industrial capacity of the men employed. . . . in proportion as emphasis is laid on its relief character and not on its commercial character, so the work degenerates from helpful, manly exertion for wages into the inefficient and lazy performance of the necessary prelude to a meal."[63] Because work-relief schemes were organized as "relief" rather than "work," "the workers were employed in their character as applicants for relief and not in their character as independent workmen."[64] Work relief compromised men's occupational identities and did not have the desired effect of restoring the manhood of the unemployed; it rather dragged down the honest unemployed to the level of the loafer. The commission damned the Unemployed Workmen's Act of 1905 on the same grounds.

As many historians have noted, the commission's reports did not have any immediate effect on the structure of the Poor Law. Policymakers and government officials looked to get beyond the Poor Law to support honest poor men who could not find work, and major legislative interventions, like the 1911 National Insurance Act, which I discuss in Chapter 3, certainly changed the landscape of unemployment assistance. In practice, however, poor law relief and public works schemes remained vital to the survival strategies of the unemployed both in the years leading up to the war and in the postwar period.

The poor law world overwhelmed

The First World War, after an initial period of disruption and work reorganization, pushed aside the "problem of unemployment." Administrative statistics showed unemployment around four per cent in 1914, but it fell below one per cent throughout the remainder of the war years.[65] The huge demand for labor in war industries and for soldiers on the battlefields meant that all men who remained without employment were regarded as shirkers who chose their condition, a theme I pick up in Part II of the book. Little sympathy existed for men out of work during wartime. The war, however, also raised further the issue of the inadequacies of the poor law world to deal with the unemployed honest poor. The immediate postwar period ushered in universal male suffrage and a limited suffrage for women, leading to increasing expectations regarding the national government's responsibility for its unemployed citizens. Additionally, the 1918 Representation of the People Act abolished the pauper disqualification that prohibited those in receipt of poor relief from voting. Soldiers and war workers received special benefits to tide them over to reintegrate them into civilian life, and already during the war the government began expanding national unemployment insurance.[66] The government promised, and working people expected, a more inclusive connection between welfare and citizenship.

This became even more pressing when unemployment reached unprecedented numbers in the early 1920s. The Ministry of Labour's *Labour Gazette* reported "a decline" in employment in September 1920, and by May 1921 more than two million workers were registered with the Employment Exchanges (the renamed Labour Exchanges) as looking for work. Black Country metal workers were hit very hard, as were coal miners, out on strike from April to July 1921, and all industries that relied on coal for fuel.[67] The new unemployment of the postwar period was much more persistent and, for many men in the Black Country, almost permanent. The *County Express* reported about Dudley in February 1921, "There does not seem to be any loosening of unemployment in the borough . . . The most pathetic side of it is that most of the real suffering is below the surface. There are those of the better artisan class who would rather die than reveal their true condition. Even those who were thrifty when the war gave them good wages are beginning to see with very painful eyes their store gradually dwindling."[68] While the rhetoric surrounding the shame of unemployment continued to be potent, the context had shifted enough that men's demands for welfare became increasingly public. Men of the "better artisan class" were forced to "reveal their true condition."

Throughout the 1920s, the Dudley and Stourbridge Boards of Guardians had to make relief decisions for very large numbers of applicants. Even as more people became eligible for unemployment benefits, restrictions on benefits meant that the unemployed continued to rely on the locally administered Poor Law. According to the Ministry of Health, in June 1922 almost 1.1 million insured workers and their dependants received outrelief, while fewer than 63,000 non-insured workers were relieved outside the workhouse, showing that the vast majority of those relying on poor law outrelief were the honest poor whose eligibility for unemployment insurance spoke to their good work histories.[69] In 1921 alone, the *Labour Gazette* reported that the Wolverhampton district (which included Dudley and environs) saw an increase in the numbers of "paupers" per 10,000 inhabitants from 115 in January, to 208 in May, to 696 in October. By comparison, London's numbers for the same months were 255, 294, and 528, while "other districts" averaged 132, 261, and 501.[70] The West Midlands saw the problem of unemployment return with a vengeance, feeling particularly the lingering lack of fuel even after the national coal strike ended in July 1921. By mid-1922, however, the West Midlands, London, and "other districts" all ranged between the high 400s and the low to mid-500s per 10,000 of their populations receiving relief. The Sheffield district and the Stockton and Tees district, where unemployment was the most severe, hovered around 1,500 per 10,000.[71]

This environment increased activism among the unemployed, when men's demands both for relief and for recognition as economic and political actors grew. By September 1921, many of the towns in the Dudley and Stourbridge Unions had their own committees of unemployed men, which held regular demonstrations, often featuring local politicians. The newspapers were filled in 1921 and 1922 with stories about unemployed men's demands, during what Matt Perry describes as one of the two major moments of political action among the unemployed in the interwar era: 1919–1922 and 1931–1936.[72] A deputation came before the Dudley Board of Guardians in early September 1921, for example, "to object to the scale of relief, which was totally inadequate, and not calculated to touch the fringe of the poverty which existed."[73] A month later another deputation protested "the way the men had been received when applying for relief . . . They called on the Board to increase the scale, and to give part in cash. They also protested generally against the applicants being treated as paupers instead of citizens."[74] The speakers for the unemployed presented themselves as willing to work and unwilling to be subjected to the humiliation of poor law relief, asserting their status as respectable citizens. The Brierley Hill Trades Council, in support of this position, unanimously agreed in October of 1921 to send a letter to the Board of Guardians "protesting against the word 'pauper' being used in the notes given to recipients of relief," because it was "degrading."[75] This language of citizenship, linked to a right to relief, spoke to the new role of welfare to working-class citizen men.[76]

Even as organizing progressed, men continued to need the Poor Law, and poor law authorities continued to require task work for outrelief. I have 28 Dataset 2 application files for the Stourbridge Union between January and August 1921 in which able-bodied men applied because they were "out of work." All of these unemployed men had to perform task work to receive relief, or "relief in work." Many of these cases indicated that the men had "no labor, no union," meaning they received no unemployment benefit and no funds from a union.[77] Because of the unsystematic nature of this collection of applications, there is no way to know how representative this group is, but as individuals these men appear in the records expressing their "needs" rather than their "rights." They accepted task work to prove their deservedness.

Unemployed men's organizations, however, contested the demonstration of deservedness through task work. The Stourbridge Board of Guardians received a large deputation of unemployed men from throughout the Stourbridge Union in September 1921 who "protested . . . against task work having to be performed." The board agreed to give up task work "except in special cases where the Board think that the test should be applied."[78] Two weeks later, another deputation pushed for an increased scale of relief, but the Stourbridge Board of Guardians turned this down.[79] By May 1922, the board's refusal to see deputations of unemployed men was routine: "Resolved . . . that no useful purpose would be served by receiving the Deputation, as it was necessary to effect economies in order to make the resources of the Board last out."[80] Perhaps guardians could no longer face these men, knowing their inability to assist them. Local boards clearly were sympathetic to the plight of men unemployed "through no fault of their own" and grew increasingly frustrated with the responses from the central government.

In the absence of acceptable alternatives, both national and local officials fell back on the work test. Government correspondence during October 1923 indicates that, while many people who ran out of national unemployment benefits moved to the Poor Law, the work test was still necessary: "relief to the able-bodied cannot be safely undertaken without the use in the majority of cases of a labour test." Yet, acknowledging that many of the honest unemployed were reluctant to apply for poor law relief, Assistant Secretary Herbert Francis of the Ministry of Health commented that task work "may of course be disguised as training, but for a large proportion of the applicants it is essential that it should be unattractive and if possible that it should be generally regarded as carrying a social stigma,"[81] indicating a desire to maintain the boundary between honest poverty and pauperism. In November, the Ministry of Health agreed to send a circular to Boards of Guardians reiterating the principle of "less eligibility" that had been codified in the New Poor Law of 1834, insisting that no one on benefit or receiving poor relief should be better off than the independent working man.[82] Guardians had to preserve the Poor Law's explicitly disciplinary framework.[83]

Utilizing task work, the Dudley Board of Guardians kept its local rates relatively under control during the crisis of the early 1920s, but in 1927 the board was forced to raise the rates and simultaneously toughen its policy on outrelief. The guardians' costs of relief were higher in April 1927 than they had been in December 1926, at the termination of the miners' strike, when unprecedented numbers had applied for assistance. The *Herald* reported that

> having had opportunities of seeing some of the men at test work, and having had so many complaints of neglect of work and the men's lazy attitude towards their work the [guardians' relief] committee thought the time had arrived when they should . . . put the relief regulation order into effect, so as to relieve able-bodied men only in the way those orders indicated – that was to 'offer them the house.' . . . [M]any of these men had settled down to continuous out-relief, and were quite content so long as they could get just sufficient to keep themselves and their families going.[84]

Weary Willy and Tired Tim continued to assert their presence in debates about the work imperative, raising doubts about the deservedness of unemployed men before the Poor Law. The Relief Regulation Order mandated that men who had been unemployed for five or more years would only be offered relief in the workhouse, although their families could apply for outrelief. The Relief Committee reported that, once this procedure was put into place, many of the men who were offered the workhouse "had found jobs,"[85] insinuating that this justified their policy, which tested men's willingness to work and culled those with a "lazy attitude."

In the nineteenth century, the foil for the honest unemployed man was the habitual pauper; in the 1920s it became the "permanently unemployed man" who might once have been honest but who had degenerated through persistent unemployment. The possibility that men could be "content" not to work as long as relief supported them was so appalling to the editor of the *Dudley Herald* that in April 1927 he devoted his leader to it. Emphasizing the Board of Guardians' efforts at "Weeding Out the Shirkers," the article commented,

> It is obvious . . . that there are many shirkers who are content to remain idle so long as they can obtain relief . . . There are many to whom a test has been applied and complaints have been forthcoming of their lazy attitude and their neglect of work. Such men have become so used to being permanently unemployed that when the opportunities occur for them to earn their own living they shirk them, and so long as they can get sufficient to carry on with they would rather remain in the ranks of the workless.[86]

Prolonged unemployment could corrupt honest poverty, turning men who had once been deserving into Weary Willies and Tired Tims who shirked their responsibilities.

Policymakers and welfare providers alike linked the ideology of the work imperative to national identity. A Ministry of Health inspector visited the Dudley Board of Guardians in September 1927 to congratulate the guardians for upholding not just the ratepayers' interests, but those of the nation: "So long as you are going to give money to anyone for doing nothing, how can you expect the ordinary Britisher to keep up his own self-respect?" He complemented "The Dudley system of giving relief [which] induced men to 'get a move on' and secure jobs."[87] Even in a period of severe economic crisis, the Dudley Board of Guardians held to the work imperative in a way that presented the union as a model. National identity was bound up with enforcing unemployed men's commitment to work.

By contrast, the Stourbridge Board of Guardians was taken to task in the summer of 1928, when H.K. Nesbit, an inspector presumably from the Ministry of Health, suggested that the board needed to adhere more strictly to the work imperative to measure deservedness. While "he knew the particular difficulties of the Stourbridge Union," Nesbit stressed that "the only thing was to tighten things up as much as possible in order to help the deserving people and sift out the undeserving, and he thought it was kindest, in the long run, to be firm. He particularly wished they would do more in the matter of test-work . . . He knew the difficulties of many applicants, whom the Relieving Officers told him were triers, and they desired to help them."[88] Even men who were "triers," who were recognized as national citizens, had to demonstrate their deservedness through the work test.

The pressure from the Ministry of Health to maintain the work test even in the face of continued chronic and mass unemployment did not sit well with many guardians or with unemployment activists. In December 1929, Wal Hannington, a founder of the British Communist Party and leader of the National Unemployed Workers Movement, wrote in the *Labour Monthly* that the Labour government had "extended" "the pernicious system of task and test work." According to Hannington, Boards of Guardians were trying to cut back on the work test as they confronted the continuing reality of local unemployment, but they were "being threatened and bullied into continuing [task work] by the Minister" of Health. Hannington offered several examples of boards that were not using task work to measure deservedness who had "received instructions from the Minister of Health insisting that task work must be imposed and that no departure from that regulation would be permitted."[89] If Boards of Guardians were committed to helping their local unemployed by relaxing work test restrictions, according to Hannington, they would suffer punishment from the central government.

Unlike Hannington, however, many unemployed men themselves believed in some kind of work test to demonstrate their deservedness. They saw work-relief projects as the best way to determine a man's commitment to the work imperative. The cry of "work not doles" spoke to the space occupied by work-relief schemes in addressing the problem of unemployment in the postwar period. In September 1921, the town councils of the Dudley and Stourbridge regions, like the poor law Boards of Guardians, were flooded with deputations from the recently organized committees of unemployed men. Councilor Robbins of the Tipton Council responded to one deputation the week of September 10, asserting that he understood that "what the men wanted, he was sure, was neither charity nor doles, but work."[90] The Dudley Town Council the next week listened to unemployed men argue to applause that "unemployment doles and poor law relief were no remedy for unemployment. They aggravated the disease . . . But the unemployed could not be allowed to starve, so the solution must be work." Sam Mulley, secretary of the local unemployment committee, stressed that "the Council would fully realise that the unemployed wanted work, not doles; they did not want charity, it stank in their nostrils . . . They wanted work, not idleness, for as Carlyle wrote: 'Idleness alone is their perpetual despair.'"[91] Only through work relief could honest men truly demonstrate their willingness to work and maintain the basis of masculine citizenship.

Yet the unemployed committees argued that the work offered to them had to be compensated at a rate signifying masculine status. At an early February 1922 meeting of the Stourbridge unemployed, the committee worried about men desperate enough to take work at unacceptable wages. The chairman D. Clarke complained,

At Lye that morning men were offering themselves for 7 ½ d an hour. He was not going to say what kind of men they were. . . . [T]he unemployed were not going to be used as tools for getting cheap labour. The trades unions would back up the unemployed if the members were men at all. . . . The Chairman said a person who would accept less money was not a man.[92]

Honest unemployed men were ready and willing to work but not under terms that unmanned them. That same week, Halesowen men on work-relief schemes complained about the pay they received, the secretary of the committee calling it "insulting." Challenging the discourse of the work imperative, the chairman argued that "they had had a good deal of talk about the shirker, but they only had the shirker because he had realized that he was not being properly paid for his work."[93] Men could only be expected to undertake work for which they were sufficiently remunerated, which raised the question of the conditions under which a man should be expected to work, a theme I explore more deeply in relation to strikes in Chapter 7.

While ideologically work relief fit the expectations of honest poverty, resources simply could not support public works on a scale that would make a difference. The chancellors of the exchequer of the 1920s had little confidence in relief works, which became increasingly discredited as a way to address unemployment.[94] For both welfare providers and recipients, however, work relief was attractive as it was recognized as a means for a man to demonstrate actively his adherence to the work imperative and his ability to meet his masculine responsibilities. Unlike work for the Poor Law's Labour Test, it was productive, and unlike the dole, it required actual physical activity.

Conclusion

"The problem of unemployment" led policymakers and unemployed men to envision a more positive role for the state in helping localities provide what was supposed to be relief without stigma for the honest poor. Yet the underfunding of work-relief schemes and the continuing suspicion of those without work as somehow responsible for their condition created significant limitations to assisting the unemployed at the local level. Men struggled to prove their welfare deservedness through demonstrations of their willingness to work, which became increasingly important as the numbers of unemployed surged and resources contracted. Policymakers, welfare providers, and unemployed men themselves all agreed on the centrality of the work imperative to working-class manhood. The question was in what ways the state would intervene to support or punish men out of work.

Chronic and mass unemployment fueled the national government's recognition that being out of work could go beyond the control of individuals and that the state could help its citizens function as productive members of society. It opened a space for welfare to bolster manhood rather than to detract from it. Unemployment, however, also drained state and local resources to such an extent that the model of less stigmatizing work relief was never fully implemented, and honest poor men operating in the poor law world were never fully comfortable with being dependent on local assistance.

3

"They were not single men": Responsibility for Family and Hierarchies of Deservedness

In the uncertain economic climate following the First World War, the Stourbridge Poor Law Board of Guardians had opened the workhouse labor yard so unemployed men could break stone to prove their willingness to work for relief. As the summer of 1919 approached and outdoor occupations became more readily available, guardian George Parkes argued that the board should close the stoneyard, because "the men would be able to find employment to tide them over until trade revived." Guardian John Downing countered that the region still suffered significant unemployment, lamenting that "there were so many men in the Halesowen and Cradley district who were in distress, and who were willing to work if they could get it." The Reverend T.J. McNulty, a long-time Liberal guardian representing Quarry Bank, agreed. He admitted,

> Some of the people who came to him were, no doubt, undeserving; but whether they were deserving or not, they were not single men, but had wives and families who were suffering acutely. The men who went from Quarry Bank to the labour yard were honest men, and only went there through sheer necessity. They felt ashamed that they had to go there to break stones; but they went there rather than see their wives and families pine away.

McNulty "implored the Guardians to keep the labour yard open a little longer," and they resolved to do so.[1]

McNulty's plea for the needs of unemployed men contains a key tension within the discourse of honest poverty that had been taking shape from the late nineteenth century. Although McNulty pointedly acknowledged that some of the men asking for help might have been "undeserving," presumably because they did not sufficiently demonstrate a willingness to work, the fact that "they were not single men" trumped doubts about their fully meeting the work imperative. Single men did not have wives and children "suffering acutely" from the male breadwinner's lack of work. The "honest men" shamed by their need to ask for assistance were married men whose need was defined above all by their positions as husbands and fathers. Their responsibility to maintain their families – their "family liability" – placed them at the top of a hierarchy of deservedness. McNulty's seemingly dismissive attitude toward the work imperative was unusual; his privileging of married men was not.

Just as the "problem of unemployment" forced policymakers to rethink how to test men's adherence to the work imperative, it also led authorities and unemployed men themselves to prioritize the welfare of the breadwinner family in new ways. As Sean Brady and other historians have argued, in the late nineteenth century, "for men to be considered fully masculine, they had to be married . . . [and] had to demonstrate their masculinity through their abilities to support their wives and families."[2] The funneling of resources to men with wives and children created "welfare heteronormativity," a system that facilitated honest men's abilities to maintain masculine status directly through their family responsibilities. While the link between masculinity and providing for a family was certainly not new in the late nineteenth century, the ways that welfare policy and practice incorporated that link into the "problem of unemployment" were. Policymakers and welfare providers saw unemployment itself as a problem of married men with families and tried to construct a system that supported married men and their dependants in positive rather than punitive ways. As was the case with the work imperative, authorities' willingness to attach deservedness to able-bodied men represented a big shift from the New Poor Law of 1834 and the crusade against outrelief of the early 1870s, which explicitly aimed to punish able-bodied men who did not have work, blaming them for their joblessness and inability to support their dependants.[3]

Poor married men asserted their status as citizens and their welfare deservedness by comparing themselves to unmarried men. All men could follow the work imperative, but only married men could demonstrate both a willingness to work and family liability. During the second half of the nineteenth century, the politics of liberalism and labor bound working-class men's citizenship closely to their status as responsible heads of household. Independence, in historian Keith McClelland's words, "was not so much the ability [of a man] to maintain himself as to be able to maintain himself and his dependants."[4] The emphasis on respectable men's breadwinner status, McClelland argues, helped secure the vote in 1867 for working-class urban householders. As Sonya Rose has shown, married men's union activism "distinguished *among* male persons" by defining "respectable manhood" as tied "to their status as husbands and fathers."[5] A single man was "suspect" and, according to Angus McLaren in his history of masculinity, "could be regarded by his peers as not having attained full adult status."[6] Unemployed married men demanded welfare that recognized the ways marriage and family differentiated them from single men as full citizens of the nation.

Guardians and other welfare authorities often conceived of deservedness as a negative: deserving men were *not* Weary Willies or Tired Tims, and they were "not single men." Not surprisingly, these were interrelated categories, since officials often assumed that tramps and vagrants were single men (or men who had abandoned their families), to whom suspicion attached.[7] Welfare policy became more expansive in order to legitimate relief to honest married men, but welfare providers continued to view single men without work through a moral lens as individual failures. The work-welfare system, in historian John Horne's words, "supported domestic masculinity as a foundation of the social order,"[8] and this hegemonic domestic masculinity had a special claim on state resources. We will see this in action in the relief politics of the Stourbridge and Dudley Unions. Policymakers and married working-class men themselves transformed the responsibility for wives and children into a right to welfare, a right that separated married from single men, even single men who were willing to work.

Profiles of poor law applicants

The Relieving Officers' Application and Report Books for Stourbridge Union, the material from which I constructed my Dataset 1 (DS1, 1871–1911),[9] show very clearly that married men applied for poor law relief on behalf of their families, and women came before poor law officials on their own chiefly when men were absent or unable to apply for themselves. The Stourbridge Union records support existing studies of the Poor Law, showing that women constituted the majority of applicants for and recipients of relief (see Table 3.1 and Figure 3.1).[10] Of the 4,321 initial applications in DS1 where gender was recorded, 55 per cent were from women. Interestingly, of the total 7,434 applications noting gender, women make up only 52 per cent, which means that, while as a whole more women than men applied once, men had more multiple applications over time. These multiple applications were

53

Table 3.1 Demographic profiles of Stourbridge Union Poor Law applicants, 1871–1911

Gender	Marital Status	16–19	20–29	30–39	40–49	50–59	60–69	70+	Unclear	Total
					Age – Primary Applicants					
Female	Married	0.0	1.5	2.5	1.2	0.4	0.4	0.2	0.1	6.4
	Single	1.5	2.7	1.2	0.9	0.8	0.7	0.4	0.2	8.5
	Widowed	0.0	1.1	4.4	4.7	3.0	10.7	15.4	0.4	39.6
Female total		1.6	5.2	8.1	6.9	4.2	11.9	16.1	0.6	54.5
Male	Married	0.0	2.4	5.3	4.8	3.7	7.2	7.4	0.2	31.1
	Single	1.2	1.6	0.8	0.8	0.6	0.4	0.2	0.1	5.8
	Widowed	–	–	0.2	0.4	0.6	1.9	5.4	0.2	8.6
Male total		1.2	4.0	6.3	6.0	4.9	9.5	13.1	0.4	45.5
Male + Female Total		2.8	9.2	14.4	12.8	9.1	21.4	29.1	1.1	100.0
					Age – All Applications					
Female	Married	0.0	1.8	3.2	1.4	0.5	0.4	0.2	0.1	7.5
	Single	1.3	2.4	1.2	1.1	0.6	0.6	0.3	0.2	7.8
	Widowed	0.1	1.1	5.0	5.5	3.4	9.6	11.5	0.3	36.4
Female total		1.4	5.3	9.4	8.1	4.5	10.5	11.9	0.7	51.7
Male	Married	0.0	2.8	6.5	5.6	4.2	9.1	7.1	0.3	35.6
	Single	0.9	1.5	0.7	0.7	0.4	0.6	0.2	0.1	5.0
	Widowed	–	–	0.3	0.3	0.8	1.5	4.7	0.2	7.8
Male total		0.9	4.3	7.5	6.6	5.4	11.2	12.0	0.5	48.3
Male + Female Total		2.3	9.6	16.9	14.6	9.8	21.7	23.9	1.2	100.0

Sources: My Dataset 1, from the Application and Report Books for the Stourbridge Union, held at the Staffordshire Record Office: from the Halesowen District, D585/1/5/27, D585/1/5/29, D585/1/5/32, and D585/1/5/35; from the Stourbridge District, D585/1/5/47 and D585/1/5/50; and from the Kingswinford District, D585/1/5/68, D585/1/5/70, D585/1/5/73, and D585/1/5/76.

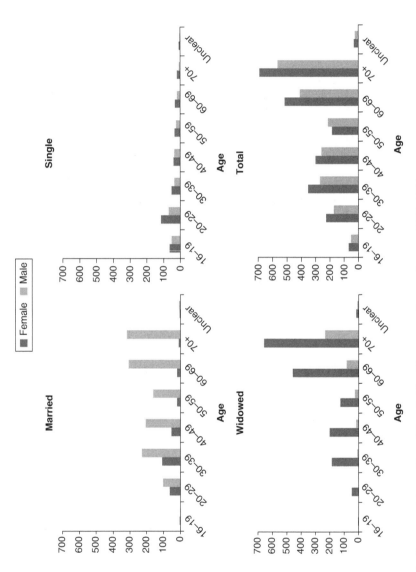

Figure 3.1 Demographic profiles of Stourbridge Union poor law applicants, 1871–1911

directly connected to men's responsibilities for families, which required repeated interactions with poor law authorities for in-kind relief. Married men predominated both among the married applicants and among the male applicants in DS1. Where the relieving officer recorded marital status, almost 38 per cent of the applicants were married. Of these married applicants, 83 per cent were men. Of the almost 1,950 applications from men where marital status is clear, more than two thirds of the applicants were married. By contrast, of the 14 per cent of applicants who were single, almost 60 per cent were women, and of the 48 per cent of applicants who were widowed, 82 per cent were women. Only 12 per cent of female applicants were married, about two thirds of whom petitioned because of the absence of their husbands (for the reasons men and women applied for relief, see Tables 3.2a and 3.2b). Tellingly, a missing spouse was the reason for only one man's appeal. Young women on their own and married men towards the end of their working years were particularly vulnerable. For applicants in their 50s, men made up 54 per cent of the initial applicants. Among the youngest age group, on the other hand, the gap between the genders is the largest, with women accounting for almost 60 per cent of applicants under 25. In my much smaller Dataset 2 (DS2, 1912–1929), 202 records are clear about both marital status and gender. In this much less representative group of applications, men predominated, making up 53 per cent of the applicants. Yet the breakdown of marital status is similar to DS1: 63 per cent of the men were married, compared to about 25 per cent of the women. Of all married applicants in DS2, almost three quarters were men.[11] Women without husbands lacked a male breadwinner, while men in their middle years struggled to meet their breadwinner responsibilities.

The vast majority of women applying to the poor law authorities were widowed or single, as these were the women without husbands to speak for them. In the local Black Country economy, where skilled jobs in coal mining and iron production were reserved for men, women worked in low-paying domestic nail- and chainmaking, as brickyard laborers (Figure 3.2), and as washerwomen and servants.[12] Single women and widows – especially those with children – could rarely earn enough to provide for themselves and their families without additional support. While the New Poor Law consistently viewed never-married mothers as problematic and positioned single women in general somewhere between the categories of "woman" and "worker," widows, especially those with small children, were perceived sympathetically as one of the groups (along with the elderly) regularly deserving of assistance[13] (for information on applicants' children, see Table 3.3). Married female applicants were most often wedded to men who had abandoned their

Table 3.2a Main reasons for Poor Law applications, 1871–1911

Gender	Marital Status (no.)	Main Reason for Application* – Dataset 1 (1871–1911)							
		Spouse absent	Illness or injury	Destitution	Age	Confinement	Death or health of child/spouse	Other/ unclear	Total
Female	Married (273)	63.4	20.5	6.6	3.7	0.4	2.9	2.6	100.0
	Single (361)	–	77.0	2.2	5.8	4.4	8.3	2.2	100.0
	Widowed (1,661)	–	41.3	17.9	35.9	0.2	3.1	1.6	100.0
Female total (2,295)		7.5	44.4	14.1	27.3	0.9	3.9	1.8	100.0
Male	Married (1,317)	–	53.1	3.3	20.3	0.2	22.4	0.8	100.0
	Single (244)	–	89.8	5.3	3.3	–	–	1.6	100.0
	Widowed (367)	–	47.4	2.7	46.6	–	2.7	0.5	100.0
Male total (1,928)		0.0	56.6	3.4	23.2	0.1	15.8	0.8	100.0
Male + Female Total (4,223)		4.1	50.0	9.2	25.4	0.5	9.4	1.4	100.0

Table 3.2b Main reasons for Poor Law applications, 1912–1929

Gender	Marital Status (no.)	Main Reason for Application* – Dataset 2 (1912–1929)							
		Spouse absent	Illness or injury	Destitution	Age	Confinement or Pregnancy	Unemployed	Other/ unclear	Total
Female	Married (26)	15.4	38.5	26.9	–	7.7	–	11.5	100.0
	Single (33)	–	42.4	33.3	3.0	18.2	–	3.0	100.0
	Widowed (34)	–	35.3	44.1	8.8	2.9	–	8.8	100.0
Female total (93)		4.3	38.7	35.5	4.3	9.7	0.0	7.5	100.0
Male	Married (74)	–	29.7	18.9	2.7	–	41.9	6.8	100.0
	Single (20)	–	40.0	50.0	–	–	–	10.0	100.0
	Widowed (15)	–	46.7	33.3	6.7	–	–	13.3	100.0
Male total (109)		0.0	33.9	26.6	2.8	0.0	28.4	8.3	100.0
Male + Female Total (202)		2.0	36.1	30.7	3.5	4.5	15.3	7.9	100.0

Note: *Can include other reasons, e.g., age also includes age plus health problems.
Applicants omitted from Table 3.2a include those with unclear (32 female, 15 male) and cohabiting (one male, one female) marital statuses.
Applicants omitted from Table 3.2b include those with unclear (nine female, eight male) marital statuses.
Sources: My Dataset 1, from the Application and Report Books for the Stourbridge Union, held at the Staffordshire Record Office (SRO): from the Halesowen District, D585/1/5/27, D585/1/5/29, D585/1/5/32, and D585/1/5/35; from the Stourbridge District, D585/1/5/47 and D585/1/5/50; and from the Kingswinford District, D585/1/5/68, D585/1/5/70, D585/1/5/73, and D585/1/5/76. My Dataset 2, from the collection SRO, D585/1/1/137, Case Papers of Individual Paupers, 1900–1926.

Figure 3.2   Women brickmakers in the Black Country, c.1902
Source: Mary Evans/Peter Higginbotham Collection.

families or who were in jail, the army, or a medical institution. Looking at it another way, women outside heteronormative families (single women, married women with absent husbands, and widows), and men within them, applied most often.

The example of Theophilus Moon, a 49-year-old glass cutter, demonstrates both the material needs of the Black Country poor and the ways that marriage helped support both men's and women's poor law petitions. Theophilus applied to the Stourbridge Board of Guardians on April 14, 1871, with a wife, Sarah, and two children under ten years old, Isabella and Philip. The relieving officer's application book describes Theophilus as able-bodied, although he had a "mind affected," which earned him a medical note to see a doctor. The following week, the relieving officer no longer defined Theophilus as able-bodied, and indeed his wife Sarah applied in his name: "husband gone into Asylum, . . . [application] for relief to wife and children." Sarah received two shillings and sixpence for six weeks as well as assistance in kind. At the end of that period, on June 2, the relieving officer started a new "case," with Sarah as the primary applicant, petitioning for assistance because her husband had been sent to Powick Asylum. The Board of Guardians renewed her pension for 12 weeks.[14]

Table 3.3 Poor Law applicants' children, 1871–1911

		Primary Applicants' Children			
Gender	Marital Status (no. in status)	Per cent with Dependent Children	Avg. No. of Dependent Children (for those who have them)	Per cent with Adult (over 15) Children	Avg. No. of Adult Children (for those who have them)
Female	Married (275)	78	3.3	14	1.6
	Single (361)	15	1.2	2	1.7
	Widowed (1,691)	28	3.2	42	2.0
Any marital status/ all women (2,327)		32	3.1	33	1.9
Male	Married (1,326)	46	3.3	32	2.0
	Single (246)	_*	_*	–	–
	Widowed (368)	7	2.8	46	2.3
Any marital status/ all men (1,940)		33	3.3	31	2.1
All men and women (4,267)		32	3.2	32	2.0

Note: *The records list one man, a single 19-year-old, as having four dependent children; because these are almost certainly not this man's biological children (likely they are siblings), the man is not counted in the table.

Sources: My Dataset 1, from the Application and Report Books for the Stourbridge Union, held at the Staffordshire Record Office: from the Halesowen District, D585/1/5/27, D585/1/5/29, D585/1/5/32, and D585/1/5/35; from the Stourbridge District, D585/1/5/47 and D585/1/5/50; and from the Kingswinford District, D585/1/5/68, D585/1/5/70, D585/1/5/73, and D585/1/5/76.

Theophilus Moon died within the month in Powick Asylum, "feeble and [in] poor condition." When Sarah applied for a renewal of her pension on July 14, the relieving officer discovered that she and Theophilus had never in fact been married: she was Sarah Downes, and "the man she called husband is dead in the Asylum but they were not married." She was awarded a temporary cash grant, but when she applied again, the Board of Guardians granted her in-kind relief and declared her children illegitimate. Theophilus and Sarah might have considered themselves married in common law, or they might have presented themselves as husband and wife to better their chances for assistance. Marriage made Theophilus deserving as a provider unable to meet his family liability and Sarah deserving as the wife of a man unable to provide "through no fault of his own."[15]

Although Theophilus Moon applied as a "glass cutter," he most likely was no longer able to work; the records, however, continued to tie his identity to an occupation. The poor law records associate men with work much more often than they do women. While the men's occupations listed in the application books universally represented paid employments, women's were more likely to represent work without pay, reaffirming women's dependence on men's earnings. Relieving officers filled in the occupation category in DS1 for 3,716 primary applications: 1,966 women (83 per cent of the women) and 1,748 men (89 per cent of the men). Reflecting the paid employment opportunities in the region, work connected to coal and iron production (Figure 3.3), as well as nail- and chainmaking, appear frequently in the applicants' lists of occupations. In DS2, 149 cases listed occupations.[16] Two thirds of these were men, many of whom were unemployed chainmakers. In both datasets, however, the "occupation" category included such employments as "domestic" and "housework," which often denoted unpaid labor and helps explain the high percentage of women applicants considered "occupied." As would be expected, in both DS1 and DS2, women made up almost 100 per cent of domestic service and housework occupations (Figure 3.4). Indeed, of all the women's occupations listed in DS1, domestic work – whether paid or unpaid – made up 73 per cent of all women's work. In DS2, of the 49 female applicants who had occupation listed, 13 had "domestic" occupations, three had "household duties," and six had their occupations listed as "housewife."

Figure 3.3 Pig ironery in the Black Country, c.1900
Source: © Dudley Archives and Local History Service, ref. p. 546.

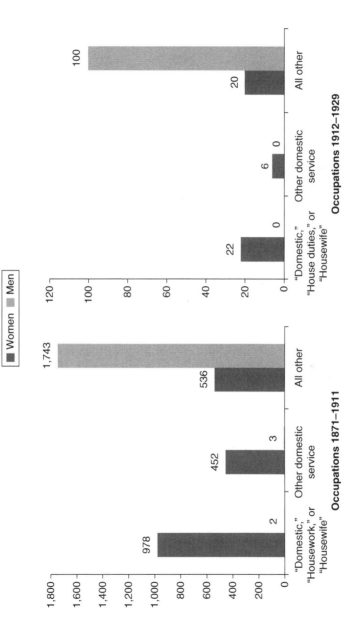

Figure 3.4 Occupations of poor law applicants by gender, 1871–1929

Sources: My Dataset 1, from the Application and Report Books for the Stourbridge Union, held at the Staffordshire Record Office (SRO): from the Halesowen District, D585/1/5/27, D585/1/5/29, D585/1/5/32, and D585/1/5/35; from the Stourbridge District, D585/1/5/47 and D585/1/5/50; and from the Kingswinford District, D585/1/5/68, D585/1/5/70, D585/1/5/73, and D585/1/5/76; and my Dataset 2, from SRO, D585/1/1/137, Case Papers of Individual Paupers, 1900–1926.

Gender, age, and marital status intersected to shape the reasons men and women turned to the Poor Law (see Tables 3.2a and 3.2b). While married women applied for relief when their husbands could not or would not provide for them, married men applied to take care of their families. Their DS1 applications show that illness, injury, and age brought married men to the Poor Law, reasons that most likely kept them from their regular occupations. Married men also applied when their children or wives needed medical care. Single people, men and women both, overwhelmingly came to poor law authoritie₃ because of health issues, which, similarly to married men, presumably kept them from wage earning. Widows and widowers also usually applied because of reasons connected to health and age. Interestingly, while "unemployment" as a category does not appear at all in the DS1 records, it becomes significant in the later dataset, reflecting the increasing incorporation of the vocabulary of unemployment into the work-welfare system. The overall portrait that emerges from the datasets is that individuals and families in the region lived in a world structured by men's family liability. Women who lacked men to provide and men unable to provide used the Poor Law to get by.

Constructing married men's privilege

In the context of the "problem of unemployment," relief providers increasingly used men's family liability in determinations of assistance and particularly of outrelief.[17] The Local Government Board's annual report for 1878–1879 noted that the large numbers of men out of work made it necessary "for the Guardians in many unions to give out-door relief to able-bodied men and their families."[18] The report made no mention of giving relief to single men. Indeed, single men have a tendency to disappear in the records of poor law decision making, except in cases where policies explicitly excluded them. For example, the chairman of the Dudley Board of Guardians indicated in early February 1879 that, to reduce expenditures, he planned to "refuse work to every single man and all boys, and only give work in such cases where it was absolutely necessary."[19] Although he left it unsaid, the chairman clearly defined "necessary" cases as those involving men with families to support. Married men's responsibilities for wives and children constructed this necessity in the eyes of welfare providers. The risk of not helping married men and their families was potential family breakdown and further demands upon the state, a subject I take up in Chapters 9. "Boys" could still be part of families who might benefit from relief afforded to their fathers. Single men, however, outside of normative families and perhaps avoiding the responsibilities of taking on dependants, were at the bottom of a hierarchy where deservedness was determined by a man's family liability.

We can follow the exclusion of single men in decisions made by the Dudley Board of Guardians in 1879. In May, struggling to deal with their relief expenditures for unemployed able-bodied men, the board's Committee on Unemployment noted

> that the number employed [breaking stone] at the Dudley Union is considerably in excess of the number of men at other unions [where] no single men or men without families [are] being employed at the present time. The Committee therefore recommend that no single men be any longer employed after the expiration of one week, and that married men without families be employed for a further period of two weeks. . . . That those men with families have 3 days work weekly for 2 weeks and that at the expiration of that time the number be gradually reduced weekly and the stone yard ultimately closed.[20]

Yet, a month later, the stoneyard was still open, and specifications of deservedness became even more precise. On June 6, the board resolved "that married men with three children have three days work per week [in the stoneyard], that with more than three children have four days work per week."[21] On June 13, the board amended its previous resolution so that married men with three or more children would get three days of work per week.[22] On July 4, the board resolved "that able-bodied men with wives and one child only be discontinued work at the workhouse and that men with wives and two children be discontinued work at the expiration of one week and that the stone-yard be closed at the expiration of two weeks from this date."[23] The stoneyard, however, did not close, and indeed the board continually awarded the yard master bonuses because of the amount of work he faced.[24] Single men, however, remained excluded from outrelief.

Similarly, in 1886, the Dudley Board of Guardians again constructed a hierarchy of deservedness based on a man's family liability. After the Local Government Board rejected the Dudley Board of Guardians' request "that their Rule as to the giving of Out Door Relief to Able Bodied Men and their Families be relaxed in necessitous cases in consequence of the great depression in trade in the district," the guardians resolved in early March to allow able-bodied unemployed men to perform task work for outrelief.[25] The *Herald* reported that the Board of

Guardians informed a deputation of about 100 unemployed men that "they would be employed at 2s. a day, men with no families to have two days work a week, with medium families to have three days, and with large families four days a week."[26] It is unclear where the board drew the line between large and medium families. However, from the previous example, "men with no families" obviously referred to married men without children. Single men fit nowhere in the framework surrounding "family." True honest poverty described a married man (with children) who was willing to work.

The reality, of course, is that men with wives and children did need additional resources, but the debates and relief decisions effaced the welfare of single men and, in some cases, all people but married men with children. For example, in July 1883, an editorial in the *Dudley Herald*, calling for a reduction of the rates by the Dudley Board of Guardians, hailed the policy in Birmingham

> where it has been . . . decided to refuse out-door relief altogether to single able-bodied men and women; to able-bodied widows without children; to married women deserted by their husbands, whether with or without families; to persons residing with relatives where the united income of the family is sufficient for the support of all its members, whether such members are liable by law to support the applicant or not; and to all those who fail to satisfy the Guardians that their destitution has not been caused by intemperance or improvidence.[27]

The Board of Guardians' linking of those outside heteronormative families with applicants whose "destitution . . . [was] caused by intemperance or improvidence" reinforced the idea that, by having families, married men demonstrated their character. The Dudley Distress Committee adopted the same perspective in 1909, when the chairman asserted that "the committee was bound to help applicants who had families. Many of the men on their books were men of good character, with good testimonials, and men who would work if they had the opportunity."[28] Implicitly, by excluding single men from relief employment, the committee also excluded them from the ranks of those with "good character . . . who would work if they had the opportunity." Relief providers associated the unmarried with Weary Willies and Tired Tims, implying doubts about single men's willingness to work.

In this way, policy and practice evolved to position honest, poor, married men as worthy of non- or less-stigmatizing welfare. While marriage itself gave this advantage to men, fatherhood only added to honest men's deservedness. As historian Joanne Bailey has argued, marriage was "an institution which conveyed privileges to men as heads of households and marked male maturity and economic independence," and fatherhood was "a consequence of marriage."[29] Welfare deservedness became one of these privileges. The sources tend to be somewhat slippery in their references to married men and married men with children, but it is clear that both wives and children bolstered married men's claims for assistance, with children being the ultimate trump card.

Unemployed men's families provoked compassion from their communities.[30] In a January 1908 letter to the editor of the *Dudley Herald*, for example, "Behind the Scenes" described eight cases of distress to persuade readers that "there has neither been drunkenness or idleness to account for the poverty in these eight families; but simply misfortune or sickness." All the cases the letter writer included were of married couples with dependent children, where husbands were unemployed or working short time.[31] The newspapers followed a script narrating the plight of un- and underemployed married men, representing women and children victimized by economic conditions.

Single men could not capitalize on the sympathy extended to married men with wives and children. At a Stourbridge Board of Guardians meeting in May 1908, for example, the Reverend McNulty, an advocate for the honest poor throughout his long tenure on the board, "complained about the manner in which the unemployed were selected for the leveling of the workhouse grounds." He worried that many "applicants were men with families, and were starving," but they were not receiving priority over single men. Guardian Meanley, living up to his rather Dickensian name, assured McNulty that single men were getting nothing: "to make up the number of men required [to work] those were selected who had families."[32] Need and deservedness became categories limited to married men with families.

As policymakers and providers determined who "required" relief, they essentially constructed a right to work relief for married men with family obligations. In January 1909, Councilor Blackbrook of the Dudley Town Council expressed his frustration with the Local Government Board's delays in funding local work schemes. He insisted that "there were four hundred children depending upon" the men who registered for work relief. He thought the Local Government Board should find Dudley deserving, for the Town Council "did their utmost to prevent those men who did not require work from receiving employment at the hands of the committee."[33] Men who "required" work were married men with families; they had a right to be able to support their wives and children, and the state should facilitate that right by providing work. Unmarried men, by virtue of being single, were actively excluded, as the council did its "utmost to prevent" them from obtaining assistance. Similarly, the Dudley Distress Committee in October 1909 discussed "How Work is Found for the Genuine Unemployed." The chairman of the committee confirmed that, of those who had been denied work, "all were single men."[34] While married men earned their right to assistance by virtue of being married, relief providers found it perfectly acceptable to cut off single men.

Interestingly, the majority report of the 1909 Royal Commission on the Poor Laws and Relief of Distress called into question the hierarchy that identified those who were "not single men" as automatically more deserving. Commission members, such as Helen Bosanquet of the Charity Organization Society, sought to reemphasize individual fault as a cause of unemployment and argued that guardians measured men's deservedness too loosely. The majority report was concerned that marriage and fatherhood automatically privileged men who did not demonstrate a real seriousness about work. From this perspective, family liability could conflict with the work imperative as a measure of men's deservedness. In regard to stoneyards, the commission complained that "the relief is not earned in proportion to effort, but is given in proportion to needs, subject to the qualification of performing a prescribed task of work. A loafer with many children may do the minimum of work required and obtain four times as much as the industrious single man, even though the latter should do four times the work of the loafer."[35] Family here illegitimately constructed deservedness, taking away assistance from men who might be more worthy, as proven by their willingness to work.

Referring to municipal relief works, the majority quoted a report from special investigators for the commission, that "the evidence seems very strong that most men on relief works do not do their best . . . Competence to do the work required should be the basis for selection of men for work, not destitution and a large family. These are very good reasons for giving relief, but not for giving work."[36] This comment suggests that having a family could justify awarding married men poor law relief but not real work. "Relief" was still stigmatized, while "work" was not. Relief helped the needy, while work should be directed to those who had proven a right to it through actively adhering to the work imperative.[37]

The majority report of the poor law commission, however, was in many ways moving against cultural currents that pushed men's family liability to the core of character and citizenship claims. If anything, the connections between family and deservedness became stronger during and after the First World War. The postwar context, as several historians have argued, put new emphasis on family as a means to return Britain to normalcy after the war, and presumably to encourage a climate of pronatalism.[38] A strand of scholarship on the postwar period, associated with the work of literary scholar Alison Light and historian Joanna Bourke, argues that the interwar years saw an explicit turn towards a domestic version of masculinity, embracing family to forget the trauma of the war.[39] This domestic masculinity reinforced a model of men's citizenship based on family liability and gave welfare authorities even more reason to support the breadwinner family at the expense of single men. The cultural context had significant material welfare implications as Britons experienced economic depression.[40]

When unemployment climbed rapidly from 1920, local authorities' discussions about relief refocused on married men's right to assistance resulting from their family need. The Tipton Council, for example, pointed out to a deputation of unemployed men in September 1921 that "in any scheme of relief the most deserving cases should be considered first. For example, married men with families."[41] The Dudley Council proudly reported in the same month that on unemployment schemes "the contractors had employed local men, giving married men the preference."[42] This preference indeed showed the validity of the scheme itself. When local authorities called attention to the obligation to relieve "necessitous cases" first, or pointed to evaluating "the necessities of the homes" or "the destitution in the homes of the applicant," they referred to the needs of families, not individuals.[43] Family liability in effect subsumed married men's individual requests, encompassing their welfare into the family unit. In these ways, unemployment policies strengthened the image of domestic masculinity, pushing unmarried men further outside the boundaries of honest poverty.

Family liability in the politics of unemployed men

Unemployed men themselves also framed the "problem of unemployment" as a problem of married men with families and focused their demands on getting assistance for married men. They did so strategically, knowing the sympathy appeals for wives and children could evoke, but their complete inattention to single men also suggests that workers' groups believed that solutions to unemployment should prioritize the deservedness of married men with families. An early example from 1878 concerns a *Dudley Herald* report of a miners' conference at Tipton discussing the "wretched" state of the coal trade in the region. A Mr. Southall lamented, "In large numbers they were walking about with empty stomachs, their wives in tears, and their children at home without shoes and crying for bread. . . . With wages at 3s a day, it was impossible to provide their families with a living."[44] Here Southall created an equivalency between the suffering unemployed and married men with their families. His portrait of economic distress omitted single men.

Deputations of unemployed men used their families to speak to guardians' and councilors' consciences and fears, raising the specter both of starving children and political revolution. In May 1911, for example, "About a dozen men" came before the Stourbridge Board of Guardians claiming "the wanting something to eat and drink for their children."[45] Ten years later, the Dudley Town Council heard a member of a deputation of unemployed men ask for work "on behalf of the kiddies who were at home with empty stomachs."[46] A deputation to the Tipton Council in 1921 also emphasized family need. One man, implying a threat of "revolution," indicated that "the unemployed did not want anything of that kind, but they and their families did want something to eat."[47] The narrative of starving children would have drawn more sympathy from the guardians and councilors, to be sure, than appeals in the name of the men's own suffering and political demands. In suggesting that revolution could be averted if children were fed, the speaker positioned men's family liability as a significant political issue and offered the councilors a reassuring domestic masculinity that prioritized fatherly responsibility over threatening political action.

The postwar period saw the political organization of the unemployed become a regular feature in the news. Having achieved universal manhood suffrage in 1918, honest poor men expected that local authorities and national political officials would listen to their demands, and their demands focused on family needs. At a September 1921 meeting to organize the Brierley Hill unemployed, for example (the *Herald* reported 1,000 people were present), one man easily collapsed all the unemployed into unemployed married men with children: "Millions of persons were starving because they had no work. The boss said he had nothing for them to do, and so they had to walk the streets while their wives and children were starving."[48] In their meeting to protest the District Council's wage for work relief, a speaker for the Halesowen unemployed in 1922 argued, "Men could not adequately feed and clothe themselves and their families upon that rate."[49] This language served to represent "the unemployed" as married men who needed to support hungry and threadbare wives and children. Where were the unmarried men? Surely the crowds of unemployed at the rallies throughout the region included single men; the rhetoric surrounding the problem of unemployment, however, did not.

Local organizations of the unemployed tried to draw the consideration of their regional Boards of Guardians and local government bodies to the trials of their families, but the politics of unemployment also played out on the national stage, and national labor organizations also contributed to identifying the honest poor by their married status and family liability. For example, a deputation from the Miners' Federation met with Andrew Bonar Law, the new Conservative prime minister, on December 2, 1922. They argued that miners' wages did not give them "an opportunity of living a respectable life. . . . In going from place to place you find a very changed appearance in the workmen generally and their wives and children."[50] In 1923, Bonar Law received a deputation from the Trades Union Congress, which was outraged that Parliament was taking a recess when the problem of unemployment was so extensive. Again the "deserving" unemployed became men with families; Mr. Smillie explained that it is "in the poorest of the districts in the various industrial centres that one really comes to realise the misery and suffering which exist. Many of the unemployed, who had spent a decent useful life for many years, have found that their children have been begging from door to door."[51] Men who lived "a respectable life" or "a decent useful life" had wives and children to support.

While the emphasis on family needs served the rhetorical purpose of making unemployed men appear respectable in the eyes of those who could potentially help them, the refrain also shaped the disbursement of resources such that single men were marginalized in very material ways, receiving very little from the Poor Law or work-relief schemes. In January 1922, for example, the committee of Stourbridge unemployed discussed the desperate circumstances in the region and wanted to assure themselves that only the deserving received assistance. Offering a plan with which to approach relief authorities, they prioritized men with large families as deserving: "A man with a big family should have preference over those with small families," relegating to the margins those without families at all.[52] Presumably, the local unemployment committees were often led by married men with families, who had roots in their communities and had established their trustworthiness. Because policymakers, welfare providers, and organizations of the unemployed all used family liability to determine deservedness, single men had no one but themselves to speak for their deservedness, and I have not heard their voices in the records of the Black Country poor. Even when they proved their willingness to work, single men could not demonstrate a claim to welfare equivalent to married men.

Family liability in crisis

Policymakers, welfare providers, and unemployed men established honest poverty as a citizenship status that recognized married men's assertions of welfare deservedness. Married men benefited materially as welfare providers moved scarce resources toward families and away from single men. However, the expectations of honest poverty placed married men under tremendous pressure to be able to maintain wives and children. Political organizing was one way to address the pressure, as married men demanded welfare to assist them in fulfilling the expectations of family liability. But unemployed men and their families utilized other strategies as well to make up for the head of household's inability to maintain his wife and children. Unable to secure sufficient resources from income or welfare assistance, men looked elsewhere. Some of them left their homes, which I examine in depth in Chapter 9. Some turned to petty theft and welfare fraud. Additionally, some men seemingly could not reconcile their breadwinner masculinity with the receipt of welfare assistance. They went to the extreme of taking their own lives, perceiving their inability to provide independently as failure.

Accused of petty theft, Black Country men used the terms of honest poverty to defend themselves, expecting sympathetic responses. "Coal stealing" was a crime particular to regions like the Black Country, where heaps of coal littered the landscape around the mines. Especially in times of heightened unemployment, the newspapers were filled with police court items about coal stealing, as men and women tried to bolster meager resources (Figure 3.5). In April 1921, when many of the local pits were closed or on short time, Joseph Hughes, aged 39, was brought before Dudley Police Court charged with coal stealing. Hughes pleaded that "he was out of work. He had a wife and nine children, and it was the first time he had done anything of the kind." The police constable supported Hughes's story, and the magistrates treated him lightly, acknowledging the "extenuating circumstances" of his large family and unemployment.[53] Granville Bowen of Dudley pleaded guilty to coal theft in February 1922. He "said he was out of employment, and had a wife and four children. He felt he was bound to do something for them

Figure 3.5 Coal pickers, Dudley, 1909
Source: © Dudley Archives and Local History Service, ref. p/104. Heaps of coal provided temptations to steal for families struggling to survive. This image suggests a colliery that allowed coal picking to occur legally during a strike.

to eat. This was his first case, and he was awfully sorry."[54] Both Hughes and Bowen stressed their histories as honest poor men, who had stolen only in desperation to maintain their families. In a March 1923 case, a man charged in Brierley Hill Police Court with coal stealing "said he had been out of work for two years. He had a child suffering from pneumonia, and he asked what a man could do when he saw so much coal wasted in the bowels of the earth, and he needed some to warm his children."[55] By pleading the needs of their wives and children, these men successfully received small fines rather than prison sentences.

Some men challenged definitions of theft itself, arguing that family liability gave them the right to steal coal and other provisions when unemployment prevented them from purchasing them honestly. In June 1926, for example, in the context of the national miners' strike, Albert Hall, a Dudley miner who had been out of work for two years, came before the magistrates for stealing timber. He claimed, "'Me and the three men working with me are risking our lives to save women and children from starvation. . . . I don't think it is stealing.'" The magistrates disagreed and fined him 20 shillings.[56] Hall seemed to believe that in "sav[ing] women and children from starvation," his actions were not criminal. Honest poverty provided Hall with a language to call civil conventions into question if they stood in the way of supporting families. Coal stealing and petty theft were common ways individuals and families sought to bolster their meager resources. A more serious offense involved defrauding welfare authorities, which included both the local Poor Law and the national insurance system. Un- and underemployed men tried to cobble together income wherever it was available, even if it meant stretching the letter of the law, which prohibited concurrent receipt of poor law relief and insurance and which refused assistance to men who were working. Men accused of fraud used their family liability to articulate their needs and contested the official definitions of what constituted "work." They used honest poverty to assert a right to state assistance.

A representative example of poor law fraud concerned Daniel Tarplee, a 43-year-old sandblaster. On July 1, 1922, the *Dudley Herald* reported in detail on Tarplee, who was being prosecuted by the Dudley Board of Guardians for "Obtaining Relief Under False Pretences." The newspaper recounted that Tarplee had applied for poor law relief on May 18, "for himself, his wife and children, in consequence of his being out of employment and without a meal." He signed a form stating "he had no employment and no income from any source whatever." On May 23, the Board of Guardians granted him "food to the value of 21s." This relief in kind was renewed over a period of three weeks. The relieving officer subsequently discovered that Tarplee had been employed the entire time he was receiving relief, and when Tarplee again applied for assistance on June 16, "he was questioned . . . as to his being at work. At first he strongly denied he had been at work, he was very strenuous in his denials, but eventually he admitted he had done work for Mrs Edwards." Yet Tarplee, "when formally charged, pleaded not guilty."[57]

Tarplee used a performance of citizenship to defend himself, claiming that while he had met the obligations of military service and honest poverty, the state had not treated him as a citizen: "The defendant declined to give evidence, and made a statement with regard to serving the Army since 1891, and in the R.I. Constabulary up to November, 1920. He justified what he had done by saying that he had a wife and seven children, and the money he received from the Guardians or for unemployment was not sufficient to maintain them." Tarplee presented himself as attempting to fulfill his duties to country and family, emphasizing that both military and domestic masculinity entitled him to the financial support that would allow him to maintain his family. The presiding magistrate told him, however, that the court was "very sorry to see you this morning, especially after the way you have fought for your country, and for the sake of your wife and children; but we have to do our duty. There are similar cases to yours throughout the country, and they are getting too prevalent. You must go to prison for one month, with hard labour."[58] The magistrates found that Tarplee's fraud voided his citizenship claims. They stressed their own "duty" as citizens to set an example to others.

Men who never imagined that their paltry earnings from irregular work could disqualify them for assistance found themselves being prosecuted for fraud. In September 1921, the *Dudley Herald* reported on eight men from Darlaston who were charged in Wednesbury Police Court for making "false representations to obtain unemployment help." The men were accused of "sign[ing] on" at the Labour Exchange as unemployed, but they had been discovered at work. One defendant claimed that

> he was a married man with four children. There had been no previous complaints against him. The small recompense he received . . . did not lead defendant to think it was necessary to state it all to the Labour Exchange. Defendant had only done three turns at his own work in 32 weeks, and he did not think he was doing any harm in trying slightly to supplement the pay he was then receiving.

This man stressed his need to provide for his family, his respectability, and his incredulity that the irregular, casual labor he could secure would disqualify him from the state assistance that would allow him to fulfill his familial obligations. The solicitor for all the men summed up that "they were only trying to eke out a little extra to supplement what they received by way of unemployment pay. They were all married men with children, and one and all had been in very low water for a long time. . . . They were all trying to live and had no intention to defraud." The Darlaston men claimed to be living lives of honest poverty, struggling to uphold their status as breadwinners. The stipendiary magistrate, however, challenged their claims and their definition of honesty, indicating they deserved "severe punishment simply because they would not tell the truth like honest men." He sentenced each of the men to 14 days in prison, "the lightest sentence he could impose," but explicitly stated that he would be much harsher in future cases.[59]

Honest poverty masculinity, like the breadwinner ideal, ignored or downplayed the fact that many wives in regions such as the Black Country contributed important earnings to family survival. When it came to making welfare decisions, however, a wife's income could put additional pressure on a man's qualification for assistance. Benjamin Hamblett, for example, in October 1922 was charged with obtaining unemployment insurance by "knowingly ma[king] a false statement in respect of his wife who, he declared was not in any occupation for profit." The authorities, however, found that she earned around four shillings a week. Hamblett's defense was that he "thought he was honestly entitled to take the money, notwithstanding the work his wife was doing, and that his conviction was an honest one. . . . He thought there could be [unemployment] pay although the wife was earning money." Hamblett, however, was found guilty and fined.[60] Hamblett's claims suggest he did not perceive his wife's work as "work," or at least he saw an argument to this effect as potentially believable. His situation would have been embarrassing both in terms of how his wife's employment challenged his ability to provide and by the appearance of fraud.

The work-welfare system put poor men in the difficult position of being forced to pretend their wives were not working to assert their own rights to assistance. When Joseph Siddaway applied for unemployment insurance in 1923, he "stated that his wife was not engaged in regular wage-earning employment." Before the magistrates, the prosecution proved that his wife had been employed for months, receiving 15 shillings a week, a sum which the magistrates thought made it a "glaring case." Siddaway initially claimed that "his wife only worked an hour and a half in the morning and he thought that was no harm." He went on to testify that "he was sorry that the 'job' had occurred. He knew nothing about it. His wife had not told him what she was getting, neither did he know when she was away from home. He thought she was only earning a few coppers."[61] He was committed to prison for a month. It seems neither Hamblett nor Siddaway conceptualized their wives' employment as work that mattered in terms of family liability – even if a family economy depended upon these women's income. Family liability set up unrealistic assumptions about men's responsibility for maintaining families that compromised both men's and women's economic citizenship.[62]

Women's income in general challenged men's obligation to be the sole, or at least primary, provider for a family, and we can see the courts' punishment of men whose wives were working as reinforcing the heteronormative family model. The Stourbridge Board of Guardians took out several summonses against men who claimed poor law relief but failed to inform the board of their wives' income. In June 1921, for example, the board went after William Hand, who had received relief but had "omitted to disclose that his wife was in receipt of a pension of

17/6 per week."[63] The board sought to prosecute John Willets of Cradley, in November 1925, for receiving relief "by making a false statement . . . on enquiry it was discovered that the man's wife had obtained 10/- unemployment benefit the day before the relief was given."[64] Husbands failed to disclose their wives' economic contributions hoping to bolster their chances for assistance. Their lies perhaps were also a psychological protection of their masculine status tied to honest poverty, which had been compromised by their inability to support their families.

Unemployed men clearly struggled with the need to prove their readiness to work and maintain their families, often internalizing their failures to achieve a masculinity tied so closely to employment and family support. As Keith McClelland has noted about the late nineteenth century, "given the centrality of paid work to the construction of men's identities in capitalism, the loss of earnings and employment probably led to a sense of 'incompleteness' and shame as men and to a loss of dignity which could not be contemplated."[65] Even with policy and cultural changes that purported to recognize no-fault unemployment and respectable welfare, "real men" were still conceptualized as "independent, self-reliant, and competent," which meant that "by definition, the unemployed were defective."[66] Although honest poverty allowed men to be dependent on public resources, some men could not accept the coexistence of welfare and their status as workers and citizens.

While married men's applications for welfare assistance and their political demands reflect the script they had created with regard to honest poverty, suicide suggests a deep internalization of the pressures associated with the work imperative and family liability.[67] According to Matt Perry, "For men 25 years and under between 1921 and 1932, the numbers of suicides rose by 60 per cent and the number of attempted suicides doubled."[68] For some men, the receipt of state assistance did not compensate for their inability to uphold the obligations of breadwinning. Additionally, some men chose to kill themselves rather than face the humiliation of turning to the Poor Law. They conceptualized honest poverty to be incompatible with poor relief.

News items connected men's suicides to unemployment fairly regularly in the postwar period. In September 1922, a headline reading "Unemployed Carter Hangs Himself" appeared in the *County Express*. The article described 72-year-old Richard Woodward as being "out of employment for some time."[69] His wife said "her husband had been out of work since the coal strike," which occurred in 1921, suggesting that his lack of employment had led Woodward to take his own life. This is especially remarkable given Woodward's age. A month later, the

County Express reported on the "Tragedy of Unemployment" in the case of Walter Cartwright, aged 47, who apparently had drowned himself in a canal. The item noted that the "deceased was very happy with his wife and three children, but during the last two years he had had hard luck in regard to employment, and at the time of his death was again on notice to cease work owing to shortage of orders." The coroner put forward that "Cartwright's mind had been unhinged by the fact that he had had no regular employment and the prospect of being out again." He lamented the situation in which Cartwright's family was left worse off than they were before, commenting on the frequency of suicides like Cartwright's: "It was regrettable that men should give way like this: in the last few weeks he had five or six similar cases, and he thought, with a little more courage, they could have pulled through."[70] Men who killed themselves because of unemployment, according to this official, were cowards, leaving their families to fend for themselves.

Newspaper headlines explicitly linked men's unemployment with suicide, such as the *Dudley Herald*'s July 1927, "'Sick of Living': Woodside Man who was Worried to Death Through Lack of Work."[71] A 1924 article described "Workless Man's Despair" and told of the suicide by drowning of Job William Richards, a 43-year-old forge-roller who had been unemployed for more than three years. His wife indicated that her husband had been "in receipt of 26s. per week as Labour pay, and this had had to keep himself, herself, and six children, the eldest of whom was 14." The article flagged Richards's respectability by mentioning that "deceased had saved some money, but only a little was now left. This had played on his mind." The anxiety of failing while playing by the rules comes through clearly: "Asked by the Coroner if deceased had any money trouble, [the widow] replied: 'He has kept us perfectly safe up till now. He owes no one anything. He has worried about being out of work. He has said he would rather work for 20s. than pick up 26s. for nothing and be a walking advertisement. He had tried hard to get work.'" The coroner ruled the death a suicide "whilst of unsound mind" and commented that "the poor man seemed to have worried over the scarcity of work, . . . He had a big responsibility, and no doubt this preyed on his mind to such an extent that he committed suicide. It was a very sad thing for the widow and six children."[72] Unemployed men might escape their failures through suicide, but the implications of their inability to provide continued after their deaths.

Without evidence from the men themselves, we cannot know what led them to take their own lives. Yet their families and the coroners framed their deaths in the context of honest poverty. These were men who did not measure up to the expectations of work and providing for their families. Even though welfare had become increasingly acceptable for an honest poor man, many men could not fit public assistance into their identities as breadwinners, which for so long had been built on ideas of independence and self-sufficiency. Working-class masculinity and a dependent status, for these men, could not coexist.

Men's unemployment and women's work

The flipsides of men's experiences of family liability were the wives who depended on men's ability to work. Poor law authorities, town councilors, and unemployed men themselves all took for granted unemployed men's identification of themselves as workers, even when they were not actually employed. Married women, however, were not conceptualized as workers but rather as victims of men's unemployment. Men's appeals to their family liability, as we have seen, continually emphasized the anguish of their wives and children. Newspaper reporting confirmed this representation. The *Dudley Herald's* reflections on Christmas 1878, for example, recognized men as workers but women and children as sufferers from unemployment: "What a contrast is this [1878] to the Christmas of 1873. Then the working men of this district were in receipt of good wages, work was plentiful, and Christmas was kept with the greatest satisfaction to all classes: but now work is nowhere to be had, men, women, and children are literally starving."[73] While expressing that men, like women and children, were starving, the item represented the workers of the district as men. Women's employment is invisible. Even more strongly, the Reverend T.J. McNulty berated his fellow guardians for closing the labor yard in January 1909, remarking "that it was a terrible thing to starve wives, mothers, and children."[74] McNulty drew a direct line between men's work breaking stones and keeping families from starvation.

Newspapers sometimes reported on women as workers, but it was usually in a negative way – as causing husbands to commit fraud (as above) and as creating illegitimate competitors with working men.[75] In 1891, in the context of parliamentary debates regarding restrictions on women's work in the nail and chain industries, the local papers gave extensive coverage to meetings of nail- and chainmakers worried about female labor and printed numerous letters to the editors on the question. Many male workers in the industries wanted legislation

Figure 3.6   Female chainmaker, c.1900
Source: © Dudley Archives and Local History Service, ref. p/1314.

Figure 3.7   Chainmaking workshop, Dudley, c.1900
Source: © Dudley Archives and Local History Service, ref. p/88. Men made the heavier, more expensive chain, while women were limited to making smaller, less valuable products.

to control women's work. Parliament eventually prohibited women from beginning work in nail- and chainmaking before the age of 16 and limited the size of chain women were allowed to make, reserving the heavier and more expensive chainmaking for men (Figure 3.6) (Figure 3.7).[76]

Yet the 1891 news stories also printed dissenting voices, acknowledging the need for women's work to contribute to the region's family economies. On April 4, an *Advertiser* editorial asserted, "Nothing can be more certain than this – that when the daughters of nail and chainmakers reach the age of thirteen or fourteen they must begin to aid in maintaining the family. They cannot all be absorbed in domestic service, and they must by very stress of circumstances go to the nail or chain block," clearly promoting the idea that young women (before marriage) were expected to work.[77] A week later, the paper received many letters on the issue, both for and against limitation on women's work. George Willetts, of the Willetts Bros. firm of chainmakers of Old Hill, wrote

> it is a noticeable fact all or most of the men who go in for legislation on female labour are men with no family or a family of sons. They have no sympathy with the man who has a family of daughters, or with women whose husbands are not chainmakers. Any fair and reasonable person will agree that any female who has been brought up to chainmaking, and who is anxious to add to the comfort of her home, ought to have the right to do so.[78]

Willetts's assessment frames women's chainmaking in the context of female domestic experiences, in a way naturalizing chainmaking as women's work because they had been "brought up to" it and worked for "the comfort of [the] home." Additionally, Willetts looks at the question of female chainmakers from the point of view of fathers, who desired the contributions of their daughters to the household economy.[79] This debate recalls Anna Clark's study of the late eighteenth and early nineteenth centuries that identified tensions between a fraternal masculine work culture that denigrated women as labor market competitors and a paternal masculine work culture that valued women as contributors to the family economy.[80] Employers themselves, of course, had an interest in encouraging women's work to keep wages low.

Expressing fears regarding the undercutting of men's wages in a context of high under- and unemployment, most coverage of female chainmakers and nailmakers reiterated familiar claims about the ways women's work hurt men's ability to support their families. This was clear to the wrought nailmakers in the region, who met in Halesowen in August 1891 to discuss a potential strike. Women featured in their discussions in two ways: as a threat to men's livelihood and as suffering wives. The nailmakers discussed how the only justification for the low wages employers were offering was that "women and children worked under the recognised prices." These presumably single women were juxtaposed with male workers' wives: the undercutting caused by (single) women's and children's work "was not very encouraging to men who had wives and families to support."[81] Single women could be construed as (illegitimate) workers, while married women relied on the work of their husbands to maintain them.

These anxieties about the impact of women's work relative to men's family liability continued to feature in the local papers throughout my period. In May 1919, for example, when demobilized servicemen and war workers demanded employment, an article titled "Women Displace Men. Stourbridge Labour Problem" worried "that married women were taking good wages and their husbands were without work and were taking the unemployment dole."[82] These married women presumably had not left their war work willingly after the war, and their employment perverted the expectations of male breadwinning: married women earned "good wages" while their husbands were unemployed. In the postwar period, and in the context of the new national unemployment acts in the 1920s, the national government increasingly recognized women as workers who could articulate their own struggles with unemployment. Married women, however, continued to have their needs categorized through their husbands, an issue I turn to in the next chapter.

Conclusion

While the work imperative identified men's honest poverty with the performance of work in the public sphere, family liability affirmed a domestic masculinity; work was how poor men maintained their families, which signified full masculine status. Family liability belied any separation between the economic and domestic spheres, emphasizing men's ability to establish themselves in heteronormative relationships in which wives (and children) depended upon husbands' financial support. As policymakers, welfare providers, and unemployed married men increasingly conceptualized deservedness in terms of family, single men starved. In many ways, welfare providers assumed married men were willing to work because having a family required it. Welfare authorities saw the unemployment of married men resulting from "no fault of their own," but they often still viewed single men through the New Poor Law lens that focused on lack of work as an individual fault, a moral rather than an economic issue. Unmarried men did not have the rhetorical power of family liability and therefore could easily become identified with Weary Willies and Tired Tims, suspicious figures who neither worked regularly nor were contained within normative family forms. They were outside the boundaries of honest poverty, a masculine status fully available only to married men.

4

"A reward for good citizenship": National Unemployment Benefits and the Genuine Search for Work

During debate on the National Insurance Bill in the House of Commons on May 4, 1911, Colonel Claude Lowther commended the Liberal Chancellor of the Exchequer David Lloyd George for introducing "a Bill which is clever, human, sound, and statesmanlike." A Conservative and staunch opponent of socialism, Lowther envisioned unemployment insurance as "free[ing] the individual from the trammels and meshes of poverty. It would inspire him with hope rather than fill him with despair, and help him instead of being a useless of member of society to become a wealth producer."[1] National insurance would be in the interests of national efficiency, whereas the Poor Law was "chaotic" and served to "breed pauperism."[2] The Poor Law stripped honest men of their self-respect, but unemployment insurance would help the poor regain their manhood:

> No man in this country is allowed to starve. The State acknowledges itself morally bound to give not only food but lodging and shelter to those who cannot find them for themselves. . . . But instead of attempting to rehabilitate the individual, instead of helping him to re-find his lost manhood and lost dignity, the State brands him with a stigma of disgrace which often causes the honest working man, out of work through no fault of his own, to sink deeper and deeper into the morass of pauperism and despair. Surely these are false economics. If the worker were helped to tide over his temporary difficulty, if he received unemployed benefits, not as a charitable dole but as a reward for good citizenship, . . . he would in time become again a useful member of the community and cease to be a burden upon the nation.[3]

While the Poor Law placed unemployed men outside the boundaries of the nation, according to Lowther, unemployment insurance would "reward" the honest poor as citizens. Not only could welfare and citizenship coexist, but the manhood of poor men depended on that coexistence. The honest unemployed had a right to "re-find [their] lost manhood and lost dignity."

The institution of national unemployment benefits, first through the Unemployment Insurance Act of 1911 and then through non-contributory schemes in the postwar period, created the possibility for a new paradigm of welfare deservedness. Historian Michael Hanagan has gone so far as to claim that the demand for a national unemployment policy "was as dramatic a change in political discourse as anything that happened in Britain in the last century."[4] These early unemployment policies were designed in large part to present a new national model of respectable assistance that moved away from the stigma associated with the Poor Law and the frustration associated with work relief. Tensions remained, however, between structural and moral conceptualizations of unemployment, and the performance of a work test continued to be both a sign of honest poverty and a punishment for those suspected of being outside its boundaries. Indeed, as the numbers relying on the system of unemployment benefits exploded in the 1920s, applicants for assistance had an increasingly difficult time proving their "right" to the "reward" of citizenship. Additionally, even while policies in the postwar period expected women as well as men to demonstrate a willingness to work, ideas about family liability meant that men and women experienced the work imperative differently.

This chapter explores the ways national policies and practices surrounding unemployment benefits extended the honest poverty work-welfare system. While the work imperative and family liability remained central to determinations of welfare deservedness, they took on different meanings in the context of national benefits. I focus on debates about unemployment and cases of men and women who appealed denials of their unemployment benefits on the grounds that they were "not genuinely seeking work." The willingness to work and family liability provided a bridge between new and traditional, national and local, models of welfare deservedness. As national responsibility for unemployment increased, however, so too did doubts about how successful public welfare could be in restoring an honest man's independence. From the local stories of the Poor Law and work relief, I turn now to the national story of "the dole."

The development of national unemployment benefits

By the first decade of the 1900s, Black Country newspapers regularly reported on local officials' frustrations with their limited resources to combat the problem of unemployment. These frustrations came to a head in the harsh winter of 1908–9. Guardians tried to displace their expenses onto the local councils, while councils looked to the national government to fund relief schemes. For example, the *County Express* reported that, during the Stourbridge Board of Guardians meeting in mid-January 1909, Mr. Rollinson "held that it was not the duty of the Guardians but the County and District Councils to deal with the unemployed." The clerk reminded the board, however, that urban councils with populations of less than 20,000 people – which encompassed many towns in the Stourbridge and Dudley Unions – were not eligible to receive national grants under the Unemployed Workmen's Act of 1905. Local bodies argued they could not support the unemployed on their own.[5]

The *Dudley Herald* complained during the same month about the difficulties local authorities experienced convincing the Local Government Board to help their region. The writer indicated that, while the Dudley Council had "made out a good case" for a national grant to assist the Dudley unemployed, "The Right Hon. John Burns [president of the Local Government Board] insists upon something more than mere generalities."[6] The *Herald* covered the town council meeting that week, when Councilor Blackbrook spoke out against the Local Government Board, pointing explicitly to the deservedness of the Dudley unemployed:

> It was not that they had not put a scheme before the Board, and it was not because they had not adopted measures the Board recommended to the Council, neither was it because they had not got honest unemployed in Dudley. . . . He was sorry that up till now nothing had been done by the Local Government Board. It was not, as he had before remarked, because the town had not got an honest claim. He did not think anybody could find a fault so far as the men were concerned, for any doubtful case was thoroughly inquired into in their committees.[7]

Blackbrook accused the Local Government Board of ignoring the honest poverty of the Dudley district, stressing the care with which the council measured deservedness. The Local Government Board's lack of response did not speak well of the national government's efforts to address unemployment, and local authorities expressed their displeasure.

The Worcester County Council during the same winter lamented the central government's denial of support for the region. The chairman "was extremely disappointed the Local Government Board had not made some grant for the people at Cradley. If they had been in Birmingham or some large town a grant would have been made."[8] The council decided to appeal to the Local Government Board to see if Burns would alter his position. On March 13, however, the *County Express* reported that their appeal was "futile."[9] The local government bodies clearly were at their wits' end trying to balance the needs of the unemployed in their districts, the ineffectiveness of national responses, and their own lack of resources.

In this context Parliament debated the bill that would become the 1911 National Insurance Act, which covered both unemployment and health insurance. The debates demonstrate conflicting ideas among members of Parliament regarding the meaning of unemployment and the ways unemployment affected honest poor men. In 1911, the central government conceptualized the unemployed as *men*, making national the gender assumptions and practices of local bodies. By addressing unemployment as a problem of national scope, however, politicians acknowledged that local solutions were not sufficient, nor were ideas about unemployment that blamed workers themselves, although the issue of blame remained fuzzy. National politicians and government officials tried to maintain clear distinctions between the deserving and undeserving unemployed, using the terms of honest poverty.

A key premise of what came to be the 1911 National Insurance Act was that a man qualified for unemployment insurance if "he [was] capable of work but unable to obtain suitable employment."[10] Ablebodiedness and the lack of "suitable" positions were thus the defining aspects of eligibility. Men who were out of work because of a trade dispute, were fired for misconduct, or left their positions voluntarily would not qualify for insurance until six weeks after their "infraction."[11] The national government, like the local guardians and town councilors, aimed to assist men who were unemployed "through no fault of their own."

An emphasis on the work imperative framed the parliamentary debate about national insurance. When Lloyd George introduced the unemployment component of the National Insurance Bill, he was careful to assure Parliament that, because workers had to contribute a portion of their wages to the scheme, "the real loafer soon drops out. The meshes of the Labour Exchange net might not catch him at first, but eventually and automatically he will work himself out, owing to the fact that he is not a regular contributor, and therefore he will come to an end of his right to obtain benefits."[12] As social policy scholar Alan Deacon describes it in *In Search of the Scrounger*, "The scrounger would inevitably be betrayed by his contributory record and no further safeguards were required."[13] This language of snaring loafers in the bureaucracy of unemployment insurance spoke to the shared assumption of those across the political spectrum that only the honest poor deserved state support. The national government now confronted the problem that had long exercised poor law authorities and town councils: how to distinguish honest poor men from Weary Willies and Tired Tims.

Indeed, the debate framed the issue of unemployment benefits around the nation's manhood in terms similar to those utilized by poor law authorities and town councils. Labour MPs pushed the government to support honest out-of-work men in a manner that would lead the unemployed to feel less humiliated by their condition. James O'Grady of Leeds, for example, in February 1911, argued "that the State should take the responsibility directly of providing employment or maintenance for the unemployed."[14] If work was not available, the government had a duty to maintain an unemployed man at a rate equivalent to wages. Labour MPs' emphasis on the right to work and maintenance sought distance from the discourse of "relief" that was tied to the poor law world: honest unemployed men had a right to state support. Pointing to his own "painful" experience, O'Grady asked his fellow MPs to "take a typical case of a skilled workman out of employment. He walks about from factory to factory, knowing his own skill, but driven away every time because his labour is not wanted. The wife has probably gone into the factory. Think of the degradation of the man's manhood that his own wife should become the breadwinner instead of himself!"[15] From O'Grady's perspective, unemployment compromised masculine identity, especially in situations when wives took over the breadwinner role. Appealing to the work imperative and men's family liability, O'Grady stressed the ways unemployment insurance could salvage working-class masculine status.

In support of O'Grady's appeal for state action, John Clynes of Manchester, bringing to mind Weary Willy and Tired Tim, assured the House that "we are not here as defenders of the 'won't works.'"[16] Categorizing the "genuine unemployed" as men with "wives and children," Clynes pushed the House to deal with the "urgency of the question."[17] The government had to take responsibility for keeping a man out of "a state of idleness and his family in a state of starvation. . . . A man cannot live well unless he works."[18] Both O'Grady and Clynes, in demanding the right to work, imagined the subject of the debate as a married man with children, juxtaposing the honest unemployed against idle "won't works."

Some outspoken Liberals, however, worried that government assistance by definition challenged the independence on which masculine citizenship rested. John Burns, the Liberal president of the Local Government Board (and the main subject of criticism by the local authorities), responded that government assistance itself demeaned the masculine status to which O'Grady and Clynes appealed: "you have no right to break the proud spirit of the poor. You have no right to undermine their sense of industry, you have no right to make inroads on their industry and on their manly independence."[19] While unemployment might challenge breadwinner masculinity, dependence on the state would be worse: state-sanctioned dependence on welfare could not coexist with masculine citizenship. The Liberal Henry Forster likewise spoke against the right-to-work principle, arguing that it took away a man's willingness to work: "To pass that into law would destroy at one blow all incentive to thrift, and would shatter that sturdy independence of character which has made the British workman famous throughout the world."[20] For these men, British identity relied on an independent masculinity.

When the National Insurance Act of 1911 became law, Britain adopted for the first time a compulsory national scheme for unemployment benefits, which required contributions from employers, employees, and the state. This provided protection for men in a limited number of trades – such as building, shipbuilding, and ironfounding – that were seen to be especially subject to cyclical fluctuations. Unemployment insurance initially covered only two and a quarter million workers. Benefits were low, allowed one week's pay for every five weeks of contributions made, and were capped at 15 weeks in a year.[21] The Act did not cover the dependants of insured men, nor casual workers, leaving central aspects of poverty unaddressed.[22] Yet, as historian John Burnett points out, "the 1911 Act was an immediate success, for even in the relatively prosperous year ended July 1914, 23 per cent of insured men claimed benefit – an indication of how irregular employment was even for skilled workers in good times."[23]

The National Insurance Act had barely been in operation when the First World War changed the terms of state responsibility for unemployment. The war made clear that the system already needed revising to include all the men – and women – who served the nation at home and abroad.[24] I consider in detail the relationship between honest poverty and the First World War in the next chapter. Here I want to highlight that the war brought into sharp relief the inadequacy of existing policies. The national government first extended unemployment insurance to munitions workers and, by the end of the war, it provided an Out-of-Work Donation (OWD) to all those who engaged in war service. The OWD required no contribution from the unemployed person, and scholars have argued that this "raised working-class expectations and thereby made it more difficult to retain a contributory system when heavy unemployment returned in 1921."[25]

The government's 1920 Unemployment Insurance Act covered all industrial workers in "insurable trades," both men and women: about 12 million people. Yet, as a Ministry of Labour memorandum put it, "Before the persons insured under the Act of 1920 could accumulate reserves of contributions, a period of severe industrial depression set in."[26] Unemployment became a major political problem, as increasing numbers of jobless men and local officials put constant pressure on the government to act (Figure 4.1). While in November 1920 unemployment stood at 3.7 per cent, by January 1921 it rose to 8.2 per cent, and

PUSHING BACK THE MOB AT THE ENTRANCE TO DOWNING STREET: A VERY SMALL POLICE CORDON RESISTING THE GREAT CROWD WHICH TRIED TO OVERBEAR THEM BY SHEER WEIGHT.

Figure 4.1 Unemployed "mob" in Downing Street, 1920. The Government increasingly had to confront the demands of unemployed men.
Source: © Illustrated London News Ltd/Mary Evans.

by March to 11.3 per cent. A national coal strike lasting from April to July 1921 raised unemployment to 18 per cent, with another 10 per cent of workers on short time.[27] These conditions rendered the insurance system unworkable, and the government had to move away from the principle of requiring contributions from workers. Throughout the 1920s, governments pulled tools from both old and new toolboxes to confront the problem of unemployment (Figure 4.2).

In March 1921, an amendment to the 1920 Act introduced "uncovenanted benefit" for people who had been employed in insurable occupations but who had not been able to make sufficient contributions.[28] The non-contributory uncovenanted benefits would be available to unemployed men and women who could demonstrate to their Local Employment Committees "that they were 'genuinely seeking whole-time employment' but unable to obtain it,'"[29] inserting the lexicon of the work imperative directly into national unemployment benefit policy. Contributory and non-contributory schemes worked together, as those who exhausted their insurance benefits could then transition to the non-contributory system. With the Labour Government's 1924 Unemployment Insurance Act, *all* applicants for unemployment benefits had to demonstrate that they were "'genuinely seeking work but unable to obtain suitable employment.'"[30] As Deacon argues, the Labour Government believed that "more generous benefits would only be possible if it could be clearly demonstrated that they were exclusively reserved for the 'deserving' unemployed, and that those less worthy were still to be left to the Poor Law. Meanwhile, the great mass of the unemployed must 'earn' their benefit by a ritualistic demonstration of their eagerness to work."[31] The somewhat perfunctory and locally variable work test of the Poor Law became a much more stringent measure of the willingness to work under the benefit system of the 1920s.

Deacon highlights that the "introduction into insurance of methods hitherto confined to the Poor Law" brought "the taint of pauperism to insurance benefits for the first time."[32] He makes this point with reference to means testing, but the genuinely-seeking-work requirement itself was very much in line with poor law theory and practice. Although Labour politicians and the unemployed both vehemently opposed means testing as humiliating, they initially supported the national government's position that benefit should be contingent on a demonstrated willingness to work. The genuinely-seeking-work test stressed a component of honest poverty that poor men held onto as central to their masculine status. If they were to receive assistance, they wanted "work not doles." The labor movement and unemployed men,

90

ALLEVIATION'S ARTFUL AID.

Dr. Lloyd George (*to Sufferer from Unemployment Epidemic*). "I DON'T SAY THESE FOUR HOT-WATER BOTTLES WILL ABSOLUTELY CURE YOU, BUT THEY SHOULD RELIEVE THE TROUBLE; AND ANYHOW THEY'RE BETTER THAN HOT AIR."

Figure 4.2 Alleviation's Artful Aid, October 1921. A commentary on the Government's frustrated efforts to "cure" the "unemployment epidemic," featuring loans to the Poor Law Guardians, funds for work relief, and unemployment insurance.

Source: © Punch Limited.

however, did come to protest the genuinely-seeking-work test when it became clear that work was not available and the experience of unemployment for many became chronic. Additionally, over the course of the 1920s, increasing numbers of applicants were denied benefit on the grounds they were not genuinely seeking work, highlighting the arbitrariness of the decisions surrounding what qualified as meeting the work imperative. Still, neither the labor movement nor the Labour Party questioned the principle that welfare dependence and masculine status could coexist only if men demonstrated a willingness to work.

Genuine work and suitable employment

In the winter of 1929–30, George Milward, a 31-year-old copper worker from Staffordshire, appealed to the Crown-appointed Umpire in charge of benefit decisions after he was denied unemployment benefits for failing to meet the "genuinely seeking work" requirement. In his petition, Milward emphasized his honest poverty to support his claim:

> My grounds of appeal are that I am on short time which is not through any fault of mine and am quite willing to work when I have work to go to and I have seen the Manager of the works this afternoon and he says when work comes in it will be there for me to go to but the thing is who is going to provide for my family, so the thing is must we all starve. So it is not that I am idle and will not work but willing to work when I get it.[33]

The Umpire declined Milward's appeal, arguing that "benefit can only be allowed to an applicant who is making genuine efforts to obtain employment when out of work, and it cannot be said in this case that the applicant has made such efforts."[34] The file noted that Milward had only done 72 days of work in the past 292 days, and he had failed to apply to any firms other than his previous employer, even after being warned by the manager at his local Employment Exchange that he needed to give more energy to his work search. He had not, according to the Umpire, proven his willingness to work, nor did his appeal on behalf of his family persuade.

Three million applicants for national unemployment benefits were denied assistance between 1921 and 1930 because they were found to be not genuinely seeking work.[35] To apply for benefit, a worker registered as unemployed at his or her local Employment Exchange. Contested cases went to local insurance officers and courts of referees, with petitions often coming through an applicant's trade association. If either the Insurance Officer or the applicant's association wanted to pursue the decision further, they could appeal to the Umpire, a Crown-appointed officer, who determined precedent regarding unemployment benefit decisions.[36] The records of Umpires' decisions exist for 1925 and 1926 in bound, published books at the National Archives, while they remain in manuscript form without as much detail for most of 1924 and part of 1929.[37] In addition to the Umpires' decisions, I examined the extant 48 case files of appeals categorized as "not genuinely seeking work," which often include the applications of the unemployed themselves as well as histories of the cases and decisions.[38]

The genuinely-seeking-work requirement raised the fundamental question of what constituted a "genuine" search for work as well as what was suitable work for a particular applicant. The cases before the Umpire reveal the various factors at play in making these determinations. In July 1926, the Umpire wrote a lengthy explanation attempting to define a claimant's genuine search for suitable employment:

> In considering whether a person is genuinely seeking work the most important fact to be ascertained is the state of the applicant's mind. If a person genuinely wants work, that is, really prefers working for wages to living on benefits, it is probable that she is genuinely seeking it. But if a person prefers benefit to wages, or is content to be without work so long as she received benefit, it may be presumed that she is not genuinely seeking work. . . .
>
> But though it is probable that a person who wants work is genuinely seeking work, it is not necessarily so . . . [S]he should be able to satisfy a Court of Referees that she is not merely looking for the particular kind of work which is most congenial to her or to which she has been accustomed, but that she is also trying to get other kinds of suitable employment if there are any for which she is qualified and which she has any reasonable chance of obtaining.

These passages put the burden on an applicant to demonstrate not only the physical effort to find work but the psychological status associated with a desire for employment. The Umpire went on:

> Regard must of course be had to the rate of wages and conditions which she has habitually obtained in her usual occupation, to her experience and training, her age and qualification, and all other points which are considered when questions arise of refusal of an

offer of suitable employment. In the case of skilled workers . . . unskilled or poorly paid work such as office cleaning would presumably be unsuitable.[39]

While compelling applicants not only to search for work mechanically, but also to desire employment actively, the Umpire also created significant interpretive space for determining what constituted suitable employment. Unlike the Poor Law, which expected honest men to go to the stoneyard to prove their willingness to work, the genuinely-seeking-work requirement could be much more discriminating in terms of the work expected of welfare applicants to meet the tests of the work imperative, recognizing some workers' occupational identities and skills.

In this lengthy explanation, the Umpire clearly spoke of a female applicant. Until the 1920s, the willingness to work was a measure of deservedness reserved almost exclusively for men, an essential marker of masculine status. Yet as unemployment benefit was extended to women in the postwar period, women too were increasingly judged by the work imperative, even though women's gainful employment was never conceptualized to be central to femininity or women's citizenship in the way that employment was to masculinity and men's citizenship. The requirements of genuine and suitable employment were structured, as Deacon and others have shown, to push women into domestic service and agricultural jobs where women's labor was needed.[40] Women never had to bear family liability in the same ways as men did. As a result, "genuine" and "suitable employment" had different meanings for men and women. These categories also had different meanings for the married and the single.

Appeals to the Umpire allowed unemployed men and women to contest definitions of what work should be expected of them and express how they positioned themselves with reference to the work imperative and family liability. While most of the records that remain of these appeals foreground the Umpire's voice, we can catch glimpses of men's and women's experiences with the benefits system, mediated by the scripts that they needed to perform to achieve their desired ends.

Work history and skill

The fundamental factor the Umpire considered when assessing an appeal was an applicant's desire for work, or the "state of the applicant's mind" regarding employment, a state that the Umpire would obviously read subjectively. Umpires carefully examined claimants' work histories, seeing in an applicant's past relationship to employment evidence of adherence to the work imperative or the lack of it. In September 1925, for example, the Umpire allowed benefit to a chain striker who had refused to take a position 120 miles away from his home. This man had been working for the same employer for 15 years. The Umpire argued that the applicant deserved benefit, because "I am not satisfied that he would have gained anything by leaving the employers for whom he had worked for 15 years."[41] The man's dedication to a single firm spoke to his deservedness. Similarly, the Umpire allowed benefit to O. Dando in August 1929, stressing that "the applicant's record is one of continuous employment at one colliery for eight years." He cited the precedent of a previous decision, regarding a female applicant, which emphasized the importance of continuous work: "If an applicant has been for many years a steady worker and there has been no change in her circumstances which relieves her of the necessity of working, the inference that she wants work is very strong."[42] A positive work history supposedly made transparent an applicant's willingness to work and satisfied the Umpire that relevant tests had been applied.

Applicants' appeals to their work histories aimed to counter the perception that they were loafers, which denial of benefit would have signified. In the case of a brass finisher who lost his position during the coal shortage of 1926, his trade union secretary testified that the applicant was a "conscientious workman. He was convinced that the applicant was unemployed solely because there was no work to be had." The Court of Referees denied the claim, and upon his appeal to the Umpire, the applicant insisted that "since his union continued to grant him unemployment pay they were evidently satisfied that he was not a shirker." The Umpire agreed, arguing that "a man who has worked for 14 years with one firm is not a man who does not want work."[43] By contrast, an applicant from London had been fired from his position after eight months "because of his unsatisfactory work and consistent laziness." He claimed that the work was "unpleasant" and "made him ill." The Umpire noted that the "applicant was warned on several occasions in regard to his failures, and it was because these warnings continued to prove ineffective that his services were finally dispensed with." He was denied benefit.[44]

Questions about skill were closely related to issues of work history and went to the heart of contests over what was a genuine search for work – predominantly for men. A 1923 Ministry of Labour memorandum to Local Employment Committees explicitly differentiated between skilled and unskilled applicants for benefit: "a stricter test is as a rule applicable to the case of the unskilled worker than to the case of the skilled worker."[45] Officials expected unskilled men to do an extensive search for employment and to accept almost any job. Having skill implied a seriousness about employment that gave advantage to skilled applicants and could justify a claimant's refusal of employments that did not measure up to his qualifications or that he insisted could damage existing skill. This was similar to arguments that criticized poor law task work for hurting men physically in ways that could deprive them of using their training once employment was available.

The Umpire tended to privilege skilled men in appeals for benefit. For example, in a March 1924 decision, the Umpire granted the application of an unemployed marine fitter, commenting that "I see no reason why unskilled work as a labourer should be regarded as suitable employment for him."[46] Similarly, the Umpire found in the case of Frederick Lark that "the applicant is a skilled man and there is not sufficient ground for saying that employment in his trade at a rate lower than the standard rate is suitable for him."[47] A lengthy case rehearsed the details of a steel worker, who lost his position in late April 1926. The Insurance Officer thought the man could have gotten work as a laborer, but the claimant retorted that "his industrial record indicated that he was a genuine workman and not a person who did not want work. He was willing to accept employment offered by the Employment Exchange, but he had not sought labouring work." The Umpire found that the man "has a good record for the last 12 years as a man can have and this raises a strong presumption in his favour;" the man should not be expected to take work as a laborer.[48] A "genuine worker" was a skilled man with a solid history of employment. These interpretations in favor of skilled men suggest that, for the Umpire, skill and the willingness to work were mutually constitutive, which disadvantaged unskilled workers, many of whom were young, unmarried men.

Men without recognized skills were pressured to search more broadly for employment to prove a genuine search for work. Thomas Stringer of Birmingham, for example, felt the Umpire's displeasure in 1924 at his refusal to accept a job that would have enabled him to develop a skill: "After 3 years' unemployment (except for 2 weeks last January) the applicant should have thankfully accepted an offer of employment which would have enabled him to become a fully skilled man in his trade."[49] Yet the Umpire was sometimes reluctant to force even unskilled workers into demeaning positions. In a 1925 case, an unemployed casual dockworker, who earned 12 shillings per day when at work, was offered employment as a potato picker at five shillings per day. He argued that this employment was not suitable, because it paid a much lower wage than he was used to. He also noted that, to obtain dock work, he had to show up at the docks every day to see if there was a position available. While the Court of Referees held that benefit should be allowed under these circumstances, the Insurance Officer disagreed, arguing that "although the work offered might not have been suitable for regular dockers, the applicant, who was only a *casual* docker, should have accepted the job offered, which would have lasted indefinitely." The Insurance Officer here followed the usual association of lack of skill with lack of deservedness. The Umpire, however, agreed with the Referees, finding the work unsuitable and seeing no evidence that the man was not genuinely seeking work.[50]

The Poor Law Labour Test insisted that men perform "unsuitable" work to prove their deservedness. This created a crisis when the numbers of honest poor men needing assistance increased from the late nineteenth century, prompting the national government's search for alternatives to poor law relief. The work test requirements for national benefits apparently were more nuanced, at least in the mid-1920s, recognizing that all labor was not equal and that a man's sense of himself tied to his employment could shape decisions about assistance. Honest poor men deserved credit for their work histories and skill, which was a way to accommodate masculine citizenship and dependence on the state.

Respectability and women's work

The Unemployment Insurance Acts of the 1920s incorporated benefits for women, which meant that women became subject to the tests of the work imperative. Whereas men's genuine searches for work tended to be evaluated in terms of skill and work history, women's cases – especially single women's cases – often drew on assumptions about respectability and female sexuality. Although the Umpire clearly wrote in Case 1404/26 that "the principles applicable to women are the same as those applicable to men: The Statutory conditions for the receipt of benefit do not differentiate between the sexes," in practice officials judged men's and women's willingness to work on different criteria.[51] Manhood was equated with work in a way that never was the case for womanhood in this period.

While men appealing denials of unemployment benefit used a language of skill to challenge the suitability of particular positions, women strategically drew on assumptions about femininity and the potential threats to their status as "honest" women with good reputations. Elizabeth Thornton, for example, turned down a job offer at a hotel arguing that it was of questionable character. The Umpire, however, disallowed her benefit in January 1925, writing that "I see no sufficient reason for thinking that the hotel at which there was a vacancy was of such a character that employment there would be unsuitable for a respectable young woman." Thornton presumably rejected the position on principle, as the Umpire wrote, "If she had been really anxious for work, she would have made further inquiry before refusing the offer."[52] Rather than taking seriously Thornton's concerns about the suitability of the job, the Umpire denied her claim that she was genuinely seeking work.

Women like Thornton appear to have used gender assumptions to try to protect themselves from unappealing jobs. These issues arose most explicitly in cases involving military canteens. Multiple Umpires' decisions indicate that young women resisted placements in canteens. Elsie Lawrey in March 1924, for example, registered at the Employment Exchange as a shop assistant and sought work in a comparable position. Denying an occupational identity for Lawrey, the Umpire noted, "The applicant had not worked as a shop assistant for some years, and has worked for a year as a barmaid. I cannot see why canteen work should be regarded as unsuitable for her."[53] Summing up his general findings on canteens, the Umpire wrote in October 1924 that "any employment in which young women are unduly exposed to risk cannot be regarded as suitable; but after careful enquiry I was satisfied that employment in canteens does not expose them to more risk than many other employments which are commonly undertaken without objection by respectable young women."[54] His inquiry involved contacting those who ran the canteens, not the women themselves.[55] The Umpire reiterated this point in the case of Amy Shead in November 1924: "I am satisfied that [the conditions of service in military canteens] are such that no respectable girl need fear to take employment in such canteens."[56]

Yet a case file from the spring of 1925 shows that the issue of women's work in canteens continued to be a point of contention. Evelyn Fulcher, who had been a shop assistant, was denied benefit on the grounds that she was offered suitable employment but turned it down. The Court of Referees, according to Fulcher, was biased against her, because in December 1924 she had "declined to accept domestic training." She had stressed that she was "entirely unsuited temperamentally and by experience" for domestic service. She also refused canteen employment and appealed the disallowance of benefit, arguing that "the environment and general conditions attaching to employment in a military camp, render such employment totally unsuitable to a girl of my age (18 years) and experience." Tellingly, she also remarked that "the continued occurrence of vacancies in these military canteens is evidence of the unsuitability of such employment for the girls who are sent to work by the Ministry of Labour."[57] This case offers a rare view of a woman aggressively challenging both the natural affinity of women for domestic work and an offer of employment that she perceived as demeaning. Her unusually articulate petition, however, did not result in benefit.

There were situations, however, where the Umpire agreed that certain positions were unsuitable for young women. In the case of Evangeline Trew of Bargood, the Umpire found that it was totally reasonable for a 17-year-old girl, upon her father's advice, not to accept employment in London without knowing the name and address of the employer. He noted, "Young women . . . are naturally afraid of going a long distance from home, and should be given more consideration than older women or men" in desiring to establish the suitability of the employment.[58] It is tempting to see this case as an appeal by the father rather than by Evangeline herself. All these examples illustrate that it was perfectly acceptable to consider reputation and safety in defining a genuine search for work for women; the Umpire might dispute a claimant's judgment about the respectability of certain jobs, but all agreed that respectability was relevant to defining suitable women's employment.[59] Unemployment for women clearly incorporated notions about "honest women."

Family liability and the gendered search for suitable employment

Although unemployed married women became eligible for the national unemployment benefits of the 1920s, their benefits continued to be contingent on the status of their husbands. The July 1923 Ministry of Labour memorandum to the local Employment Exchanges, for example, stated that "the claim of the wife will be refused or allowed according as the earnings of the husband are or are not regarded as sufficient to maintain the wife and *any dependent children* [emphasis in original]."[60] While wives' earnings were also supposed to be taken into account in the cases of their unemployed married husbands, "there must . . . be greater latitude in the treatment of such claims." The Ministry placed no conditions on a husband's responsibility to support his family through employment. For a wife to be considered responsible for her family, "The intention is to apply the rule only in a case where the wife is a regular worker; disallowance [for an unemployed married man] would not be justifiable if the wife was only in casual or intermittent employment, or if she only entered employment on account of the continued unemployment of her husband."[61] Men's work toward family maintenance was taken for granted; women's was conditional. These rules reflect a discomfort with making a man dependent upon his wife; better that his unemployed status be recognized through the receipt of a government dole. Yet, as the fraud cases I discussed in the previous chapter suggest, these rules could be bent, and men could be denied benefit if their wives were engaged in casual employment.

National policies on uncovenanted benefit also handicapped married women by requiring that they be "capable of and available for insurable employment and reasonably likely under ordinary circumstances to obtain such employment."[62] Eligibility for benefits was based on being able to prove a historical or current connection with insured positions, which most married women did not have. According to the Ministry of Labour, the test of being "capable," "available," and "likely under ordinary circumstances" to find an insurable position would bar most married women from benefit. Married women, even if they had been in an insured occupation previous to marriage, "in view of their present circumstances [must] be regarded as outside the ordinary industrial field," meaning that marriage took them away from the regular work force. Married women, the Ministry assumed, would generally be disallowed benefit on these grounds.[63]

As they considered their cases, Umpires drew on established assumptions about family liability and gendered familial roles in assessing suitable employment and a genuine search for work. The applications raise very few questions concerning the norm of men's family liability, but economic pressures challenged the exemption of some married women from work. Even though the Umpires' decisions demonstrate the new expectation that women had to adhere to the work imperative, they also show that men continued to bear the burden of family liability.

In defining suitable work for a man, Umpires clearly measured his ability to support a family. In a case from 1926, the Umpire decided in favor of benefits for a man who left his job hoping he could find something closer to home, writing, "I do not think that a married man with a family can be reasonably expected to pay out of the wages of a labourer both for lodgings and a substantial sum for daily traveling."[64] Frank Pygott, a boilermaker from Lincoln, had his appeal allowed in March 1924, the Umpire noting that "it appears his wife is ill and he has 3 young children and on that ground I think it is unreasonable to expect him to live away from home."[65] Their positions as heads of households put unemployed married men in the same awkward position with benefit as they were relative to the Poor Law: on the one hand, relying on "the dole" challenged their masculine status by acknowledging their inability to support their families independently; on the other hand, needing to provide for a family bolstered a man's claim for assistance, especially in comparison to single men. Their family liability spoke for their honest poverty, which enhanced their claims for assistance.

The Umpire's decisions also show, however, that married men's references to their family responsibilities were not universally successful. In another decision from March 1924, the Umpire's explanation for a disallowance mentioned that "the suggestion that the applicant's wife had been recently confined appears to be unfounded."[66] The Umpire denied Herbert Parfitt's appeal in April 1924, because "the applicant's wife does not appear to me to have been so ill as to make it unreasonable to expect him to take work away from home."[67] Men seem to have played the family liability card to argue mitigating circumstances in defining a genuine search for work, but for the Umpire in these cases, the willingness to work won out – especially, it seems, when he suspected an applicant used his family as a cover for shirking employment.

While marriage for a man meant the additional responsibility of family liability and therefore an urgent need for employment, marriage for a woman created an obstacle to continuing employment. In many regions, employers explicitly excluded married women, and officials took this into account in assessing a married woman's genuine search for work. Lucy Hollyoak of Birmingham, for example, appealed a disallowance of benefit to the Umpire in 1925. Hollyoak was married, with a baby, and indicated on her initial application for benefit that her grandmother could watch the child to facilitate her employment. The Court of Referees accepted that she was genuinely seeking work but noted, "There is, of course, some doubt, as the number of firms who employ married women are few."[68] The Insurance Officer and Umpire denied her claim, believing that she should have registered for domestic work, which was clearly available for married women.

Some female applicants used the typicality of the marriage bar to bolster a benefit claim. For example, anticipating her impending marriage, a woman left the laundry works where she had been employed, assuming that the employer did not allow married women to work. Her claim for benefit was disallowed, the officials deciding she had voluntarily left her employment and thus shown an unwillingness to work. She told the Court of Referees that she had not asked the employer point blank whether married women were kept on, but the employer confirmed for the Referees that "it was not the custom to engage married women whose husbands were in a position to support them, but each case was considered on its merits." The employer expected husbands to maintain their wives but acknowledged that situations existed where this would not be the case. The Court of Referees allowed benefit, finding that "the applicant was genuinely of the opinion that she would not be allowed to remain at work after marriage." The Insurance Officer and the Umpire disagreed, arguing that because she did not ascertain whether she would be let go, she was not genuinely seeking work.[69]

Clearly cases did exist where married women were prohibited from employment. In the spring of 1925, the marriage bar affected a group of "young women," who were forced to leave their factory positions to get married. They then claimed unemployment benefit, arguing they were unable to find other suitable employment. The case was brought to the Umpire by the Insurance Officer, who maintained that a woman who gave up employment to get married should not expect the state to support her if she failed to secure other work:

> where it was known that the employer did not employ married women, a woman who intended to get married should first seek other employment, and if she could not obtain such she would leave her employment without hope of being able to obtain unemployment benefit. In his opinion, the unemployment fund should not be resorted to by women as a means of enabling them to get married to men whose earnings are not sufficient to support them.[70]

Married women were responsible for finding suitable employment or finding suitable husbands who could support them, leaving very little space for them to be eligible for benefit.[71] The Umpire, however, commented that "it is obvious that it cannot be laid down as a universal rule that recently married women are not genuinely seeking work." He reasoned, "It may be that many employers now do not employ married women . . . and that consequently a woman by marrying diminishes her chance of getting work." This fact, however, did not prove that a woman did not desire employment. He declined to evaluate the Insurance Officer's point that women should wait for marriage until their prospective husbands could support them, saying this was really a question for Parliament: "The Unemployment Insurance Acts do not impose any disqualification for unthrifty marriage."[72] In this fascinating case, the Insurance Officer tried to use benefit to police women's marriage choices, telling women to find good husbands who could provide for them or be faced with the prospect of continuing to be wage earners. Yet an obvious solution seems not to have been considered: getting rid of the marriage bar.

In most cases, married women without children were under pressure to find employment that would suit their circumstances. For example, in 1925 two "young married women" had left their employment as packers to get married; they then refused as unsuitable work at a jam factory 18 miles from their homes: "They stated the distance was too great . . . They did not wish to work away from their homes, but were willing to work in the district from 8 am. to 5 or 6 pm." Presumably, this would allow them time for their domestic responsibilities. The Umpire disallowed the claim, writing, "The applicants were recently married and have no children. If they claim to be genuinely seeking work, and ask for benefit, they must accept the hours and conditions of work on the same basis as single women. . . . [A] young married woman should either look to her husband to support her or be ready to take work on the same conditions as single women."[73] Again, married women's benefit depended on their husbands' employment circumstances as much as their own; a woman who chose an unworthy husband would be punished by being treated as if she were not married at all, forced to demonstrate an extensive search for work.[74]

Another 1925 case suggests that even a married woman with children could be expected to work. The Umpire decided it was not sufficient for an applicant to search for work only when her husband was unemployed. Upon her application for benefit, the local Employment Exchange found that her usual occupation as a machine barker was "obsolete" in the district. She had been working on and off in domestic service, and then in a pulp works, depending upon whether or not her husband was in regular employment. The couple had two children, but the wife indicated that her mother was able to watch them while she was at work. The Court of Referees found that "the claim for benefit should be allowed. They were of the opinion that the applicant's domestic circumstances were sufficiently strong to provide an incentive to the applicant in seeking employment, although they doubted whether she had made all the efforts she might have done to secure employment." The Insurance Officer disagreed, feeling that she had not undertaken a genuine search for work, and appealed to the Umpire, who disallowed her claim. Interestingly, he commented that he was reluctant to disagree with the Court of Referees, "who have seen the applicant and know the local conditions," but he found the case against her to be compelling.

He wrote that "the applicant seems genuinely to have wanted work when her husband was unemployed but not when he was at work. . . . In my opinion, an applicant who was genuinely seeking work would be able to show that she had done more than the applicant shows."[75] Perhaps because the applicant's mother could care for her children, the officials insisted on a more aggressive effort to secure employment.

While men's searches for work were closely connected with their training and skill, officials assumed that all women could naturally turn to domestic service. The Umpire took a harsh view of the situation of Lilian Hopley, noting, "The applicant's marriage makes it very difficult for her to get employment in the occupation which she had previously followed [as a cigarette packer]. She must be prepared to take work of a kind which married women can normally obtain and should register for that work." He found her not genuinely seeking work, since she had been offered a position in domestic service.[76] She indicated she would take any factory work but not domestic service. The Insurance Officer commented, "The pretext on which the work was refused seems frivolous."[77] Ruth Watson's marital status is unclear in the record, but the pressure to accept domestic service is not: "After 6 months' unemployment the applicant should have been prepared to take domestic service. If she prefers to remain unemployed until she finds some employment more to her liking she must do so at her own expense."[78] The Umpire, however, could be sympathetic to the difficulties married women faced in finding work. Emily Hopkins had to leave her live-in employment in December 1923 when she got married. The Umpire commented, "Residential employment is not generally suitable for a married woman who wishes to live with her husband, and I think she had just cause for leaving."[79] Married women, it went without saying, should be at home to produce domestic comforts for their husbands.

Seeing to their husbands' domestic needs was rarely construed as "work" for women, but the need to care for young children usually exempted a married woman from an extensive search for work. The Umpire, for example, allowed benefit to Elizabeth Jeffers of Liverpool, reflecting that "as a married woman with a young child the applicant cannot be expected to leave her home."[80] Elizabeth Stanistreet "had a breast-fed infant and the employment was two miles from her home." The Deputy Umpire here found that "in accordance with previous decisions it must be regarded as temporarily unsuitable for her."[81] Married women's roles as mothers seemingly overrode their roles as workers. For married men, however, fatherhood was contained within the category "worker" – they fulfilled their roles as fathers by working to provide.[82]

Although employment at a distance may have been counted as "unsuitable" for the married, this was not the case for the unmarried.[83] Single men and women, seemingly with or without children, were expected to leave their districts in a search for work, particularly if they had been unemployed for a considerable period. As the Umpire indicated in a case from October 1924, "An applicant is allowed a reasonable time in which to find employment in his or her own district before being expected to accept employment away from home, and it has usually been held that one week is reasonable time for this purpose."[84] Indeed, the Umpire's decisions suggest a high level of micromanagement of single people's public and private lives. Ida Hill, for example, left a position in which she had "given satisfaction for over a year." The brief notes imply that she was unhappy with her living arrangements and so chose to seek another situation. According to the Umpire, "Instead of leaving she should either have put up with the discomfort of staying with her Aunt or have taken lodgings at 25/- a week until she found more suitable occupation."[85] The Umpire denied her appeal. In a case from January 1924, the Umpire considered the appeals of 11 "young unmarried men who have been unemployed for a considerable time." These men apparently had found work, but it was far from their homes, so they did not accept the positions. The Umpire, however, found "they were not unable to obtain suitable employment" and denied their benefits.[86]

The Umpire constrained single people's work choices, disallowing benefit in circumstances similar to those in which married men's and women's appeals were allowed. The extent to which unemployed single people's choices were limited was clear for Christopher Hardon in 1924. The Umpire found "no reason for thinking that the hut accommodation which would have been provided for the applicant would have been dirty or so uncomfortable that it was unreasonable to ask the applicant to avail himself of it until other lodgings could be found."[87] A 24-year-old seaman argued in 1925 that work as a laborer was unsuitable because "I am doubtful as to my success in labouring ashore, as I have never tried it before as all my time I have been employed at sea." The employment he was offered was also 80 miles from his home. His refusal of the position was "considered unreasonable," since more than 100 seamen were unemployed in the area, and there were not enough jobs at sea for all of them.[88] Even Mabel Alice Elliott, a single woman with a child, had to deal with the Umpire's finding that "the applicant had been unemployed for 9 months and had no prospect of employment at home. She was offered permanent employment in another district and I think she should have taken it and made arrangements either to take her child with her or leave it with her relatives as she found most convenient."[89] The demands on widows and widowers with children were more ambiguous. A case from 1925 suggests how the Umpire might have measured men's marital status and responsibility for children. The case concerned a widower with a 12-year-old son, who rejected an offer of training for skilled work because it was 150 miles from his home. He appealed that "the rate of wages was £2 per week, which was the standard rate applicable to single men under the Scheme." To support his child, the applicant "contended that the wages offered were insufficient, and that he should be paid the 2s. 6d. per day subsistence allowance applicable to married men under the Scheme. . . . the cost of rail fare, and the removal of his furniture would have been considerable. In the circumstances, he contended that the employment offered was unsuitable." While the Court of Referees disallowed benefit on the grounds of not genuinely seeking work, the Umpire disagreed with the decision: "He was offered training away from home at a rate which is usually paid to unmarried trainees, and which is no doubt calculated to enable a single man to live away from home. He could not get the married man's additional allowance as he was a widower. But he has a young son for whom he must find a home and he would no doubt require for this purpose at least the equivalent of a married man's allowance." Under these conditions, it was not suitable employment.[90]

Conclusion

The national unemployment benefit system created the possibility for new models of welfare deservedness that could better incorporate women and unmarried men. The government, however, built the work imperative and family liability into the national benefits system such that married men continued to sit atop the hierarchy of deservedness. Indeed, by foregrounding the occupational identities of skilled men in benefit determinations, the national system contributed to even firmer associations between welfare and citizenship for particular (mostly married) men. Gender and marital status intersected to put extra pressure on single men and women to prove their "genuine search for work," while married women's assistance was defined primarily by the status of their husbands. The state's insistence that single people search far and wide for employment suggests that their unemployment was not considered firmly blameless – if only they looked harder, they would find work. Married men and women with children, however, benefited from the state's recognition of their family status, which opened opportunities for government officials to see them in domestic as well as working roles.

In many ways, the governments of the 1920s lost control of unemployment benefits, as they compromised the insurance principle and increased the amounts allotted to unemployed claimants. Bureaucrats, however, used the genuinely-seeking-work test to try to regain some of that control and limit the terms by which applicants were considered deserving. The work imperative, read through the lens of family liability, constricted men's and women's abilities to demonstrate deservedness. The policies of the 1920s forced unemployed men and women to shoulder the burden of their unemployment, assuming a lack of deservedness unless an applicant could prove otherwise. The Unemployment Act of 1930 changed the burden of proof, "making unemployment benefit a right unless just cause could be shown why it should not be paid."[91] Throughout the 1920s, governments saw potential shirkers everywhere – perhaps a holdover from the rhetoric of the First World War. The next chapter will further explore that possibility.

Part II
Honest Poverty in National Crisis

5

"Married men had greater responsibilities": The First World War, the Service Imperative, and the Sacrifice of Single Men

On October 9, 1915, the *Dudley Herald* devoted a full page to "Recruiting Rallies in Dudley and District," where soldiers, politicians, and local notables gathered Black Country men to urge them to enlist. Britain had declared war against Germany in the late summer of 1914, and, immediately, military recruiters began traveling the country to persuade men of the necessity of signing on. At the rally in Brierley Hill, a featured recruiter, Mr. Avers, cheered on married men's enthusiasm to fight the Germans, while calling into question single men's commitment to the war:[1]

> A large proportion of men who had joined the ranks were married men, and why? Leaving on one side minor reasons, [Avers] thought the primary reason was that the married men had greater responsibilities. They had wives and children to think of, and they knew what it would mean to those who were dear to them should the Germans succeed in the struggle. The men without responsibilities and ties did not look upon the war in the same serious aspect as the married man.[1]

According to Avers, family responsibilities created men who understood the greater implications of the war. Protecting the nation was essentially family liability writ large, and, framed in these terms, married men were more invested in the military effort than were single men. Single men's lack of family liability blinded them to the "seriousness" of the situation, so they needed to be made aware of their "responsibilities" to fight.

Yet, rather than pointing to something in unmarried men's lives that might spur them to enlist, Avers appealed to an assumed shared knowledge of the centrality of family life to Britons and to single men's future family obligations: "it was for the young unmarried men who had not yet obeyed the call to think that they themselves in the next generation might have dependents and homes, and their duty was to see that future generations should have the same privileges and liberties which people of this country enjoyed to-day."[2] Single men had the responsibility to maintain the promise of British domestic life for the future.[3] The "privileges and liberties" of the British people (men) centered around having "dependents and homes." Ironically, the fact that single men did not have "dependents and homes" made them the ideal candidates for the dangers of military service, whether or not they understood the moral significance of enlistment that recruiters emphasized.

Because military service remained voluntary until January 1916, convincing men to sign on was a defining practice of the early war years. Initially, men joined the army in droves (Figure 5.1). After September 1914, however, when 460,000 men enlisted, recruiting lagged, with just over a million men having joined up by the end of the year.[4] With disastrous campaigns in the late summer and fall of 1915, the British suffered massive casualties and, in historian R.J.Q. Adams's words, "enlistments,

Figure 5.1   Marketplace, Dudley. Blessing the recruits, c.1914
Source: © Dudley Archives and Local History Service, ref. p/371.

quite understandably, continued to decline."[5] It became clear that existing measures were not going to result in the needed manpower. The government debated and then instituted the draft. Conscription only intensified the public and political discussions that had erupted during the period of voluntary enlistment about which men should be sent into combat.[6]

The propaganda of recruitment and the debates surrounding conscription have received a good deal of attention from scholars, who have examined the social and cultural impacts of recruitment efforts as well as the political ramifications of voluntarism and conscription.[7] Historian Nicoletta Gullace has emphasized that the culture of the war created a dichotomy between those who served and those who did not serve as a means of assessing citizenship status, allowing women who engaged in a wide variety of war work to claim their place in the nation. By contrast, men who did not serve, and particularly conscientious objectors, were disenfranchised. The willingness to serve, Gullace argues, trumped all other markers of citizenship and national belonging during the war.[8]

How did this emphasis on service intersect with the discourse of honest poverty during the First World War? Because the problem of unemployment virtually disappeared during the war, the period interrupted the narrative of continuity that I advance in Part I of this book, challenging any simple structure to the story of family liability and the work imperative as the defining features of masculine status for poor men. Military service created a new, sometimes competing, claim to good citizenship for men, which was experienced differently by the employed and the unemployed, the skilled and the unskilled, and, most importantly, the married and the single. In the early years of voluntarism, recruiters targeted the unemployed and converted the work imperative into a service imperative, devaluing the willingness to work relative to the willingness to serve and creating tensions for many men working on the home front. With the draft, men's marital status became an even more significant marker of differentiation during the war than it had been in the prewar years – a matter of life and death. Without wives and children to "protect" them, single men were fully able to prove their deservedness as masculine citizens only by heading to the front lines.

Constituting the service imperative

The transition to the wartime economy disrupted daily life in the Black Country. Ten days after war was declared, the *Dudley Herald* reported on "mobs of men and women, infuriated beyond control in consequence of the advanced prices of food stuff."[9] The Dudley Board of Guardians saw an increase in outrelief expenditure, and the Dudley Town Council set up improvement schemes to deal with the anticipated unemployment.[10] Newspapers emphasized workers' donations to the Prince of Wales Relief Fund for civilian distress as well as workers' collections aimed specifically at the dependants of fellow workmen serving abroad.[11]

Yet fairly quickly the war became a boon to many depressed areas like the Dudley and Stourbridge Unions, as local manufacturing was well suited to war production. In his 1929 history of the region, George Allen indicates that many of the larger engineering factories were able to transition easily into munitions production. Other local industries, including most of the hardware trades, had to adjust their plants and products but then also could take on munitions work. The area benefited from the removal of foreign competition during the course of the war so that demand for Black Country-produced glass, nails, and chain, for example, increased and was sustained for the duration.[12] In March 1915, the *Herald* could report on the "prosperity now existing in the coal trade," and an item on the Prince of Wales's Dudley Fund in April claimed that "fortunately employment on the whole has been so good that it has only been found necessary to distribute some £50 in the relief of civil distress arising out of the war."[13] Because the region was so heavily invested in munitions and fuel production, many Black Country men remained on the home front rather than being called to combat.[14] The *Dudley Herald*'s retrospective for 1915 noted, "The war has opened up many avenues of labour, and workers have not been 'wanting.'"[15]

While the war rapidly deferred the "problem of unemployment," the historical experiences of poverty in areas like the Black Country initially provided a context in which the government planned military recruiting. Government correspondence suggests that officials wanted the recruitment process to seem part of an organized state response to economic circumstances and used languages of recruitment that fit with the broader conversations about unemployment. For example, immediately after the war declaration in August 1914, Umberto Wolff, of the Office for Labour Exchanges and Unemployment Insurance, received a memo regarding the use of Labour Exchanges for military recruitment. The memo suggested that "since there is this great stress of unemployment it will be far better to draft them [through Labour Exchanges] than to have them about starving. On the whole I think we can be of great service here."[16] As men showed up to exchanges looking for work, recruiters could grab them for the military. A Ministry of Labour memo on recruiting commented, "From the point of view of national relief, it is obviously infinitely preferable to have a fair number of men employed full time and a fair number of men enlisted, than to have a large number working half time only."[17] War service could thus be seen as a solution to the problem of unemployment. Officials considered how to use men's economic anxieties to encourage enlistment. While not getting to the point of directly equating war service with employment, Wolff pondered how unemployment benefits could be used to the military's advantage:

> While it is not clear that it would necessarily be right to refuse Unemployment Benefit even to single men on the ground that enlistment is open to them, I think we might possibly consider paying unemployment benefit for the maximum period to unemployed men in the Insured Trades who enlist . . . It would of course be clearly understood that the benefit would be paid to the man's family.

Wolff carefully thought about the ways the government could manipulate unemployment benefits to encourage men to enlist, although he had doubts about the extent to which the state could withhold benefits to those who did not sign on – "even . . . single men." Notably, Wolff conceptualized the potential relationship between unemployment benefits and military service positively relative to married men – if insured married men enlisted, their families would receive allowances. Yet, for single men, Wolff only referred to the possible refusal of benefits to drive them into service. Wolff also noted that "the Local Government Board Committee have laid it down that they will not pay [poor] relief to persons of enlisting age until all others have been looked after."[18] Thus, while national benefits could serve as a carrot to service, the withholding of poor law relief could be the stick to push into the military men authorities believed should enlist.

Not only did men need to sign on; employers of war workers needed to be willing to release men to join the military. By September 1915, 6,000 men were already doing official war work in the town of Dudley alone, and these numbers continued to increase. The *Herald* stressed that "Dudley must now be regarded as a munition area,"[19] meaning it was essential to supplying the military effort. Recruiters had to convince both working men and employers that industrial workers could be spared for combat. At the end of February 1915, for example, the *Herald* reported that the Worcesters, a regional military regiment, wanted 300 recruits and urged Dudley men "to support their own local companies . . . The patriotism of employers and employees is alike appealed to, so that they should do all they can in response to the appeal."[20] Because the region had such a high concentration of industries devoted to the war, tensions surrounding the relative value of war work at home and military service ran high and fed a conversation about what constituted patriotism.

These tensions erupted at a recruiting rally in Dudley in October 1915. Quartermaster-Sergeant Wheatcroft, a soldier wounded at the front, led off the rally calling on men of "all trades and ages up to fifty" to sign on. He said that, while walking around the city that day, "he had accosted many young and eligible men in the streets. Many of them said: 'Oh! We're munition workers.' So he asked them to produce their badges, but the invariable reply was: 'Our firm ain't got 'em yet.' 'No, nor never will have 'em,' shouted the Quartermaster. 'I don't call them men.' (Loud applause)." In relating this exchange, Wheatcroft criticized men he suspected of falsifying their work status to avoid military service. Wheatcroft continued his chastisement of non-soldiers, claiming, "Some men said they had got jobs worth £2 10s and they're 'Not going to give that up.' Those men are cowards. What would they do with their fat jobs if the Germans came? (Loud applause)."[21] The war shifted the discourse of masculinity and cowardice away from the work imperative and toward a service imperative. Men who valued wage earning over military service could be marked as less than men. In this way, military service challenged work in determinations of masculine status.

Yet the government needed men in occupations considered work of national importance. Some recruiters tried to emphasize the equal value of men's war work at home and soldiers' military service, but this equivalence was never fully successful. For example, at a "Patriotic Demonstration at Brierley Hill" in August 1915, Colonel Sir Arthur Boscawen, Conservative Member of Parliament for Dudley and military garrison commander, insisted, "They wanted men and more men every day. It was the duty of every man in Brierley Hill who was fit and could be spared to at once and without any palavering, offer himself to the colours and contribute his share to the great victory that ultimately awaited them." Boscawen, however, also acknowledged that men were needed on the home front:

> There were many men in the pits and works who were doing their bit just as much as if they were actually fighting in the trenches. These men were doing their duty and would have their reward; and

he hoped they would get the medal as the soldiers would. . . . but if there were suitable men doing work which old people, youngsters or women could do, then it was their duty to make way for others to do that work and to at once enlist in the Army and to shoulder the rifle. . . . If they were fit for the nation's work they would not be proud of themselves when the war was over.[22]

This powerful speech attempted to assure men in essential industries that their work was equivalent to soldiers' service. However, Boscawen simultaneously identified "the nation's work" explicitly as military service and associated domestic war work with women, old men, and children.

Newspaper items on summonses for "neglect of work" suggest that not all Black Country men bought into the call to service, whether on the home front or the battle front. While neglect of work cases appeared in the papers throughout the period of this study, they took on new meaning during the war. In March 1915, for example, an item on "Workmen's Duty in War Time" discussed the prosecution of two boatmen from Tipton who had "absent[ed] themselves from work without notice." The stipendiary magistrate granted the firm's claim for 15 shillings from each man and warned the boatmen, "Men are short in the country. If you don't do your duty by going to the front you ought to do all you can for the trade of the country."[23] The magistrate clearly represented military service as the most important work a man could take on, a national duty that should have trumped work at home. Doing "all you can for the trade of the country" took second place.

The value of employment came up in another case where two Cradley Heath iron workers were prosecuted at Old Hill Police Court for neglect of work in September 1915. In addition to leaving work, the men went "on the spree" and got drunk. The prosecutor stressed, "He wanted the Bench to impress upon the men the importance of sticking to their work, to keep the front supplied." The magistrates fined the defendants 20 shillings and the court costs, concluding that "it was a serious thing for men to leave work as they had done. It meant prolonging the war." Individual behavior took on national significance. Yet the men themselves challenged their value both to their workplace and to the war effort. One said "his absence did not stop the furnaces at all," and another complained, "If we are working on Government work, why don't they pay us the minimum wage, and not 3s a day? We should know then when we were on Government work."[24] According to this man, if the government valued his work, it should have paid him to show it.

Patriotic rhetoric came to the fore in these cases, connecting the willingness to work with a commitment to the war. In Halesowen Police Court in September 1915, 23 "youths" were summoned for leaving their positions at Coombs Wood Tube Works, which was engaged in war work:

> Mr T Cooksey, who appeared for the plaintiffs, explained that on the date in question the senior men engaged at the works made an application to the directors for permission to leave the furnaces at mid-day, owing to the heat. The directors reminded the men that their brothers were working and suffering in Gallipoli and Persia under heat beyond all comparison to that which they were asked to work in. It was suggested to them that they ought not to make such a request, and very properly they withdrew their application and decided to continue at their work.

In this case, it appears that the senior tube workers accepted the solidarity with soldiers constructed by their employers as well as the equating of war work and military service: since servicemen could not leave their positions, tube workers should not request to leave theirs. However, younger workers at the firm did not express this solidarity. The men accepted their guilt and offered apologies to the court. The magistrates' chair, however, stressed the seriousness of the situation, warning them that "the country was being roused up to do its duty, and if defendants neglected their work in that fashion they would be taken as soldiers. He had no patience with shirkers like them."[25] Interestingly, the magistrate implied that men's work at home protected them from military service, an issue that would become more contentious after the government instituted the draft.

The single and the married

While recruiters, employers, and working-class men contested the significance of the work imperative when weighed against military service during the period of voluntary enlistment, opinions about family liability relative to war responsibilities were more uniform. Civilians and military representatives alike preferred single men for the military, assuming the unmarried had fewer ties to home, and families would be less disrupted by their absence. Single men, in effect, were more disposable for their home communities, because they did not have wives and children dependent upon them. Just as policymakers and relief providers demonstrated married men's value to the nation by prioritizing their welfare needs, the military recognized the value of married men by "protecting" them from the front. This protection can be seen as another privilege granted to men with family liability.

The government worried about both the short-term impact of married men's absence on their families and the long-term impact should married men be killed and leave their families without support. Historians have shown that the unusual circumstance of so many men away fighting opened up possibilities for women to inhabit the public sphere in new ways and to take over as heads of households, "replacing" men who were at the front.[26] However, wartime welfare and employment policies aimed at keeping the gender order in its prewar form as much as possible and particularly at promising a return to "normality" at the end of hostilities. Some of the most important of these strategies involved assuring men that they would have their jobs when they returned, at the expense of women employed during the war, and creating separation allowances that had the state assume family liability in the absence of a male breadwinner who was serving the nation. As the *Dudley Herald* put it in an item about poor relief, a dependant "must not be any worse off by reason of the breadwinner having gone to fight his country's battles."[27]

Policy discussions certainly addressed how to make service more attractive and practical for married men. Especially in the period before the draft began, separation allowances promised married men who enlisted voluntarily that their wives and children would be guaranteed non-stigmatizing support. Historian Susan Pedersen has argued that these "universal, need-blind" separation allowances, which the government instituted at the beginning of the war, were the roots from which the gendered welfare system codified in the post-1945 welfare state grew.[28] According to Pedersen, "Allowances were important for the way they committed the state to a 'logic' of social citizenship structured around maintaining the domestic rights of the male citizen."[29] The government promised to take on absent married men's family liability, maintaining the family until the husband's hoped-for return. Yet, as Janis Lomas emphasizes, the government also stood in for the husband by investigating the "honesty" of the wives of soldiers and war widows to determine deservedness.[30] Women's honesty determined the terms on which they could receive these supposedly universal allowances.

Although the government was concerned with supporting married men's enlistment, there is no question that the state and the public thought single men should be the ones on the front lines. Newspapers promoted the protection of married men from combat, routinely printing soldiers' letters concerning the injustice of sending married men to fight when single men were still available. In July 1915, the headline "To Single Men" prefaced a Brierley Hill soldier's letter printed in the *County Express*: "I think it is a shame for married men with children to look after to have to come here to fight while so many single young men are remaining in England; the boys out here don't like it."[31] Two weeks later, the *County Express* printed a letter from a soldier to his friend under the heading "Hasbury Soldier's Appeal to Single Young Men":

> I don't think you ought to enlist; you have a wife and child to think of, and there are hundreds of thousands of young single men still walking about. I think the Government ought to study these things. Why not put the married men on munition making and send the single ones out? We have at least 800,000 married men fighting, and yet there are millions of single men at home. There are married men out here over 40 years of age with large families. It's a shame to see some of them.[32]

Whether this letter and others like it were "plants" of recruiters or not, the message was clear: married men could participate in the war effort at home, while single men should fight in the more dangerous combat conditions. The letters juxtaposed single men's supposed reluctance to fight against married men's supposed urgency, painting a picture of married men's greater patriotism.

This contrast between married men fighting and single men "walking about" created a forceful perception that married men were more valuable to the nation in occupations other than serving as soldiers. Surprisingly, little scholarly attention has been given to this extremely significant marker of difference during the First World War. Gullace has stressed that, for men, volunteering for service was considered much more meaningful than being conscripted through the draft: Britons viewed a man who enlisted voluntarily as having undergone "an inner transformation, one that enlightened him to the duties of citizenship."[33] The citizenship conferred by service, however, meant very different things for single and married men. Even in the desperate context of the First World War, many believed that married men did not need to be "enlightened to the duties of citizenship": that enlightenment had already taken place when they got married. Shirking was essentially a problem of single men (Figure 5.2).

The preference for single men's service shaped discussions of enlistment through the Derby Scheme, the last gasp of voluntarism,

"WAR? WELL, WOT ABART IT?"

Figure 5.2   Loafers in the park. "War? Well, wot about it"
Source: © Illustrated London News Ltd/Mary Evans.

introduced in October 1915 by Edward George Villiers Stanley, Earl of
Derby, whom Liberal Prime Minister Asquith had placed in charge of
recruiting. Under the Derby Scheme, all men between the ages of 18
and 41 had to "attest," to promise that when the government needed
them to enlist they would do so. There were two lists of attestation, one
for married men and one for single men. According to historian R.J.Q.
Adams, single men assumed (most likely correctly) that these separate

lists meant they would be called up first and "shunned the attestation forms like the plague, while married men – sure of their immunity to immediate call-up – signed up in droves."[34] These responses would only have confirmed the wider perception that married men were more patriotic than single men.

Asquith spoke to the House of Commons about the scheme, hinting that he was open to drafting single men to prevent married men from volunteering for combat: "so far as I am concerned I should certainly say the obligation of the married man to serve ought not to be enforced or held to be binding upon him unless and until, I hope by voluntary effort, if it be needed in the last resort, as I have explained by other means the unmarried men are dealt with."[35] This "pledge" to protect married men ultimately shaped conscription policy and maintained the centrality of marital status in the politics of military service.

Lord Derby presented a report on attestation to the Cabinet in December 1915, which "revealed that more than half a million single men were neither attested nor employed on work essential to the war effort."[36] The Cabinet thus had "proof" that single men were not doing their part. This report led Asquith to make a specific "Appeal to Unmarried Men" in front of the House of Commons on December 21, 1915.[37] Asquith began by reaffirming his pledge that married men would not be called up until after all single men had enlisted. He commended married men "who have responded, on the whole, so well to the call of patriotic duty" but worried that "there are parts of the country where the young unmarried men have not come forward as they should have done in response to the national call."[38] Asquith requested an additional million men for the military, which led to a heated discussion in the House that lasted until after 5:00am the next morning, resulted in no resolution, and continued the following day. Among other things, this debate revealed significant differences among MPs regarding the relationships between masculine citizenship and marital status.

Some MPs agreed very strongly that single men were more expendable and should be sent to the front before any more married men. Henry Duke, Conservative for Exeter, reiterated that "the young married men have the protection of the solemn pledge of this country that they shall not be called to serve until the unmarried men in this country have done their duty." He essentially demanded that Asquith release the married men who had already attested until the "young and robust men in this country who regard it as a sacred duty not to defend it" came forward to do their duty.[39] For Duke, even married men who voluntarily enlisted should not have been sent into combat until single men were forced to sign on. In bringing to the fore married men's willingness to serve, politicians like Duke and Asquith suggested that marriage for men was a transformative act, that their "greater responsibilities" made them recognize their duties as citizens.

Other MPs, however, argued vociferously against marital status as a measure of a man's worth, challenging the idea that marriage automatically conferred a different masculine citizenship. The Labour Party's Charles Stanton of Merthyr Tydfil, for example, argued in favor of a draft, claiming, "There are slackers! There are young men, and young married men – some of whom married to dodge their responsibility, and who are not ashamed to slink behind the garments of their womenfolk. Are these the people who are to breed future Britishers? I think it is shameful."[40] Marriage, according to Stanton, could in fact signify a man's cowardice rather than his manhood. It would be better, Stanton hinted, that these shameful, slinky men be sent to die rather than "breed future Britishers." In less evocative language, the Liberal Richard Holt of Hexham supported Stanton's line of reasoning, indicating, "I rather protest against the aspersions which are so readily cast upon single men. After all, single men are of exactly the same flesh and blood as married men, and surely it cannot be suggested that the mere fact of getting married immediately converts a lazy man or a shirker into a full-blooded patriot."[41] Yet, as I have argued, in many ways this is exactly what was suggested. Marriage, in creating family liability, transformed a man, integrating him more fully into the state.

John Dillon, of the Irish Parliamentary Party, protested to his colleagues that the issue of enlistment was being framed around "whether a few alleged unmarried slackers are to be conscripted or not." He indicated that "according to the theory that is common to the readers of the 'Daily Mail' and of that Press you would imagine that the average Britisher was more or less a coward until he provided himself with a wife, and then he became a hero, eager for the field of slaughter. I can only assume that the theory emanated in the mind of some man whose marital experience was extremely unhappy."[42] With dismay, Dillon complained:

> There are an enormous number of groups [under the Derby Scheme]: Group 1, single men of eighteen; Group 24, married men of eighteen. Therefore, if a man gets married at the age of eighteen, without any provision for a living, he is then a privileged person. I submit that

the classification is preposterous and is perfectly indefensible and absurd. It comes to this: that in twenty-three groups single men up to forty are to be called out before the married men of eighteen. Under this grouping the man who is a waster and a slacker, and who is married at eighteen, gets into a privileged class of men, while the man who is waiting until he can provide a home for his wife is called out first.[43]

According to Dillon, singleness was in no way a sufficient sign of a man's lack of responsibility. Indeed, it could denote just the opposite, a thoughtful effort to avoid family obligations before a man was financially stable. Marriage, similarly, was not a transparent signifier of a man's ability to provide; it should therefore not confer the privilege associated with honest poverty. Even more significantly, marriage could offer cover for Weary Willies and Tired Tims.

Robert Outhwaite, Liberal member for Hanley, also worried about using marital status to differentiate between men. He lamented, "I cannot understand how the State can say to one man, 'You are unmarried and therefore you shall undertake this obligation and shall risk your life,' and to say to another man, 'You are married and therefore you shall escape'." He linked this approach to military service explicitly with the place of family liability in welfare:

I have seen a letter in the Press recently in which it was said that a married man [killed in service] might leave a wife and perhaps children who might become dependant [sic] on the State, whereas an unmarried man would leave no such dependants, and that, therefore, to send a married man to be killed leaving dependants on the State would cause an increase of taxation in the future. That is the genesis of this demand that married men shall not go and that unmarried men shall; it is the fear of the rich that if the married men go and get killed they will have to provide for those left behind. That is the origin of it, and if that is the only reason you can find for it, then I say it is a most unfair distinction.[44]

Rather than seeing the protection of married men as tied to their greater investment in the nation, Outhwaite aimed to expose a more base economic justification for the policy of sending single men first.

Several MPs challenged the use of family liability at all as a measuring stick of a man's worth, arguing instead that the work imperative should determine privileged status with regard to military service. Unskilled men, whether married or single, in this vision made up the group of most disposable men. For example, Holt asked whether

> commercial people [have] been consulted in any way as to which men can best be spared? I think the Army ought to be satisfied with the residuum not only in quantity but also to a certain extent in quality. . . . When we are carrying on the trade of the country we do not inquire whether the clerks we engage are married or not. That is not a relevant question at all. The question is, can they perform their duty properly, and the employer very often does not know whether or not the clerk is married.[45]

Holt stressed a version of the work imperative that measured men's value through their productivity. The "residuum," those who were unemployed or employed in unproductive capacities, contained the men who could be sacrificed to the war. Good workers, by contrast, should be reserved for the benefit of the nation. Marital status did not define whether a man was a good worker.

James Thomas, Labour member for Derby, made a similar argument about the need to account for the type of work a man did when discussing enlistment. While Asquith equated "single men" with men "with the least responsibility," Thomas disagreed: "I dissent from the suggestion that the single man is not to have a conscience as well as the married man. . . . Would anyone who believes in this talk about the married men suggest that a single munition worker should go before a married unstarred man?"[46] Starred and badged men were those doing the essential work of the war, and these categories more than marital status should have determined enlistment priorities.

Appealing to a more inclusive model of family liability that recognized single men's roles in maintaining their elderly parents or other family members, Thomas wondered,

> Could anyone suggest that the young man who has got a widowed mother, or whose father and mother being dead takes the responsibility of maintaining the younger children – has he not any moral obligation? Is he not in precisely the same position as the married man? Take the thousands of homes in this country where there are two and three sons already fighting. Mothers have written to me and said, 'Save me one of the boys.' Are these men cowards? Are these men slackers? Are these men to be pilloried without there being an opportunity to examine the case?[47]

The Poor Law established a long history of sons being responsible for dependent parents, and the war provided a moment when single men and their advocates tried to claim this responsibility to their benefit. Single men's liability for their parents and siblings might seem equivalent to married men's liability for their wives and children, but, as we will see in Chapter 8, these different forms of liability had very different cultural meanings. Single men's dependants were not dependants of choice, and therefore single men did not prove their responsibilities in the same ways as married men. By marrying wives and creating families, men chose the burden of taking on dependants. Just as Gullace argued that it was volunteering for military service that transformed a man, so too was it volunteering to take on dependants through marriage that "enlightened [him] to the duties of citizenship."

Family liability as national service

While the context of voluntary enlistment produced tensions surrounding the comparative patriotism and citizenship claims of married and single men, conscription forced the issue of whether marital status would matter in compelling military service. The Military Service Act of January 1916 mandated that all men between the ages of 18 and 41 could be called up for active service. However, the significant exceptions to this mandate included married men and widowers with children as well as men who were serving in war industries and a few professions, such as clergy. Single men who had been reluctant to enlist voluntarily were now compelled to do so. Yet Parliament quickly abolished the marital status restrictions on conscription when, as of May 1916, a revised Military Service Act brought in general compulsory service. Subsequent acts added to the categories of men deemed eligible for conscription, steadily increasing the age and "starred" occupational groups that could be called up until the final Act in April 1918 extended the ages of men who could be drafted to between 17 and 51.[48]

With the institution of conscription, the national government set up local tribunals to consider men's applications for exemptions from military service. The tribunals contained representatives from local government and business as well as military representatives who were above all interested in providing men for the forces. In his history of the tribunals, James McDermott writes that each case received about five minutes before the tribunal, and decisions usually came quickly "following very brief, whispered conferences."[49] If the local tribunal did not grant a desired exemption, a man could appeal to his county tribunal.

Most exemptions were temporary, giving a man time to organize his home or business to ready for his departure, although the tribunals did grant a very few absolute exemptions that lasted for the duration of the war. Certain occupational exemptions – the starred and badged men – were separate from tribunal exemptions. These, according to P.E. Dewey, increased from about 1.4 million men in October 1916 to 2.3 million men two years later. Tribunal exemptions "fluctuated at about the three-quarter million mark for the last two years of the war."[50]

In this section, I use Black Country men's applications for exemptions from military service to explore contests over work, family liability, service, and citizenship. As Gerald E. Shenk has written about the United States draft during the First World War, "Individuals needed to make their interactions with Selective Service officials into scripted performances of race, gender, and sexuality as they jostled with one another and with officials to get what they wanted."[51] In Britain, this jostling very much drew on the terms of honest poverty. While historians have certainly examined the politics of conscription during the First World War, they have given less attention to the local tribunals. The major work on the tribunals is McDermott's 2011 *British Military Service Tribunals, 1916–18: A Very Much Abused Body of Men*, a thorough study of the Appeal Tribunals in Northamptonshire.[52] McDermott notes that the limited historiography stems from the national government's order for all "borough, district, metropolitan and county councils in England and Wales to destroy all files, minute books and other records relating to the Tribunals' work." He argues that this represented a "symbolic repudiation" of a very fraught institution.[53]

However, newspapers provide another rich source on exemptions. The Stourbridge and Dudley newspaper coverage of the tribunals took up much of the weekly papers during the war years, with columns devoted to the cases sitting side by side with pictures and obituaries of local men killed at the front. I constructed a dataset with tribunal reports from the *County Advertiser*, the *County Express*, and the *Dudley Herald*, using the first newspaper of each month (all were published on Saturdays) for 1916, 1917, and 1918 when the tribunals were in operation.[54] The newspaper record is unclear as to which cases editors chose to print. Many of the reported exemption cases are very brief, without any demographic data or information regarding why an applicant was asking for exemption. Coverage might simply say, for example, "Eight notices of claim had been lodged by employers, and three by attested men. . . . All the claims were dealt with by the tribunal in accordance with the decisions of the military representative."[55] Lack of specifics and several men applying for exemption at the same time are common, especially in the early coverage or when many cases were before a particular tribunal. My dataset of 2,997 exemption records is therefore inconsistent with regard to available details, but it is helpful in creating a loose profile of exemption cases in the region.

Some missing information in the newspapers was purposeful. The early coverage suggests that exemption applications were not seen positively by the public, and the newspapers therefore hid the case details. At the Brierley Hill Tribunal in mid-March 1916, for example, "The Chairman announced that the Tribunal desired him to renew the request made at their first sitting that the Press would not publish the names and addresses of applicants appealing for exemption. They felt that hardship might ensue in some cases if names were given."[56] The same month, a "Mother Who Would Not Feel Proud of Such Sons" wrote a letter to the editor decrying the operation of the tribunals, complaining that men gamed the system: "It makes a mother's blood boil to think we have such young men who claim the title of Englishmen. . . . In my humble opinion the only way of dealing with these young men whose hearts, if they have any, are out of place, is by putting them all under military law at once."[57] The tribunals themselves could provide fodder for criticism, especially as they were associated with conscientious objectors.[58]

The coverage of the tribunals reveals that tensions surrounding service and marital status continued, and were even exacerbated, with conscription. About 41 per cent – 1,240 – of the cases clearly indicated marital status. Of these, almost 70 per cent (850) of the men applying for exemption were married, only about 30 per cent (380) were single, and less than one per cent (9) was widowed. Breaking down these numbers over the three years during which the tribunals operated during the war produces interesting observations. In 1916, while there was still a preponderance of married men, the difference between married and single was not as great: 63 versus 36 per cent (181 versus 104); in 1917, the relationship was 67 to 32 per cent (448 to 215); and in 1918, 77 to 21 per cent (221 to 61). The numbers suggest that exemptions for single men were increasingly hard to come by, especially as the categories of accepted exemptions shrank as the war went on. I cannot explain the utter absence of widowed men, except to speculate that they were counted under either the married or single category (perhaps with dependants they were married and without they were single).

Men applied for exemptions from service based on four broad categories: occupational need, domestic hardship, medical incapacity, or conscience (Table 5.1). My dataset includes all of the reasons an applicant

Table 5.1 Total reasons for military exemption applications by year, 1916–1918

Reason	1916 (1,688 reasons)	1917 (1,300 reasons)	1918 (706 reasons)	Total (3,694 reasons)
Business	52.8	53.2	43.8	51.2
Conscience	2.0	0.2	0.4	1.1
Domestic/children/personal	18.0	18.5	17.3	18.0
Medical	4.5	6.6	4.0	5.1
Work of national importance*	16.4	9.8	8.9	12.6
Unclear/unspecified	6.3	11.6	25.6	11.9
Total	100.0	100.0	100.0	100.0

* Includes agricultural certificate, certified, and protected.
Sources: Tribunal reports from the County Advertiser, the County Express, and the Dudley Herald, using the first newspaper of each month (all were published on Saturdays) for 1916, 1917, and 1918.

offered for his exemption claim (for example, some men argued poor health and responsibilities for dependants), so the number of reasons is actually greater than the number of total cases (3,694 reasons and 2,997 cases). Where reasons are clear, by far the largest number of claims – 64 per cent – fell under the occupation category, just one per cent was based on conscience, about five per cent on medical reasons, and 18 per cent on domestic hardship, with the rest being unclear. Where both the reason for the claim and the outcome of the application were recorded, about 25 per cent of domestic claims were refused compared with about 18 per cent of business claims. The few men basing their appeals on conscience were also refused about a quarter of the time. If a man could produce a medical certificate testifying to poor health, his exemption was almost always approved.

Most applications by all categories of men led to temporary exemptions, from one week up to 12 months.[59] The purpose of these temporary exemptions was to allow men time to prepare themselves to leave their homes and businesses. Sixty per cent of all applicants where the exemption was clear received a three-month exemption. Some exemptions were predicated on a man volunteering for home service. Absolute exemptions were extremely rare in this dataset: only 20 men received exemptions for the duration of the war, with 19 of these awarded in 1916 (see Table 5.2). The majority of these men won their absolute exemptions based on occupational appeals, claiming they were doing work of national importance, had some "rare skill," or were essential to the operation of

Table 5.2　Tribunal outcomes by year, 1916–1918

Outcome	1916 (1,303 outcomes)	1917 (1,085 outcomes)	1918 (609 outcomes)	Total (2,997 outcomes)
Adjourned	6.4	7.2	8.9	7.2
Conditional	10.7	5.6	4.4	7.6
Refused*	20.0	17.2	10.0	17.0
Temporary	48.7	57.4	55.8	53.3
Other**	5.4	1.7	2.6	3.5
Unclear***	8.7	10.9	18.2	11.4
Total	100.0	100.0	100.0	100.0

*Includes refused, revoked, and overturned.
**Includes absolute, appealed, badged/certified, referred, no jurisdiction, deferred, continued, renewed, withdrawn, and amended.
***Includes unstated or unclear outcomes, complex outcomes listed in a comments field, and no action taken.
Sources: My dataset with tribunal reports from the County Advertiser, the County Express, and the Dudley Herald, using the first newspaper of each month (all were published on Saturdays) for 1916, 1917, and 1918 when the tribunals were in operation.

their firm. Some domestic claims also garnered absolute exemptions, such as that of Wilfred Hill, an ironplate worker, whose widowed mother appealed for him before the Lye Tribunal in June 1916. Mrs. Hill claimed that one of Wilfred's "brother[s] had been killed in the Dardanelles, and another brother had been twice seriously wounded, being totally blinded." The tribunal granted Wilfred an absolute exemption, expressing "sympathy" to Mrs. Hill.[60] The fact that the dataset shows only one absolute exemption in 1917 and none in 1918 demonstrates the increasing need for servicemen and the inability of men to make persuasive claims for total exemptions. As the military representative warned the Halesowen Tribunal in March 1916, "he was against absolute exemptions. He thought such cases should be periodically reviewed."[61]

The newspaper reporting on the tribunals suggests that marital status was a key factor in exemption decisions (Table 5.3). Single men were refused exemptions more than twice as often as married men. Covering the second meeting of the Dudley Tribunal in March 1916, the *County Advertiser*, under the heading "The Rights of Married Men," reported on the case of a clerk "in a Government controlled works, who was the sole supporter of his mother and an invalid sister," who was refused an exemption. Colonel Higgs-Walker, the military representative, argued that "now the married groups were to be called up [in May], he thought single men in circumstances like applicant should be regarded in the

Table 5.3 Military exemption application primary reasons and outcomes by marital status, 1916–1918

Marital Status	Primary Reason (no. of outcomes)	Outcome (per cent of total for each reason)						
		Adjourned	Conditional	Refused*	Temporary	Other**	Unclear***	Total
Single	Business (242)	5.0	5.8	28.9	48.3	2.0	9.9	100.0
	Conscience (3)	–	–	–	–	33.3	66.7	100.0
	Domestic/children/personal (54)	7.4	7.4	33.3	46.3	3.8	1.9	100.0
	Medical (22)	40.9	4.5	13.6	27.3	–	13.6	100.0
	Work of national importance**** (24)	12.5	4.2	33.3	25.0	–	25.0	100.0
	Unclear/multiple (36)	2.8	2.8	27.8	50.0	5.6	11.1	100.0
	Total (381)	**7.6**	**5.5**	**28.6**	**45.1**	**2.6**	**10.5**	**100.0**
Married	Business (527)	6.8	10.1	11.0	64.5	1.7	5.9	100.0
	Conscience (1)	–	–	–	100.0	–	–	100.0
	Domestic/children/personal (119)	7.6	7.6	19.3	54.6	1.6	9.2	100.0
	Medical (35)	34.3	8.6	11.4	34.3	8.6	2.9	100.0
	Work of national importance**** (90)	4.4	7.8	7.8	33.3	2.2	44.4	100.0
	Unclear/multiple (78)	6.4	9.0	11.5	65.4	2.6	5.1	100.0
	Total (850)	**7.8**	**9.3**	**11.9**	**58.7**	**2.1**	**10.2**	**100.0**

*Includes refused, revoked, and overturned.

**Includes appealed, badged/certified, referred, no jurisdiction, deferred, continued, renewed, withdrawn, and amended.

***Includes unstated or unclear outcomes, complex outcomes listed in a comments field, and no action taken.

****Includes agricultural certificate, certified, and protected.

Sources: My dataset with tribunal reports from the County Advertiser, the County Express, and the Dudley Herald, using the first newspaper of each month (all were published on Saturdays) for 1916, 1917, and 1918 when the tribunals were in operation.

light of married men. It was only fair to the married men."[62] Even though this clerk clearly had family liability, it was not seen as equivalent to that of a married man.

Tribunal members consistently asked single applicants to weigh their circumstances against those of married men. In April 1916, James Kennedy Ward, an unmarried packer and motor car driver, claimed serious hardship as he was the only support of his dependent mother and sister. Refusing his application, the chairman of the tribunal asked, "You don't think your case would be harder than that of the married men who will have to leave their wives and children?" Ward replied, "I think I am worse off."[63] Later the same month, the tribunal refused Ernest Brooks, a button maker, who also stated his widowed mother needed him at home. According to the *County Express*, "In reply to the Chairman, applicant admitted his case was not so hard as that of married men who must leave wives and families." Someone in the room, criticizing the applications of single men, yelled, "It is a shame, a scandalous shame," forcing the chairman to call the tribunal to order.[64] Under the heading "Single Men's Responsibilities and Married Men's Claims," the *County Express*, also in April 1916, recounted the case of George Wood, of Cradley, who, as in the other cases,

> applied as being the sole support of his widowed mother. . . . Asked by the Chairman if he would like to serve his country, applicant said he would not like to leave his mother. – The Military Representative: Do you think your case ought to be given preference to the married men who are being called up and will have to leave their wives and children? – Applicant: Having no father, my case is a serious hardship. – The married men will be leaving their homes; wouldn't you be ashamed as a single man, to see your next door neighbour, probably a married man, with two or three children, sent out to fight for you?[65]

Refusing to fight and tied to his mother, Wood did not compare well with married men with children. The construction of the heteronormative family is evident here, with the military representative ͻ identification of the imaginary neighbor as a married man with children. Some applicants must have internalized this effort to shame single men for protecting themselves while married men fought. Not surprisingly, the tribunal refused Wood's application.

According to the newspaper coverage, tribunal members were clearly interested in shielding married men from combat. At the Dudley

Tribunal at the end of March 1916, "Mr. Round urged that the utmost consideration should be given to married men. He noticed that other Tribunals were putting back these men for several months, and it would not be fair to take all the men from Dudley. . . . Mr. W. Bradford, speaking in regard to the married men, thought Dudley should act uniformly with other tribunals. . . . [T]he tribunal should grant married men equal privilege to those allowed in other districts."[66] The *County Express* in April reported on "Fetching up the Single Men" in Stourbridge, where the tribunal told the unmarried Owen Grove that "he ought to be in the army if that was possible. . . . Major Trinham said it was very difficult for them to have these young men going about when they were taking married men with responsibilities."[67] By implication, single men "going about" had no responsibilities.

Apparently the tribunals were under a good deal of pressure from both the public and military authorities not to grant single men exemptions. In August 1916, the *County Advertiser* called the continuing presence of single men at home "The Single Men Scandal," reporting that Joseph Parsons of the Halesowen Tribunal "complained that many single men were still unaccounted for by the military authorities. Men whose applications had been refused by that Tribunal were walking about the streets. The Chairman replied that the Tribunal had done their work, and it was up to the military authorities to see that the men were secured for service."[68] The tribunal members did not want the military to blame them for giving single men exemptions.

Married men themselves complained to the tribunals that the government was not making good on its promise that single men would serve first. At the Kingswinford Tribunal in March 1916, 24-year-old William Thomas Adams received a three-month temporary exemption, but he protested that "he was a young married man and voluntarily attested thinking it his duty to do so with an assurance that he would not be called upon before the unmarried men were."[69] In April, Thomas Henry Reece told the Halesowen Tribunal that he would serve "when all the single men had gone," to which those present replied with a general "hear, hear."[70] In March 1917, "a young married man" came before the Rowley Regis Tribunal, refusing to give up his war work certificate, even though the Ministry of Munitions had released him for combat. The man indicated that "he did not consider it fair to release him, when there were single men and men who never worked in their lives being retained on the same work."[71] This applicant asserted that both his marital status and his work history should have protected him from the front; unmarried men and those who did not adhere to the work imperative were disposable.

Employers and managers in non-starred workplaces also found themselves caught up in the politics of marital status. They wanted to keep their skilled men from being called up, but the tribunals pitted marital status against skill, in many cases exempting married workers while insisting that skilled single men be released for service. For example, an Amblecote foundry manager claimed exemptions for two workers, one single and one married. The military representative "asked for Davies," the single man. The manager indicated that Davies was more important to the functioning of the foundry, but the representative "expressed the view that they ought to have every single man who was not in a certified occupation." The tribunal refused Davies's exemption but granted the married man three months, which explicitly went against the appeal of the employer.[72] The *County Express* printed a Halesowen Tribunal case from April 1916 in which a button manufacturer appealed for three of his workers, all married men "doing work formerly done by single men." The military representative queried whether the firm could "give up any more single men," and the manufacturer replied, "We have no more you have every one."[73] These decisions most likely created incredibly tense situations in workplaces where men working side by side had their relative safety determined by marital status.

In this environment, tribunal members worried that men used the protection of certain occupations to avoid being sent to the front. As a military representative complained to the Stourbridge Tribunal in March 1916, young men "were walking about and bragging how they had got off at the tribunals."[74] This issue came through pointedly at the Halesowen Tribunal, when the Halesowen Cycle and Perambulator Company applied to have four employees exempted, because many of their workers had "gone into munitions factories." A tribunal member queried whether this was "to get higher wages or to get under the umbrella" of protected occupations, and the representative of the company indicated there were rumors that men were seeking to avoid the front and "ought to come out." Again the issue came down to sheltering single men when married men were vulnerable to being called up: a tribunal member stressed, "If we exempt these men we shall have the married men in the trenches before the single men have gone. We have all got to make sacrifices."[75] Single men, knowing the risk, strategically used "the umbrella" of war work to position themselves more favorably relative to the draft, which further called their patriotism into question.

The tribunals were well aware of this structural problem. A Halesowen Tribunal member worried in March 1916 that "there are hundreds of single men securing badges and exemption who are doing nothing of importance to the country. I am sorry to sit in judgment on any man, but the Government ask for men. We can't keep letting these single men off. You will have the married men here shortly [with the new Military Service Act including them] and you will not have the same consideration for them."[76] The same week, the military representative Mr. Dudley requested that the Kingswinford Tribunal remove the badged status of 26-year-old Edward Harry Harley, "who had been in a clothing shop all his life until he went, for one month, to a munition works, and whilst there he was starred."[77] Ernest Brooks, who lost his appeal, asked, "Is there any reason why I should go whilst others are hiding behind the munition factories?"[78]

This suspicion of men who took on starred occupations continued throughout the war. The chairman of the Rowley Regis Tribunal revealed in March 1917 his frustration that single men appeared to be getting away with shirking: "he was opposed to sending the last son in a family when single men in the district who had no relatives serving had absolutely flounced the Tribunal and gone into the munition factories."[79] Similarly, in April 1917, the military representative at Rowley commented that a bricklayer who had taken on work for a "firm of odd work manufacturers" was "'a regular shuffler,' and said he had taken up the work to make himself safe."[80] Men's work in protected occupations, it appears, could not be read automatically as a willingness to work. Rather, the willingness to work could be used to mask an unwillingness to serve, calling attention to a man's failure as a man and citizen in the context of war.

Similarly, getting married and taking on family liability could also be seen as a strategy to avoid the front. Just as men could seek the shelter of an occupational umbrella, according to tribunal members, so too could they find "the umbrella of marriage." The Military Service Act of January 1916 had exempted married men, but only if they had been married before November 1915, meaning the government anticipated that men would indeed seek the "umbrella of marriage" to keep them from combat. Mr. Westwood, of the Halesowen Tribunal, argued in April 1916 that, since an applicant "had been married since the war commenced, . . . he had gone under the umbrella of marriage instead of the umbrella of munitions."[81] At the Dudley Tribunal in early May 1916, a case titled "Married and Single" shows that men who married after the war started were legally treated as if they were single. The applicant, who was a cutter in a clothing shop, "was married and single as far as the Act was concerned." A tribunal member commented, "He's single for us."[82] Similarly, in a case from August 1918, the military representative at Tipton pointed out in a case of a married coal dealer that the applicant "was single for the purposes of the Act."[83] The government armed itself against men who would use marital status to protect themselves from military service.

While tribunal members certainly doubted the veracity of married men's exemption claims, the central message coming out of the tribunals continued to be that forcing married men to serve while there were still so many single men available was a problem. In June 1917, a headline for the Rowley Regis Tribunal stressed again that "Single Men Should Go First." After the military representative spoke against an exemption for a 34-year-old married man, another member of the tribunal "strongly protested against calling for men of that age when there were hundreds of single young men walking the streets." The tribunal granted a three-month exemption, with the chairman commenting "that the tribunal considered there were many single men who ought to serve before the married men."[84] Even in May 1918, Arthur Hadley, a 40-year-old bootmaker from Cakemore, could complain to the tribunal that they should "look outside the picture palaces and see the young men that ought to be taken." He received two months' exemption, on condition he join the volunteers.[85] The language describing these cases remained the same throughout the war, positioning single men who did not join the military as shirkers and supporting the notion that married men were more invested in national concerns.

The knowledge of local circumstances, however, could lead tribunal members to be sympathetic even towards single men's claims for exemption. Indeed tensions between local sympathies and military needs are obvious in these cases. The War Office instructed the local tribunals to "use proper and reasonable discretion" when considering the claims of single men with dependants.[86] In July 1916, a "single Blackheath filer, aged 25, said he was keeping his home going, his father being an invalid. He had two brothers, both of whom were married, but they did not support the parents." He was granted a three-month exemption.[87] The tribunal members had compassion for single men's domestic claims but in some ways had little room to maneuver, being required to weigh single men's circumstances against the promise to protect married men. At the Rowley Regis Tribunal in March 1917, an applicant claimed "he had three brothers serving, and he was the only one to keep on the home for his sisters. – A member objected to sending the fourth and last of a family when there were families who had lost none." The tribunal granted three months, but the military representative indicated he would appeal.[88]

Sensitive to some applicants' family responsibilities, tribunal members countered men's domestic claims by pointing to the support the state was willing to provide dependants. At Stourbridge in March 1916, the Mayor told a roadman who was refused an exemption to care for his widowed mother that "you will be better off in the army; you can make an allowance for your mother."[89] Similarly, at the Amblecote Tribunal in April 1916, a widow applied for an unmarried son, claiming "he was her sole support." She indicated that "she did not wish to debar her son from doing his duty, but she wanted to be assured of a living." She was refused, with a tribunal member indicating that she "would receive an allotment allowance, and really be better off."[90] The existence of dependants' benefits compromised the claims of single sons who emphasized their family liability. The separation allowances granted to the wives of married servicemen, by contrast, did not challenge the notion that single men should go first.

Married men's marital status generally spoke for itself; their responsibilities for wives and children did not need to be articulated in the same ways that single men's support of their parents did. As I explore further in Chapter 8, sons' support of their parents did not have the same cultural significance as husbands' support of their wives, as it did not enhance the familial norm. Yet consideration of separation allowances also appears to have weighed on the minds of tribunal members, who understood the heavy financial commitment of the government to the allowances. For example, in February 1917, the owners of a quarry firm applied to the Rowley Regis Tribunal for exemptions for six of their employees. The military representative indicated that "the only man he could ask for was the one with six children, he being the youngest of the lot." In response to this, the chairman of the tribunal noted that, because of the size of the family, "the allowance for the man's wife would be 38s. per week. He would be a dear soldier." The larger the family, the larger the allowance would be, suggesting a financial motivation for "protecting" married men. In this case, all six men received three-month exemptions.[91]

Married men continued to have some protection throughout the war, although it became increasingly tenuous. In June 1918, for example, a 42-year-old cabinet maker applied to the Rowley Regis Tribunal, presumably based on the needs of his family of seven children. His request was granted, with the *Herald* recording a tribunal member's comment "that his family had saved him."[92] Perhaps, at this point in the war, a remark like this reflected an ironic commentary on the ways family could "save" married men from what the public and government alike saw as the death factory of combat. In a case from very late in the war, August 1918, the military representative at the Rowley Regis Tribunal opposed the exemption of a married bricklayer with eight children. He argued that "the children would be well provided for," with the separation allowances, and "there would be no hardship in the case, and he had to ask for the man in spite of his eight children." Members of the tribunal disagreed. One member argued, "It is a tremendous obligation to leave a family of eight children." Another asserted, "I shall not vote to send a man with eight children into the Army." The tribunal members outvoted the military representative, who then "gave notice of appeal."[93]

Conclusion

During the First World War, the nation's need for men in many ways replaced the work imperative with a service imperative, which measured men's deservedness and status as citizens by their willingness to fight for their nation. Even though there was great need for workers, such as those associated with the industries in the Dudley and Stourbridge Unions, to remain on the home front doing what was considered work of national importance, this work did not compare with combat service as a sign of masculine citizenship status. No matter how much politicians, recruiters, and tribunal members stressed the significance of men's war work, their language suggested a clear hierarchy of value that measured men's citizenship above all by their willingness to serve.

Yet marital status further complicated this entire system of meaning during the war. While military service blurred the work imperative, family liability very much continued to determine men's relative wartime responsibilities. Indeed, the context of the war heightened scrutiny of marital status, calling obvious attention to the differences between married and unmarried men. The press fostered the notion that married men felt compelled to fight to keep their families safe, but many Britons also believed that single men should be forced to enter combat first. The vulnerable wives and children that supposedly drew married men to serve actually should have afforded these men protection from battle. Married men were privileged by being married, and this privileged status shaped efforts to protect them from combat during the war. Single men, by contrast, could be sacrificed in the name of protecting the wives and children they did not have, highlighting their existence on the margins of the hetero-norm. Single men also cost less, since married men's wives and children were due the expensive separation allowances.

Thus marital status created a paradox during the First World War, where married men were considered willing to serve because family responsibilities made them conscious of their investment in the nation, but single men were considered more suitable to serve because of the impossibility of their embodying full masculine citizenship through family responsibilities. Service itself would be the vehicle through which single men could prove their worth. Single men's military sacrifice could transform them into full citizens, a sacrifice not required of married men, whose family status already was read as a sign of national belonging. Family liability was a matter of life and death.

6

"The whole world had gone against them": Ex-Servicemen and the Politics of Relief

The wartime economy provided regular occupations for soldiers and civilians alike, but the First World War did not usher in any long-term solution to the "problem of unemployment." Rather, when grim economic circumstances returned in the fall of 1920, the situation created new anxieties about the particular demoralizing effects of unemployment on veterans. At a mass meeting in Halesowen in February 1924, for example, the national secretary of the British Legion indicated that "the question of unemployment was causing great concern at headquarters, for they were finding out many cases where the unemployed were degenerating into unemployables. Some of the men had become so despondent that they felt the whole world, including the country for which they had fought, had gone against them."[1] The Legion considered the employment question central to veterans' status, "because they felt it was hard to know that a man who had been a good workman had lost the chance of earning his livelihood because he had been away fighting so that others might live." Councilor Robbins, secretary to the West Midlands area British Legion, argued that "if a man was good enough to fight he ought to be maintained until employment could be found for him."[2] In many cases, however, the national government fell short in providing either maintenance or employment. Ex-servicemen were in danger of becoming Weary Willies and Tired Tims.

Following the First World War, Britons felt obligated to assist veterans to secure jobs as a means of honoring their service to the country. The economic realities of the times, however, as well as the government's decreasing investment in ex-servicemen, led to much disappointment and frustration among veterans and their allies.[3] David Lloyd George's promise to create a "land fit for heroes" has become famous, as much for its rhetoric as for its failure.[4] The war raised expectations on a variety of levels, not least because of a strong wartime economy and improvements in welfare provision. In his history of *Poor Citizens*, David Vincent has argued, "During the war the working class had been implicitly protected from the degrading embrace of the Poor Law, and the families of servicemen had received the formal assistance of separation allowances, which unlike the insurance system, provided benefits for wives and children." With demobilization, the government felt compelled to continue this protection, instituting the Out-of-Work Donation (OWD), which "enshrined the principles of non-contributory, non-Poor Law support for the unemployed, and the maintenance of their families."[5] Not only did veterans, and many civilians as well, receive this non-contributory, non-pauperizing assistance, but they did so in the context of the new universal male suffrage granted with the 1918 Representation of the People Act. The war thus ended with the promise of political, economic, and social citizenship for those who served their nation.[6]

The presence of unemployed veterans visibly called into question the government's ability and desire to fulfill its promises. Politicians and civil servants sweated over the problem of unemployed veterans, who haunted both the imaginations of policymakers and the rooms of Labour Exchanges, renamed Employment Exchanges after the war. The Employment Exchanges kept separate records of civilians and ex-servicemen registered as unemployed, which highlighted the problem of unemployment for veterans throughout the 1920s. The *British Legion Journal* reported in its inaugural edition in June 1921, for example, "On January 1st this year there were 20,000 disabled men unemployed, and 270,000 non-disabled discharged men in a like condition. To-day there are 23,000 disabled men unemployed and 449,374 non-disabled discharged men."[7] According to Niall Barr's study of the British Legion, "roughly 300,000 unskilled ex-servicemen throughout the interwar period" were unable to secure jobs, a clear sign of both the government's failure of policy and the omnipresence of unemployment.[8]

Tensions surrounding the deservedness of ex-servicemen erupted almost immediately upon demobilization and became worse with the general increase in unemployment. Veterans had to shift the terms on which their masculine status was based. The soldier expressed his citizenship by actively serving his country during war; the ex-serviceman, by contrast, entered civilian life and confronted already-existing expectations about how men should behave, expectations that emphasized the breadwinner ideal. As Deborah Cohen has argued, veterans "looked forward to the hallmarks of masculine independence: a steady job, a home of their own, a wife, and perhaps even children . . . More than anything else, soldiers looked forward to domestic life."[9] Organizations like the National Federation for Discharged and Demobilized Sailors and Soldiers (NFDDSS) and other veterans' groups constantly reminded the government and the press that veterans were, "by reason of their service," disadvantaged to meet the expectations of male breadwinning and therefore deserved special state assistance. They demanded preference in unemployment work schemes and for training and benefit when they could not obtain employment.[10]

The reliance of ex-servicemen on poor law relief and the principle of preferences for veterans became primary sites around which Britons debated ideas about postwar unemployment, welfare, and masculine citizenship. A nation of ex-soldiers dependent on poor law relief should have been unthinkable in a world praising the sacrifices of veterans as well as dealing with the guilt surrounding those sacrifices. Ex-servicemen, however, did turn to the Poor Law, and particularly to workhouses, throughout the postwar period, compromising the national government's representation of itself as benevolent but also creating a space to doubt the deserving status of veterans. Additionally, the principle of preference for honest poor married men in welfare schemes was already well established and conflicted with preference for ex-servicemen in the postwar period. The government was slow, and ultimately unable and unwilling, to follow through on its commitment to veterans for employment and training. Officials quickly became suspicious of demobilized men in the cities and towns who joined the ranks of casual laborers or remained unemployed. They questioned veterans' willingness to work and contested the state's liability to provide for men who seemed outside the boundaries of honest poverty.

Ex-servicemen and the poor law

The press forced national government officials to confront the fact that ex-servicemen were turning to the Poor Law when, in June 1918, the *Daily Express* reported that two disabled veterans were in the Bath Union workhouse infirmary. A clipping in the government file on the case fumed that "to reduce men who have been broken in the nation's service to the level of paupers is an insult not only to them, but to the whole community."[11] A workhouse was the last place veterans deserved to be, and it was the government's fault that it had happened. A few days after it broke the story, the *Daily Express* castigated the War Pensions Committee at Bath for essentially watering down the problem to the fact that "the men had to be somewhere and the workhouse infirmary was the only institution available." The article pointed out that this only emphasized "the need for some special provision for such men in order to keep them free of the taint of the Poor Law."[12] Receiving poor law relief, especially workhouse relief, condemned veterans to needy pauper status that called their citizenship into question. Even if a veteran was willing to apply for poor law relief, it was in the government's interest to prevent this from happening. The clerk to the Bath Board of Guardians explained to the Local Government Board that one of the ex-soldiers in the workhouse had been nursed at home by his wife, but, when her own health deteriorated, "he was willing under the circumstances [to go to the workhouse infirmary] and there was no alternative." The clerk emphasized, however, that, both on economic and moral grounds, "the Guardians feel very strongly that such cases ought not be obliged to resort to the Poor Law," a pointed criticism of government provisions.[13] As Cohen has shown, the public, through voluntary efforts, did much more for disabled ex-servicemen than did the government, which was not prepared for the scope of veterans' needs. The public was certainly incensed to see the respectability of veterans compromised through their association with the workhouse. Sir John Collie of the Ministry of Pensions wrote at the end of June that "the feeling seems to be that under no circumstances should a man who has been a soldier, even should he desire it, ever enter a Poor Law infirmary."[14] Veterans' reliance on workhouses could both call their own deservedness into question and expose the government's inability to follow through on its promises.

The publication of the Bath case embarrassed the Ministry of Pensions, which complained in a letter to the assistant secretary of the Local Government Board that it was really the fault of the Bath Board of Guardians themselves for neglecting to report that veterans had applied for relief. Instead of going to the Pensions Committee, the Bath board had "passed a formal resolution of protest and taken steps to see that the Local Press were informed that a discharged man was being treated in the Infirmary."[15] According to the Ministry, the burden was on the guardians not only to be informed about the service status of their applicants, but also to contact the Pensions Committees when ex-servicemen applied. Veterans were a national, not a local, responsibility and should immediately be transferred from local to national officials. Minutes from Black Country Boards of Guardians demonstrate that the boards indeed referred cases of ex-servicemen to Pensions Committees, but, until they heard back from the committees, the boards continued to maintain veterans through local poor law resources.[16]

Various constituencies expressed dissatisfaction about disabled veterans' reliance on the Poor Law. While the war was still being fought, a London branch of the NFDDSS held a mass meeting on September 1, 1918, to protest this perceived slight on their service to the nation. The association,

> while re-affirming our Loyalty to His Majesty's Person & Throne, and our determination to see this War through, emphatically protests against the pledges given by His Majesty's Government to the manhood of the nation, when asked to come forward to serve their King & Country, being violated wholesale by . . . [permitting Discharged Soldiers] to enter and die in the Workhouse infirmary their pensions being claimed by the Guardians.[17]

Not only did poor law relief erode "the manhood of the nation," but it also threatened patriotism and indeed national strength. In the Midlands, the NFDDSS was concerned that ex-soldiers and their dependants be protected from the stigma of the Poor Law. At a meeting of about 200 people in July 1920, Douglas Pielou, local councilor and chairman of the Tipton Branch of the NFDDSS, urged all ex-servicemen to join the Federation, "to prevent the scandal of the kiddies of dead soldiers being sent to the workhouse, as some nine hundred of them had already been sent."[18] The memory of veterans' service was further tarnished by the government's neglect of soldiers' children.

Communications among national government officials reveal a growing frustration with ex-soldiers themselves, or at least with the position in which ex-soldiers were putting the government by turning to the Poor Law. In 1922, C.F.A. Hore, the assistant secretary to the Minister of Pensions, received a memo worrying that the Ministry

> have had from Boards of Guardians a great number of resolutions, which are still being received (some of them in indignant terms), and which appear to be based on the assumption that the Ministry has a duty to any ex-service man who happens to be ill or destitute. I think it would save much waste of time and paper if Guardians were made to understand the criterion of attributability or aggravation due to service which is the basis of our functions.[19]

While the Boards of Guardians were clearly upset about finding themselves accountable for veterans (for financial as much as ideological reasons), the tone of this correspondence suggests that certain bureaucrats were losing patience with the idea of an automatic association between ex-servicemen, even disabled ex-servicemen, and welfare deservedness as a right deriving from their service. The Ministry felt the need to reassert that a veteran garnered special treatment only from issues resulting directly from the war, not from anything that befell him once the war was over.

As Cohen has shown, Hore was consistently opposed to extended state support of veterans.[20] His efforts to restrain the Ministry of Pensions are obvious in memos from March 1924 concerning whether the government should order a survey of the numbers of ex-servicemen receiving poor law assistance. Hore was strongly against this survey, fearing,

> It would undoubtedly be used . . . to foster an agitation in favour of State provision for all ex-service men who are obliged to resort to public assistance. I cannot conceive of any justification for this. It could only end in the creation of a privileged class of the community who could acquire a right to assistance out of State funds, because they had at one time been mobilised for war service.[21]

A survey, Hore feared, would reveal that a good many veterans did indeed rely on the Poor Law, which would make the government look bad. Yet Hore at this point essentially accepted that veterans would need the Poor Law, since the state clearly could not – or would not – take responsibility for non-pauperizing relief. Conceptually, for Hore, war service did not automatically confer deserving status that needed to be protected from the "taint" of the Poor Law. Indeed, veterans had no "right" to agitate for the privilege.

The problem of veterans and the Poor Law came up repeatedly in the 1920s in the House of Commons, where the Minister of Pensions was pressed on his knowledge of the circumstances of disabled ex-servicemen and their dependants in various local workhouses.[22] In November 1925, Captain Reginald Terrell asked the Minister of Pensions about veterans who were "forced to frequent the casual wards of Country," because they were unable to get their pensions in a timely fashion. Sir F. Flannery followed up by wondering, "in cases where ex-service men apply for relief to workhouses, could not the master be instructed to deal with him specifically and not put him along with paupers who have not served their country."[23] Both politicians were concerned above all with the "taint" of the Poor Law and the possible reduction of veterans to the status of common paupers. Veterans, like all honest men, could not be allowed to degenerate into regular paupers.

Yet, as the economy continued to struggle, the government pulled back even on its limited special provisions for veterans. The Ministry of Pensions increasingly emphasized that the government was only responsible for disability based on war service and made it more difficult for veterans to prove their conditions resulted from the war. As Major G.C. Tryon stated in the House of Commons in 1926, "Any assistance that may otherwise be required by ex-service men in consequence of ill-health or unemployment necessarily falls to be provided under the arrangements in operation for the civil population at large."[24] Service alone did not qualify a man for preferential treatment.

Interestingly, as early as December 1918, Hore had raised the possibility that military service would not guarantee the state's liability for the welfare of ex-servicemen. Always trying to justify limited state responsibility, Hore worried about the "question of the vagrant ex-soldier or of the vagrant posing as an ex-soldier." Although Boards of Guardians and Local Pensions Committees had been ordered "not to let discharged soldiers remain in Poor Law institutions," this had referred specifically to disabled ex-servicemen; according to Hore, "the vagrant ex-soldier was not specially in view when these arrangements were made in the early part of last year," suggesting that this group of men was not deserving of protection against the Poor Law, even though they had served their country. Hore warned that the government should "unquestionably in the next few months be prepared for . . . the vagrant ex-soldier; and . . . the silver-badged man asking for assistance."[25] Veterans' vagrant status underscored a questionable relationship to the work imperative and deservedness.

The issue of "fit" ex-servicemen was not even supposed to be a concern of the Ministry of Pensions, which dealt specifically with questions of disability. As John Collie wrote to Hore in January 1919, "We seem to be very much at cross purposes on this question of able-bodied discharged men in Poor Law Institutions. This Division is not concerned with able-bodied pensioners who find their way into Poor Law Institutions, but only with those pensioners who are sent to a Poor Law Infirmary on medical grounds."[26] Disabled status was the key here, as it defined a man's dependency. "Fit" men, according to pension policy, were more responsible for their own condition and, particularly, for their efforts to find employment. The issue of these vagrant, non-disabled ex-soldiers became increasingly urgent. As Robert Humphreys has written, "From 1920 casual ward numbers multiplied rapidly. During the next 12 months, difficulties brought by the sharp economic depression with unemployment approaching 17 per cent were compounded by the social instability of disillusioned ex-servicemen."[27] Single, able-bodied, unemployed veterans wandering the streets created particular anxieties for the government.

In addition to worrying about these "fit" veterans winding up in workhouse casual wards, Hore stressed in his December 1918 comments that the government had to anticipate men posing as ex-soldiers to receive preferential assistance. He urged that they had to find a way to "sift their cases and to provide for those who were genuinely in need."[28] Three weeks later, however, Hore received a handwritten note questioning whether or not it really mattered if a man could prove his veteran status; if he was a vagrant, he belonged in the workhouse: "The habitual vagrant cannot be kept out of the workhouse. The silver badge has nothing to do with it." Yet the Ministry also had to take public relations into account, since the perception that ex-servicemen were forced to rely on workhouses could damage the government. The note suggested, "To satisfy public opinion (1) Men should not be described as discharged soldiers in the records of the workhouses, unless they could produce discharge papers which should be carefully scrutinized; and (2) . . . prove that they are not V.C. or D.C.M. heroes as they often claim, but only home service men with only very little service indeed."[29] Still, some in the Ministry of Pensions thought, "There would be much to say for a scheme which would insure that no man who has fought for his country should get into the workhouse."[30]

The potential problem of vagrant ex-soldiers seemed threatening enough to the Ministry in January 1919 that it warned the Home Office of the "discharged soldier, whether disabled or able-bodied, who goes from one district to another either genuinely in search of work or because he prefers to tramp, and I have no doubt at all that this class of man will loom very large in the next few months and, to some extent, permanently."[31] Even those "genuinely in search of work" could potentially cause problems because of the numbers of men concerned. Hore worried about the public perception that the government was not taking care of these vagrant ex-soldiers, fearing that "we shall have complaints that men who have served their country should not be allowed to go to the casual wards." He argued that employment committees and authorities should "work together so as to give the man an early chance of getting off the road if he really wants work." If men refused work, they would have to go to the casual wards and be entered upon a black list. The big fear was "that the man who may take to the road in the first instance with the genuine idea of getting work should not degenerate into a tramp with constant recourse to the workhouse."[32] Deservedness, as we have seen, was a fragile state; honest men's proximity to those unwilling to work could infect their own deserving status.

Even the British Legion worried that ex-servicemen who remained out of work were at risk of "degenerating into unemployables."[33] They wanted no confusion between veterans and vagrants. The Legion's "Manifesto on Unemployment" of 1923 criticized both charity and government doles, arguing that work alone was the solution to the country's ills and, specifically, to the revitalization of veterans dragged down by reliance on public assistance.[34] The Legion did not want to emphasize veterans' neediness but rather to enhance their right to function as masculine citizens.

The pressing question of vagrant ex-soldiers did lead to the survey of ex-servicemen receiving poor law relief that Hore had been concerned about in the spring of 1924. The survey revealed that more than 87,000 ex-servicemen relied on poor law assistance. Hore, however, found it notable that this made up only 0.8 per cent of the total adult male population, while the 235,553 non-ex-servicemen receiving poor law relief accounted for 2.14 per cent of that population. Adding to his positive interpretation of the numbers, Hore indicated that, while veterans made up about 41 per cent of the adult male population of England and Wales, they constituted only 27 per cent of the total number receiving poor law relief: "only in the cases of vagrants does the proportion of ex-service men exceed the proportion of ex-service men to population, in this case the % is 43, but the total numbers are small (only 3,500 are ex-service men)."[35] Hore's explanation of the numbers raises several interesting issues. On the one hand, public relations concerns for the government were not necessarily going to be defused by seeing these numbers; the fact that more than 87,000 ex-servicemen needed poor law relief was distressing enough. Additionally, the link between demobilization and vagrancy was sustained by the survey, although 3,500 seems like an extremely small number of ex-service vagrants. The numbers might reflect the ways local Boards of Guardians kept records, particularly if they lumped ex-servicemen together with other casual paupers.

The Ministry was quite pleased with the outcome of the survey. Hore received a message, for example, expressing "surprise . . . to find the proportion [of veterans in workhouses] so small."[36] Whether or not the numbers indicated the actual proportion of veterans relying on the Poor Law, the question continued to be significant throughout the interwar period. According to Barr, a 1929 estimate showed that one quarter of the people relying on poor law relief were veterans of the First World War.[37]

The politics of preference

While veterans' reliance on the Poor Law raised questions about ex-servicemen's vagrancy and status relative to the work imperative, preferential treatment for veterans in benefit and unemployment schemes brought questions about family liability to the fore. On the one hand, the state had established its responsibility for the welfare of veterans on the principle that war service conferred a citizenship right to assistance. The government stressed that ex-servicemen would receive industrial training, non-contributory unemployment benefits, and preference in hiring schemes. Although this principle applied most forcefully to disabled ex-servicemen, it was not, as the Minister of Labour noted in May 1920, "limited to the disabled."[38] Yet local authorities explicitly, and the national government implicitly, had already established principles of preference for honest poor married men and especially married men with children. How did these two preference principles work together in the postwar world? In other words, which groups of men had the primary right to state resources?

Men who were disabled through military service gained their preferential treatment through their bodily sacrifice.[39] Able-bodied ex-servicemen earned their preferential treatment because their military service "deprived [them] of the opportunity of establishing themselves in a definite vocation."[40] However, according to Cohen, the British state, and particularly the Ministry of Pensions and the Treasury, "sought to restrict the state's responsibility for rehabilitation and employment. . . . [M]ost British officials argued that the state had acquitted its obligations through the distribution of pensions."[41] The government's promise to ex-servicemen "'for special industrial training, and their return to civil life under conditions worthy of their services to the country'"[42] was, according to Cabinet minutes in June 1920, "being construed by ex-Service men as an unqualified pledge to provide training for every ex-soldier, including the able-bodied, who requested it."[43] Facing at least 200,000 yet-to-be-employed, able-bodied veterans, the government feared growing discontent if it did not respond to veterans' demands, especially as they anticipated that the special benefits for veterans would be running out when unemployment began to soar.[44]

Two related debates about ex-servicemen's welfare, both of which took place primarily in 1920 and 1921, highlight tensions surrounding the principle of preference for veterans. In these debates, marital status and family liability shaped ideas about veterans' entitlement to welfare preference. The first debate concerned the government extension of a postwar veterans' benefit, the OWD, and the possibility of limiting the benefit to married veterans alone. The second debate focused on policy struggles over the implementation of grant-aided unemployment relief schemes, which moved from universal preference for ex-soldiers to admit married civilians. These examples also show that the government incorporated single veterans grudgingly into their efforts to deal with unemployment. While married unemployed ex-soldiers were automatically characterized as deserving, the national government and local authorities worried about unemployed single veterans causing disorder and degenerating into vagrants. Marital status intersected with veteran status in determinations of welfare deservedness.

Out-of-Work Donation

The government intended the OWD to be a temporary expedient to ease the transition from military service to civilian employment. The Donation came into operation on November 25, 1918, when, within their first 12 months after being discharged, ex-servicemen (and civilian war workers, including women) were allowed 26 weeks of support at a rate of 29 shillings per week, additional benefit for dependent children, and a further 13 weeks at a reduced rate of benefit.[45] These were far more generous terms than existed under unemployment insurance. Yet the vision of the OWD proved inadequate, as many thousands of veterans remained unemployed and dependent on the benefit when it was about to expire a year later. Until the new Unemployment Insurance Act of 1920 was in place, the government wound up creating several special extensions of OWD that excluded civilians, reduced veterans' benefits, and eliminated children's allowances.[46]

In the fall of 1919, the government undertook an inquiry "to ascertain what Classes of Ex-Service Men are Remaining on Donation for Long Periods and Why their Unemployment Continues."[47] As the framework of this inquiry suggests, even though eligible women war workers also received the OWD, government debates about the donation completely neglected the question of women's unemployment. Indeed, assumptions about family liability shaped OWD decisions; historian Susan Pedersen has claimed that the OWD "transformed [male war workers and veterans] into 'breadwinners' and their wives into 'dependants' . . . whatever their earlier [or present] patterns of earning."[48] In this context, the government could observe from its 1919 investigation that the OWD was most used by the very different categories of the young casual laborer (assumed single) and the married breadwinner with children. They also noted a "very marked tendency" among recipients to move from highly skilled and heavy labor to less skilled and lighter labor.[49] The continued support of married men with dependants seemed justifiable, but maintaining veterans who were slipping from skilled into unskilled labor, and those who had been irregularly employed before the war, raised red flags concerning the deservedness of single men. The OWD was expensive, but it became clear that the government had to extend the scheme before implementation of the planned new Unemployment Insurance Act. At this point, Minister of Labour Robert Horne seems to have been on his own questioning ex-servicemen's special benefits, worrying in November 1919, "On social grounds there is some objection to the perpetuation of the distinction between ex-service men and others. . . . if [donation] preference is extended for a further period, it might be regarded as establishing a claim to such a preference for all future time."[50] While Horne advised against any extension, the Cabinet decided that preference was justified by agreeing to continue the donation until March 1920 but only to veterans, not civilian war workers, and at a reduced rate of 20 shillings without dependants' benefits.[51]

After a further extension of the OWD in March, which was to end in July 1920, when 143,000 men were still receiving it,[52] the Coalition Government tried to limit the benefit further. The most obvious way was to cut off the single men who had no family liability and who seemed to be staying on benefit rather than adopting civilian responsibilities and finding employment. Chancellor of the Exchequer Austen Chamberlain insisted that the government had been generous to unmarried men so far. He felt that "it is difficult to believe that any but extremists would condemn the Government for now refusing an extension of rights to single men or even to married men without children."[53] Veterans' deservedness contracted as those without children were seen as less deserving of maintenance. Indeed, it was "extreme" to expect the government to support unmarried men.

The Cabinet, however, received multiple memos from the more liberal Thomas Macnamara, now Minister of Labour, cautioning the government not to limit the extension too much. On July 17, 1920, Macnamara worried that most of the men who would be dropped off benefit were unskilled men, congregating in large towns and likely to cause a threat. He remarked that some of these men "no doubt have not been very active in their endeavour to find work," but he acknowledged that there was not a great demand for unskilled labor. Many men adhered to the work imperative but were unable to obtain employment.[54] Arguing for the continuation of the donation on existing terms,

Macnamara warned the Cabinet that he anticipated "agitation" from veterans aiming to maintain the OWD for all ex-servicemen, who were vulnerable to "extremists."[55]

As the government was debating what the OWD extension should look like, Macnamara received a letter from J.R. Griffin, the General Secretary of the NFDDSS. Griffin stressed that official statistics did not reflect the depth of unemployment among veterans and that, if the OWD was stopped, "then the whole of the ex-service men who by reason of their service are out of employment will become entirely dependent either on the charity of friends or on some sort of casual employment." He argued that, in fighting the government's war, young men had been unable to train for an occupation or to save for unemployment. Ex-servicemen were "destitute" "by reason of the services to the State."[56] If employment was the basis of masculine status and civilian men's citizenship claims, the state owed its veterans the opportunity to establish themselves as honest men and citizens.

It is unclear whether Macnamara's subsequent advice to the Cabinet was in direct response to Griffin's letter or not, but, in correspondence dated July 24, he expressed his discomfort with his previous recommendations and was pointedly nervous about the ramifications of withdrawing benefit from unskilled, single men:

> I have most seriously considered whether we could equitably leave the single men out of a further extension. *The more I examine it the more I am compelled to abandon the idea.* These single men are practically all unskilled; and nearly two thirds of them are congregated in the 10 or 12 big centres of population. Some probably have not made very much effort to get work. . . . *But undoubtedly many have, and failed. The unskilled market in their areas is full. We cannot refer these men to the Poor Law.*[57]

The Poor Law, as we have seen, was not considered an appropriate venue for veterans, nor were poor law resources capable of absorbing them. However, in this discussion, Macnamara highlighted the potential discontent and danger only of single men. Unmarried veterans were not, in this framework, deserving on their own account; rather, the government feared what would happen if they were cut off from benefit, both in terms of public relations and in terms of social disorder.[58] The Cabinet decided to grant a further extension of the OWD on the same basis as it existed (eight weeks' donation at 20 shillings per week). However, they also agreed "that an immediate examination should be made of the military records of all ex-Service men on Donation Benefit, with a view to restricting any further extension after November 8 which might be necessary to men who had served overseas and whose military records were good."[59] Increasingly, the terms under which the government was willing to acknowledge an ex-soldier's deservedness on principle were shrinking.

Even as the government sought to restrict the parameters of veterans' deservedness, the differentiation between ex-servicemen and civilians remained clear, with preference for veterans expressed in more certain and more generous benefits. This principle was articulated when the government was faced with the possibility – and then the brief reality – of a national strike of miners in the midst of the 1920 debate about the OWD extension. The Chancellor of the Exchequer concluded that the government could not withhold the benefit to veterans who would become unemployed by the strike, even though the numbers would increase dramatically. The only responsibility to *non* ex-servicemen, however, would come from unemployment insurance:

> If an ex-service man falls out of work from any cause, then, no matter how many months he has been in civil employment, he is entitled to draw out of work donation at 20s. a week for 8 weeks. In similar circumstances the non-service man would get nothing unless he were one of the 3 or 4 million workmen covered by the old Unemployment Insurance Act in which case he would get 11s. a week unemployment benefit.
>
> The strike makes no difference to this except that it enormously increases the number of ex service men who are likely to claim out of work donation. *Despite the time which has elapsed since the Armistice there should be no great difficulty in giving separate treatment to ex service men* at any rate up to November 8th when the new Unemployment Insurance Act comes into force.[60]

Veteran status was still a clear mark of privilege. In the event, the OWD was extended until March 1921, and the new Unemployment Insurance Act made special provisions for veterans.[61] As a principle, preferential treatment for ex-servicemen remained.

The debates around the OWD extension reveal that the decision to keep extending benefits, particularly to single ex-servicemen, had as much to do with fear of discontent and bad publicity as with any true perception of unemployed ex-servicemen's deservedness. The government had serious doubts about unmarried veterans, who they clearly perceived both as marginally deserving and potentially degenerating into what were called unemployables. As with the questions surrounding veterans' relationship to the Poor Law, service alone did not protect veterans from doubts about their deservedness. As the entitlement to benefits contracted, an ex-soldier's marital status was in some ways more important than his service in determining whether or not he should receive assistance. This point is even more obvious in debates surrounding preferential hiring.

Preferential hiring

While the government struggles with the OWD used marital status to measure veterans against each other, policy discussions surrounding preference in hiring and work-relief schemes became even more complicated as married civilian men entered the conversation. The public pressured the government to help disabled ex-soldiers find employment.[62] The largest program of preferential hiring was the King's Roll, instituted in September 1919. This was a scheme of moral suasion, whereby an employer who voluntarily took on a certain proportion of disabled veterans was listed in a royal honor roll and was allowed such perks as the use of the royal seal on stationery.[63] Deborah Cohen has shown that the government resisted compulsory preference programs, and, as economic conditions worsened, this resistance became even more pronounced.[64] According to Joanna Bourke, disabled ex-servicemen "rapidly lost their claim to special consideration," partially because of the tightening employment market but also from a cultural fatigue with encountering disability.[65] Economic and cultural factors combined to challenge disabled veterans' claim to preference.

As was clear in the OWD debates, neither the national government nor the local authorities wanted to deal with masses of disaffected, unemployed ex-servicemen. Yet, by 1920, there were clear signs of discontent with government efforts to find ex-soldiers employment. A deputation from the NFDDSS met with Prime Minister David Lloyd George on February 6, 1920, to voice its concerns, which were dominated by preferential hiring. The Federation pushed for the voluntary system of the King's Roll to become compulsory, to obligate firms to take on disabled ex-servicemen as workers. As it stood, the deputation argued, there was a "penalty upon patriotism," for employers who did not adopt the scheme had more "fit" workers and were therefore more competitive.[66] Lloyd George raised the point that, even if trade union leadership had recommended it, rank and file unionists had already voted down compulsory hiring.

The work imperative framed much of this debate. The Prime Minister argued that pushing disabled men into positions would cause trouble among unionists, as "a man who is forced into works and who has thereby a statutory right is not always very helpful." In other words, the promise of a position would not motivate a man to work; he could become a Weary Willy. The President of the NFDDSS agreed that "to give an individual man a guarantee of work throughout his lifetime might be a dangerous thing." Lloyd George commented that "it would be dangerous to the man himself. After all, there are all sorts amongst us. If a man to whom his foreman spoke felt that he had an Act of Parliament behind him, he would snap his fingers and it would really destroy the discipline of the works." Having a preferential, statutory right to a position was an enormous threat to the principle that men gained their masculine status through their willingness to work. Griffin responded, however, that the more than 353,000 ex-servicemen who were still unemployed "are men who, as far as can be gathered, have shown their willingness to work by attending regularly for employment at the Labour Exchanges, and so far as can be ascertained they have been officially approved as men who are genuinely seeking employment."[67]

While most of the public conversation about veterans and unemployment focused on disabled ex-servicemen, the government was quite concerned about able-bodied men as well, particularly those who had gone to war before they had the opportunity to acquire occupational training and had therefore come back from service with no marketable skills. In the context of increasing competition for scarce employment opportunities, the government implemented a variety of limited schemes to assist able-bodied veterans. In May 1920, the Committee on the Re-Employment of Ex-Service Men "decided in principle in favour of facilities for training . . . being given to *non-disabled* ex-service men whose opportunities for entering definite employment had been prejudiced owing to their service."[68] They presented a formal recommendation that "the Committee are impressed by the numbers of young ex-service men, of 20 years of age and upwards, who, though not disabled, are unable to obtain employment because they have no skill or experience in any definite occupation."[69] Notably, Thomas Phillips of the Ministry of Labour worried that, when they were discharged, veterans "require a man's pay, but have little to offer an employer in return and unless some assistance is given towards giving them a footing even in a semi-skilled occupation their case is really desperate."[70] Because of a deficiency in training, veterans could not command a "man's pay" and thus lacked the capacity to take on family liability.

The 1918 election manifesto suggested a promise of preference to all ex-servicemen, whether disabled or able-bodied. In addition to the King's Roll, designed to benefit disabled veterans, the government attempted to compel the hiring of able-bodied ex-servicemen through adopting the principle of preference on all government-supported relief projects. From December 1920, the Unemployment Grants Committee (UGC) was responsible for assessing applications from local authorities for national government funding of work-relief schemes, and the UGC operated assuming that all these schemes would adhere to a preference for ex-servicemen.[71] Preferential hiring schemes came up against issues of skill and lack of training, against some trade unions who objected to the employment of veterans who had not served apprenticeships, and against preexisting ideas that preference in unemployment schemes should go to married men with families.

But what exactly constituted preference for ex-servicemen? The UGC detailed that "the Committee had from the first taken the view that the term 'preference' was intended to mean 100 per cent preference, or in other words, that so long as an ex-service man was available for work upon 'assisted' relief works, that man was to receive employment in preference to all civilians."[72] However, another national relief scheme, run by the Ministry of Transport to construct arterial roads, operated with a different preference principle, holding that up to 25 per cent of men hired on could be civilians, a position favored by the Ministry of Labour.[73] In March 1921, the Cabinet decided that all government relief schemes should "maintain the principle of preference but . . . look favourably on the employment of a small proportion of civilians if requested to do so by Local Authorities." The civilians in question, unsurprisingly, were married men with dependent children. The Ministry of Transport decision to hire up to 25 per cent civilians had "met the objections of Local Authorities to the engagement of unmarried ex-service men who had perhaps not served overseas, while married civilians with dependent children remained unemployed."[74] The local authorities pressured the national government to recognize that the family liability of married civilians could override military service, especially in cases where unmarried veterans had not been fully engaged in combat.

The Cabinet decision led the UGC and the Ministry of Transport to agree that "preference should be given to all ex-service men over civilians, but that if a Local Authority so desired, married civilians might be engaged upon State-aided relief works up to a number not exceeding 25% of the whole."[75] In January 1922, the UGC took over all decision making relative to government grants and loans to assist the unemployed, and its policy was that "the proportion of ex-Service men employed was at least 75 per cent." A report the UGC issued in 1922 acknowledged, "At first this was 100 per cent; it was subsequently reduced to 75 per cent to allow of the employment of a proportion of married men other than ex-Service men."[76] While the preference principle for ex-servicemen obtained, government policy evolved to recognize that honest married civilian men deserved a claim on welfare resources that challenged the universality of veterans' entitlement.

The British Legion was not happy with this outcome, worrying about a slippery slope that would put even the 75 per cent preference at risk. In an October 1921 meeting with the Minister of Labour, the British Legion asked the government to compel local authorities applying to the UGC to maintain a 75 per cent preference for veterans. It argued, "We detest the permissive clause because in the actual operation of this the Local Authorities can get around it," suggesting that local bodies had priorities other than veterans. Yet H.J. Wilson, Secretary of the Ministry of Labour, responded that compulsion would simply keep local authorities from applying to the UGC, which would not benefit the unemployed.[77] The British Legion argued from both moral and material standpoints. Preference was a right veterans gained from their sacrifice to the nation, but it was also compensation for veterans' lack of employment training because of their war service, which prevented them from achieving an occupational identity or the ability to take on family liability.[78]

Local authorities, however, constantly faced the claims of all the unemployed men in their areas. They insisted "that with the volume of unemployment, and its long duration numbers of men are married men with dependent children who would ordinarily be given preference, whereas many of the ex-service men are young and unmarried."[79] In the early 1920s, unemployed men's organizations kept up pressure on their local authorities to prioritize the welfare of honest married men. For local authorities, the competing principles of preference – for married men over single men and for veterans over civilians – came into stark conflict. As the war receded and the circumstances of prolonged mass unemployment continued, local authorities felt it unjust that the newer politics of preference trump the older system of honest poverty, especially when married civilian men had dependants to support. The historical experiences of local bodies with unemployment relief schemes forced the national government to acknowledge the deservedness of civilian men's family liability, even at the expense of unmarried veterans' welfare.

A local context

As politicians and government bureaucrats struggled over competing principles of preference, local communities also had to decide where veterans fit into their schemes to help the unemployed. In the Dudley and Stourbridge Unions, the Employment Exchanges consistently revealed high numbers of unemployed ex-servicemen. In February 1921, the Stourbridge Employment Exchange showed veterans constituted 387 (45 per cent) of 860 men on the register.[80] In Cradley Heath, 50 per cent of more than 1,000 men on the register in early March were ex-servicemen.[81] Local pressures such as this contributed to fraught discussions surrounding national policy.

These issues came to a head in the Black Country when local officials debated the preferential employment of ex-servicemen for a relief scheme in Brierley Hill. In mid-February 1921, Brierley Hill established a Relief Committee to deal with the approximately 2,000 unemployed in the town, of which about 400 were ex-servicemen. The vice chairman of the committee stressed that ex-servicemen had a particular right to their assistance, as they had been "unable to put anything by, and he considered the first claim upon any fund established in the town would belong to these men,"[82] echoing the position of the British Legion. On Monday, February 21, "a large party of ex-service men hitherto unemployed, commenced work in laying out at Church Hill, the park given to the town." To provide employment to as many ex-servicemen as possible, the committee "proposed that these should work in gangs of 50, for a fortnight at a time."[83]

In early March, after the relief scheme had been operating for a few weeks and the numbers of unemployed in the town had grown to about 3,000, tensions erupted around the comments of Harry Bullus, a representative of the Amalgamated Society of Engineers. Bullus submitted a resolution from the society to the Brierley Hill and District Trades and Labour Council, objecting to "relief measures being on a charity basis,"[84] a statement that implicitly criticized the preferential hiring of ex-soldiers at the expense of trade union men and more overtly attacked the running of assistance schemes by the Relief Committee rather than the Trades and Labour Council itself. The *County Advertiser* reported on March 5 that, at a meeting of the Brierley Hill Relief Committee, when a Mr. Warne "mentioned that ex-Service men were being employed on a scheme, Mr. H. Bullus enquired why ex-Service men should have any preference." When the chairman replied that "those who had not served had had opportunities to earn good money," Bullus was reported to have answered, "I know all about that," suggesting that he was impatient about veterans' preference issues.[85]

A week later, the *Dudley Chronicle* reported on a committee meeting of the Brierley Hill branch of the NFDDSS, which had convened specifically to discuss Bullus's remarks. The chairman, Stanley Harley, reported that

> Mr. Bullus had asked why ex-service men should have the preference over married men in the matter of employment at the park. It was pointed out for the information of Mr. Bullus that some of the ex-Service men were married. They were not all single, and Mr. Plant moved that the branch protest against the remarks and ask Mr. Bullus through the press if he spoke on his own behalf or through the Trades Union he represented.[86]

Here the hierarchy of deservedness with regard to unemployment relief is very clear: Harley assumed that Bullus's main concern was that single men – less deserving men – were receiving preference over married men. Their service, in some ways, was incidental. Even more significantly, "it was explained that one ex-Service man had declined a job at the new park because he was single and could afford to make room for a married man. This explanation was considered most gratifying from the ex-Service man's standpoint, for no one had so far stated that some civilians had also refused work at the park."[87] Not only had this single man sacrificed by serving his nation, he was willing to sacrifice his own livelihood to support a civilian married man.

An early April letter to the *Chronicle* defended Bullus. The writer, who identified himself as "an unmarried ex-Service man," indicated that he "personally interviewed Mr. Bullus, and his opinion has been falsely represented. His statement was this, that single ex-Service men must not have preference to married men with families, and at the same time states that married ex-Service men should have preference to all." The writer stressed that he was "absolutely in agreement with this, and I don't doubt for a minute my fellow comrades of the war understand it is only right." He concluded by attacking another letter to the editor that had criticized Bullus, asserting that, if the correspondent did "not agree" that married men deserved preference, "he had better take his abode in a country where home life is not so prized as in Britain."[88] Home life, marriage, and children were the very things that veterans had been told they fought for in the First World War, so challenging their primacy by giving preference to single men was questioning the very values of the British nation.[89]

Conclusion

The Bullus controversy highlights a community weighing preference policies that pitted honest married men with family liability against unmarried veterans for unemployment assistance. The youth and singleness of many ex-servicemen told against them with regard to both national and local strategies for unemployment relief. Many unmarried ex-servicemen found themselves unable to successfully reintegrate into civilian life, socially or economically. As studies of the emotional and physical impact of the war have shown, the experiences of the war in addition to the economic circumstances of the 1920s made it almost impossible for many veterans to get work or establish a "normal" home life.[90] Yet the economic realities of unmarried veterans' experiences could not ultimately stand up to already-existing policies and practices that gave preference to married men with children. Married men's histories of honest poverty in some ways trumped the deservedness of unmarried veterans. As resources became increasingly stretched, hierarchies of preference delegitimized the needs of single ex-servicemen, many of whom became exactly what the government feared: vagrants and casual, unskilled laborers who relied on the Poor Law.

By the early 1920s, the relationship between welfare deservedness and military service had all but collapsed, and the government reverted to the familiar terms of honest poverty to determine priorities in expending its resources. Military service had provided an alternative path to deservedness, one that competed with honest poverty. It presented a different system of meaning regarding masculine status and welfare that, in the 1920s, had little staying power. The government continued to award pensions to disabled veterans, to be sure, but able-bodied veterans, many of whom were young, single men, remained on the margins of welfare deservedness grounded in the work imperative and family liability.

7
"No right to relieve a striker": Trade Disputes and the Politics of Work and Family in the 1920s

In May 1926, the Trades Union Congress, the national organization of trade unions in Britain, called for a general strike in support of the Miners' Federation dispute with employers, who sought to reduce wages and increase hours. The General Strike lasted nine days, during which time much of Britain's transport and industrial base was shut down.[1] Anticipating the large numbers of resulting relief applicants, the Stourbridge Board of Guardians held a special meeting to discuss strategies relative to the strike. The *County Express* reported that a "crowd of several hundred people gathered in the vicinity of the [poor law] institution" on the day of the meeting, and the board had about 900 applications for assistance. When the Reverend C.D. Banks-Gale asked how the board was going to handle applications from the men on strike, the clerk answered "that the Guardians were not dealing with the strikers at all, but with their wives and families."[2] As its minutes recorded, the Board of Guardians resolved "that the applications of strikers be considered as for, and on behalf of, the wives and children."[3] Two months later, with the General Strike over but the miners' strike continuing, the Board of Guardians still faced "emergency circumstances." In response to a complaint by a deputation of miners that the relief offered to strikers' families was inadequate, the board noted that the law tied its hands. The board's clerk assured the deputation that "the scale of relief being paid was more than the Guardians really ought to give at the present time. It was a scale which practically included the man – the striker – himself, and the deputation were aware that the Guardians had no right to relieve a striker."[4]

According to the honest poverty work-welfare system, an able-bodied man who participated in a trade dispute compromised the conceptualization of masculine citizenship built around the willingness to work and the maintenance of family. While state authorities might have wanted to punish striking men, whom they perceived as refusing to take available work, officials were not ready to extend this punishment to strikers' wives and children, whom they regarded as innocent victims of the circumstances. Thus the Stourbridge Board of Guardians insisted that it was dealing only with the strikers' wives and children, not with the strikers themselves. By denying public support, welfare policies marked striking men as agents of their condition: strikers chose not to work, so their unemployment was not blameless. Wives and children, by contrast, were seen as unable to choose their condition: they depended on husbands and fathers to provide for them and were therefore still deserving of assistance when men failed to provide. This was a major departure from the 1834 New Poor Law mandate that the families of able-bodied male paupers followed the husband/father's condition.

Strikes were fundamentally a contest about the conditions under which the work imperative should matter. Men involved in industrial disputes did not see themselves as Weary Willies who were unwilling to work; rather, they argued that employers unmanned workers by forcing them to accept wages that challenged men's abilities to provide for their families. As a deputation from the Miners' Federation put it to the Prime Minister in December 1922, the government needed to make sure that miners were "properly paid, because an industry such as this ought to be able to pay wages which we, as citizens, have a right to expect, and we ask the Government that we should be paid as citizens and that we should be given an equal opportunity with other citizens."[5] Strikes were a central means through which honest poor men sought to assert their rights as citizens. While these issues came into play throughout the period of this study, the conditions of the 1920s brought into sharp relief questions regarding aid to striking men. In particular, the national coal strike of 1921 and the General Strike and miners' strike of 1926 created policy problems for the British government surrounding interpretations of honest poverty. Striking men challenged employers who used the work imperative and family liability to justify poor work conditions and low wages.

Family welfare and the Merthyr Tydfil decision

The 1921 coal dispute began when Parliament ended government control of the coal industry, giving mine owners the power to set wages district by district as opposed to following national scales. Coal mining had been taken over by the state during the First World War, and the government's decision to turn the industry back to private hands provoked miners to contest the wage reductions they knew employers would impose. As the London *Times* forecast the week before the strike, "the pits will open on Friday for men to work at the wages which the industry in any particular district can afford to pay, but the men may refuse to cut coal on these terms."[6] The Miners' Federation argued that the wage rates being proposed by the owners were a regression back to the days before the war and would significantly harm miners' standard of living. This was especially the case in the context of the already existing trade depression.[7] The 1921 strike lasted for three months, but the consequences of the dispute carried through the remainder of the year and beyond.[8]

Even before the strike began on April 2, the year had started badly for Black Country inhabitants.[9] The *Dudley Chronicle* on February 12 worried that "unemployment has reached a most acute state . . . practically every industry is now feeling severely the effects of the depression."[10] The already high numbers of unemployed in the West Midlands jumped from about 202,000 on April 8 to almost 242,000 on April 30; "the large addition to the figures in this period is due primarily to the coal stoppage,"[11] claimed the *Dudley Herald*, which also described the "Black Country as a silent wilderness at the present time."[12] The fallout from the coal dispute went well beyond the collieries, affecting the industries – such as glass making and the small metals trades – that relied on coal for fuel, decimating Black Country manufacturing. As one colliery owner told the *Herald* the week the strike was declared, "The situation is the most serious we have ever been faced with in the Black Country."[13]

Unsurprisingly, the strike caused increasing numbers of people to turn to the Poor Law. In the first three months of 1921, the Dudley Board of Guardians already was relieving 300 more people per week than in the previous year.[14] The numbers receiving poor law relief in the Dudley Union during the strike ranged between about 1,500 early in April and 2,700 when the strike ended in early July (compared to between 1,000 and 1,100 the year before). But the ramifications for the region lasted much longer, with flooded mines keeping miners out of work and coal in limited supply. The worst month of 1921 was November, when as many as 9,500 people were in receipt of relief in the Dudley Union (compared to 1,100 the year before). By January 1922, the numbers had dropped below 6,000, still a staggering number.[15]

These figures included the large numbers of workers out of jobs because of a lack of fuel to support their industries and families made destitute when the mines shut down. Did they, however, include strikers themselves? The postwar debate about relief to striking men focused heavily on whether the Poor Law legally enabled Boards of Guardians to help able-bodied strikers. The debate drew on the context of an earlier legal decision on the question, the Merthyr Tydfil judgment of 1900, which ruled that relief to strikers could not be accommodated within the Poor Law. Specifically, the Appeals Court found that the Merthyr Tydfil Board of Guardians in southern Wales had acted illegally in giving relief to able-bodied men involved in trade disputes, because work was indeed available in the region.[16] The finding prohibited striking men from receiving outrelief because the court considered them to blame for their unemployment. Simultaneously, however, the Appeals Court decided that the wives and children of striking workmen were still eligible for poor law assistance, as were the men themselves if they had become so destitute that they were physically unable to work.[17] Able-bodied strikers also could be liable to prosecution under the 1824 Vagrancy Act for refusing to maintain themselves and their families.[18]

The Merthyr Tydfil decision and the policy discussions about relief to strikers in the 1920s drew on the long history of the poor law work tests required of men to demonstrate their commitment to the work imperative. The problem for the strikers in Merthyr Tydfil, according to the Appeals Court, was that the miners had been "physically fit to work and able to obtain work at wages sufficient to support themselves and their families, but [they] had refused to perform such work."[19] In "refusing" work, they did not adhere to the work imperative. Essentially, "The exclusion of strikers [from poor law relief] on the ground that they were able-bodied meant they were to be treated no differently from any other able-bodied men who, for whatever reason, refused work."[20] Men who refused work were seen as neglectful husbands and fathers, willing to sacrifice the health of wives and children to the trade dispute. (This also had the effect of turning women into victims, denying them any agency in supporting strikes.) Government policy clearly implied that men on strike were undeserving, thus repudiating the legitimacy of industrial actions.

During the 1920s, the Ministry of Health was anxious to ensure that local Boards of Guardians would not assist men involved in trade disputes, but this raised thorny political issues. Some Boards of Guardians were sympathetic to their local men on strike and provided them with outrelief. Additionally, after 1894, the boards were democratized by allowing elections of women and working-class men as members. "Thus," according to Patricia Ryan in a study of the Poor Law and the General Strike of 1926, "Boards of Guardians, as elected relief agencies, were . . . directly responsible to popular control by claimants, and by

Figure 7.1 A Staffordshire miner handing in his lamp before the October 1920 strike
Source: © Illustrated London News Ltd/Mary Evans.

people who . . . were likely to be in receipt of relief at some period of their working life."[21] *The Times* reported that the Durham Board of Guardians, in one of the most coal-heavy unions, did not abide by Merthyr Tydfil: "Several members [of the Board of Guardians] declared that they did not care if they were surcharged a thousand times over. They would not allow thousands of children to starve."[22] Guardians in communities sensitive to strikers' circumstances found themselves at odds with national government policies.[23]

In an effort to contain the conflict with local authorities, the Ministry of Health under Alfred Mond distributed circulars during the national strikes of the 1920s, reminding Boards of Guardians of the Merthyr Tydfil ruling. However, while emphasizing the illegality of relieving striking men, the Ministry also acknowledged the ways in which the judgment itself was essentially unworkable in principle and practice. Specifically, Mond pointed to inconsistencies in law and in implementation regarding the separation of the striking head of household from his dependent wife and children when rendering relief decisions.

A lengthy 1921 Ministry of Health memorandum on "Relief to Strikers" worried that the Merthyr Tydfil decision had incorporated a fundamental flaw into poor law policy by allowing relief to strikers' families. The Merthyr Tydfil judgment, the memo argued, was "inconsistent with the existing statutes," because "under the Poor Law Acts the father of a family is held to be constructively relieved when relief is afforded to any of his dependents." Because wives and children were dependants of their husbands/fathers, authorities assumed these dependants would only be relieved when the male provider was unable to maintain them and needed assistance himself. The Merthyr Tydfil decision effectively attempted to separate the welfare of wives and children from that of husbands/fathers. Mond stressed that the families of striking men needed to be treated like any other family where the breadwinner refused to work, which meant going into the workhouse as dictated by the 1834 New Poor Law.[24]

In addition to the issues of policy, Mond pointed to the practical problem of the Merthyr Tydfil decision, which he contended left too much discretion to Boards of Guardians' interpretations of the circumstances. The Minister called differentiating between relief to a family and to the man himself "practically impossible to put into operation." How, he asked, could relief to wife and children not benefit the striking husband?: "clearly, if outdoor relief is afforded to the wife and children, it is scarcely possible to prevent the striker's receiving a share of the relief." Mond was also concerned that since relief scales were tailored to serve the needs of the wife and children alone, "the only effect of not relieving the striker is to reduce the resources of the whole household below the level which the Guardians consider necessary to relieve destitution."[25] In practice, Boards of Guardians wound up increasing the amount of relief for women and children to be able to support the whole family, knowing that the male head of household would be drawing on the resources. This was obviously illegal and subject to penalty from the Ministry.[26]

Boards of Guardians were "confused" regarding how to deal with strikers and their families. In some cases, boards gave payments "to the striker as the agent of his family," who was then liable to repay the relief as a loan. In other areas, "the wife has been treated as the legal head of the household."[27] One strategy maintained the husband's family liability, requiring a striking man to take responsibility for poor law relief of his dependants for the duration of the strike by repaying whatever assistance his family received. The other strategy, however, undermined men's family liability, making women the "head of the household," explicitly punishing men who placed themselves outside honest poverty based on the work imperative and family liability and positioning women as responsible agents.

Knowing the difficulties the Merthyr Tydfil decision presented to the Boards of Guardians, the Ministry of Health desired above all to revoke the decision or revise it significantly. Alternatively, if the Merthyr Tydfil decision remained in force – which it did – the Minister argued that "the only practicable course seems to be to press Boards of Guardians to afford relief as far as possible in kind [rather than in cash] and in such a manner as will preclude its being converted to the man's use."[28] The Dudley Board of Guardians followed this practice, agreeing on May 6, 1921, to give relief only by food tickets to local grocers and to consider that relief as a loan.[29] The amount of attention paid by the Ministry of Health to relieving striking men suggests unease not just about issues of economy but also about the moral questions of a man's responsibilities.

In light of the confusion around the actual application of the Merthyr Tydfil decision, Mond presented a question to the Law Officers of the Crown.[30] Mond was concerned that, as Boards of Guardians requested national loans to supplement their inadequate local resources if the 1921 strike continued, the Ministry of Health would essentially be sanctioning loans that boards would use to give illegal relief to strikers. Mond pointed out that the Merthyr Tydfil decision was based on the principle that "the applicants for relief" should be denied assistance if they were able "to obtain work 'at wages sufficient to support themselves and their families.'"[31] He believed this judgment opened up space for sympathetic Boards of Guardians to make their *own* decisions about what constituted sufficient wages and available work. He argued that the boards "gave or withheld relief in accordance with their views as to the merits of the dispute and as to the proper standard of living for wage-earners."[32] Additionally, boards had to decide whether work was available in the district, which could also turn on political opinions and perceptions. The Minister wanted to close down this space for interpretation by insisting that "*no* poor relief is to be given to persons on strike, and that the relief is not to exceed a certain *fixed* scale."[33] This, he hoped, would prevent Boards of Guardians from creating new scales for wives and children that would benefit the strikers themselves.

Additionally, Mond again emphasized that the Poor Law Amendment Act of 1834 held that all relief granted to a man's family was supposed to be treated as relief given to the man: "Relief to the wife of a striker is, therefore, in law relief to the striker himself, and if the latter is illegal, the former would seem on a true construction of the Act to be illegal also. . . . But certain Boards of Guardians, while declining to grant relief to strikers, have substantially increased the amount of relief granted to their wives."[34] While I have not found a response from the Law Officers of the Crown to these queries, the fact that the issues were still present in 1926 suggests that Merthyr Tydfil remained untouched.

With 1921 behind it, the Ministry of Health was more prepared to address the problems concerning poor relief for strikers when workers went out on a general strike in 1926. The issues regarding the application of the Merthyr Tydfil judgment had not been resolved, however, and the government again confronted the contradictions it posed. The General Strike began near midnight on May 3, 1926, when the Trades Union Congress called for other unions to support the miners, whose wages and conditions of work were again threatened. The General Strike ended on May 13, but the miners remained out throughout the fall, refusing to accept wage reductions and longer hours at work. By the end of 1926, however, the strike was over with nothing gained; many miners returned to work, but many also remained unemployed, because jobs were no longer available to them as mines damaged during the strike were abandoned.[35]

Anticipating a large increase in poor law applications with the commencement of the General Strike, on May 5 the Ministry of Health once more sent out a circular to Boards of Guardians regarding what to do when strikers applied for relief:

> The questions for the consideration of the Guardians on any application for relief made by a person who is destitute in consequence of a trade dispute are questions of fact, namely, whether the applicant for relief is or is not a person who is able-bodied and physically capable of work: whether work is or is not available for him and if such work is not available for him, whether it is or is not so unavailable through his own act or consent.

Where the applicant for relief is able-bodied and physically capable of work the grant of relief to him is unlawful if work is available for him or he is thrown on the Guardians through his own act of consent and penalties are provided by law in case of failure to support dependants, though the Guardians may lawfully relieve such dependants if they are in fact destitute.[36]

Nothing had changed since 1921. Emphasizing the "facts" of the situation, the Ministry was still obviously worried about Boards of Guardians' discretion. The facts for the Ministry were that able-bodied striking men made the illegal choice to refuse available work, neglecting their dependants. This in turn disqualified them from any state assistance. Yet the government still would not let wives and children suffer as a result.

As in 1921, local Boards of Guardians in 1926 had to negotiate their approach to the strike in light of the Ministry of Health warnings. The Stourbridge board on May 7 "unanimously resolved that no relief be granted this week to strikers. It was decided that workmen locked out be treated in the usual way, and not as strikers until some official discussion on the point is arrived at."[37] This illustrated the national government's concern: the board left itself space to distinguish a strike from a lock-out and to make relief decisions accordingly. Men who were locked out as opposed to on strike could "be treated in the usual way," meaning as eligible for outrelief. The Board of Guardians would decide for themselves through "official discussion" how to differentiate between strikers and men locked out of work. The Dudley board was more firm than its Stourbridge counterpart in its initial approach to the strikers. Its Unemployment Committee met on May 6, and the committee's members reminded themselves of their success dealing with the 1921 situation. They resolved to suspend test work during the strike, to limit applications (if possible) to two days a week, and to give relief only in kind and on loan. They told the clerk to be prepared to hire additional staff if needed to deal with the circumstances.[38]

The numbers created urgency. While the General Strike ended on May 13, the miners' dispute continued, and by mid-June about 5,000 people had received outrelief in the Stourbridge Union, compared to around 2,200 the year before at the same time.[39] In early July, the Board of Guardians received a deputation from the Lye and Wollescote Distress Relief Committee, which had been set up at the beginning of the General Strike. The representatives "complained that relief given by the Board to miners' families was inadequate." Mr. Perrins, the Distress

Relief Committee spokesman, told the guardians that the committee "had been dealing with cases of direct distress first, and with people whose pride would not allow them to come to the Board of Guardians." He condemned the board's recent adoption of an inferior scale of relief and argued that "we feel you are not relieving destitution, and that you are simply starving these people." The Board of Guardians' chairman replied that they were "dealing with each case on its merits . . . We are not starving anyone."[40] A government memorandum concluded that "public sentiment" was ranged against the admission of strikers' families to the workhouse, so Boards of Guardians almost exclusively provided outrelief and in-kind relief to strikers' families.[41] Yet, in July, the *Herald* noted, "Some of the Boards of Guardians in the district are bemoaning the large amount of money it has cost the ratepayers in giving out-relief to the miners and others,"[42] suggesting that the boards were relieving striking men and not just their families.

The issue of relief to strikers became so fraught that the national government had to address relieving officers who refused to carry out what they perceived to be illegal orders for relief given by Boards of Guardians. A deputation from the National Association of Relieving Officers voiced their concerns to Herbert Francis, Assistant Secretary of the Ministry of Health, on July 26, 1926.[43] Francis assured the relieving officers that they could not be punished for holding to the letter of the law. Yet, simultaneously, Francis reminded the relieving officers that they "would be held responsible for a case of death from starvation."[44] Relieving officers were only allowed to dispense relief in cases of urgent necessity. With regard to the strikers, this only applied to men who had been so reduced by their destitution that they were deemed incapable of working.

A February 1927 memorandum on the 1926 coal dispute summarized some of the key issues.[45] The report highlighted both "the essential 'elasticity' of the English Poor Law System in its ability to cope with an emergency of this magnitude" and "certain inherent weaknesses of the system and the unsatisfactory state of the law as regards the relief of persons participating in an industrial dispute,"[46] presaging the abolition of the Boards of Guardians in 1929. The memorandum specifically addressed the practical problems posed by the Merthyr Tydfil judgment, acknowledging that "it is obvious . . . that even though the relief was given in kind, there was no guarantee that it was not shared by the Striker-husband, and the resources of the family thereby reduced below the adequate scale."[47] Interestingly, this point stresses both the impossibility of compartmentalizing the family/household in the way envisioned by the judgment and the necessity of providing relief sufficient for subsistence.

Definitions of work and family welfare

Strikes clearly called the components of honest poverty into question. What did the willingness to work mean during a strike? What were the implications for family liability? In the discussions about relief to striking men, policymakers, poor law authorities, and men involved in the disputes publicly represented the striker as a married man with wife and children to support. For the government, strikers were married men who irresponsibly abrogated their deservedness by refusing work to support their families. For strikers themselves, strikers were married men who deserved to demand good working conditions and fair wages in the interests of their families. Both sides used family liability to describe how a strike related to the willingness to work.

The categorization of a trade dispute itself spoke to the honest poverty of the men involved. At the beginning of the 1921 national coal stoppage, Frank Hodges, the secretary of the national Miners' Federation, claimed, "The stoppage in the mining industry has been caused, not by a strike of the miners, but by a lock-out on the part of the coalowners. . . . The miners have been locked out. Work cannot be resumed until the mineworker is assured of at least a living wage for the hard and dangerous work he is required to do." Miners were willing to work but not on terms that would "require cheap coal at the cost of the men who produce it under conditions of great physical strain and risk, and of the women and children who are dependent on them."[48] Comparing the owners' terms to slave labor, in late May 1926, Mr. Cook for the miners stated that the coal owners' "only desire is to reduce the conditions of their employees, the miners, to abject slavery. They declare without a blush in favour of both longer hours and lower wages, and refuse absolutely to consider any proposals for reorganizing the industry."[49] These were not conditions under which any "man," any citizen, should be willing to work.

Locally, Alderman Henry Parker of Dudley, during the third week of the 1921 coal dispute, spoke to a crowd of between 400 and 500 mine workers, calling the struggle a "lock-out" that revealed to the world the value of mine workers. He stressed that "the miners deplored as much as anyone the fact that industries had become paralysed through lack of fuel, and that in thousands of homes there was no warmth for women and children, but they felt that their claims were so just that until they were conceded the withholding of their labour must be continued."[50] Parker argued that employers, not miners, caused the suffering of women and children. The *Herald* reported, just a week into the strike, that "many . . . notably those with large families, and the improvident, have already begun to feel the pinch,"[51] strangely coupling the distress of deserving and undeserving.

The "starvation" of miners' dependants became central to the discourse of strike politics in both 1921 and 1926. A formal joint "manifesto" from the Parliamentary Committee of the Trades Union Congress, National Executive of the Labour Party, and the Parliamentary Labour Party insisted in early May 1921 that "the mineowners and the Government have declared war upon the miners. Their weapon is starvation, their first victims women and children. It is to be a war of attrition. They count upon hunger forcing the miners back to work."[52] Evan Williams, the president of the Mining Association, clearly took offense at this kind of language: "It is suggested that the owners are 'making war' against the men and against the women and children as well. This is a travesty of the owners' position."[53] In 1926, Winston Churchill, Chancellor of the Exchequer, "den[ied], on the authority of the Ministry of Health, that there was any serious distress due to lack of food among the mining community." Indeed, Churchill expressly referred to miners' family liability to reverse the accusations:

> There is no truth whatever in this starvation tale. (Cheers.) It seems to me that you could not put a greater insult on the mining community, who are a great mass of manly, well-respecting people, than to suggest that they would let their wives and families starve week after week, as we are told, and suffer all the acute physical injury of deprivation of food, rather than work an eight-hour day for a wage which the great majority of this country would gladly receive.[54]

Miners, as "manly" citizens, surely would not refuse work if doing so compromised their family liability. Churchill placed blame firmly on the men whom he saw as neglecting their responsibilities.

The local Black Country newspapers emphasized that neither employers nor strikers wanted to see women and children suffer because of a trade dispute. While in 1921 the miners were prepared to wait out the strike, "they regretted that the suffering should apply to the women-folk and children."[55] Meanwhile, colliery owners themselves were subscribing to relief funds to help miners' families. According to the *County Advertiser* in late June 1921, mine owners "intimated that though the men were on strike they could not allow the wives and children to suffer unduly."[56] Perhaps a bit of the reality of the situation comes through in an Old Hill distress committee meeting, which in mid-May 1921 discussed the need to feed children at the schools since many children, especially miners' children, were "very much underfed."[57] Family needs defined the understanding of the strike's consequences for all parties involved (Figure 7.2).

This focus on family needs put unmarried men in a particularly awkward situation relative to strike relief policy. While married men could benefit – illegally – from the relief given to their wives and children (and many Boards of Guardians operated to facilitate this process), single men had no such opportunities. The government, however, did not specifically consider the implications of their policies for single men until 1926. A May 18, 1926, note from Assistant Secretary Francis of the Ministry of Health stressed the "difficulty about single miners." Francis indicated that he could not recall similar problems in 1921 but suggested that the lack of trouble for single men in 1921 was because

Figure 7.2   Distribution of food during miners' strike, Derbyshire, 1926. Women and children wait in line for free soup during the 1926 strike
Source: Mary Evans/Sueddeutsche Zeitung Photo.

strike pay had still been available. He worried about "the young men with no standing or claim on the hospitality of the people with whom they lodge."[58] Single men, in this account, were more vulnerable than married men, precisely because the unmarried had fewer family and community ties. Yet Ministry officials agreed that, as with married men, single men were barred from relief under the terms of Merthyr Tydfil.[59] Francis reiterated to a deputation of relieving officers in July 1926 that "relief given to single miners was given on their own responsibility. A Relieving Officer giving such relief was liable to surcharge."[60]

Because they had less flexibility in dealing with unmarried strikers, local officials pressed the national government to change policy. Prime Minister Stanley Baldwin in 1926 received resolutions from Boards of Guardians protesting "against the action of the Ministry of Health in withholding relief from single men and widowers affected by the dispute in the Coal industry" and demanding that "the Government . . . bring about an alteration of the law under which single men concerned in industrial disputes can be given relief in kind before they are broken down in health."[61] The Birmingham Trades Council "denounce[d] the Government's policy of starvation" as a means to get the miners back to work.[62] The concern about single men's wellbeing suggests that married men did benefit from relief to their families. Otherwise, local officials would have been just as worried about the health of married strikers. Even though the Ministry rhetoric stressed the illegality of relieving striking miners altogether, it is clear that married men received relief, either on their own or through inflated relief scales for their wives and children. Single men did not have that luxury.

Striking men and unemployment benefit

While the Merthyr Tydfil decision expressly forbade poor law relief to striking men, Boards of Guardians used their discretion, pushed the boundaries of legality, and assisted married strikers through their families and seemingly as individuals as well. Similarly, the Unemployment Insurance Acts prohibited men involved in strikes from receiving benefit, but the law left room for interpretation. The relevant statute came from the 1920 Unemployment Insurance Act. Under "Disqualifications for Unemployment Benefit," section 8(1) indicated,

> An insured contributor who has lost employment by reason of a stoppage of work which was due to a trade dispute at the factory, workshop, or other premises at which he was employed shall be

disqualified for receiving unemployment benefit so long as the stoppage of work continues, except in a case where he has, during the stoppage of work, become bona fide employed elsewhere in the occupation which he usually follows or has become regularly engaged in some other occupation.

Where separate branches of work which are commonly carried on as separate businesses in separate premises are in any case carried on in separate departments on the same premises, each of those departments shall, for the purposes of this provision, be deemed to be a separate factory or workshop or separate premises, as the case may be.[63]

In the case of unemployment benefit and the 1920s strikes, the interpretive confusion surrounded the determination of whether a man was involved in a trade dispute, whether he had taken on an occupation unrelated to the strike, whether his work at a colliery was actually separate business, and when a trade dispute ended. All of these points revolved around understandings of the work imperative: whether the act of striking meant a man displayed an unwillingness to work. My examination of the Umpire's decisions for 1926 sheds light on how various constituencies addressed these questions.

The Umpire's assessment of an applicant's relationship to a strike was far from straightforward. Men asserted their rights to benefit, but if the Umpire found that an applicant had interest in the strike outcome or history as a miner, he would likely disallow benefit. For example, in a case from August 1926, two men who had been working as tip laborers at a colliery appealed their benefit disallowances, claiming they did not belong to any trade union. Stressing their adherence to the work imperative, they insisted they "were prepared to work if there was work for them to do." Even so, "they agreed that their wages were subject to fluctuation in the miners' rates of wages." Apparently this sealed the deal: the Deputy Umpire found that "there seems to be no dispute as to the facts" that the men could benefit from the strike, and the "evidence does not show that they do not belong to a grade or class of workers members of which are participating in or financing or directly interested in the dispute."[64] This double negative emphasizes the difficulty applicants faced persuading the Umpire that they had no investment in the strike.

Membership in a mining union, likewise, almost automatically disqualified an applicant from receiving benefit. Edwin Bithell appealed to the Umpire, claiming "I have not lost my employment by reason of a Trade

Dispute. . . . There is no dispute between me and my employers. . . .
I may say that I personally am not concerned in the cause of the stoppage of work as I have had no contract of service with the Colliery
Company and only with the men." The Umpire disagreed, finding that
"the applicant is a member of the Miners' Association, and presumably
is participating in the dispute, even though he himself may not be
directly interested in it."[65] While Edward Dempsey, a surface worker,
"had no direct interest in the dispute," the Umpire wrote that "he does
not satisfy me that he was not financing the dispute [through union
dues]. Although no strike pay was being paid it is difficult to believe that
the Union had not some funds which were used in some way for payment of salaries and traveling expenses, or otherwise in financing the
dispute." Dempsey's union argued to no avail that "Dempsey was stood
off work by the management through no fault of his own . . . he was
not off work through a 'Trade Dispute' nor . . . contributing to a Trade
Union connected with the dispute."[66] The Umpire disagreed.

If, however, the Umpire decided an applicant's occupation was
unconnected to the strike, this meant that being unemployed was not
a "choice." To convince the Umpire of their willingness to work, non-
miners employed at collieries had to prove their distance from strikers.
For example, in the case of a colliery overseman who appealed benefit
disallowance in July 1926, the Umpire concluded that "the applicant
belonged to a grade of workers members of which were not participating
in or financing or directly interested in the trade dispute. He may have an
indirect interest but not a direct interest."[67] The Umpire overturned the
Court of Referees and allowed benefit. Comparing this case to the cases
above, the only salient difference seems to be that Bithell and Dempsey
were union men, which presumably meant the oversman was not. In
another appeal, Henry Flint of Darlington contested the disallowance
of his benefit, arguing he had no interest in the 1926 strike outcome.
Flint claimed he was a construction worker, employed by a contractor
separate from the colliery at which he was working. In his appeal, Flint
insisted, "I have nothing whatever to do with this dispute between the
Miners and Owners. The work I was on is in no way involved in this
dispute. The Colliery Management having stopped the job until such
time as this dispute is settled [sic]. I might say I am prepared to return to
my work at any time." The Umpire agreed and allowed benefit, finding
that the work Flint did was indeed a "separate business."[68] Flint had no
control over his unemployment and therefore deserved benefit.

The language in these appeals clearly reflects contests over the work
imperative, and, in many ways, the appeals confirmed the association

between being on strike and being unwilling to work. A composi-
tor, for example, whose union supported the 1926 strike, refused
work that was "unsuitable" because the employer did not hold to
union standards. The Umpire, however, decided that suitable work
was available and disallowed benefit. Once the dispute was over, the
applicant "was offered re-engagement in his former position, one of
the conditions of re-engagement being that the employer's works
were, in future, to be regarded as an 'open house' which gave all
employees the option of being members of trade unions or otherwise." The man refused this condition, "because it was contrary to the
trade union rules." The man's union appealed to the Deputy Umpire,
"submitting on appeal that the employment of non-union men was
contrary to the National Agreement, reached on the termination of
the General Strike." The Deputy Umpire, however, upheld the Court
of Referees, arguing that "it has been held in many previous cases
that the employment of non-unionists does not make employment
unsuitable."[69] This model of the work imperative operated to close
down men's ability to challenge their working conditions legitimately
through union membership.

Indeed, many non-union men stressed their willingness to work in
ways that implied striking men were not in fact blameless. Frederick
Scrimshaw, a joiner and carpenter who fixed houses for a colliery,
insisted in his appeal that "I am not a trade unionist and so was not
called out on strike. Nor have I had any Desire to be away from my work
and Further Proof of this is that I have been looking all around for work
and have at last succeeded in getting work temperly [sic] at Southwell
until the strike is over." The Umpire accepted these arguments and
awarded benefit.[70] Arthur S. Hill, a wagon builder at Cannock, argued
that he and other wagon builders, "Being in no Trade Union we
are not drawing any Benefits, therefore, I claim we are entitled to
Unemployment Benefit on the ground of being suspended through no
fault of our own." An additional note of appeal added "Having paid
into the Unemployment scheme since I started and not having had
any benefits out before, I think it is unjust that we should be disallowed through no fault of our own." The Umpire agreed, finding that
wagon building was really its own business, not connected to the trade
dispute.[71] Hill's emphasis on his blamelessness and his history of work
in an insurable occupation spoke to his honest poverty. Applicants continued to draw on the language of blameless unemployment to assert
their deservedness, which challenged the legitimacy of strikers' claims
that they were willing to work.

Men combined stories of their good work histories with their distance from trade unions to claim deservedness. The engineer Thomas Carruthers, for example, appealed denial of benefit, insisting that

> I am entitled to unemployment benefit as I have been 6 years past September at the engineering trade. . . . I have been signing on [at the Employment Exchange] twice every week which means me walking a distance of 7½ miles every time I sign on and I am notified I receive no money of any description during this dispute. I am willing to work at any minute and have been all the time. This is the first time I have asked unemployment benefit. I am a member of no trade union.

The Umpire agreed with the claim that the applicant's employment was not connected to the trade dispute and awarded him benefit.[72] Carruthers argued that his regular contributions to the unemployment fund and his lack of a history of dependence should signify his deservedness.

Even men in non-mining unions used the willingness to work to compare themselves to miners: Henry Moore, a plater, had temporarily taken work as a boiler cleaner at a colliery because there was little available in his trade. The boiler makers' association spoke for him upon his appeal of benefit denial, arguing that their union was not involved directly in the miners' strike or the General Strike. They asserted, "Claimant's idleness is involuntary, it having been forced upon him by the Colliery Owners, and we therefore contend he is entitled to State Unemployment Benefit." The Umpire agreed.[73] Unemployment, in this case, resulted from an employer's rather than a worker's "choice"; the worker was, in effect, locked out.

To bolster their possibilities for benefit, some men who had been miners argued that they had left mining for other jobs. As with the military tribunals, which accused applicants of seeking an "umbrella" of marriage or munition work to protect them from military service, the Umpire's decisions reveal doubts about the authenticity of men's claims of taking on non-mining occupations. Arthur Houlston listed his employment as a road man, but the Umpire concluded, "The applicant has been employed as a miner for many years and I am not satisfied that he has become regularly engaged in some other occupation."[74] Similarly, the Deputy Umpire found in the case of a collier who had been a special constable during the General Strike that "I cannot agree that one month's service as a special constable during a temporary emergency, constitutes regular employment in some other occupation . . . so as to remove the disqualification imposed on account of the trade dispute."[75] The Umpire, in denying the appeal of Harry Newall of Oldham, stated, "During the stoppage of work the applicant . . . obtained a good deal of casual work on odd days as a labourer, but has no regular work," meaning he did not develop another occupation outside of mining and was therefore not eligible for benefit.[76] Being a miner or being associated with mining, as these cases suggest, trumped other identities during the strikes.

Back to work?

Questions about striking men's willingness to work were not necessarily solved at the conclusion of the strikes, as new issues regarding deservedness arose when the miners began returning to work in 1921 and 1926. Many collieries did not need all their miners back after the strikes. The Brierley Hill Trades Council bemoaned in August 1921 that, even though the strike ended in July, "many miners were still out of work locally. Some of the mines had not re-opened and others had not taken on all the former workmen."[77] The Trades Council Secretary pointed out that these men were "walking about without any means of subsistence except charity. They were getting nothing from the trade unions, and were still debarred from receiving unemployment benefit. Although they were anxious and ready to work, the pits had not been re-opened." He called on the council to help them figure out the situation with unemployment pay.[78] In December 1921, the fate of these men was still unclear. The *County Express* printed an official statement from the South Staffordshire, East Worcestershire, and Old Hill collieries

> that the dispute was at an end and advised the men to present themselves for work at the collieries where they had been formerly employed. Failing to get such employment the men were advised to sign on at once at the Employment Exchange for the purpose of securing Unemployment Benefit. Whether the men presenting themselves for work and not being "taken on" will be entitled to the unemployment pay is a point which is not quite clear, but in official quarters it is expected that the men will become entitled to the "dole."[79]

Here were miners willing to work but potentially being prevented from doing so, because the work that was available before the strike was no longer there. Yet because their initial "unemployment" was caused by the trade dispute, their eligibility for state assistance continued to be compromised.

The Umpire ruled on these issues in Case 4665 in November 1926, deciding that, if employers no longer needed all their previous employees once a stoppage of work was over, then those employees should be eligible for unemployment benefit: men could receive benefits "when the employers have got all the workers they require – that is, when work is no longer being stopped or hindered by the refusal of men to work on the employers' terms, or the refusal of employers to employ men on their terms."[80] Miners could not be denied benefit forever if their previous employers no longer needed them, even if a trade dispute had initially caused their unemployment.

Other points of contention involved mines damaged by the lack of maintenance during a strike, which had to be repaired before work could resume, and mines that were so damaged that owners decided to abandon them. Memos within the Ministry of Labour in the late fall of 1926 reveal the Ministry's desire to bring a test case before the Umpire regarding the permanent closure of mines and benefit to former employees of those mines. A 1921 Umpire's decision had found "that, although there might be a settlement of the dispute which brought about the stoppage of work, it did not follow that the disqualification ended when the dispute ended," if the mines had been destroyed by the dispute.[81] However, the memos also indicated that, in practice, "the Umpire has in each case found as a fact that the abandonment of the mine was due to causes independent of the dispute."[82] Apparently, the Umpire found it hard to sustain benefit disallowances once a man's workplace no longer existed.

The government tried to assure post-strike miners that they would be eligible for benefit, even though the Unemployment Insurance Acts were much more ambiguous. The Executive Committee of the Miners' Federation met with the Cabinet Coal Committee in mid-November 1926 to discuss issues surrounding the end of the strike. Because of several statements at this meeting, the Executive Committee understood that the government supported the committee's position that, as men were attempting to return to work, if their jobs were no longer available, the miners should be eligible for benefit. The Minister of Labour, Sir Arthur Steel-Maitland, for example, indicated that "when pits re-open which have been closed because of the stoppage, those who are then unemployed providing nothing else comes up, will be able to get unemployment insurance." Lord Birkenhead went even further, asserting "that no Court in this country" would treat miners any differently

from other workers with regard to benefit; "if I am wrong then the Government is committed by my opinion and matters can be put right."[83] These statements called into question the Umpire's ruling of 1921 that declared miners' benefit claims should be disallowed if their workplace was closed because of the strike.

Nevertheless, in mid-December 1926, Ministry of Labour records reveal that, not only were thousands of miners being refused benefit, but also the Ministry had sent a circular to local insurance officers reminding them of the 1921 Umpire's ruling "that where the stoppage itself was the cause of [the] non-resumption [of work] (e.g. owing to disrepair of pits above or below ground), the men were disqualified from benefit."[84] The Miners' Federation Executive Committee was, not surprisingly, confused because of the government's seeming "promise" that miners would be eligible.

When the Miners' Federation Executive Committee met again with the Minister of Labour on December 15, Steel-Maitland insisted that he had offered no promises. Herbert Smith, the Miners' Federation president, told the Minister that "the miners had been deluded by what was said by the Government on November 11th." Mr. Varley of the Miners' Federation pointed out that the miners were at a significant disadvantage because "in giving decisions the statutory authorities relied almost entirely on the words of pit managers, who were in many cases of a vindictive nature" toward the miners who had been on strike, adding that "while these cases were being argued the men were being half starved."[85] Miners had lost the ability to define what constituted a willingness to work.

For the next month, correspondence shows that Smith consistently sought to meet with the Prime Minister and the Cabinet Coal Committee. In making the miners' case, Smith stressed that "the men were ready for work and had offered to sign on."[86] Yet, in the case of trade disputes, differences surrounding definitions of the willingness to work meant that Smith's assertion had no purchase. All Smith's requests for additional meetings in December 1926 and January 1927 were denied, and it is unclear whether the issue was resolved in any way but the passage of time, which allowed ineligible miners to be eligible for benefit again.[87]

Conclusion

Strikes politicized the terms of honest poverty and brought into sharp relief contests over the meaning of the work imperative and the state's

relationships to family liability. According to the government, striking men gave up their claims both to poor law relief and national benefits when they refused to take available work to support their families. They no longer met their responsibilities as honest, poor citizens, and the state would not maintain them. The government, however, considered wives and children to be blameless in trade disputes and thus did not challenge their deservedness with regard to welfare. This was a big change from the nineteenth-century Poor Law, which tied women's welfare much more closely to the actions of their husbands. Merthyr Tydfil undercut husbands' family liability by differentiating between relief for a man and for his wife and children, challenging men's control of marriage. Yet authorities saw wives as victims rather than agents of industrial disputes and did not take into account wives' own views of the strikes. Women and children deserved the support of the state when their husbands "neglected" them. As we will see in the final chapter, the "protection" of women from the bad behavior of their husbands became an increasing concern of social policy.

Yet men on strike certainly did not understand themselves to be behaving badly; they clearly held to a different definition of honest poverty than did employers and national government officials. From the strikers' perspective, the willingness to work had to be measured by the conditions of employment. By striking, they indicated they were not willing to work at low wages or under conditions that they felt debased them. Their willingness to work was predicated on being offered a "man's work." Poor law Boards of Guardians in the 1920s sometimes shored up this alternative definition: in giving relief to men on strike, they supported striking men's claims that the wages on offer were not sufficient to maintain the breadwinner and his family. The Umpire was less likely to be convinced by this argument, seeing men as strikers first and as unemployed second.

Neither the 1921 nor the 1926 strike ended well for the miners. Their attempts to use the terms of honest poverty to achieve a better standard of living and improved working conditions were ineffective. While the work imperative and family liability were not the only concepts framing understandings of the strikes, they were central to both sides' justifications of their positions. In the end, mine owners and government authorities succeeded in labeling strikers as men unwilling to work and therefore as men neglecting their families. The lesson working men might have taken away was that unions could hurt rather than help their citizenship claims by marking them as undeserving of state welfare, outside the bounds of honest poverty.

Part III
Honest Poverty and the Intimacies of Policy

8

"Younger men are given the preference": Older Men's Welfare and Intergenerational Responsibilities

Maurice Joyce came before the Umpire in 1925 to appeal the decision to deny his unemployment benefit on the grounds he was not genuinely seeking work. Joyce, "an old man," was a union cooper. The Court of Referees had refused his benefit, because they thought he should have been looking for a different occupation, since he was no longer physically able to handle the tasks of a cooper. Joyce was appealing the decision that he was too weak or old to perform his usual duties. He stressed, "I am quite fit to carry on with my usual occupation as a cooper," insisting that it was not his physical ability but the lack of available work that prevented him from obtaining employment. The Umpire, however, upheld denial of benefit, finding that Joyce's "chance of obtaining work [as a cooper] is remote while there are a number of younger men unemployed. The work calls for a good deal of physical exertion and younger men are given the preference." The Umpire disallowed Joyce's benefit, deciding that Joyce was "capable of work and should try to get some work suitable for a man of his age."[1]

Men like Maurice Joyce fit awkwardly into the honest poverty work-welfare system: often they were willing to work, but their working lives had changed as a result of age and infirmities. As they aged, many men saw their role relative to family welfare shift; no longer bearing the burden of liability for others, older men became objects of family liability, with sons expected to become accountable for elderly parents' economic needs. Some older men, like Joyce, pushed back against changing perceptions of their physical capacities, suggesting their status as workers was incredibly important to them or that they feared having their working independence challenged. Even receiving unemployment benefit connected these men to employment, because benefit signaled the hope of eventual re-employment. Older men who were no longer working continued to identify themselves with their former occupations – as did the welfare authorities who recorded their applications for assistance. However, many older men could not prove a willingness to work through employment itself. Rather, a life history of adherence to the work imperative and family maintenance spoke to older men's deservedness.

Expectations of intergenerational liability

Historically, the aged poor faced particular vulnerabilities as many became increasingly unable to work due to bodily infirmities and decreasing productivity in tight labor markets.[2] As historian Pat Thane, among others, has demonstrated, older people "package[ed] together survival from a variety of sources,"[3] including co-residence, sick clubs, poor law relief, charitable resources, and their own income and that of their wider families. From January 1909, they were also eligible for old age pensions (OAPs). Welfare authorities viewed contributions from adult children as the primary form of maintenance for the aged poor. Indeed, Richard Wall stresses in a study of intergenerational relationships, that only recently "it has become unusual for elderly persons to be supported both by a state pension and the earning of a younger adult."[4] In the late nineteenth and early twentieth centuries, those administering welfare regarded state assistance for the elderly as supplemental. If adult children could care for their parents, the state had an interest in finding them.

Poor law officials paid a great deal of attention to finding the children of the elderly poor. The "crusade against outrelief" of the early 1870s, among other things, led poor law authorities to be much more exacting in their attempts to enforce the Poor Law's "liable relatives clause," which had originated in the Elizabethan statutes.[5] This clause mandated that, in the unfortunate circumstances of intergenerational neglect, "fines, distress warrants, or imprisonment act as substitutes for gratitude and love,"[6] in effect legally compelling relatives to take care of each other. The enforcement of adult children's maintenance of their parents varied over time and in different regions, but the last third of the nineteenth century saw a national effort to police it rigorously.[7]

In order to contain their growing expenses, poor law authorities aggressively sought to identify relatives they could hold responsible for maintaining family members. Thane has pointed out that "the existence of liable relatives suspected of being able to provide support often determined whether outdoor relief was given and how much. . . . It was taken for granted that any older paupers would live with relatives who could not afford wholly to support them, and rates of relief were fixed with this expectation in mind."[8] M.A. Crowther reminds us, however, that "families were not responsible for their adult, able-bodied members, and could not be brought to law for their maintenance."[9] Yet, as I will show in the following chapter, this changed in the late nineteenth century: able-bodied wives could bring their husbands to court to demand maintenance orders, meaning that maintenance was not gender neutral. Neither was provision for elderly parents: since welfare administrators did not normally classify women as economically independent, they did not see daughters as having family liability under most circumstances.

The Poor Law was a major source of support for the elderly poor.[10] The records of poor law applications in my Dataset 1 (DS1) reveal that the percentage of applicants aged 60 and older (where age was recorded) steadily increased in the late nineteenth and early twentieth centuries, jumping from 43 per cent in 1871 to 70 per cent in 1901.[11] This increase can be read as a sign of the increasing vulnerability of the aged in the declining economy of the Black Country and the reluctance of younger people to apply to the stigmatized Poor Law through the usual channels. The increase in elderly paupers also reflects some of the efforts by poor law authorities to create less harsh conditions for the aged poor, such as allowing couples to be together in the workhouse.[12] The numbers of older paupers dropped precipitously after OAPs for those 70 and older became available, with DS1 applicants aged 70 and above falling from 47 per cent in 1901 to only four per cent in 1911 (Figure 8.1). Of the less representative 221 case records in my Dataset 2 (DS2) poor law applications, 69 (31 per cent) were from applicants aged 60 and older, and 27 (12 per cent) were from applicants aged 70 and older.[13]

The demographic portrait of elderly applicants highlights the interrelationships among gender, marital status, and welfare that I have underscored in other contexts in this study. In DS1 where marital status was noted, 66 per cent of the elderly applicants were listed as widowed, but the large majority of the elderly widowed were women: 78 per cent. Married people made up 30 per cent of the elderly, with a striking 96 per cent of these being male applicants. Only 78 of the 2,178 elderly applicants with marital status recorded were single, with almost two thirds of them being women. These figures for the elderly applicants exaggerate the overall relationship of gender to marital status in the dataset: men applied to the poor law authorities as parts of couples, while women came single or widowed.

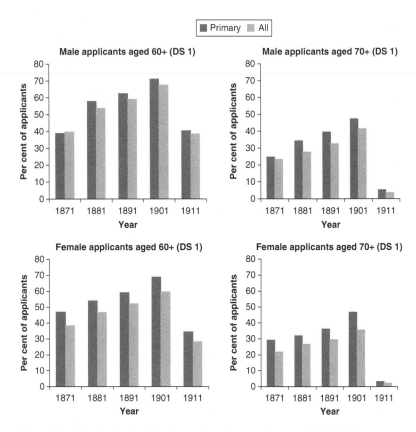

Figure 8.1 Elderly Stourbridge Union Poor Law applicants, 1871–1911

With the increasing percentage of elderly relief recipients came an increasing interest among poor law officials to compel liable relatives to contribute a share of maintenance. DS1 contains 473 records of primary applicants aged 60 and older that provide information about adult children contributing to their parents' support; 257 of these were for parents 70 and older. In 1871 the Stourbridge Union relieving officers responsible for recording applicants' petitions rarely filled in names under the column to register "Observations and Names of Relations Liable by Law to Relieve the Applicant." With the exception of the 1881 records (for which I only have data from the parish of Kingswinford, where the relieving officer seemingly did not record liable relatives), DS1 shows a large increase in children contributing to elderly parents over time, until the OAP system was in operation (Table 8.1). While

Table 8.1 Elderly applicants with children contributing, 1871–1911

Gender	Age	1871	1881	1891	1901	1911	All Years
Female	60–69	14	8	34	50	37	27
	70 or older	11	1	25	56	10	21
Female 60 or older		12	4	28	54	35	23
Male	60–69	9	3	22	43	30	19
	70 or older	13	1	27	55	8	20
Male 60 or older		11	2	25	51	27	20
Male & female 60–69		12	6	29	47	34	23
Male & female 60 or older		12	3	27	53	31	22
Male & female 70 or older		12	1	26	56	9	20

Sources: My Dataset 1, from the Application and Report Books for the Stourbridge Union, held at the Staffordshire Record Office: from the Halesowen District, D585/1/5/27, D585/1/5/29, D585/1/5/32, and D585/1/5/35; from the Stourbridge District, D585/1/5/47 and D585/1/5/50; and from the Kingswinford District, D585/1/5/68, D585/1/5/70, D585/1/5/73, and D585/1/5/76.

there is no systematic way to break the DS2 figures down chronologically because of the small number of records, the figures suggest the continuing significance of assistance from liable children, although that assistance diminished sharply from the high point at the turn of the century before OAP.

According to DS1, most elderly petitioners applied to the Poor Law half-yearly and were awarded their relief pensions for 26 or 27 weeks. Guardians and relieving officers only required more frequent applications from aged petitioners whose histories relative to honest poverty they viewed as questionable, whereas younger applicants had many more repeated interactions with the poor law authorities and received much more in-kind aid. Relieving officers and guardians granted elderly Black Country poor law petitioners monetary pensions more than any other type of relief, although they also provided medical aid, burial expenses for spouses, food, and linen. Some of the applicants also benefited from money from clubs or lodgers and, as expressed in the 1911 records, from OAP.

The amounts the aged poor received from the Boards of Guardians, however, could not have sustained them, and, even with children contributing, older people did not have much to live on. From 1871 to 1891, pensions of one shilling or one shilling sixpence were common for the aged, and these small amounts still appear through 1911. In fact, 75 per cent of all awards to elderly applicants whose adult children also contributed were two shillings or less a week, and only six per cent received four shillings or more. In DS2, cash awards ranged between two shillings and six shillings a week for applicants with children contributing. Most of the support given by children to their older parents came in cash, rent payment, and housing provision. The records show little evidence of other types of family contribution. While amounts of poor law relief varied little over the period for which I have data, DS1 shows that contributions from children ranged from sixpence a week to as much as 16 shillings a week, although that higher amount was rare. DS2 reveals similar contributions from children, ranging from one shilling a week to help defray the cost of indoor relief to 12 shillings a week, even into the 1920s. Nevertheless, the combination of support from children and the Poor Law would still have amounted to very little.

The records suggest that poor law officials generally viewed assistance from liable adult children as a sign of an applicant's respectability that enhanced a petition for relief.[14] In the parish of Cakemore in 1891, John H. and his wife Elizabeth, both 75 and infirm, had several sons in their 40s assisting them, yet they received a pension of three shillings weekly poor law relief.[15] The 58-year-old Edward L. of Kingswinford applied in June 1911, noting that his wife had left him. His case indicates that one married son "helps his parents considerably." Edward was granted two shillings a week for 16 weeks.[16] Some cases are more ambiguous. Edward S., for example, applied with his wife for assistance in May 1891. He was 70 years old and defined as not able, because he suffered from rheumatism. Edward was initially granted four shillings a week but only for a four-week period. He applied again when his award ran out, but the relieving officer ascertained that he was "now supported by his sons" and denied relief. Edward returned in September, applying for a renewal of relief. On his first application, he was denied; on September 17, after being "under observation," the relieving officer granted assistance in kind. A week later, on further application, he was awarded three shillings for two weeks as well as assistance in kind. It is unclear if his sons continued to contribute.[17]

The liability of sons

Just as marriage "protected" some men from serving in the military, it could also protect them from being liable for financial contributions to their elderly parents, especially if they had unmarried brothers. Authorities pressured single sons into assisting parents more often than their married brothers and expected married sons without children to help more often than those with children. Because married men already had liability for their wives and children, welfare providers assigned unmarried sons primary liability for dependent parents. As Pat Thane has stated, "Obligations downwards to children did come before those upwards to parents."[18] An unmarried son was expected to express his masculine status by financially maintaining his parents, since he had no wife or children for whom to fulfill family responsibilities.

Poor law applications demonstrate this hierarchy of maintenance in which wives and children came before parents in expectations of masculine responsibility: officials seemingly did not often require married sons with children to support their elderly fathers and mothers. The 92-year-old widower James A. of Cradley had five sons, all of them nailmakers with families, which apparently relieved them of liability on James's application in 1891.[19] Also from Cradley and applying in 1891, Frederick F., a 77-year-old widower, had two sons, one a 47-year-old chainmaker with six children and another aged 36 with eight children. The Board of Guardians awarded Frederick two shillings for 27 weeks, not asking for contributions from his married sons.[20] Lucy P., a 60-year-old nearly-blind widow from Brettell Lane, applied in March 1911. The relieving officer's notes indicate that Lucy had one unemployed married son who could not contribute as he had to support a child. Lucy received two shillings for 26 weeks.[21]

Even though authorities tracked down these married sons, they did not pressure them to contribute to their parents' maintenance. In none of these cases does the record make clear whether the applicants had any daughters, suggesting that poor law authorities did not conceptualize daughters as liable relatives, a point to which I will return. However, the structure of the documents and the information the relieving officers provided show clearly that married sons with children were generally not obligated to support their parents if they already had a hard time maintaining their families of marriage. Poor law officials did not exempt married sons from parental liability, but they were much more interested in assuring married men could care for their wives and children.

On the other hand, poor law authorities definitely expected unmarried sons to help their elderly parents. The case of Elizabeth T., for example, reveals the ways having a non-contributing, unmarried son could shape a less-than-desirable welfare outcome. Elizabeth, a 71-year-old widow from Stourbridge, applied for relief in April 1871. Her application indicates that she was a non-able-bodied charwoman suffering from general debility. Her age and infirmity should have made her a likely candidate for a pension. Yet the record reveals that Elizabeth had an unmarried son, James, whom the relieving officer believed "ought to do a little." Assuming the son's ability to provide for his elderly mother limited the type of assistance given to Elizabeth. Instead of providing monetary relief to be used as Elizabeth needed on her own terms, the relieving officer offered the workhouse, perhaps as a way of coercing her son into contributing.[22] Alternatively, Elizabeth might simply have been unable to care for herself, so the workhouse provided the only option if she could not afford to pay for home nursing. James still would have been expected to contribute for his mother's maintenance in the workhouse.

When poor law authorities were unable to convince sons to support their parents, their cases often played out in front of the magistrates' courts. Boards of Guardians could use the courts to compel sons to contribute to their parents' welfare or to insist that sons repay funds the boards had already expended on elderly parents. In February 1876, for example, the *Dudley Herald* reported on "A Son Summoned for the Support of His Father." Thomas Arnold's father was receiving two shillings a week outrelief, and Thomas had been summoned to contribute this same amount, essentially repaying the Board of Guardians. The *Herald* described Thomas as a glass blower who earned "about 23s a week, and was a single man." This flagging of marital status was the key to the story, since Thomas complained that he was supposed to contribute while his brothers were not. One of the magistrates stated definitively that "the defendant's brothers were all married and had families, therefore it was impossible for them to bear any share of their father's maintenance." Thomas was ordered to pay the two shillings a week.[23]

Single and married brothers could clearly expect different outcomes when magistrates decided these cases. At Brierley Hill Police Court in September 1906, for example, the Stourbridge Board of Guardians summoned two brothers from Kingswinford, demanding support for their father, who was receiving relief. The relieving officer indicated that three other brothers already contributed "to the support of the old man," and if the two before the court would help out, the board would raise the father's allowance from two to three shillings a week.[24] When sons did contribute, it seems to have helped their parents' claims for aid, emphasizing the mixed nature of the welfare economy. The brothers, however, "refused to contribute anything." The presiding magistrate castigated the brothers, saying "it was a great pity these sons should have to be summoned in order to give support to their aged father. They ought not to have allowed him to have gone on the rates for support." The court ordered the unmarried brother to pay one shilling a week and the married brother sixpence, also making the men responsible for court costs.[25] Older parents themselves tried to use the Poor Law and the courts to force their sons to help financially. William B. and his wife Elizabeth, both in their sixties, applied to the Stourbridge relieving officer in April 1915. They were behind in their rent and had debts amounting to about two pounds. While they had nine children of working years, their appearance before the poor law authorities in 1915 aimed to compel their son, James, a single 23-year-old who had refused to assist them, to contribute to their support. The outcome is unclear, but perhaps James was summoned before the magistrates.[26] Clearly the issue of intergenerational family liability could place parents and their adult children in an antagonistic relationship. In 1908, the Stourbridge Board of Guardians was clearly so fed up with the negligence of liable relatives that it formed a Collection of Contributions from Relatives Committee, Guardian Warr stating that "the responsibility of relatives to contribute should be brought home to them."[27]

When officials pursued married sons to help their parents, men pointed to the difficulties they encountered from the dual liability for parents as well as wives and children. In December 1929, John Thomas Dudley, who was brought up on arrears to the Board of Guardians for support of his father, told the court that the relieving officer "can pick up my wages to-night, if he will keep my wife and children," suggesting that he saw a tradeoff between providing for his father or providing for his wife and children. The relieving officer indicated that, because Dudley had six children, the maintenance payment for his father was only one shilling and sixpence a week. The magistrates' clerk "pressed" Dudley to "make some offer," and Dudley said he would pay two shillings and sixpence a week until he covered the arrears.[28] Apparently Dudley was the only son and did not have unmarried brothers on whom the Board of Guardians could rely.

The maintenance of parents could bring wives and husbands together to protect their own family resources. When married men were held liable for their parents, wives frequently testified to their husbands' financial difficulties, illnesses in the family, or other circumstances that they claimed challenged their husbands' ability to contribute outside the marital household. In July 1879, for example, the Stourbridge Board of Guardians' minutes show that "the wife of Joseph Woodhall attended before the Board and applied for a reduction of the amount of 1/6 which her husband has to contribute to the support of his father," but the board refused the request.[29] The Dudley board brought Charles Cooper before the magistrates in September 1908, demanding support of his 67-year-old father Isaac, who was in the workhouse. Cooper was a pikeman at a pit, and the relieving officer indicated that he earned the decent sum of one pound, 12 shillings, and ten pence a week. Attempting to show hardship, Cooper's wife testified that "her husband had been out of work for six months." The magistrates, however, argued, "if that were the case defendant could have appeared before the Board of Guardians to ask for leniency." Cooper was ordered to pay one shilling a week to maintain his father in the workhouse.[30]

Liable relatives pushed back against the Poor Law's expectation that they care for elderly parents. We see this clearly with Ann H., an 84-year-old widow suffering from "senility and dry cancer of the face," when her case was created in April 1918. The application suggests that Ann had been in the workhouse and had been removed by one of her daughters, who "took her to Wolverhampton Station then put her in a cab" to go to a sister's house. Ann spent one night with the sister, who "then brought her back to the workhouse." Without an order for admission, Ann was refused entrance to the workhouse and had to see the relieving officer, who commented, "It appears that none of the family want the old woman. No alternative but to admit her at least pending interviewing the available portion of the family as to what they intend to do." A relieving officer from West Bromwich Union was sent to investigate the circumstances of Ann's sons but "had a great deal of trouble to obtain the information; the wives, whom he interviewed in both cases being very defiant. The Officer had to make three journeys to one of the homes before he could see anyone." The case indicates that at least one son did wind up contributing to Ann's upkeep in the workhouse, but he appealed to have his payment reduced. Ann H. died in the workhouse in August 1919.[31]

Unemployment insurance complicated the measurements by which sons were held accountable for their elderly parents. Old age pensions were already in place when the 1911 Unemployment Insurance Act made no provision for dependants. In November 1921, the government introduced the Unemployed Dependants (Temporary Provision) Act, which required an additional contribution from the insured person and allowed five shillings for dependent spouses and one shilling for each dependent child. These provisions were made permanent in 1922, but they did not include dependent parents.[32] The Dudley Trades Council submitted a letter to the Minister of Labour in early 1922 complaining that the Act created a particular hardship for single men: "When a single man is the main stay of the home, and his mother is dependent on him, he is unable to claim the dependent's allowance under the Unemployed Dependants (Temporary Provision) Act. We feel sure that when you consider the great hardship this entails, in quite a number of cases, that you will recommend the Government to amend the Regulations, and make it possible, where cases of hardship can be proved," for single men to receive extra benefit for their parents. The Minister of Labour responded that, "in view of financial considerations, it was found impracticable to extend the scope of the Act so as to include dependants other than those to which the Act at present relates."[33] While the council at the local level saw clearly the impact of parental liability on single sons, the national government did not acknowledge it was a problem deserving attention. Single men were both the least likely to receive state assistance on their own and the most likely to be targeted by the state as the primary financial contributors to elderly parents.

The invisibility of daughters

Officials could have reinterpreted the masculine nature of family liability by making daughters as well as sons responsible for their parents' welfare. Both poor law records and newspaper reporting on the magistrates' courts demonstrate, however, that women did not have the same liability for their parents that men did. Although daughters provided assistance to their parents in money, in kind, and in care, they were not held accountable for this assistance. Sons, and particularly unmarried sons, had the burden of supporting their parents, while daughters' contributions often went unrecorded. Additionally, nowhere did I find cases of brothers arguing that their sisters should be financially liable for their parents. The absence of women in the records both confirms assumptions about men's family liability and renders invisible the non-monetary support and domestic work that women historically have provided, such as cooking meals, doing laundry, and cleaning house.[34] As historians have shown in so many other contexts, women's household and caring work has often not been counted as work.[35] Adult female children, older mothers, and mothers-in-law do not appear nearly as frequently in DS1 as male relatives as potential sources of support, and I did not find a single instance of a daughter summoned to the magistrates' court for parental liability.

The poor law archives make it very difficult to situate adult daughters as members of family economic units – adult being defined by the Poor Law as aged 16 and over. Edward Higgs and others have demonstrated the tendency of nineteenth-century recordkeeping to undercount women's economic activities because of assumptions about male bread-winning and female dependency.[36] The Stourbridge Union application and report books illustrate this undercounting, as the relieving officers unsystematically recorded the existence of adult daughters unless those daughters were directly contributing to parental maintenance. Even then, however, relieving officers describe sons' circumstances in much more detail. For example, the relieving officer noted upon the application of Edward R. and his wife Mary Ann, both in their late 70s, that they had a 51-year-old son with three children, who was a tailor in Yorkshire; another son, a 47-year-old pikeman with two children, who gave his parents two shillings a week; and a 37-year-old son, a coal miner with five children. The record also simply indicates that two daughters paid the applicants' rent of three shillings sixpence.[37] In this case, adult daughters directly contributed to maintaining their parents, but we learn nothing of the women's ages, occupations, or marital statuses, although I presume they were single or widowed.

While authorities expected daughters to look after their parents, little evidence suggests they pressured daughters to provide financially. More than 2,700 adult children are identified in DS1, and, accepting the data at face value, sons far outnumbered daughters in Stourbridge Union families at a time when women outnumbered men in the English population.[38] Of the adult children listed as potentially liable to contribute, 86 per cent (where gender is clear) were sons: 892 sons to 142 daughters. The absence of daughters is more striking in some parishes than in others. The first day of the quarter beginning March 27, 1891, in the parish of Kingswinford, the relieving officer recorded 267 adult sons as potential sources of assistance and only one adult daughter.[39] Taking one example, Sarah N.'s 1891 poor law application registers only her son, a laborer with four children.[40] The Census of 1881, however, shows that, in addition to her son, Sarah had three daughters, who in 1891 would have been in their mid- to late 20s and able to contribute to her maintenance.[41]

Almost uniformly, the records of the period show officials looking to sons as the primary source of income for elderly parents and contribute to a picture of women as non-economic actors. The Stourbridge Board of Guardians minutes of 1891 mention seven cases where adult children were summoned to pay for the support of parents receiving outdoor relief or being maintained in the workhouse; all were sons.[42] Similarly, the 1911 book of the Stourbridge Union House Committee, which was in charge of workhouse affairs, only refers to sons who needed to be tracked down to support parents in the workhouse. The language seems clear: on February 24, "Mr. Thompson [a relieving officer] was directed to report as to the ability of the sons of Mrs. [T.] to contribute towards her maintenance"; on June 30, it was "recommended that the sons of John [A.] be ordered to contribute to his maintenance in workhouse"; on October 6, "Stephen [E.] was ordered to leave the House with a view to getting his sons to find him a home"; and on December 15, "Mr. Woodall [a relieving officer] was directed to report as to the ability of the son of Jane [D.] to contribute towards her maintenance."[43] Of course it is possible that the children of these workhouse inmates were all male, but the records are consistent with the construction of family liability as a man's responsibility.

The one place where daughters appear to have predominated as liable relatives was in providing homes for their elderly parents. Here we have an overt case of the ways gendered assumptions about family liability shaped the records. Overall, the relieving officers' books of DS1 show 201 relatives "finding homes" for elderly applicants.[44] Of these, 47 were sons-in-law, who presumably were married to the applicants' daughters. The application books show Ann C., a 74-year-old widow, for example, living with her son-in-law. The relieving officer also recorded that Ann had a son, a nailmaker with bad health. Nowhere does the record show the existence of her daughters.[45] These are difficult numbers to assess precisely. The application and report books generally do not include the names of sons-in-law, so finding corresponding household structures in the census records is difficult. A general assessment of the 1881 census, however, confirms my assumption that, when parents lived with married daughters, they were registered as in-laws – for example, as mothers-in-law rather than mothers. In these cases, co-residential parents had their primary relationships defined in terms of a daughter's husband, rather than the daughter herself. Poor law authorities assigned sons-in-law this responsibility because the home "belonged" to the husband. Relieving officers and Boards of Guardians did not see married daughters as workers or earners and thus did not conceptualize them as liable for their parents' welfare.

Single adult daughters, by contrast, do appear in the records of DS1 as potential providers, although not as frequently as adult sons. When an unmarried daughter was earning wages, the relieving officer registered her income in the application and sometimes her occupation as well. For example, Mary Ann G., a 53-year-old widow with three dependent children in 1901, had a daughter considered liable to contribute. She was a single, 19-year-old brickyard hand who lived with her mother and contributed six shillings weekly. Mary Ann had three sons as well, two of whom were clearly married with children and therefore seemingly less liable than the unmarried daughter.[46] In DS2, nine daughters and 23 sons were listed as assisting their parents. Of the nine daughters, five contributed in money or rent payment, while the other four either lived with the elderly parent (all mothers) or "looked after" her. The five sons all contributed in money or rent.

In 1920, women became eligible for unemployment insurance as workers, rather than as dependants of men, meaning that authorities recognized them as independent earners. Historically, the Poor Law's interest in women as workers tended to be punitive, a means to push them off relief. As Lynn Hollen Lees and Pat Thane, among others, have shown, part of the crusade against outrelief in the 1870s included a new emphasis on single women's "duty to work."[47] This, however, apparently did not translate into like treatment with regard to parental liability. While single women might have been expected to support themselves independently of state assistance, poor law officials still targeted wage-earning men to maintain families. This expectation had material as well as ideological backing, for usually women's wages could barely sustain the women themselves, let alone families. Of the women between the ages of 16 and 55 in DS1 whose wages were recorded in the application and report books,[48] only five per cent earned more than seven shillings a week. The median weekly wage was four shillings, with 26 per cent getting two shillings or less a week, incredibly meager earnings across the period.

Interestingly, it is much easier to identify in the application and report books daughters whom the Poor Law classified as dependants, meaning under the age of 16. An applicant for relief was required to name all dependants, and when a dependent daughter was employed, relieving officers recorded her earnings and occupation as contributing to the family economy. For example, 58-year-old Joseph D. and his wife Maria had two children, a 17-year-old son working as a collier and earning four shillings a week as well as a 13-year-old daughter earning one shilling sixpence as a nurse.[49] Eliza Y., a 59-year-old domestic, applied in July 1901. Her two adult sons – one a soldier in South Africa, the other a chainmaker with eight children – were unable to contribute to her maintenance. A 14-year-old daughter, however, was recorded as earning seven shillings a week as a blower for a chainmaker.[50] Here we have the details that are often missing for adult daughters. Thus gender is seemingly less salient in examining the work histories and contributions of children under 16, as the earnings of both sons and daughters were expected to be part of wider family survival strategies.[51] These were children considered dependent on their parents, and yet dependent daughters were actually more "liable" to help their parents before they reached "independence."

The small size and random nature of the DS2 collection means that the figures regarding liable relatives do not reveal clear patterns. Read qualitatively, however, the material suggests authorities increasingly saw daughters, and especially unmarried daughters, as potential liable relatives for their parents. Joseph T.'s application in 1924 included a 39-year-old widowed daughter among five children listed as liable relatives.[52] Also in 1924, Thomas G., an 82-year-old farm laborer, applied to be admitted to the workhouse after being injured by a horse. This "very respectable person" had four daughters and one son listed as liable relatives. The information about the son, as is the case throughout the application records, focuses on occupation and earnings; the information about the daughters, however, also includes the occupational and earning statuses of their husbands, suggesting again that sons-in-law rather than daughters were regarded as more directly liable for their elderly in-laws.[53] Still, as women became identified as workers with eligibility for unemployment insurance, it makes sense that they would also be considered as liable relatives by authorities looking to lessen their welfare burden.

Old age pensions

The expectation that sons and, to a much lesser extent, daughters, would assist their elderly parents stayed constant even when the state took responsibility for OAPs with the 1908 Old Age Pensions Act. The institution of OAPs explicitly acknowledged that, once they reached a certain age, women and men alike entered a stage of dependency and were no longer expected to work. While it fit within the gender norms of honest poverty for elderly women to need assistance, for elderly men the lines were not as clear. For an older man to become a deserving dependant, welfare authorities had to recognize that he was no longer able to work; his deservedness would no longer be measured by the willingness to work or his ability to provide for a family. The very fact that a man could receive assistance without proving a willingness to work constituted a major life change that, as is clear from the case of Maurice Joyce with which this chapter opened, was not always welcomed.

The Poor Law in practice had long provided elderly men and women with relief designed not to stigmatize them, as the half-yearly outrelief pensions awarded by the Stourbridge authorities suggest. The Local Government Board more officially acknowledged the deservedness of the aged poor from the 1890s, issuing circulars in 1896 and 1900 that approved outdoor relief for the "'worthy aged poor'" to address in a non-deterrent way relief to men and women who could no longer work to support themselves.[54] The poor law records show, however, that, before OAPs were instituted in 1908, there was no obvious age at which a man became "old," meaning that he was no longer required to work or maintain family. On October 24, 1873, for example, the Stourbridge Board of Guardians' minutes referred to William M., who "although 94 years of age[,] is able and will work." The clerk recorded that William survived on a combination of his own earnings of about two shillings a week, poor law relief of two shillings a week, and sixpence a week "from a Lady." The minutes further indicate that William's only son "is 50 years old and has a wife and 4 children and is himself suffering from phthisis, and has only worked 1 week in the last 5 weeks and at present is under medical treatment and would be compelled to seek relief for himself but for his own children."[55] In this case, the elderly father was more "able" to work than his son.

The poor law confusion regarding the role of age in determining working ability and relief is clear in the case of Joseph H. of Brierley Hill, who was receiving outdoor relief from the Stourbridge Board of Guardians in 1902. Mr. Rollinson, a guardian from the Kingswinford district, indicated that Joseph should have been getting "sick benefit from the Foresters Lodge on account of illness." The Foresters were a mutual benefit society meant to assist members when they were unable to work because of illness. Rollinson, however, complained that "the doctor certif[ied] that the man was suffering from 'old age' [so] the Foresters Lodge declined to give sick pay." A designation of "old age" disconnected Joseph from his working life in a way that illness would not have and meant that the Foresters were no longer obligated to offer sick pay. After discussion, the board decided there was nothing they could do.[56]

Age and work histories also came together in the poor law applications of widowed and single women, such as 65-year-old Elizabeth T., whose application for relief in 1912 indicated that she "worked very hard when she was able."[57] The 1912 application of the unmarried 67-year-old Mary M. noted that she "can do very little work now."[58] Emily H. applied for relief in 1923. She was a 64-year-old widow who usually worked at the Gibbons Tile Works. She turned to the Poor Law when illness kept her from her employment, but "she is able to manage when at work."[59] These examples reaffirm that women and welfare authorities expected women without husbands to be responsible for their own maintenance, but this was different from seeing single and widowed women as breadwinners or liable relatives.

Just as it was questioning the utility of the Poor Law to assist unemployed men, by the end of the nineteenth century, the national government was realizing the limits of existing structures to assist the elderly. The Royal Commission on the Aged Poor, which reported in 1895, and the Select Committee on the Deserving Aged Poor, which reported in 1899, both endorsed some type of OAP.[60] A bill put forward in 1901 recommended that pensions be situated under the Poor Law, with Boards of Guardians in charge of pension determinations. The early bills proposed that a person in receipt of poor law relief would be disqualified from national pensions and stressed that pension eligibility be restricted to men and women who had not relied on poor law funds (with the exception of medical relief) for 15 or 20 years before applying for a pension. Also, from the outset, any applicant who had not "endeavored to the best of his ability, by his industry or by the exercise of reasonable providence, to make provision for himself and those immediately dependent on him" would be "struck" off the list of eligible applicants.[61] Although the bills framed OAPs as gender-neutral benefits, applicable to men and women, they consistently constructed deservedness around the terms of honest poverty, based on a male applicant.

The OAP bills explicitly attempted to address the problem of disenfranchisement associated with the Poor Law. Taking the recommendations of the 1899 Select Committee on the Aged Deserving Poor, a memorandum prefacing each bill articulated that, even though poor law authorities would administer OAPs, receipt of a pension "shall not involve any electoral disability, nor convey the reproach of pauperism."[62] Interestingly, while not losing the national franchise, an old age pensioner would be excluded from voting locally for poor law guardians, presumably because there might be a conflict of interest.[63]

The distancing of pensions from the Poor Law increased even further in 1906, with an Old Age Pensions Bill that proposed a pensions committee for every poor law union. Committee membership would be determined partially by the national treasury rather than the local constituency, moving OAPs to some degree under national control.[64] These gradual changes over the first decade of the twentieth century reflected the government's increasing realization that it needed to position old age pensioners outside the poor law framework as honest, deserving citizens. The requirement that an applicant demonstrate a history of solid employment and support of dependants remained throughout, in effect constituting the "pensioner" as an honest poor man in a rhetorical move very similar to the one simultaneously shaping "unemployment." The recognition that a man could not be expected to work forever was finally codified with the Old Age Pensions Act that received royal assent on August 1, 1908, and came into operation in January 1909.[65] The parliamentary debates surrounding the Act put honest poverty at the center of the new legislation.[66]

The debates over the pensions bill reveal a significant shift in attitude toward outdoor relief since the crusade against outrelief of the 1870s. Several Members of Parliament (MPs) expressed their discomfort with proposed relationships between OAPs and the Poor Law, worrying that "deserving" people who had received outdoor relief would be excluded, while "undeserving" people who had been turned away from the Poor Law would qualify. If the outdoor deserving poor were excluded, MPs argued, then people would starve themselves avoiding the Poor Law to meet the requirements for a pension, and Boards of Guardians would have an incentive to administer relief harshly to older people by urging them to wait for assistance until they were eligible for an OAP.[67] It made no sense to exclude outdoor paupers when the goal of the bill was "to relieve the poorest of the poor, and the poorest of the poor outside the poorhouse were those in receipt of outdoor relief."[68] Hugh Law of Donegal asserted that the "distinction between paupers and other poor people was entirely unreal. In many country districts there were numerous people who received outdoor relief from time to time, but who for the greater part of their lives were ratepayers."[69] According to Sir George White of Norfolk, "outdoor paupers . . . covered a large number of the most deserving poor."[70] For these MPs and others, using the Poor Law was not an adequate indicator that someone was dishonest.

Because of this kind of confusion, some MPs asserted the need to separate OAPs from the Poor Law completely. Ramsay MacDonald, for example, pointed out that it was precisely the taint associated with the Poor Law that led the Labour Party to argue in favor of OAPs: pensions were meant to solve the problem that old people who "apply for pauper relief . . . lost their independence and their civic rights."[71] The Conservative Edward Goulding of Worcestershire argued that "outdoor relief was largely given to those who had endeavoured to live thrifty lives," placing them in the "category of deserving citizens."[72] These points reflect an important development from the 1870s and 1880s, when no one really suggested that pauperism could coexist with citizenship; rather, in the earlier period, solutions to the citizenship issue aimed to keep men off poor law relief entirely. In the OAP debates, we see a recognition that the Poor Law could be a regular part of people's survival strategies, that outdoor relief did not necessarily mark a recipient as undeserving, and that structural unemployment forced government officials to make these connections. As Sir Walter Foster of Derbyshire pointed out, since a pension bill of 1892, "there had been a great change of opinion. A feeling had grown up that poor law relief should under certain conditions not be a barrier to the receipt of a pension."[73] Sir Francis Channing went so far as to conceptualize the OAP as a means for poor law relief recipients to "[re-attain] the citizenship with which they had parted with deep sorrow and regret."[74]

Because they continued to define deservedness through the work imperative and family liability, MPs wondered what women's eligibility for pensions would look like. Sydney Buxton, for example, indicated that "it might be difficult for a woman to show that she had worked according to her ability, opportunity, and need for the maintenance of herself and those legally dependent upon her." He proposed that they "insert the words 'or benefit'" after "maintenance" to make clearer that this provision "applied to women as well as men."[75] As I argued earlier in this chapter, women could contribute to maintenance, but they were not regarded as primarily responsible for family liability. Austen Chamberlain progressively suggested that women's domestic work at home should count as "work" in this context, pointing out that "married women who had kept house respectably and well, but who technically it might be said had not worked for the maintenance of themselves or those dependent upon them" were already included in the bill.[76] In justifying a wife's receipt of a pension by virtue of a husband's qualification, David Lloyd George explained, "It was very often owing to the wife's care and good housewifery that the man had been able to save any money and pay his subscription to his friendly society, and she ought to have a fair share of the benefit to it. If the woman had been one who squandered her husband's means, he would not have been able to save anything at all."[77] These discussions denied women's agency as workers and providers but at least recognized that women's housework facilitated men's economic stability.

Members of Parliament acknowledged the conflicts some men could experience with regard to intergenerational maintenance, when they were expected to provide both for their wives and children and their elderly parents. They argued that OAPs would mitigate this difficulty. George Roberts of Norwich indicated he had investigated the circumstances of the elderly men in a Norfolk village, finding that "whilst they [as younger men] were bringing up their family, and adding to the wealth and productivity of the nation, they had to contribute 1s. a week towards the maintenance of their aged parents." They were, in his words, "worthy citizens," but their contributions to their aged parents when they were younger had prevented them from saving for their own old age.[78] Charles Masterman, in support of the final reading of the bill, emphasized that "in thousands of humble homes it [OAP] will remove the desolate and cruel choice of the wage-earner between the needs of the parent on the one hand and the needs of the child on the other."[79] Without OAPs, working men were sandwiched between dependent generations.

The final law stated that men and women 70 years old and above qualified for pensions of up to five shillings a week (Figure 8.2). Pensions were graduated based on a yearly income, and anyone who earned over 31 pounds ten shillings a year was not eligible. The OAP democratized assistance processes and aimed to remove the stigma of relief for the elderly. Individuals picked up their pensions from the Post Office rather than from the poor law authorities, which drew a line between different types of assistance. Still, the Act held that anyone receiving poor law relief was disqualified from receiving a pension, and it expressly indicated that, unlike poor relief, the OAP would not "deprive the pensioner of any franchise, right, or privilege, or subject him to any disability."[80] The state recognized age 70 as the end of a man's working life and the beginning of a new status with regard to honest poverty. The pauper disqualification was amended in 1911, allowing the elderly who had been receiving poor law outrelief to move to the OAP. In January 1911, for example, the *County Express* reported that "between 700 and 800 [people] will, in the whole [Dudley] Union, go from ordinary relief to old-age pensions."[81]

While the OAP was not tied to the performance of task work and did not require a pensioner to prove willingness to work, the work imperative still featured in the 1908 Act in ways suggested from the 1890s. An applicant's negative work history could disqualify him from benefit. According to the Act, "If, before he becomes entitled to a pension, he has habitually failed to work according to his ability, opportunity, and need, for the maintenance or benefit of himself and those legally dependent upon him," he would not receive a pension. The disclaimer added the exception that "if claimant has been paying into some trade union or benefit society to support him or wife out of employment or for sickness," he could qualify for benefit, acknowledging that not all who were willing to work were able to work. The OAP expressed the

203

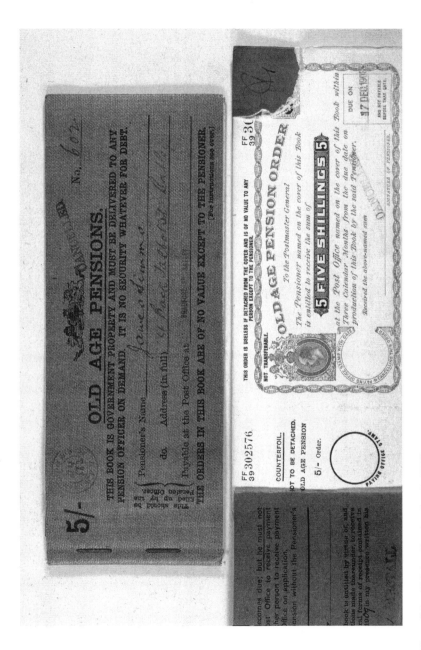

Figure 8.2 Old Age Pension book, 1909
Source: Mary Evans Picture Library/BRUCE CASTLE MUSEUM.

expectations of honest poverty, requiring at least a willingness to work and responsibility for dependants.

Significantly, even though women as individuals were eligible for benefit and would be the primary recipients of OAPs, the language of the Act framed the "pensioner" as a man.[82] The OAP contributed to a recognition that men reached a point in their lives when their dependence could be expected. Eligibility for a pension marked a man as no longer a worker. In April 1926, the Dudley Board of Guardians affirmed the repackaging of elderly men from workers to pensioners, with its Unemployment Committee resolving "that men of 60 years of age and upwards shall be treated as not able-bodied cases."[83] Although these men would not qualify for a national pension for ten more years, the local guardians knew that older men could not compete for jobs when "younger men are given the preference."

Conclusion

Before Old Age Pensions, older men who no longer were physically capable of working or able to support their wives found themselves in an awkward position relative to honest poverty. They could not be blamed for their inability to work or their failure to support their families, but no welfare system provided non-stigmatizing assistance. Historically, the poor law authorities awarded routine pensions to the elderly poor, but these pensions took the vote away from men once they had been enfranchised. If elderly poor men were blameless in their lack of work, this blamelessness was acknowledged by the Poor Law only unofficially.

Although poor law officials played an important role in the relief of the elderly, they assumed that sons, and predominantly single sons, would take on the family liability for their elderly parents. In determinations of family liability, poor law authorities weighed married and single sons' responsibilities against each other and, as in so many other cases, found single men wanting. Because married sons already had wives and children, authorities pressured single sons to take up the financial support of their elderly parents, to take on family responsibility. In this way, the work-welfare system again sustained heteronormative institutions by prioritizing the state of marriage. Yet, presumably, the money expended on their parents placed unmarried sons in a precarious position relative to future marriage, as it depleted the savings they might accrue.

The expectation that sons should provide for their parents was an obvious one in the honest poverty regime. However, while the Poor Law increasingly emphasized that women – and especially single women – had a duty to work, this work was not understood as breadwinning, which implicitly contained a notion of family liability. Materially, women's low wages often precluded any large financial support for relatives, but the evidence suggests that women did contribute to maintaining their families. Still, gender assumptions influenced the records in such a way as to minimize or even erase women's support. Married women's legal and customary dependency not only covered over the ways they might act as independent providers for elderly parents, but also it wiped out their independent identity in the poor law records and even in unemployment records that represented them as workers. Poor law authorities placed the pressure of full-time independence solely on adult able-bodied men, whose construction as always-potential breadwinners made them highly visible to officials seeking to cut back state assistance. The fate of elderly parents frequently rested on the willingness of sons to provide, on poor law authorities' ability to force sons to contribute, and on the often invisible assistance supplied by daughters.

9

"He did not realise his responsibilities": Giving Up the Privileges of Honest Poverty

From 1917 until 1929, Emma Jane C. of Dudley appeared at least seven times before local officials to ask for assistance because of her husband's neglect. My first record of Emma is as an applicant to the Stourbridge Board of Guardians in early August 1918. Her case notes indicate she was 32 years old and the mother of two young children. She owed five shillings and nine pence for bread she had received on credit and had rent payments in arrears. Her husband, Horace, was a lathe hand, earning 22 shillings and sixpence per week as well as receiving an army pension of 16 shillings. In December 1917, the Brierley Hill magistrates had ordered Horace to pay Emma maintenance of 12 shillings and sixpence a week, but Horace had not complied, and a warrant had been issued for the back payments. Horace, the relieving officer's notes indicate, "neglects to maintain." The Board of Guardians granted Emma relief in kind, which continued from August 1918 until May 1919, when she applied anew for assistance because she had injured her hand at work. Although the record does not specify whether she was offered continuing assistance or a new form of relief, it does again stress that she was "awaiting compensation. Husband neglects to maintain," even though the outstanding order against Horace for 12 shillings and sixpence a week remained in force.[1]

I found Emma and Horace C. again in September 1921, when the *County Express* covered their case at the Stourbridge Police Court. Horace was summoned for over five pounds arrears in his maintenance payments and was committed to prison for 22 days, but the magistrates said they would not act on the imprisonment warrant as long as Horace paid Emma 15 shillings per week.[2] We do not know if he kept to this agreement, but Emma again applied for poor law relief in June 1925 because "husband was absent from house." She received in-kind relief through

July 1925 and also from March 1928 through January 1929. Horace was again summoned to police court, this time in Brierley Hill, on March 2, 1928, to deal with his arrears, but still in January 1929 the case notes indicate "non-compliance with maintenance order."[3]

In early July 1920, John Thomas R., a 35-year-old disabled ex-serviceman from Netherton, was summoned by his wife Edith for a maintenance order. Edith claimed that John "had never made an effort to provide a home for her. He was always getting drink and he had recently left her. She absolutely refused to live with him again." John very much wanted to keep the marriage together, but Edith refused. The magistrates granted Edith a separation with maintenance of two pounds a week, which would come out of John's pension and his wages from a fireclay works.[4] By the end of the month, John was already in arrears from being out of work. He said, "He was anxious to support his children, but did not know how he was to do it." The magistrates indicated that they did not want to send John to jail, "but he did not realise his responsibilities, and he must do something to support his family." John paid part of the existing arrears, and the case was adjourned for two weeks for John to arrange steady payments or face going to prison.[5]

John R. was again in the magistrates' court in September 1920, charged with failing to pay the 32 pounds he owed his wife "under a maintenance order for payment of £2 a week." John "pleaded inability to pay" because of the miners' strike, which had kept him out of work from early April to early July. He indicated "he had paid what he could," but his wife stressed that his payments had been insufficient, since she needed to support three children as well as herself. The magistrates adjourned the case when John promised regular payments in the future.[6] Two months later, on November 26, however, the *Herald* reported that John was back before the local court,

> having failed to pay a maintenance order in regard to his wife and three children, who had been in receipt of poor relief. The arrears were stated to be £41 5s. The defendant said he was handicapped by his inability to get full wages, but the Magistrates Clerk pointed out that he had never made any attempt to pay. He was committed [to prison] for two months.[7]

The *Herald* again reported on the couple in April 1922: John was again out of work and "found it impossible to pay 35s. to his wife out of the money he was getting at present, and he did not see any prospect of their coming together." Edith argued that John's employment status did not really matter: "When he has got the money he will not pay it." The clerk reminded John that they had imprisoned him before for non-payment of maintenance. The magistrates decided to reduce the order temporarily to 23 shillings per week, "until [John] was in a position to pay his wife a larger sum. The chairman urged him to see that he kept up his payments regularly," to which John responded, "I will do it."[8] Whether he did "do it" is unclear.

The stories of these two couples illuminate the ways husbands' neglect of their family liability resulted in wives repeatedly seeking assistance from welfare and legal authorities for their survival and that of their children. Women like Emma C. and Edith R., whose husbands failed to support them, applied for poor law relief, which then led Boards of Guardians to summon negligent men to the magistrates' courts. Before the magistrates, women sometimes asked for separation orders from their neglectful husbands; more often, they wanted the magistrates to compel their husbands to uphold the obligation to support them. Married women who applied for poor law relief did not fit within normative gender and familial relations, because their husbands were "absent." Their situations call attention to the awkward position of women seeking welfare on their own and the punitive attitude towards married men who did not abide by the work imperative or fulfill their family liability. The expectations of honest poverty put husbands and wives in competition for welfare deservedness when men did not "realise their responsibilities."

Just as cash-poor Boards of Guardians attempted to rein in their expenses by tracking down sons to support elderly parents, they also chased men whose wives and children had become reliant on poor law relief because of the male breadwinner's desertion and neglect. The moral messages attached to sons' liability for their parents, however, never sounded as loud as those attached to husbands' liability for wives and children. "Being a husband," as historian Ellen Ross has written, "was synonymous with providing support,"[9] suggesting that a man who did not maintain his wife was not really a "husband." The state aggressively pursued husbands and fathers who rejected the masculine norm by ignoring the work imperative or family liability. Married women, not wanting to be left to the Poor Law, partnered with poor law authorities and magistrates to drive negligent men back to the fold of honest poverty. While poor married men used family liability to enhance their claims to citizenship, their failure to live up to the terms of honest poverty condemned them as unsuccessful men and inadequate citizens.[10]

Neglectful husbands and women's poor law relief

Deserted and neglected women faced an ambivalent Poor Law, which simultaneously sought to compel husbands' family liability and historically treated abandoned women with suspicion. Only 12 per cent of the Stourbridge Union female poor law applicants in my Dataset 1 (DS1) were married. Sixty-three per cent of these women applied because of absent husbands, when their positions most resembled single and widowed women. Without a male breadwinner, women were clearly economically vulnerable. Married women alone with children were a particularly important group of poor law applicants; not only was there an absent husband, but an absent father as well (see Table 3.3). In DS1, women with dependent children constituted 32 per cent of all female applicants 16 years of age and older. Among married female applicants, 78 per cent had dependent children. Not surprisingly, because they tended to be older, only 28 per cent of widows had dependent children. What is surprising, however, because the New Poor Law itself was so focused on the problem of single mothers and their "bastard" children, is that only 15 per cent of single women applied with children.[11] The Stourbridge Union officials were much more caught up with what to do about married women applying without husbands, particularly those who had children to care for. Authorities were obviously reluctant to take on liability for this group of applicants who supposedly already had husbands to maintain them.

Poor law authorities looked very carefully at the appeals of married women on their own and weighed their petitions in moral as well as economic terms. They tended to see married women through the lens of their husbands' actions. According to historian Jane Humphries, officials judged married women's petitions believing that "families had to bear some responsibility for the 'misconduct' of their husband and father."[12] The "crusade against outrelief" emphasized that authorities should wait at least a year before granting outdoor relief to abandoned wives, also promoting a prohibition of relief for wives whose husbands were in jail.[13] In July 1883, the Dudley Board of Guardians commended the Birmingham Guardians for denying outrelief "to married women deserted by their husbands, whether with or without families," among other groups of people considered less than deserving.[14] While honest unemployed men were rarely condemned to workhouse relief, women whose husbands left them continued to be offered the workhouse, demonstrating the Boards of Guardians' discomfort with offering neglected women "honest" relief.[15]

The application records reveal relieving officers' constant uncertainty about how to regard the status of a married woman on her own: Was her husband gone for good? Was he looking for work, planning to return to her? Thirty-year-old Elizabeth Y., a married woman with two children, for example, applied for relief in September 1871, saying her husband had deserted the family. The relieving officer's comments indicated otherwise: "I visited and made inquiries and saw the husband returning home from his work." Needless to say, she did not receive assistance.[16] Here, the relieving officer understood the husband's presence as evidence that he assumed liability for his wife and children. Doubting the veracity of Elizabeth's application, the relieving officer did not consider the possibility that her husband, even though in the home, did not provide for his family.

Even in clear cases of desertion, authorities were suspicious of abandoned women's characters. Phoebe K., for example, applied to the Stourbridge Board of Guardians initially in April 1923. She was listed as having no occupation but supporting five children between the ages of five and 17. She received relief in kind on and off from mid-1923 until June 1926. Phoebe's husband had deserted her and had "not been heard of for some time." Yet the record flagged that "she is a woman addicted to drink etc (a case not to be recommended). The daughter Violet has illegitimate child." In 1925, the relieving officer noted that the husband was in prison for six months.[17] While Phoebe's situation as a mother alone with five children was obviously a difficult one, questions about her moral status clearly shaped constructions of her welfare deservedness and seemingly played as big a role in determinations of her relief as did her husband's neglect.

By contrast, the poor law records portrayed Lena P., a Stourbridge woman with two young daughters, as a woman victimized by an irresponsible husband. She applied for relief in April 1915, claiming her husband deserted her. Comments on her application indicate that her living area was "in good condition," suggesting her own good character. The relieving officer recorded in May, "Husband drunken and has left her and her family and gone to live with a sister on same street and will not send anything up for their maintenance." The husband agreed to repay the relief the Board of Guardians provided, but in August Lena was awarded a separation order with maintenance, revealing that the relationship was not salvageable and that her husband would not support her without compulsion.[18]

Liability and the law

Lena P.'s case wound up before the local magistrates' court, as the Board of Guardians summoned her husband for repayment of relief and eventually for separation and maintenance orders. Married women relied heavily on legally mandated maintenance payments when their husbands neglected them, and I conceptualize maintenance orders as an important component of the honest poverty work-welfare system. Since destitute women turned to the Poor Law when their husbands did not provide for them, poor law authorities sought to use maintenance orders to transfer their welfare burden back onto husbands who did not fulfill their family liability.

The local newspapers provide an excellent source to examine struggles over men's family liability in the magistrates' courts. In 1868, Boards of Guardians gained the power to use the local courts to enforce a man's maintenance of a wife who had become reliant on poor law relief and to demand repayment of any "loan" for her assistance.[19] To facilitate my analysis of these issues, I constructed a Maintenance Dataset of 332 magistrates' court cases, compiled from Stourbridge and Dudley Union newspapers. Reporting on the maintenance cases was usually in district news sections of the newspapers and, later, more regularly under police court items, which also included petty crimes such as assault, drunkenness, public nuisance, and theft. The maintenance cases sometimes received the barest notice, while at other times they could take up an entire column or more. My dataset contains details from fuller cases that provide insight into the circumstances of the people involved. Without reference to the original magistrates' records, it is difficult to judge why some cases and not others were printed, especially those that contained little information and thus did not appeal much to public interest.

What is clear is that wives and poor law authorities used the courts and newspapers to expose neglectful husbands' failures as honest poor men. The newspaper coverage depicted husbands who were violent, lazy, and unemployed, who evaded their legal and cultural obligations, and who pauperized their families (Table 9.1). Maintenance cases taught men a lesson: magistrates, as historian George Behlmer has shown clearly, had "great latitude" in dispensing summary justice and used these cases to urge responsibility on husbands, not hesitating to make examples of neglectful men.[20] The publication of these cases in the newspapers made private matters public, displayed men to their communities as failing to provide, and put additional pressure on men to uphold their family obligations.[21] Jennifer Davis has argued, "Frequently, the wife hoped the mere act of appearing before the magistrate and taking out a summons without returning for trial would be sufficient to frighten a recalcitrant husband into mending his ways."[22] Even cases that did go to trial could end with wives deciding to give their husbands another

Table 9.1   Reasons for summons to maintenance proceedings, 1871–1929

Reason	Frequency
Arrears of maintenance payments	116
Deserting family	89
Leaving wife/family chargeable to poor law union	55
Neglect or failure to provide sufficient support	43
Domestic violence, cruelty, or threatening	31
Separation or application for separation	29
Variance of maintenance order	33
Husband and wife reconciled	1
Vagrancy	1
Total	**398**

chance, which suggests wives used the courts to bolster a lack of power in their domestic situations.[23]

The Poor Law worked in tandem with Common Law to support women's claims against their husbands. As a 1910 guide for justices and magistrates put it, "The duty of maintaining wife and family is a moral obligation imposed by the law of nature, and as such is recognised by Common Law." However, the guide explained, "affection will not always induce the discharge of this [maintenance] duty," so legislation had become necessary "both to define the relationships to which such duty shall extend, and also to regulate the means by which natural obligation shall be enforced."[24] Even after the Married Women's Property Acts of 1870 and 1882, which gave women the right to retain their own property and earnings within marriage, Common Law still held a husband accountable "to provide necessaries for his wife," just as sons were held accountable for dependent parents.[25] Wives with separate property could be compelled to maintain their children or parents and, on rare occasions, husbands who had become reliant on poor law relief, but husbands' family liability for their wives was the near-universal rule.[26]

Just as the problem of unemployment was making it more and more difficult for poor men to work and maintain their families, marriage law created stronger incentives for them to do so. Before 1878, although poor law authorities could obtain orders of maintenance against liable relatives and a man could be prosecuted for refusal to work under the Vagrancy Act of 1824, a poor woman whose husband neglected to maintain her during marriage had no recourse to the courts to demand support.[27] This changed with the Matrimonial Causes Act of 1878, which empowered women to summon their husbands before the magistrates for separation with maintenance orders on the grounds of domestic violence.[28] This Act responded to two fundamental problems for poor women: the high costs and other inconveniences of divorce in the High Court, and the lack of social and legal provision for abused wives.[29]

The Married Women (Maintenance in Case of Desertion) Act of 1886 legislated that a woman could obtain a maintenance order of up to two pounds a week from the magistrates if she showed her husband refused or neglected to support her when able to do so. (In 1920, a new statute added ten shillings for each child a woman had to maintain.)[30] The careful interest of poor law authorities in marriage law is evident from a petition in favor of the 1886 bill circulated to Boards of Guardians: "The petition stated that the Guardians, in their administration of poor relief, found abundant evidence to show that the measure proposed was much needed, and would produce beneficial results." The chairman of the Stourbridge Board of Guardians, among others, was happy to sign on behalf of his board.[31] Since poor law officials confronted the problem of abandoned and neglected wives firsthand, they pushed for legislation to force husbands to uphold their family liability and prevent women from relying on poor law union funds.

Consolidating the acts of 1878 and 1886, the Summary Jurisdiction (Married Women) Act of 1895 gave magistrates general power over marital relations – with the exception of divorce, which remained in the High Court.[32] By the turn of the twentieth century, wives could sue for separation based on domestic abuse, desertion, assault, persistent cruelty, neglect, and habitual drunkenness, and "any married woman . . . whose husband shall have deserted her or whose husband shall have been guilty of . . . wilful neglect to provide reasonable maintenance for her or her infant children whom he is legally liable to maintain" could go to magistrates' courts for maintenance orders.[33] While divorce laws were liberalized in 1923, allowing women to sue for divorce on the same grounds as men, it was not until the later twentieth century that divorce became accessible enough that poor people frequently used it.[34] From 1870 to 1930, separation and maintenance remained the legal framework under which the poor negotiated their marital problems. Significantly, separation (as opposed to divorce) precluded remarriage, thus constraining financial and emotional couple relationships among the poor.

The late nineteenth-century marriage laws gave "working class wives a statutory right to maintenance against their husbands,"[35] and, once this legal apparatus was in place, poor women used it. While divorces until 1918 numbered in the hundreds per year,[36] separations numbered in the thousands, and the figures for maintenance orders jumped from 6,583 in 1900 to 11,602 in 1920.[37] By the early 1920s, marital separations reached 22,000 a year.[38] Many men were imprisoned for failure to comply with maintenance orders: 1,288 went to prison in 1900, 2,265 in 1910, and 2,403 in 1920.[39] The state was increasingly willing to punish men who did not uphold their responsibilities for their wives. The development of marriage laws that explicitly and forcibly sought to compel men to maintain their families is another sign of the increasing centrality of family liability to masculine citizenship. As poor men became incorporated into the nation with the expanding franchise and unemployment benefits, the state more closely monitored the economic, social, and cultural markers of belonging.

The domestic politics of family liability

Women seeking maintenance orders from their husbands had to demonstrate their own adherence to the rules of marriage. While husbands were legally liable to maintain their wives, the magistrates' court cases show that, to be deserving of maintenance, wives were culturally liable to fulfill an expectation of wifely industriousness that included housekeeping, cooking, and making a comfortable home. Above all, a wife had to abide by sexual norms. Doubtful wifely credentials might override a husband's legal liability or at least stay the court's hand temporarily. While honest poverty for men focused on men's status as workers and providers, honest poverty for women centered on women's status as domestic and sexual beings.

According to both Common Law and the statutes on matrimonial causes, an adulterous wife gave up any claim to her husband's support.[40] On June 10, 1871, for example, the *Dudley Herald* covered the maintenance case of the forgeman John Tyler, whose wife became reliant on poor relief. Tyler testified that "his wife for years had lived a dissolate [sic] life, and he had overlooked her faults, until about eighteen months ago, when her own daughters found her in the act of adultery. He then left her." One of the daughters spoke in support of this story, and the relieving officer who brought the matter to court "withdrew the case," seemingly embarrassed, "remarking that . . . had the facts of the defence been known to him before, he would not have appeared before the bench."[41] In a similar situation, James Meanley, an ironworker, was in March 1876 accused of forcing his wife to turn to the Poor Law because of his neglect. Meanley argued that his wife was adulterous, and even though she countered that her husband was abusive, "the

Bench considered that the complainant had been guilty of adultery and dismissed the case."[42] Although poor law authorities were interested in recouping money spent maintaining neglected families, they would not enforce husbands' liability for "dishonest" wives.

Magistrates also judged poor women's deservedness in terms of the performance of domestic duties. Doubts about a wife's domestic habits often resulted in an adjournment to see if the couple could work things out, even if a wife accused a husband of abuse. Frederick Jones, for example, when charged with assaulting his wife Elizabeth, defended himself in Halesowen Police Court in July 1886 by claiming that Elizabeth did not regularly get his meals to him at his place of work. The magistrates found that "it was the duty of the wife to see that the husband got his meals, and that it was a case which should have been made up between the husband and wife."[43] Ignoring Elizabeth's claim that her husband assaulted her, the magistrates saw her appeal as trivial, something to be addressed in the domestic sphere.

In a similar case, the *Dudley Herald* devoted a long column to John Albert Cartwright, whose wife Fanny brought him to Brierley Hill Police Court in January 1921, accusing him of abuse and asking for a maintenance payment of two pounds a week. Fanny indicated, "Ever since the marriage day she had been led an awful life. She had been afraid to tell her own people because she did not want them to know how badly her husband treated her." She stressed that John earned the healthy wage of three pounds and 15 shillings a week and had ten shillings from an army pension. Fanny had left John and was living with her brother. John, however, emphasized Fanny's lack of domestic skills:

Defendant proceeded to blame his wife for the discomfort of the home, and added that he had always tried to pay his way.

Complainant stated that defendant had never given her a wage since the marriage day. She had never had a wife's place. She had to go out without a halfpenny, and if she ordered any goods she had to go and ask defendant for the money with which to pay for them.

. . . He complained that his wife nagged him. He was what could be called a home bird, and he looked for comfort when he came home from work, but he never got it. Defendant said he was willing to have his wife back if she would give him the comfort he wanted.

At this point, the magistrates' clerk intervened, stressing that John was not abiding by the rules of marriage. He "stated that 99 out of 100 or even, he might say, 999 out of 1000 husbands gave their wives the housekeeping money. The women were really the chancellors of the exchequer of the home." A woman could not be expected to maintain a household without financial support, and the clerk reminded John of these gendered expectations. John, however, accused his wife of being a bad money manager. Surprisingly, Fanny agreed to try to work things out with John, as long as he attempted to find them a house away from his family. The magistrates did award her a maintenance payment of two pounds a week.[44]

Magistrates agreed with female petitioners that it was a husband's duty to find the family a proper home. "Of all the dreams dreamt by working-class women," argues Joanna Bourke in her history of working-class cultures, "marriage followed by full-time housewifery was the most widely shared."[45] Home was one of the few venues that conferred status on a woman; it was, as Bourke has claimed, a source of power and control in a working-class world dominated by men.[46] Neglecting to provide a home was a strong mark against a man. Joseph Round, a chainmaker from Cradley Heath, was before the magistrates in March 1921 for assaulting his wife and for desertion. According to the prosecutor, Joseph failed miserably in his responsibilities: "defendant had never found a home for his wife, neither had he given her a penny piece for housekeeping purposes. They lived with his mother . . . Instead of giving his money to his wife, he handed it all to his mother." The magistrates adjourned the case for five weeks "in order that the defendant could carry out his promise" to find a home. Joseph was ordered to pay 15 shillings maintenance in the interim.[47] In November 1921, the magistrates found in favor of Annie Kate Plant against her husband John, arguing "that in four years defendant ought to have provided a home. She was justified in refusing to live with his people and it was natural she should want a home of her own." As in the Rounds' case, the magistrates adjourned the case for six weeks to give John the time to find his wife a home but insisted that John pay his wife's maintenance.[48] Men's liability extended to fulfilling women's "natural" desire for their own homes.

Broken marriages clearly strained the finances of husbands and wives in separate households and raised the chances that families would have to rely on poor law relief. The magistrates did everything they could to pressure husbands and wives to keep their families together and, as historian James Hammerton has argued, "avoid the fragile division of slender economic resources"[49] The *County Advertiser* of April 23, 1921, for example, reported that 19-year-old Annie Gauden applied at the

Stourbridge Police Court for an order of separation against her husband Harry, a 20-year-old collier. The couple had a nine-month-old child. Annie related how her husband had "struck her and jumped on her chest after his boots had been taken off. For six weeks she had had no money from him. She left him because she was afraid, as he had threatened to 'kill' her." Harry claimed that he "was on strike and had no money. It was not a case of desertion," meaning that he did not intend to abandon his wife; rather, economic circumstances prevented him from supporting her. The magistrates disagreed, finding for desertion, but adjourned the case for two weeks, "to see if the parties could be brought together again."[50] The court did not comment on Annie's fear of her husband's abusive behavior.

The extent of violence in these cases exposes the fault lines of patriarchal privilege in working-class marriages.[51] While historians have stressed the development of a more companionate model of marriage, they have also acknowledged the ways economic difficulties could heighten the continuing patriarchal nature of the institution, particularly as women had very little power relative to abusive relationships.[52] "Most women," according to Hammerton, "were unable to live and support their children on the inevitably small maintenance payments," and some made the choice – dangerous in cases of domestic violence – to return to their husbands anyway.[53] Husbands, however, also had an interest in keeping a marriage together: even the small payments a man had to surrender for maintenance could constitute a significant portion of his means. Remaining in an unhappy marriage meant benefiting from family economies to which wives and children also contributed.[54] It also upheld a man's privileged position as head of household.

Women used the heteronormative framework of honest poverty to argue their cases, actively drawing on the law to demand the financial support they understood to be due to them as wives. Yet the available strategies to use the work-welfare system to their advantage involved getting authorities to speak for them. The cases show that poor wives whose husbands did not provide often had to become paupers to garner assistance. Sometimes legal authorities were explicit about women's lack of choices: in November 1894, for example, the Old Hill magistrates dealt with a couple whose case had been adjourned a month earlier. Sarah Bradley, asking for a separation and maintenance order, told the court that she and her husband, John, had been living together, but he had "not provided her with any food or fire for a week." The clerk and a magistrate informed her, however, that "the Bench could not make an order, seeing the parties were living together, but they advised complainant to apply to the relieving officer for relief, and then the Guardians would take the case up."[55] To prove destitution caused by a neglectful husband, a married woman could be compelled to pauperize herself. Thus, at the same time local authorities were discussing ways not to pauperize honest men in light of increasing unemployment, they were encouraging honest women to use the Poor Law. Questions about political citizenship were irrelevant for women, who had no vote to lose if they received poor law relief.

Men's work and women's maintenance

Through maintenance payments, women continued to depend on men's support even when a marriage was broken, but, as we have seen, men did not always abide by the terms of their family liability. Some men actually preferred going to jail to paying maintenance, since a prison sentence, no matter how short, erased whatever maintenance arrears were owed to their wives.[56] According to Iris Minor in a 1979 essay on marriage law reform, "It was not unknown for men to leave reasonably well-paid jobs and take some ill-paid and irregular work in order to plead an inability to pay before the magistrates."[57] Less rare, however, and much more easily, men could leave town without disclosing their whereabouts to their wives; as Olive Anderson states in her study of judicial separation, "'Leaving' was always the commonest male response to domestic problems."[58] Women and their children gained very little from maintenance orders that husbands were unwilling to honor (Figure 9.1).

Magistrates evaluated maintenance cases assuming that men should work and provide for their families; men defended themselves by emphasizing the obstacles to their abilities to provide. Wives stressed that their husbands were lazy and neglectful, willing to abandon their families. Husbands, by contrast, tried to convince the courts of their good intentions as providers. Magistrates had to decide whose story to believe. A man who legitimately could not support his family because of his own destitution was not legally liable for maintenance. If he was searching for work, he could be seen to embody the cultural and legal expectations of honest poverty. He would not be found guilty under the Vagrancy Act for refusing work or neglecting to support his family.

Husbands who had work or were able to work but were not properly maintaining their wives, however, were frequently accused of being idle and selfish, men who had degraded their masculine status. For example, in 1871, the *County Express* reported that Noah Roberts of Old Hill was charged with leaving his family to the Poor Law. The primary evidence

Figure 9.1 Backyard chainshop, Cradley Heath, early twentieth century. Women and children had little means to survive on their own
Source: © Dudley Archives and Local History Service, ref. p/83.

against Roberts came from his mother-in-law, who claimed that Roberts, a collier, "could earn 4s 6d per day, but was too lazy to work." Roberts was fined four shillings and the court costs "in default of two months' imprisonment, with hard labour."[59] Pursuing their own interests, wives and their relatives contributed to representations of husbands as unwilling to work. In December 1921, John C. Pearson was charged with not paying maintenance to his wife Lily and their children, accruing arrears of about 12 pounds. John "pleaded that he could not get work, and that he had been out of work for some time, but his wife told the Bench that he had given up a job because it was too hard for him. . . . The Bench commented on this fact, and pointed out that he would not have been out of work now if he had, a young strong fellow, been willing to do work that other men would do to support their families." The magistrates committed John to jail for two months unless he was willing to pay all of what he owed his wife.[60] This case explicitly compared John's unwillingness to work with the norm of "other men" who used their "young strong" bodies to uphold their family responsibilities.

Magistrates were not shy about reminding a man that he "must recognise his responsibilities and maintain his wife and child" to sustain his masculine status.[61] A 1901 case from Brierley Hill drew the headline

"Unmanly Conduct of a Husband." The miner Daniel Hickman was charged with persistent cruelty to his wife Mary Ann and neglecting his four children. Mary Ann indicated, "He was always violent in his language when she asked him for money, as he wanted it for gambling, horse racing and drinking . . . Defendant was able to get good money and could work regularly." Mary Ann was awarded a separation and maintenance of 15 shillings a week.[62] The *County Express*'s identification of Daniel as "unmanly" served to affirm the connection between masculinity and family liability. Daniel's "gambling, horse racing and drinking" presumably were shared with other men at the expense of his family obligations.

Even when a woman had an income of her own, her husband was still liable for her maintenance. Mary Louisa Price summoned her husband Hezekiah for desertion in March 1919, and, although she worked in a brickyard earning an average of one pound a week, the magistrates granted a separation order and maintenance from Hezekiah of 15 shillings a week.[63] A year later, he was sent to prison for failure to pay.[64] Edward Armstrong, in February 1922, was brought before the magistrates by his wife Nellie for separation and maintenance. While Edward was unemployed, his wife had been earning money and said "her husband had been constantly a 'henpecker' because she had not, while he was out of work, brought in all her wages." Here the traditional gender roles were reversed, with Edward chasing after his wife to provide for him. While the magistrates did not agree to a separation, they did order Edward to pay five shillings a week for maintenance and the court costs.[65]

Wives and relieving officers usually made convincing cases against men who could not successfully defend themselves against accusations of laziness or explicit negligence that spoke to a reduction in their masculine status. The authorities could be persuaded, however, by men who tried to present themselves as "'good' husbands,"[66] embodying ideas about the willingness to work and family liability. The miner Joshua Greenway of Cooper's Bank, for example, attempted to demonstrate his honesty. His story, reported in an August 1883 *Dudley Herald*, was that "owing to the ironworkers' strike he was thrown out of employment. He afterwards left the district in search of work, but had been unable to procure any. He very much regretted that his wife had been compelled to apply for relief." The case was adjourned for a month, "to give the prisoner an opportunity of paying something towards the amount due and the costs incurred."[67] The newspapers frequently reported that husbands said they were sorry, which was most likely expected of them, but this is the only case I found where the husband's regret was specifically directed towards his family's receipt of poor law relief, which probably had the effect of marking Greenway as honest in front of both the magistrates and the poor law authorities.

In periods of particularly high unemployment, the magistrates were more likely to be lenient towards a man's claim of seeking a job outside the district to provide for his family. Indeed, magistrates emphasized that "there was a great deal of difference between a refusal to pay and not being able to pay."[68] The editor of the *Dudley Herald* in 1894 sought to explain for his readers this difference between "professional tramps" and "the unfortunate *bona-fide* working man who is compelled to take to the road to search for employment." He argued that these honest poor men "should be shown indulgence" and went so far as to argue, "In a degree they are heroes," presumably because they did not pauperize themselves, but went far and wide searching for work.[69]

Yet being away from home on a search for work could also associate a man with vagrancy, which called his deservedness into question. The 1878–79 *Annual Report* of the Local Government Board, for example, acknowledged an "increase in the number of vagrants relieved . . . [which] is mainly attributable to the continued depression of trade in the coal and iron mining districts, which has caused large numbers of men to leave those neighbourhoods in search of work and to avail themselves on their route of the accommodation afforded in the vagrant wards of the several workhouses."[70] Unemployed men's need to use workhouses while trying to find work made fuzzy the line between the honest poor and the traditional vagrant, even though the Local Government Board acknowledged the reason for the increased "vagrancy" was structural.

Men who left their towns to look for work risked having their motives misread. During the very difficult year of 1886, the *County Express* reported on "A Caution to the Guardians," where the magistrates actually castigated the poor law authorities for their prosecution of the miner William Waterfield. Waterfield claimed he had left the area to look for work "because his family would have starved if he had waited for work in this district." He related that he had found a job but lost it when the Board of Guardians had him arrested. The magistrates were sympathetic and "thought it was a cruel thing that when a man went away and got work he should be brought back without being allowed a chance. It was perfectly clear that the defendant intended supporting his wife and family as soon as he got work. . . . [I]n these bad times . . . the Guardians might exercise a little more common sense."[71] Here was a man doing what he was expected to do when poor law officials misinterpreted his absence.

In many instances, sympathetic magistrates, poor law guardians, and local councilors altered their practices to account for extraordinary economic distress. Judge Tebble of the Dudley County Court, for example, during the 1921 coal strike ordered the adjournment of "all [maintenance] cases in which miners and others engaged in industries which were dependent on the coal supply [were involved] for three months."[72] The newspaper reports show this sympathy in action: the *Herald*, on May 14, 1921 reported that Andrew Harthill, a 23-year-old miner, was summoned to Dudley Police Court for a maintenance order, "but owing to the crisis, an adjournment was made."[73] While the national government treated strikers as unwilling to work, local officials did not consistently punish striking men for failure to maintain their families or force them to pay maintenance. Perhaps local magistrates did not appreciate wives summoning their husbands for maintenance during a strike.

Magistrates' sympathy for men, however, meant less financial support for women. A January 1922 item in the *County Express*, for example, addressed the "problem of out-of-work husbands keeping up payments ordered by the Court for the maintenance of their wives from whom they are separated . . . In several instances the justices solved the knotty problem by adjourning the cases, with a suggestion that the men should pay half their unemployment doles to their wives."[74] Magistrates were even willing to help men get rid of their maintenance arrears during an economic crisis: sending them to prison for one day erased whatever arrears of payment were owed. This was the situation for Percey Robinson, who, in November 1921, owed over twelve pounds on his maintenance payments. Being out of work, Robinson wanted the order reduced, and the bench agreed. Additionally, "in order that the husband might not be encumbered with the arrears, he was committed to prison for one day. The Magistrates' Clerk explained that that meant defendant could leave the Court, and that the arrears were wiped out."[75] This could not have helped Robinson's wife and nine month-old child. Indeed, if women did not receive their maintenance payments, they probably stayed dependent on the Poor Law. Magistrates' protection of honest poor men's status could easily come at the expense of wives and children.

The courts sometimes even castigated wives for pursuing maintenance claims when it was difficult for honest men to pay. For example, as reported in the *County Express* on May 28, 1921, 56-year-old John Thomas Leddington was summoned by his wife Jane Ellen to the Brierley Hill Police Court for payment of maintenance arrears: "Mr. W. W. King [the clerk] remarked: 'You bring him up at a bad time. He has given you money out of his unemployment pay, and it's not so bad. Very few do it.' Defendant said he had done his level best, and in order to pay what he could he had impoverished himself." Here the clerk presented the husband as the wronged party. John, unlike most men, tried to fulfill his family liability even when unemployed and even at the expense of his own wellbeing. In the end, the magistrates held off on a warrant for John's imprisonment as long as he paid "7s 6d a week out of his unemployment pay, [with the] contribution to be increased by 10s immediately [when] he resumed work."[76]

While economic crises could make magistrates lenient towards men unable to pay maintenance, husbands' claims of searching for work were sometimes seen as excuses to avoid financial responsibilities. Joseph Jilliver, for example, in November 1871, was charged with deserting his family and leaving them reliant on the Board of Guardians: "The accused pleaded that he went away in search of work. [The relieving officer, however,] stated that [Joseph] left his family chargeable in like manner two or three times a year on an average," making him untrustworthy.[77] In similar circumstances 30 years later, in October 1901, the *County Express* reported on the case of Thomas Wellings. The Board of Guardians had been supporting his family for a year and a half, and his neglect had cost the union 12 pounds and 18 shillings. Thomas claimed he had gone away to find work and was afraid to "send home, fearing he would be arrested." The relieving officer, however, countered that the defendant had quit his job: "He and his wife had a quarrel, and defendant having been previously sent to gaol for thrashing her, went off to avoid being summoned." The Board of Guardians "had no faith" in Thomas's promises to pay, and the magistrates committed him to prison for three months with hard labor.[78] Again, punishment of a negligent husband did not contribute to a destitute wife's welfare.

Maintenance as an imperial problem

Local authorities' frustrations with men's abrogation of family liability became an imperial problem as domestic unemployment pushed more and more men to seek work abroad. In 1912, the minutes of evidence before the Royal Commission on Divorce and Matrimonial Causes raised the issue that husbands not only left their towns, but also the country, to elude their maintenance responsibilities. Numerous magistrates, judges, barristers, and solicitors testified about husbands departing for the United States and the colonies – particularly Australia and Canada – with the explicit intention of escaping maintenance orders. Questioners and respondents alike noted the struggle to track down men who had left Britain to set themselves up overseas. As C.M. Atkinson, stipendiary magistrate for Leeds, testified, "Men frequently disappear . . . [and] the [maintenance] order is of no value; it is a mere piece of paper."[79] John Gilbert Hay Halkett, stipendiary magistrate for Hull, put it even more bluntly: "The men bolt [out of the country] if they have an order to pay."[80] The empire created space for neglectful husbands to make themselves invisible to the authorities back home. Men's liability to support wives and families expanded out of the realms of national policy and local practice to occupy a central place in defining the imperial masculine citizen.[81]

Along with the United States, the Dominions, with their promise of employment, drew men from districts such as the Black Country where un- and underemployment were regular features of the economic landscape.[82] Indeed, the British government viewed the Empire as a means to help with the increasing problem of unemployment in the late nineteenth century, with subsidized emigration schemes focusing on settling men in the Dominions, which were hungry for their labor.[83] Yet these plans focused on single men, who posed problems at home but who might find family-supporting work in the broader English-speaking world. Married men, however, also sought prosperity overseas, often leaving behind their families to pursue the possibility of work.

Some men who traveled abroad for employment did indeed send money to support families at home. Economist Gary Magee and historian Andrew Thompson, for example, have argued that "migrants made regular and sometimes vital contributions to family budgets and demonstrated that those who had been left behind had not been forgotten."[84] They emphasize that remittances signified important family relationships: "Despite the fact that migrants were separated from their family by such great distances, they frequently expressed a sense of responsibility for wives and children, aged parents, and other dependent relatives, some of whom they would shortly see on a return visit, yet others perhaps whom they would never see again."[85] Yet connections could much more easily be severed than sustained, with distance facilitating negligent behavior.

Poor law guardians regularly relieved wives whose husbands had left the country. Sarah T., for example, applied to the Stourbridge Board of Guardians for a pension renewal in March 1891, as her husband Joseph was still "abroad." Her application identifies her as a molder with three dependent children, although she was unable to work due to illness. She and the children were living with her mother. Joseph had sent Sarah three pounds recently, but his payments were inconsistent, and she was awarded a pension of two pounds a week.[86] Julia P., a married "housewife," needed help in June 1915 because her husband was in the United States. He had "sent no money for weeks."[87] Twenty-two-year-old Ethel H. of Brierley Hill applied for poor law relief in the spring of 1923. Her husband had "gone to America to seek work." She had been receiving intermittent unemployment benefit but had "insufficient means" to support herself and her infant son Harry. She received casual relief for several months.[88]

Well into the 1920s, poor law officials received applications from women whose husbands' travel overseas left their wives in limbo. Florence Ada C., for example, a 32-year-old married woman with three young children from Brierley Hill, applied in June 1923, claiming her husband had stopped supporting her. According to the application, "applicant's husband is in America[,] has been there 12 months but has not sent his wife any money for four weeks. Applicant lives with her parents. . . . A very respectable family." She was granted five shillings and relief in kind. Florence applied again in July 1924, her "husband absent from home" and she with "insufficient means." Her husband James had sent home ten dollars in May, but she had not heard from him since. In June 1925, James "returned from Canada," and the Board of Guardians stopped relieving Florence.[89]

While local authorities fretted over how to support women and children whose husbands had gone abroad for work, the British government tackled how to find men throughout the empire whose families had become destitute.[90] During the first decade of the twentieth century, both the Colonial Office and the Local Government Board received communications from poor law guardians asking for help finding absent husbands. Dudley specifically appeared in interdepartmental notes as one of two cases where the problem of overseas desertion previously had been investigated.[91] In July 1907, in a letter to the High Commissioner for South Africa and Governor of the Transvaal, Britain's Colonial Secretary acknowledged the problems facing poor law officials when men left home. He called attention

> to the fact that authorities responsible for the administration of the poor law [in England] sometimes incur considerable loss owing to their not being able to take proceedings or if proceedings have been successfully taken, to enforce the judgments of the Courts against men who obtain employment in South Africa and leave their wives and children chargeable to the parish at home.[92]

He also noted that the South African states already had legislation "for reciprocity in enforcing orders made by a magistrate against a man who deserts his family," and indeed three states provided "for a reciprocal arrangement being made 'with any other part of His Majesty's dominions.'" While portions of the Dominions already addressed maintenance as a problem without territorial borders, the United Kingdom had "no provision . . . under which reciprocal arrangements could be carried into effect."[93] The Empire provided British men with the means to escape their family liability, and, as it stood, there was very little British authorities could do about it.

Domestic pressure from poor law guardians, however, merged with the interests of Dominions officials in legislation that would protect wives and children from absconding husbands. At the Imperial Conference of 1911, Sir Joseph Ward, the Prime Minister of New Zealand, put forward the resolution, "That in order to relieve both wives and children and the poor relief burdens of the United Kingdom and her dependencies, reciprocal provisions should be made throughout the constituent parts of the Empire with respect to destitute and deserted persons."[94] As *The Times* reported it, "The wish of the proposers was that no man should be able to escape the responsibility of providing for his family by simply deserting it and migrating to a Dominion."[95] Here was a transnational condemnation of men who neglected their families and gave up their claims to honest poverty.

Dominion officials argued that reciprocal legislation was urgently needed to enforce men's maintenance of their wives and children. Australia and New Zealand were already moving towards reciprocal legislation that would make maintenance orders issued in one state's courts valid in the other's, and the South African Union Government was planning "to introduce uniform legislation for the whole of the Union."[96] Broader maintenance legislation agreements would foster imperial cohesion as well as protect women and children. Some Imperial Conference attendees raised concerns about bringing proceedings against men who would not be present to defend themselves and about the costs of reciprocity in practice. In the end, the interests of constructing a deterrent message about desertion as well as promoting "Imperial co-operation"[97] won out over the interests of cost. The Australian Prime Minister articulated this position explicitly, quoting from a paper submitted by the Scottish Local Government Board that "considerations of public policy outweigh the question of expense. . . . [W]hen it becomes known that a man cannot escape his natural and legitimate liabilities by merely going to Canada, Australia, South Africa, or New Zealand, a great deterrent force will result."[98] Men had to be reminded of the consequences of "their natural and legitimate liabilities" that tied them to their families back home.

The emphasis on justice and protection underscored women's vulnerability and dependence upon men for support at a time when women throughout the empire were actively campaigning for greater public roles and economic opportunities.[99] Yet, while reinscribing women's subordination, the maintenance debate was above all a conversation about policing masculine citizenship. While men abandoning families and poverty in one state might be seeking new lives in another, government officials wanted the neglect of their liabilities to follow men throughout the Empire. Andrew Fisher, the Australian Prime Minister, asserted that reciprocal arrangements "would be protecting our own communities against people who are manifestly dishonest or even worse than dishonest, who desert their own issue and their own kith and kin." In this view, Fisher affirmed that "we want a simple process of law by which deserters shall be compelled to do what worthy citizens would do to support a dependent wife and child."[100] The expectations of honest poverty defined imperial citizenship status.

The Scottish Local Government Board paper on reciprocal maintenance arrangements provided Imperial Conference attendees with perhaps the strongest condemnation of "dishonest" men. It asserted that "generally . . . the type of person who, after emigration, allowed his dependants to become destitute was usually an undesirable citizen, and . . . he would be of as little benefit to his new country as he had been to that which he had left."[101] Men who defaulted on their family responsibilities could not be trusted to uphold their other citizenship responsibilities, such as obtaining employment or keeping law and order. The memorandum maintained that Scottish officials "are persuaded that no Colony would benefit by the retention of a person unwilling to fulfil his most elementary and natural obligations."[102] Men who denied their family obligations had no place in the imperial community.

These concerns about irresponsible men shaped the Imperial Conference's final resolution on the "Provision for Deserted Wives and Children," which read, "That, in order to secure justice and protection for wives and children who have been deserted by their legal guardians either in the United Kingdom or any of the Dominions, reciprocal legal provision should be adopted in the constituent parts of the Empire in the interests of such destitute and deserted persons."[103] This language differed significantly from the original resolution by pointing directly to states' responsibilities to protect deserted women and children rather than simply to relieve them. The final resolution also explicitly blamed the "legal guardians," the negligent men who forced the Empire's governments to act.

After the Imperial Conference, the British government prepared a draft bill to "facilitate the enforcement in the United Kingdom of Maintenance Orders made in other parts of His Majesty's Dominions and vice versa."[104] The onset of the First World War stalled the legislation, and it was not until 1920 that the British Parliament began discussing the issue. Lord Birkenhead, the Conservative Lord Chancellor who championed divorce law reform, argued to the House of Lords that the concerns expressed at the 1911 Imperial Conference had only been "immeasurably aggravated by war conditions."[105] He indicated that, in 1919, more than 30 local Boards of Guardians had sent a resolution to the Colonial Office, "That a Court should be established in this country and in each of the British Colonies to consider matrimonial causes in which one of the parties is resident in another part of the Empire, and that the authority of such Courts should be enforceable in all parts of the Empire."[106] Lord Buckmaster, the former Liberal Lord Chancellor, who also advocated for divorce reform, commented that the bill was "a small and long over-due instalment of a debt which I think society owes to women who have been deserted by their husbands."[107] The desire to get back to "normal" after the war included a push on many fronts to return to rigid gender roles, with women out of the public sphere and dependent on responsible men for their welfare.[108] The state had a clear stake in protecting women from men who did not meet the standards of British manhood. The bill passed to the House of Commons and was read for the third time on August 20, 1920, passing without amendment.[109] It became the Maintenance Order (Facilities for Enforcement) Act of 1920 and was operative in regions that also endorsed reciprocal arrangements.[110]

While the 1920 legislation was seen as an act of justice for women and children, the specter of unworthy – and particularly adulterous – wives haunts almost all the documents, just as it does the reporting on local Black Country maintenance cases. From the very beginning, in the Colonial Office's 1907 letter to the South African Governor, British officials expressed the possibility that reciprocal legislation would be unfair to men. If husbands were not present to defend themselves, particularly on the grounds of their wives' immorality, justice would not prevail. In an Interdepartmental Conference leading up to the bill of 1913, a Home Office official "pointed out that grave hardship might arise if process were granted on application while the defendant was not in a position to prove that his wife was leading an immoral life and was no longer entitled to maintenance."[111] The representative of the Scottish Local Government Board, however, was not as concerned about this potential problem, arguing that "a man who deserted his wife and children was, *prima facie,* in the wrong, and if he were . . . at a disadvantage in raising defences that might otherwise be open to him, that was a disadvantage in which he had placed himself."[112] This position suggested that a neglectful husband gave up his rights, even to the point of overlooking his wife's adultery. The 1920 Act, however, took the middle ground: by enacting that maintenance orders in cases of reciprocal arrangements should be provisional until a husband was given the chance to testify, Parliament hoped to press its expectations for men while satisfying fears about disreputable women who did not merit the Empire's protection.

By 1920, men's responsibility for maintaining their families was so central to masculine citizenship that Parliament considered including affiliation orders in the reciprocal legislation.[113] This would have meant that unmarried women making financial claims on the putative fathers of their children would have the backing of imperial governments in seeking the men who did not follow through on payments. Even Leo Amery, the Under-Secretary of State for the Colonies, who was not in favor of reciprocal affiliation orders, referred to deserted unmarried women and their children as "cases of hardship,"[114] showing sympathy for unmarried mothers.

The First World War unquestionably brought the question of affiliation orders to attention in new ways. Charles Palmer, member for Wrekin in Shropshire, advocated that the Maintenance Orders Act should include affiliation orders, stressing the impact of the war on welfare priorities:

> I have had many cases in my own experience in which young women, owing to circumstances into which we will not inquire but due to the peculiar circumstances of the War, have been left with children, while the fathers have escaped either to Canada or Australia, and evaded the terrible responsibilities that we all agree rest on any man who is the father of an illegitimate child.[115]

What is so intriguing about this passage is Palmer's downplaying of women's sexuality; in fact, he was willing not to "inquire" into women's sexual behavior at all, but rather to focus on the "terrible responsibilities" of men who had fathered children. While the 1920 Act did not include affiliation orders in the end, the language in the parliamentary debate did not blame women for becoming pregnant outside of marriage. Rather, Members of Parliament focused on men who failed in their adult responsibilities. Unmarried mothers certainly did not receive the sympathy or welfare benefits accorded to married mothers, but the very fact that political debate could frame single mothers as potentially deserving is significant. Women, especially women with children, whether married or single, needed to be protected from men who failed to "realise their responsibilities."

Conclusion

Policy and legislative debates about women's welfare all represented poor women's wellbeing as best supported in marriage. However, husbands had to fulfill the expectations of marriage to support their wives. Men who neglected their wives or deserted their families challenged the domestic masculinity of honest poverty, which privileged married men over single men. Magistrates almost universally punished men's abrogation of their family liability as an obvious sign of their diminished status as men and citizens, and the victimization of women by unworthy men came to dominate the framework in which authorities discussed women's welfare. The publication of the maintenance cases in newspapers reinforced the punitive attitude toward men who gave up the benefits of honest poverty by ignoring their families. Men who approached work with a lazy attitude or refused to use their earnings to support wives and children compromised their own claims to deservedness, while neglected wives' deservedness depended upon their ability to demonstrate the failures of their husbands as men.

On another level, however, the magistrates' cases show very clearly that some men were simply unable to fulfill their maintenance obligations because of difficult economic circumstances. Magistrates showed sympathy for men who were unable to maintain their wives through no fault of their own and, especially in periods of particularly high unemployment, tended to adjourn cases rather than award a wife maintenance payments. Magistrates' willingness to help men erase arrears of maintenance payments suggests that their priorities rested with punishing undeserving men rather than ensuring wives and children received support. The sympathy extended to honest poor men had a negative impact on poor women's welfare, since, without a maintenance order, neglected wives remained in the position that brought them to court in the first place. They most likely continued to rely on poor law relief.

Women and the authorities who spoke for them were tested most decisively by men who left their families and went abroad for work or to "bolt" from maintenance responsibilities. When the Dominions' leaders raised the specter of the unsuitable imperial citizen escaping family liability by migrating throughout the empire, the heads of state prioritized a deterrent moral message about men relinquishing their honest poverty privileges over economic arguments about the burden posed by women and children left behind. Parliament dictated that women deserved protection from men evading their obligations. Legislators even considered the question of affiliation orders for unmarried women in conjunction with maintenance orders to protect married women, suggesting their priority had shifted from punishing women who fell outside heteronormative institutions to punishing the men who put them in that position.

Conclusions

As I conclude this book in the enduring fallout from the global recession, policy sympathy for those without jobs is stretched thin. Britain's Work and Pensions Secretary Iain Duncan Smith, for example, warned his fellow Conservatives at their October 2012 conference of the current "culture of entrenched worklessness and dependency" and called for "a renewal of personal responsibility within the welfare system."[1] With reforms in 2014, Duncan Smith introduced what he referred to as "the final nail in the coffin for the old 'something for nothing' culture," essentially reinstituting a genuinely seeking work requirement for people applying for benefits.[2] In March 2014, United States Senator Paul Ryan, a regular Republican voice on poverty issues, was even more explicit, identifying a "tailspin of culture . . . of men not working and just generations of men not even thinking about working or learning to value the culture of work."[3] While women today are recognized as workers in a way they were not in the late nineteenth and early twentieth centuries, the "problem of unemployment" is still articulated in terms of a problem particularly affecting men,[4] and the assumption that men need work to fulfill family responsibilities remains strong.[5] To politicians like Duncan Smith and Ryan, long-term unemployment figures suggest growing numbers of loafers. They see people with histories of consistent employment turning into Weary Willies and Tired Tims, who prefer "dependence to independence."[6]

The public in many ways shares this attitude: Duncan's Smith's spring 2013 introduction of a cap on benefits was "according to opinion polls the government's most popular welfare policy."[7] With the benefits cap, after a certain point, claimants are cut off from eligibility for a variety of programs, including the jobseeker's allowance, income support, and housing benefit, among others.[8] Rather than bringing to the fore structural causes of poverty, these approaches highlight individual fault and negative moral meanings attached to welfare. According to Duncan Smith and Ryan, both of whom exercise significant influence on public discourse and social policy, dependence on state resources is fundamentally incompatible with full citizenship, as those who use benefits become lazy and irresponsible. This is no "welfare state."

In the late nineteenth century, a number of policymakers, welfare providers, and members of the British government questioned these attitudes, challenging prevailing opinions that blamed the poor for their poverty. Confronting visibly increasing unemployment among men who presented themselves as the honest poor, they decided that these masses of men without jobs, some of whom had been newly enfranchised, did not have control over their unemployed status. Politicians, policymakers, and unemployed men alike produced economic explanations for unemployment that recognized structural reasons for joblessness.

In the face of new economic and political realities, a remarkably broad consensus developed around a model of working-class masculinity that incorporated dependence on welfare, promising honest poor married men who could not fulfill the normative breadwinner ideal a status that identified them as citizens, not as moral failures who deserved to be shamed. Receiving government assistance, indeed, became a sign of an honest poor man's citizenship status, evidence that the state recognized that unemployment was not his fault and that he deserved resources to help him become independent again. While creating hope for some men, honest poverty remained a limited vision of citizenship tied to welfare. No one was particularly outspoken in regard to the deserving status of "regular paupers" or "unemployables." Because "honest" men agreed that the willingness to work was a necessary sign of deservedness, they did not challenge policy and provider rhetoric about the "residuum." Indeed, they supported the idea that a group of men existed who could be blamed for their condition. And, in bringing forward the deservedness of married men alone, married unemployed men and the state fostered "welfare heteronormativity," marginalizing single men's welfare and filtering women's welfare through marriage.

What did working-class men actually gain from the attempts to rethink masculine status in relationship to welfare dependence? In the context of the poor law world, a man identified as part of the honest poor was separated from "regular paupers" and received less stigmatized poor law relief. Rather than being condemned to the punitive workhouse, honest poor men could perform task work for a cash award or in-kind relief. The poor law world, however, did not really support honest poverty as a masculine citizenship status, because men lost their vote no matter what kind of poor law relief they received, and the work itself was monotonous and unproductive. Even if men could be differentiated through a hierarchy of assistance types, in socio-political terms, all men dependent upon the Poor Law were paupers not citizens. This tension continued throughout the entire period covered by this study, since, although welfare for honest poor men evolved, many men still had to fall back on poor law relief. Even though the 1918 Representation of the People Act abolished the pauper disqualification from the franchise, cultural understandings refused to combine the terms "pauper" and "citizen."

The government also sought to separate honest poor men from those considered undeserving by offering them relief projects outside the poor law framework entirely. In 1886, the Local Government Board proposed public works schemes as an alternative to the Poor Law, to protect honest poor men from the taint of poor relief. Productive "work" rather than "relief" supported masculine citizenship, but work schemes were underfunded and could not address the extent of unemployment in the crises of the mid-1880s and the mid-1890s. Even after the Unemployed Workmen Act of 1905, which instituted national grants to facilitate local public works programs, honest poor men still found themselves demeaned by the types of work provided for them, work which was often little different from the stonebreaking of the Poor Law. Unemployed men and local government bodies alike pressured the national government to do more nationally for the honest unemployed, to find a way to provide assistance that honored the occupational identities of the men in their communities, who deserved to be treated like citizens.

Both poor law task work and local public works schemes required men to perform active, physical labor to demonstrate their welfare deservedness through adherence to the work imperative. Willingness to work was supposed to differentiate honest men from loafers. In this way, local bodies did not construe assistance as a right, but rather something that a man (literally) had to work for. These work tests themselves, however, were still a privilege, since they were not available to men identified by those in power as outside the boundaries of honest poverty. These relief strategies suggest that it was almost impossible for a man who had been labeled a Weary Willy or Tired Tim to rehabilitate himself. Indeed, authorities constantly worried that honest men would be corrupted by the "culture of entrenched worklessness" associated with loafers.

The persistence of unemployment eventually led to the National Insurance Act of 1911, through which the national government took responsibility for contributing to the welfare of honest unemployed men. Eligibility for benefits, which required men to pay into the insurance fund, was a clear mark of privilege protecting an initially small group of honest men from what were recognized as economic forces beyond their control. Honest men could now claim unemployment benefit as a right, different from the neediness associated with the Poor Law. When the numbers of unemployed men and women in the post-First World War period made the insurance system untenable, the government introduced new benefits that no longer required contributions from workers. This meant that authorities had to develop new ways of distinguishing the honest poor from the undeserving. Claimants no longer had to perform task work to receive benefits, but they had to prove a history of adhering to the work imperative and demonstrate a genuine search for employment. The state materially privileged men who had long histories of occupational identities and skills that spoke to their seriousness about work, meaning the unskilled and young men had a more difficult time claiming a right to welfare.

While all honest men could differentiate themselves from loafers through task work for outrelief and public work schemes, and all honest men and women could in theory receive national unemployment benefits, in practice honest poverty was a status that fully supported only married men with responsibility for families. Poor law guardians gave married men the opportunity to undertake task work much more frequently than single men; sometimes they allowed only married men with children to work for outrelief. Similarly, local councilors reserved the few available public works positions for married men. Married men had an easier time than single men convincing officials that their searches for work were genuine, and they used their family liability to assert their deservedness. Authorities read men's marital status as a fundamental mark of differentiation with regard to welfare deservedness.

The honest poverty work-welfare system fostered a hegemonic masculinity that was both patriarchal and heteronormative, assigning privilege to men over women and to married men (especially those with families) over unmarried men. Single men's unmarried status frequently delegitimized their willingness to work, and welfare providers often saw single men as loafers and ignored their welfare needs. Because marriage (and fatherhood) signified a man's full integration into the community, the lack of wife and children undermined single men's welfare rights. The overall aim of state assistance was to return men to independent breadwinning, so men who had no family liability – no one to win bread for – were marginalized ideologically and economically. Hegemonic breadwinner masculinity – a cultural construct – had negative material consequences for men who did not have family responsibilities. The state's investment in married men went beyond providing them with direct welfare advantages. Poor law guardians and local magistrates put the burden on single men to provide for their needy elderly parents, freeing up poor married men's resources for wives and children. Authorities could have understood single men's liability for their parents as a mark of mature responsibility that garnered points in terms of masculine status, but they did not because sons did not choose the burden of parental liability. Rather, single men's support of their parents released their married brothers to accrue the privileges of honest poverty. The privilege afforded to married men was perhaps most significant during the First World War. Public and political discourse alike called for single men's sacrifice to shield married men from combat. While this military sacrifice was framed as a path to citizenship for single men, it often cost them their lives.

Single men could, of course, get married to enhance their status in the honest poverty work-welfare system. Taking on responsibility for a wife and children provided a man with welfare rights claims. Yet honest poverty in many ways trapped single men in their subordinate state. Poor law authorities, local councilors, magistrates, and the national government all pushed resources toward married men, leaving single men to struggle on their own, often unable to establish themselves in their communities. The expectation that single sons should support their parents also depleted the savings poor unmarried men might build up. The war exacerbated single men's problems, as many unmarried veterans returned home without having trained in an occupation before enlisting or being drafted. Unskilled and unmarried, they became stuck outside the boundaries of honest poverty.

In addition to ignoring single men, honest poverty reinforced the gender divide at a time when an alternative presented itself. In many households, wives were able to find employment when their husbands could not. Wives' income was fundamental to family survival, but, as the maintenance cases reveal, wives' earnings were discounted to the point that unemployed men were held responsible for supporting women who made enough to support themselves. No one challenged work as the basis of masculine worth; it was part of what separated men from women. Women might need to work to obtain basic necessities, but work was certainly not understood as a central aspect of their identities as it was for men. The unemployment benefits system regarded wives' income as supplementary, and while men were required to report their wives' earnings, women's wage contributions to the household were rarely used to withhold benefits from their husbands. Authorities, by contrast, told wives to find husbands who could support them and denied women benefits on the grounds that they were not careful enough in their marriage choices. Women's welfare should come through marriage, while men's should come through employment.

Sitting atop the hierarchy of welfare deservedness, married men indeed garnered privilege in the honest poverty work-welfare system. That privilege, however, was also easily lost. In very explicit ways, the state reprimanded men who refused to abide by the work imperative and family liability. A married man who did not work to provide for his family or who deserted his wife and children to fend for themselves drew the wrath of government bureaucrats and welfare providers. Through the withholding of welfare benefits and the use of the courts, the state disciplined men who visibly fell outside norms of marriage. Although authorities essentially ignored single men's needs, they actively sought to punish married men who had had the advantages of honest poverty and had given them up. They did not want them to be British citizens.

While policymakers and welfare providers drew on the assumptions of honest poverty to measure applicants' deservedness, poor men and women actively used the language of honest poverty to demand relief and benefits. Married men with good work histories claimed the values of honest poverty to declare their own welfare deservedness at the expense of single men. Neglected wives challenged their husbands' honest poverty to serve their own interests. Committees of unemployed men confronted welfare providers with their members' honest poverty to insist that being out of work was no fault of their own. Unemployed men – at least those whose voices come through the records – helped to construct honest poverty as a masculine citizenship status built on the willingness to work and family liability. They did not contest the centrality of employment and family responsibility to working-class masculine citizenship.

The various constituencies involved in discussions of welfare, however, did not always agree on how to define the terms of honest poverty. Unemployed men wanted to use honest poverty not only to assert their rights to welfare resources but to claim fair wages and better working conditions. They argued, for example, that refusing to work in an environment that "unmanned" them did not show they were unwilling to work and undeserving of assistance. It meant that employers denied their rights as citizens. In the end, however, those with the power to make policy and shape practice won the definitional battle. The meanings they attached to the willingness to work and family liability determined which men and women received which material outcomes, and, indeed, who should count as a full citizen.

Why end this story in 1930, before the Great Depression? On one level, 1930 provides a convenient ending for a poor law historian because of the elimination of the Boards of Guardians, creating, in historian Anthony Brundage's words, "a clear sense that an era had passed."[9] Guardians' responsibilities were moved to newly-created local public assistance committees, and, within a few years, to a national Unemployment Assistance Board.[10] More significantly, honest poverty was no longer relevant. Moving into the early 1930s, unemployment, and particularly long-term unemployment, got even worse. While the Labour Government abolished the genuinely seeking work test in the Unemployment Insurance Act of 1930, the 1930s saw the introduction of means tests to determine benefits for those who had used up their eligibility for unemployment insurance.[11] The shift to means testing explicitly challenged the honest poverty ideal that men who proved their willingness to work and responsibility for family had a right to welfare; rather, means testing was simply a humiliating quantifiable measure of need. It did not promise to set honest poor men on a path to achieve independent breadwinner masculinity. It did not try to rehabilitate citizens.

Honest poverty as a masculine citizenship status was constructed to rescue men from the blame and failure that the ideology of the New Poor Law attached to men without work. Yet it was never a sustainable status, even for those it privileged. Poor men who claimed a right to welfare simultaneously called out their deservedness and their failure to achieve hegemonic masculinity. Rather than produce a collectivist vision of the state, honest poverty provided a bridge between the nineteenth-century liberal independence assumed by the Poor Law and the post-1945 vision of the welfare state, when *everyone* regardless of income level had a right to state benefits, a vision which now has pretty much dissolved. Between 1870 and 1930, the British state was moving towards "social programs [that would] offer assistance as a right of citizenship, rather than as an alternative to it, as was the case with poor relief."[12] Honest men, however, needed both the Poor Law and the national benefits system, which continually disrupted the construction of welfare as a right. Additionally, men who relied on the state were, in the end, dependent and subordinate, never fully achieving breadwinner status at a time when independence remained the predominant marker of masculinity. The efforts by unemployed men and policymakers to replace the moral meanings of joblessness with economic ones were clearly unsuccessful in the long run, and the story of honest poverty can be regarded as the story of a failed struggle to separate structural and moral understandings of unemployment.

The attempts to solve the "problem of unemployment" in the late nineteenth and early twentieth centuries highlight tensions among economic circumstances, prevailing ideologies and cultural beliefs, and people's everyday lives. They underscore the inconsistencies of policy and practice as government officials, bureaucrats, and welfare providers struggled to weave their ways through the conflicts produced by implementing national policies in local contexts where they did not necessarily make sense. These tensions and inconsistencies produced complaints about Weary Willies and Tired Tims that tended to neglect the circumstances in which people experienced poverty and decided to apply for state assistance. For the "honest" poor men in this study, asking for help never became normalized, and they struggled with the shame of being without work. Even though they and their policymaker allies attempted to "de-moralize" unemployment, the negative associations of being without work and relying on the state remained. They remain today, and those who assert the constructive power of state welfare fight an uphill battle to defend the position that people can indeed be out of work, in President Barack Obama's January 2014 words, "through no fault of their own."[13] As politicians and programs compete for national resources, it is perhaps easier to blame unemployed people for their circumstances than to challenge long-held assumptions and think expansively about how to confront "so much honest poverty."

Notes

Preface

1. "Inaugural Address by President Barack Obama," The White House, accessed February 23, 2014, http://www.whitehouse.gov/the-press-office/2013/01/21/inaugural-address-president-barack-obama.
2. Rowena Mason, "Benefit Reforms Will End 'Something-for-Nothing Culture,' says Duncan Smith," *The Guardian*, October 1, 2013, accessed February 19, 2014, http://www.theguardian.com/politics/2013/oct/01/benefit-reforms-iain-duncan-smith-unemployed.

1 "So Much Honest Poverty": Introduction

1. "Further Unemployment Demonstrations in Dudley," *Dudley Herald*, September 17, 1921, 2.
2. "Quarry Bank. Poor Unemployed," *Dudley Herald*, March 27, 1919, 10.
3. There is a large literature on the male breadwinner ideal. Studies particularly relevant to my argument include Sara Horrell and Jane Humphries, "The Origins and Expansion of the Male Breadwinner Family: The Case of Nineteenth Century Britain," *International Review of Social History* 42, Supplement 5 (1997): 25–64; Angelique Janssens, "The Rise and Decline of the Male Breadwinner Family? An Overview of the Debate," *International Review of Social History* 42, Supplement 5 (1997): 1–23; Wally Seccombe, "Patriarchy Stabilized: The Construction of the Male Breadwinner Norm in Nineteenth Century Britain," *Social History* 11, no. 1 (1986): 53–76; Anna Clark, "The New Poor Law and the Breadwinner Wage: Contrasting Assumptions," *Journal of Social History* 34, no. 2 (Winter 2000): 261–81; Marjorie Levine-Clark, "Engendering Relief: Women, Ablebodiedness, and the New Poor Law in Early Victorian England," *Journal of Women's History* 11, no. 4 (2000): 107–30; Susan Pedersen, *Family, Dependence, and the Origins of the Welfare State in Britain and France, 1914–1945* (New York: Cambridge University Press, 1993); and Mary Daly, *The Gender Division of Welfare: The Impact of the British and German Welfare States* (New York: Cambridge University Press, 2000).
4. Mike Savage, "Class and Labour History," in *Class and Other Identities: Gender, Religion, and Ethnicity in the Writing of European Labour History*, ed. Lex Heerma van Voss and Marcel van der Linden (New York: Berghahn Books, 2002), 61. I thank Sonya Rose for pointing me to this concept.
5. On this mixed economy of welfare, see, for example, Martin Daunton, ed., *Charity, Self-Interest and Welfare in the English Past* (London: UCL Press, 1996); Jane Lewis, *The Voluntary Sector, the State & Social Work in Britain: The Charity Organization Society/Family Welfare Association since 1869* (Aldershot: Edward Elgar, 1995); Donald T. Critchlow and Charles H. Parker, eds, *With Us Always: A History of Private Charity and Public Welfare* (Lanham, MD: Rowman and

Littlefield, 1998); and Steven King and Alannah Tomkins, eds, *The Poor in England, 1700–1850: An Economy of Makeshifts* (New York: Palgrave, 2003).

6. For an introduction to the long historiography of the New Poor Law, see Lynn Hollen Lees, *The Solidarities of Strangers: The English Poor Laws and the People, 1700–1948* (New York: Cambridge University Press, 1998); and Anthony Brundage, *The English Poor Laws, 1700–1930* (New York: Palgrave Macmillan, 2001).

7. See, for example, Clark, "Breadwinner Wage," and Levine-Clark, "Engendering Relief."

8. The workhouse system has received a good deal of scholarly attention. See, for example, Karel Williams, *From Pauperism to Poverty* (Boston: Routledge, Kegan, and Paul, 1981); M.A. Crowther, *The Workhouse System, 1834–1929: The History of an English Social Institution* (Athens, GA: University of Georgia Press, 1982); and Felix Driver, *Power and Pauperism: The Workhouse System, 1834–1884* (New York: Cambridge University Press, 1993).

9. This process reflects James C. Scott's arguments about the importance of states' making local circumstances legible, rationalizing local practices to establish centralized control: *Seeing like a State: How Certain Schemes to Improve the Human Condition Have Failed* (New Haven, CT: Yale University Press, 1998).

10. See, for example, Mary MacKinnon, "English Poor Law Policy and the Crusade against Outrelief," *Journal of Economic History* 47, no. 3 (1987): 603–25.

11. Gareth Stedman Jones, *Outcast London: A Study in the Relationships between Classes in Victorian Society* (New York: Oxford University Press, 1971), 11.

12. Noel Whiteside gives an excellent introduction to the development of unemployment as a category in "Constructing Unemployment: Britain and France in Historical Perspective," *Social Policy and Administration* 48, no. 1 (February 2014): 67–85. See also Sean Glynn, "Employment, Unemployment and the Labour Market," in *British Social Welfare in the Twentieth Century*, ed. Robert M. Page and Richard Silburn (New York: St. Martin's Press, 1999), 184.

13. Booth's work was published in 17 volumes between 1889 and 1903. For the early work, see *Life and Labour of the People in London* (London: Macmillan and Co., 1892); and Seebohm Rowntree, *Poverty: A Study of Town Life* (London: Macmillan, 1901).

14. Matt Perry, *Bread and Work: The Experience of Unemployment, 1918–1939* (London: Pluto, 2000), 23.

15. See, for example, Geoffrey Finlayson, *Citizen, State, and Social Welfare in Britain, 1830–1990* (New York: Oxford University Press, 1994), 114, 120; and Bentley B. Gilbert, *British Social Policy, 1914–1939* (Ithaca, NY: Cornell University Press, 1970), 51.

16. See, for example, Stedman Jones, *Outcast London*, 301–5.

17. Robert Pinker, "New Liberalism and the Middle Way," in *British Social Welfare in the Twentieth Century*, ed. Robert M. Page and Richard Silburn (New York: St. Martin's Press, 1999), 84–91; and Finlayson, *Social Welfare in Britain*, 155–6, 160–2.

18. William Beveridge, *Unemployment: A Problem of Industry* (London: Longmans, Green, and Co., 1909).

19. Ann Shola Orloff, "Gendering the Comparative Analysis of Welfare States," *Sociological Theory* 27, no. 3 (2009): 317.

20. Jane Lewis, "Gender and Welfare in Modern Europe," *Past and Present* 1, Supplement 1 (2006): 40.
21. For an introduction to this scholarship, see, for example, Orloff, "Gendering the Comparative Analysis"; Lewis, "Gender and Welfare"; Ann Orloff, "Gender in the Welfare State," *Annual Review of Sociology* 22 (1996): 51–78; Jane Lewis, "Gender and the Development of Welfare Regimes," *Journal of European Policy* 2, no. 3 (1992), 159–73; and Seth Koven and Sonya Michel, "Womanly Duties: Maternalist Politics and the Origins of Welfare States in France, Germany, Great Britain, and the United States," *American Historical Review* 95, no. 4 (October 1990): 1076–108. On men and welfare, see Jennie Popay, Jeff Hearn, and Jeanette Edwards, eds, *Men, Gender Divisions, and Welfare* (New York: Routledge, 1998).
22. My analysis aims to complement the excellent studies of gender and social policy in the United States and France by Alice Kessler-Harris, *In Pursuit of Equity: Women, Men, and the Quest for Economic Citizenship in 20th-Century America* (New York: Oxford University Press, 2001); and Laura Levine Frader, *Breadwinners and Citizens: Gender in the Making of the French Social Model* (Durham, NC: Duke University Press, 2008).
23. John Tosh, *Manliness and Masculinities in Nineteenth-Century Britain* (Harlow, UK: Pearson Education, 2005), 14.
24. Anna Clark, *The Struggle for the Breeches: Gender and the Making of the British Working Class* (Berkeley: University of California Press, 1995); and Sonya Rose, *Limited Livelihoods: Gender and Class in Nineteenth-Century England* (Berkeley: University of California Press, 1992) still provide some of the best illustrations of this point.
25. The main theoretical assumptions that I bring to my work are that social policy and law are fundamental locations where gender (a social construct) becomes naturalized (made to seem natural); and that historical actors' choices regarding their actions, roles, and identities are constrained by the material conditions and discursive constructs in which they are situated. People act within these constraints, performing roles that both reinforce and challenge norms. I am interested in the relationships between structure and agency, and discourse and lived experience. See, for example, Pierre Bourdieu, *Outline of a Theory of Practice* (New York: Cambridge University Press, 1977); Judith Butler, *Gender Trouble: Feminism and the Subversion of Identity* (New York: Routledge, 1990); Michel Foucault, *The History of Sexuality. Volume I: An Introduction* (New York: Vintage, 1990); Denise Riley, *'Am I That Name': Feminism and the Category of Women in History* (Minneapolis: University of Minnesota Press, 1987); Joan W. Scott, "Gender: A Useful Category of Historical Analysis," *American Historical Review* 91, no. 5 (1986): 1053–75; and Kathleen Canning, *Gender History in Practice: Historical Perspectives on Bodies, Class, and Citizenship* (Ithaca, NY: Cornell University Press, 2006).
26. Kathleen Canning and Sonya O. Rose, "Introduction: Gender, Citizenship, and Subjectivity: Some Historical and Theoretical Considerations," in *Gender, Citizenship, and Subjectivities*, ed. Kathleen Canning and Sonya O. Rose (Oxford: Blackwell, 2001), 1.
27. Canning and Rose, "Introduction," 5.
28. Linda Kerber's *No Constitutional Right to Be Ladies: Women and the Obligations of Citizenship* (New York: Hill and Wang, 1998) provides an excellent

discussion of the relationships between rights and obligations with reference to gender.

29. T.H. Marshall, "Citizenship and Social Class," in *Inequality and Society*, ed. Jeff Manza and Michael Sauder (New York: W.W. Norton and Co., 2009), 149–50.
30. Marshall, "Citizenship and Social Class," 149.
31. Marshall, "Citizenship and Social Class," 149. Nancy Cott has argued that "The whole system of attribution and meaning that we call *gender* relies on and to a great extent derives from the structuring provided by marriage. ... The unmarried as well as the married bear the ideological, ethical, and practical impress of the marital institution, which is difficult or impossible to escape." *Public Vows: A History of Marriage and the Nation* (Cambridge, MA: Harvard University Press, 2000), 3.
32. Feminist scholars long have been interested in questions of gender and citizenship. See, for example, Carol Pateman, *The Sexual Contract* (Stanford, CA: Stanford University Press, 1988); Gisela Bock and Susan James, eds, *Beyond Equality and Difference: Citizenship, Feminist Politics, and Female Subjectivity* (New York: Routledge, 1992); Ruth Lister, *Citizenship: Feminist Perspectives* (New York: New York University Press, 2003); and Sasha Rosenheil, ed., *Beyond Citizenship: Feminism and the Transformation of Belonging* (New York: Palgrave Macmillan, 2013).
33. Tosh, *Manliness and Masculinities*, 35.
34. R.W. Connell, *Masculinities*, 2nd ed. (Berkeley: University of California Press, 2005), 37, 67–86.
35. Linda Gordon has argued that "Needs have often been feminine, while earnings and rights, speaking of power in the economy and the state, have more often been masculine." *Pitied But Not Entitled: Single Mothers and the History of Welfare* (New York: Free Press, 1994), 11. Gordon (10–12) provides a brief introduction of the rights versus needs theories. See also Jane Lewis, *Women and Social Policies in Europe: Work, Family and the State* (Brookfield, VT: Edward Elgar, 1993), 12–14.
36. Samantha Williams, in her study of the Old Poor Law, differentiates lifecycle paupers who needed assistance at specific life crises from lifetime paupers who regularly relied on the Poor Law for survival. *Poverty, Gender, and the Life-Cycle under the English Poor Law, 1760–1834* (Rochester, NY: Boydell Press, 2011).
37. Connell, *Masculinities*, 80–1. Tosh frames these two pillars of masculine status as setting up and maintaining a household and earning income from dignified work. *Manliness and Masculinities*, 36–7.
38. Joanne Bailey, "Masculinity and Fatherhood in England, c. 1760–1830," in *What Is Masculinity? Historical Dynamics from Antiquity to the Contemporary World*, eds. John Arnold and Sean Brady (London: Palgrave Macmillan, 2011), 168.
39. John Gillis, *For Better, For Worse: British Marriages, 1600 to the Present* (New York: Oxford University Press, 1985), 229.
40. See for example, Clark, *Struggle for the Breeches*; Sonya Rose, "Respectable Men, Disorderly Others: The Language of Gender and the Lancashire Weavers' Strike of 1878 in Britain," *Gender and History* 5, no. 3 (1993): 382–97; and Keith McClelland, "'England's Greatness, the Working Man'," in *Defining the Victorian Nation: Class, Race, Gender, and the British Reform Act of 1867*, ed. Catherine Hall, Keith McClelland, and Jane Rendall (New York: Cambridge University Press, 2000), 71–118.

41. Margot Canaday, *The Straight State: Sexuality and Citizenship in Twentieth-Century America* (Princeton, NJ: Princeton University Press, 2009).

42. Chrys Ingraham, ed., *Thinking Straight: The Power, the Promise, and the Paradox of Heterosexuality* (New York: Routledge, 2005), 4. This collection offers multiple approaches to thinking about the institutionalization of heterosexuality and heteronormativity.

43. Heteronormativity, according to the sociologist Stevi Jackson, "defines not only a normative sexual practice but also a normal way of life." "Gender, Sexuality, and Heterosexuality: The Complexity (and Limits) of Heteronormativity," *Feminist Theory* 7, no. 1 (2006): 107. See also Kristen Schilt and Laurel Westbrook, "Doing Gender, Doing Heteronormativity: 'Gender Normals,' Transgender People, and the Social Maintenance of Heterosexuality," *Gender and Society* 23, no. 4 (2009): 440–64, especially 441.

44. José Harris, *Unemployment and Politics: A Study in English Social Policy, 1886–1914* (Oxford: Clarendon Press, 1972), 148.

45. Lees, *Solidarities*, 182.

46. Lees, *Solidarities*, 242.

47. Elizabeth Hurren, *Protesting about Pauperism: Poverty, Politics, and Poor Relief in Late-Victorian England, 1870–1900* (Rochester, NY: Boydell Press, 2007). Lees, *Solidarities*, also has emphasized the ways the poor asserted their entitlement to poor law relief.

48. Quoted in D.M. Palliser, *The Staffordshire Landscape* (London: Hodder and Stoughton, 1976), 197.

49. Richard H. Trainor, *Black Country Elites: The Exercise of Authority in an Industrial Area, 1830–1900* (New York: Oxford University Press, 1993), 26. For an in-depth discussion of the Black Country economy, see G.C. Allen, *The Industrial Development of the Black Country, 1860–1927*, (1929; repr., New York: A.M. Kelley, 1966). See also George Barnsby, "The Standard of Living in the Black Country during the Nineteenth Century," *Economic History Review* 2nd series 24 (1971): 220–39; George Barnsby, *Social Conditions in the Black Country, 1800–1900* (Wolverhampton: Integrated Pub. Services, 1980); Harold Parsons, *Portrait of the Black Country* (London: R. Hale, 1986); and Charles Elwell, *Aspects of the Black Country: Black Country Social and Economic History* (Kingswinford: Black Country Society, 1991).

50. Barnsby, "Standard of Living," 220.

51. Allen, *Industrial Development*, 272; Dudley Archives and Local History Service, David Faulkner, "Chainmaking and Nailmaking: The Domestic Industries of the Black Country," unpublished manuscript, 19.

52. Barnsby, *Social Conditions*, 5. See, for example, Kathrin Levitan, "Redundancy, the 'Surplus Woman' Problem, and the British Census, 1851–1861," *Women's History Review* 17, no. 3 (2008): 359–76.

53. Barnsby, *Social Conditions*, 7–8.

54. Barnsby, *Social Conditions*, 8.

55. Barnsby, *Social Conditions*, 8–9.

56. Carol Morgan, *Women Workers and Gender Identities, 1835–1913: The Cotton and Metal Industries* (New York: Routledge, 2001), 105–107. See also, Sheila Blackburn, "Working-Class Attitudes to Social Reform: Black Country Chainmakers and Anti-Sweating Legislation, 1880–1930," *International Review of Social History* 33, no. 1 (1988): 46–7.

57. Barnsby, "Standard of Living," 233. This figure is quoted in Trainor, *Black Country Elites*, 294; and Morgan, *Women Workers*, 98.
58. See, for example, Barnsby, *Social Conditions*; and Allen, *Industrial Development*.
59. Allen, *Industrial Development*, 381–3.
60. Palliser, *Staffordshire Landscape*, 199.
61. The archival collection on which this dataset is based is the set of Application and Report Books for the Stourbridge Union, held at the Staffordshire Record Office (SRO); from the Halesowen District, D585/1/5/27, D585/1/5/29, D585/1/5/32, and D585/1/5/35; from the Stourbridge District, D585/1/5/47 and D585/1/5/50; and from the Kingswinford District, D585/1/5/68, D585/1/5/70, D585/1/5/73, and D585/1/5/76.
62. SRO, D585/1/1/137, Cases of Individual Paupers, Stourbridge Union, Parts 1, 3, and 5.

2 Not "Weary Willies" or "Tired Tims": The Work Imperative in the Poor Law World

1. "The Demon of Unemployment," *Dudley Herald*, November 21, 1908, 9.
2. "The Demon of Unemployment," *Dudley Herald*, November 21, 1908, 9.
3. Lew Stringer, "Blimey! It's another blog about comics! A tribute to Tom Browne," accessed February 2013, http://lewstringer.blogspot.com/2010/03/tribute-to-tom-browne.html.
4. Multiple newspaper reports characterized honest men's unemployment as being "through no fault of their own." See for example, "Christmas," *Dudley Herald*, December 21, 1878, 5; "Distress in Dudley," *Dudley Herald*, October 29, 1921, 4.
5. See, for example, Noel Whiteside, "Constructing Unemployment: Britain and France in Historical Perspective," *Social Policy and Administration* 48, no. 1 (February 2014): 67–85; and George R. Boyer, "The Evolution of Unemployment Relief in Great Britain," *Journal of Interdisciplinary History* 34, no. 3 (2004): 393–433. Earlier unemployment crises, such as that associated with the Lancashire Cotton Famine of the 1860s, also led Boards of Guardians to relieve men affected by the particular circumstances in non-stigmatizing ways, but this did not lead to the systemic analysis of unemployment that would emerge in later decades. See George R. Boyer, "Poor Relief, Informal Assistance, and Short Time during the Lancashire Cotton Famine," *Explorations in Economic History* 34, no. 1 (1997): 56–76.
6. Act for the Relief of the Poor, 1601, 43 Eliz. 1, c. 2.
7. Vagrancy Act, 1824, 5 Geo. 4, c. 83, 698.
8. Robert Humphreys, *No Fixed Abode: A History of Responses to the Roofless and Rootless in Britain* (New York: St. Martin's Press, 1999), 81.
9. See, for example, John Tosh, *Manliness and Masculinities in Nineteenth-Century Britain: Essays on Gender, Family, and Empire* (New York: Routledge, 2004), 36.
10. José Harris, *Unemployment and Politics: A Study in English Social Policy, 1886–1914* (Oxford: Clarendon Press, 1972), 2.
11. On the development of the New Poor Law, see Anthony Brundage, *The English Poor Laws, 1700–1930* (New York: Palgrave Macmillan, 2001).

12. Poor Law Commission, "General Out-Door Labour Test Order," in *Eighth Annual Report of the Commission*, 1842 (389), 103–4.
13. Deborah Valenze, *The First Industrial Woman* (New York: Oxford University Press, 1995); and Marjorie Levine-Clark, *Beyond the Reproductive Body: The Politics of Women's Health and Work in Early Victorian England* (Columbus, OH: Ohio State University Press, 2004).
14. On the "crusade," see Elizabeth Hurren, *Protesting About Pauperism: Poverty, Politics, and Poor Relief in Late-Victorian England, c. 1870–1914* (Rochester, NY: Boydell and Brewer, 2007); Karel Williams, *From Pauperism to Poverty* (London: Routledge and Kegan Paul, 1981); and Mary MacKinnon, "English Poor Law Policy and the Crusade against Outrelief," *Journal of Economic History* 47, no. 3 (1987): 603–25.
15. Lynn Hollen Lees, *The Solidarities of Strangers: The English Poor Laws and the People, 1700–1948* (New York: Cambridge University Press, 1998), 268.
16. Keith McClelland, "'England's Greatness, the Working Man,'" in *Defining the Victorian Nation: Class, Race, Gender, and the British Reform Act of 1867*, ed. Catherine Hall, Keith McClelland, and Jane Rendall (New York: Cambridge University Press, 2000), 117.
17. Richard H. Trainor, *Black Country Elites: The Exercise of Authority in an Industrial Area, 1830–1900* (New York: Oxford University Press, 1993), 306.
18. Lees, *Solidarities*, 262; and Local Government Board (LGB), *Fourteenth Annual Report*, 1884–85, xl, xvii.
19. National Archives (NA), MH 32/52, Report to the Local Government Board, Poor Law Inspector Francis D. Longe, February 15, 1879, 4.
20. NA, MH 32/52, Report to the Local Government Board, Poor Law Inspector Francis D. Longe, February 15, 1879, 23–38.
21. Harris, *Unemployment and Politics*, 374. These statistics do not include all trade unions, only some that provided unemployment benefits and maintained monthly unemployment registers. Government Statistical Service, "Unemployment Statistics from 1881 to the Present Day," *Labour Market Trends* (January 1996): 8.
22. "The Distress in the District," *Dudley Herald*, December 21, 1878, 5.
23. "Christmas," *Dudley Herald*, December 21, 1878, 5.
24. "Dudley Board of Guardians," *Dudley Herald*, January 18, 1879, 4.
25. "Dudley Board of Guardians," *Dudley Herald*, February 1, 1879, 5.
26. "Dudley Board of Guardians," *Dudley Herald*, February 1, 1879, 5.
27. "Dudley Board of Guardians," *Dudley Herald*, March 1, 1879, 5.
28. Harris, *Unemployment and Politics*, 374.
29. John Burnett, *Idle Hands: The Experience of Unemployment, 1790–1990* (New York: Routledge, 1994), 146.
30. Burnett, *Idle Hands*, 145–8; and McClelland, "'England's Greatness, the Working Man'," 72–7. Gareth Stedman Jones's *Outcast London: A Study in the Relationships between Classes in Victorian Society* (New York: Oxford University Press, 1971) remains the most definitive study of middle-class responses to the "residuum" in London.
31. "Stourbridge Board of Guardians," *County Express*, March 13, 1886, 5.
32. Lees, *Solidarities*, 295.

33. "Stourbridge Board of Guardians," *County Express*, March 13, 1886, 5.
34. "Stourbridge," *County Advertiser*, January 3, 1891, 5.
35. Harris, *Unemployment and Politics*, 75–8.
36. Local Government Board (LGB), *Sixteenth Annual Report*, 1886–1887. Appendix 1: "Pauperism and Distress: Circular Letter to Boards of Guardians," March 15, 1886, 5.
37. LGB, "Pauperism and Distress," 6.
38. LGB, "Pauperism and Distress," 7.
39. LGB, "Pauperism and Distress," 7.
40. "Tipton. The Authorities and the Poor," *Dudley Herald*, March 6, 1886, 7.
41. "Coseley Local Board. Annual Meeting," *Dudley Herald*, April 24, 1886, 7.
42. Harris, *Unemployment and Politics*, 90.
43. House of Commons, "Second Report of the 1895 Select Committee on Distress," vol. 8, 234.
44. House of Commons, "Second Report of the 1895 Select Committee on Distress," 103, 106.
45. See, for example, Daniel Pick, *Faces of Degeneration: A European Disorder, 1848–1914* (New York: Cambridge University Press, 1993), Part 3.
46. House of Commons, "Second Report of the 1896 Select Committee on Distress," vol. 9, iii.
47. House of Commons, "Report of the 1896 Select Committee on Distress," vi.
48. House of Commons, "Report of the 1896 Select Committee on Distress," xiv.
49. House of Commons, "Report of the 1896 Select Committee on Distress," xiv.
50. Neal Blewett, "The Franchise in the United Kingdom 1885–1918," *Past and Present* 32, no. 1 (1965): 27–56. The extent of disqualification has been challenged by Eric Briggs, "The Myth of Pauper Disqualification," *Social Policy and Administration* 13, no. 2 (1979): 138–41.
51. House of Commons, "Report of the 1896 Select Committee on Distress," vii.
52. House of Commons, "Report of the 1896 Select Committee on Distress," viii.
53. Bentley B. Gilbert, *British Social Policy, 1914–1939* (Ithaca, NY: Cornell University Press, 1970), 51–2.
54. *Parliamentary Debates*, 4th ser., vol. 151 (1905), col. 760.
55. "Dudley Distress Committee. How Work is Found for the Genuine Unemployed," *Dudley Herald*, October 23, 1909, 11.
56. "Dudley Town Council," *Dudley Herald*, January 9, 1909, 9.
57. *Report of the Royal Commission on the Poor Laws and Relief of Distress*, Cd. 4499 (1909).
58. *Report of the Royal Commission on the Poor Laws*, 364.
59. *Report of the Royal Commission on the Poor Laws*, 365.
60. Sidney and Beatrice Webb, ed., *The Break-Up of the Poor Law: Being Part One of the Minority Report of the Poor Law Commission* (London: Longmans, Green, and Co., 1909).
61. *Report of the Royal Commission on the Poor Laws*, 333.
62. *Report of the Royal Commission on the Poor Laws*, 380.
63. *Report of the Royal Commission on the Poor Laws*, 381.
64. *Report of the Royal Commission on the Poor Laws*, 378.
65. Government Statistical Service, "Unemployment Statistics," 6.
66. Gilbert, *British Social Policy*, 54–61.

67. Ministry of Labour, *Labour Gazette*, October 1920, XXXVIII, no. 10: 538; June 1921, XXIX, no. 6: 280.
68. "Doings in Dudley," *County Express*, February 26, 1921, 8.
69. Ministry of Labour, *Labour Gazette*, August 1922, XXX, no. 8: 325.
70. Ministry of Labour, *Labour Gazette*, February 1921, XXIX, no. 2: 101; June 1921, XXIX, no. 6: 322; November 1921, XXIX, no. 11: 610.
71. Ministry of Labour, *Labour Gazette*, August 1922, XXX, no. 8: 349.
72. Matt Perry, *Bread and Work: The Experience of Unemployment, 1918–1939* (London: Pluto, 2000), 104.
73. "Dudley Board of Guardians," *Dudley Herald*, September 10, 1921, 7.
74. "Dudley Board of Guardians. Deputation of Unemployed," *Dudley Herald*, October 8, 1921, 9.
75. "Brierley Hill Trades Council," *Dudley Herald*, October 1, 1921, 4.
76. Sonya Rose has identified this language of "respectable dissent" in late nineteenth-century labor politics, "Respectable Men, Disorderly Others: The Language of Gender and the Lancashire Weavers' Strike of 1878 in Britain," *Gender and History* 5, no. 3 (1993): 382–97.
77. Staffordshire Record Office (SRO), D585/1/1/137, Cases of Individual Paupers, Stourbridge Union, Part 5.
78. SRO, D585/1/1/59, Stourbridge Guardians Minutes, September 30, 1921, 216.
79. SRO, D585/1/1/59, Stourbridge Guardians Minutes, October 14, 1921, 228.
80. SRO, D585/1/1/59, Stourbridge Guardians Minutes, May 26, 1922, 392.
81. NA, HLG 30/32, Memorandum to Lord Eustace Percy and Sir Aubrey Symonds, October 1923.
82. NA, HLG 30/32, "Note on Discussion at the Ministry of Health," November 29, 1923.
83. Michel Foucault's arguments concerning discipline certainly apply to the Poor Law throughout this period, in this case, as a means to create bodies disciplined for work. *Discipline and Punish: The Birth of the Prison* (New York: Vintage Books, 1995).
84. "Relief to Unemployed," *Dudley Herald*, April 16, 1927, 8.
85. "Relief to Unemployed," *Dudley Herald*, April 16, 1927, 8.
86. "Weeding Out the Shirkers," *Dudley Herald*, April 16, 1927, 6.
87. "Out-Relief Administration. Dudley Guardians Policy Commended by Ministry," *Dudley Herald*, September 24, 1927, 11.
88. "Out-Relief and Test Work. Stourbridge Guardians' Discussion," *County Express*, June 16, 1928, 9.
89. Wal Hannington, "Unemployment and the Labour Government," *Labour Monthly*, December 1929, 738.
90. "Tipton Unemployed. Deputation to the Council," *Dudley Herald*, September 10, 1921, 8.
91. "Dudley Town Council. Deputation of the Unemployed," *Dudley Herald*, September 17, 1921, 8.
92. "Stourbridge Unemployed," *County Express*, February 4, 1922, 9.
93. "Halesowen Unemployed," *Dudley Herald*, February 4, 1922, 8.
94. G.C. Peden, "The 'Treasury View' on Public Works and Employment in the Interwar Period," *Economic History Review* 37, no. 2 (1984): 167–81.

3 "They were not single men": Responsibility for Family and Hierarchies of Deservedness

1. "Stourbridge Guardians," *Dudley Herald*, May 29, 1919, 3.
2. Sean Brady, *Masculinity and Male Homosexuality in Britain, 1861–1913* (New York: Palgrave Macmillan, 2005), 46. For more on this version of masculinity, see Keith McClelland, "'England's Greatness, the Working Man,'" in *Defining the Victorian Nation: Class, Race, Gender and the Reform Act of 1867*, ed. Catherine Hall, Keith McClelland, and Jane Rendall (New York: Cambridge University Press, 2000), 71–118. See also Anna Clark, *The Struggle for the Breeches: Gender and the Making of the British Working Class* (Berkeley, CA: University of California Press, 1997), and Sonya Rose, *Limited Livelihoods: Gender and Class in Nineteenth-Century England* (Berkeley, CA: University of California Press, 1992).
3. See, for example, Lynn Hollen Lees, *The Solidarities of Strangers: The English Poor Laws and the People, 1700–1948* (New York: Cambridge University Press, 1998), and Karel Williams, *From Pauperism to Poverty* (London: Routledge and Kegan Paul, 1981).
4. Keith McClelland, "Masculinity and the 'Representative Artisan' in Britain, 1850–80," in *Manful Assertions: Masculinities in Britain since 1800*, ed. Michael Roper and John Tosh (New York: Routledge, 1991), 82.
5. Sonya O. Rose, "Respectable Men, Disorderly Others: The Language of Gender and the Lancashire Weavers' Strike of 1878 in Britain," *Gender and History* 5, no. 3 (1993): 389.
6. Angus McLaren, *The Trials of Masculinity: Policing Sexual Boundaries, 1870–1930* (Chicago, IL: University of Chicago Press, 1997), 55, 252n69. See also John Tosh, *Manliness and Masculinities in Nineteenth-Century Britain: Essays on Gender, Family, and Empire* (New York: Pearson Longman, 2005), 36; Brady, *Masculinity*, 26; and Rose, *Limited Livelihoods*, 128. For further discussion of the breadwinner ideal in its relationship to welfare in Britain, see Sara Horrell and Jane Humphries, "The Origins and Expansion of the Male Breadwinner Family: The Case of Nineteenth Century Britain," *International Review of Social History* 42, Supplement S5 (1997): 25–64; Wally Seccombe, "Patriarchy Stabilized: The Construction of the Male Breadwinner Norm in Nineteenth Century Britain," *Social History* 11 (1986): 53–76; Anna Clark, "The New Poor Law and the Breadwinner Wage: Contrasting Assumptions," *Journal of Social History* 34, no. 2 (Winter 2000): 261–81; Marjorie Levine-Clark, "Engendering Relief: Women, Ablebodiedness, and the New Poor Law in Early Victorian England," *Journal of Women's History* 11, no. 4 (2000): 107–30; and Susan Pedersen, *Family, Dependence, and the Origins of the Welfare State in Britain and France, 1914–1945* (New York: Cambridge University Press, 1993).
7. The negative assumptions attached to transients in terms of sexual and gender nonconformity are discussed in both Nayan Shah, *Stranger Intimacy: Contesting Race, Sexuality, and the Law in the North American West* (Berkeley, CA: University of California Press, 2011) and Margot Canaday, *The Straight State: Sexuality and Citizenship in Twentieth-Century America* (Princeton, NJ: Princeton University Press, 2009).
8. John Horne, "Masculinity in Politics and War in the Age of Nation-States and World Wars, 1850–1950," in *Masculinities in Politics and War: Gendering*

Modern History, ed. Stefan Dudink, Karen Hagemann, and John Tosh (Manchester: Manchester University Press, 2004), 34.

9. The archival collection on which this dataset is based is the set of Application and Report Books for the Stourbridge Union, held at the Staffordshire Record Office (SRO); from the Halesowen District, D585/1/5/27, D585/1/5/29, D585/1/5/32, and D585/1/5/35; from the Stourbridge District, D585/1/5/47 and D585/1/5/50; and from the Kingswinford District, D585/1/5/68, D585/1/5/70, D585/1/5/73, and D585/1/5/76.

10. See, for example, Lees, *Solidarities*; and Pat Thane, "Women and the Poor Law in Victorian and Edwardian England," *History Workshop Journal* 6 (Autumn 1978): 29–51.

11. My much smaller Dataset 2 (DS2) comes from the collection, SRO, D585/1/1/137, Case Papers of Individual Paupers. This set of records is completely unsystematic: a bundle of application files, seemingly surviving randomly in the archives.

12. On women's work in the Black Country, see Carol Morgan, *Women Workers and Gender Identities, 1835–1913: The Cotton and Metal Industries in England* (New York: Routledge, 2001); and Sheila Blackburn, "Working-Class Attitudes to Social Reform: Black Country Chainmakers and Anti-Sweating Legislation, 1880–1930," *International Review of Social History* 33, no. 1 (1988): 42–69.

13. On classifying paupers, see Lees, *Solidarities*, 142–3; on women in particular, see 196–210.

14. SRO, D585/1/5/47, Application and Report Book, Stourbridge Union, Stourbridge District, April 14, 1871; April 21, 1871; June 2, 1871.

15. SRO, D585/1/5/47, Application and Report Book, Stourbridge Union, Stourbridge District, July 14, 1871; July 21, 1871; and Worcestershire Record Office, 489:16, parcel 13, Admission Register for Powick Asylum, 1870–74. The 1871 census shows the Moon family composed of Theophilus, Sarah, a 20-year-old son, Jonathan, and two children under ten, Philip and Isabella. Ancestry.co.uk, 1871 Census, accessed October 10, 2013.

16. I do not include "none" or "not employed" as occupation categories, although this suggests applicants who expected to be working.

17. This is notably different from the findings in Samantha Williams's study of the Old Poor Law in Bedfordshire, *Poverty, Gender, and the Life-Cycle under the English Poor Law, 1760–1834* (Rochester, NY: Boydell and Brewer, 2011).

18. Local Government Board (LGB), *Eighth Annual Report*, 1878–79.

19. "Dudley Board of Guardians," *Dudley Herald*, February 1, 1879, 5.

20. Dudley Archives and Local History Service (DALHS), G/Du/1/14, *Dudley Guardians Minute Book*, November 1878–July 1880, 202–3.

21. DALHS, G/Du/1/14, *Dudley Guardians Minute Book*, November 1878–July 1880, 216.

22. DALHS, G/Du/1/14, *Dudley Guardians Minute Book*, November 1878–July 1880, 226.

23. DALHS, G/Du/1/14, *Dudley Guardians Minute Book*, November 1878–July 1880, 247.

24. See, for example, DALHS, G/Du/1/14, *Dudley Guardians Minute Book*, November 1878–July 1880, 290.

25. DALHS, G/Du/1/19, *Dudley Guardians Minute Book*, 1885–86, 111.

26. "Dudley Board of Guardians," *Dudley Herald*, March 6, 1886, 8.

27. "Out-Door Relief," *Dudley Herald*, July 14, 1883, 4.
28. "Dudley Distress Committee. How Work Is Found for the Genuine Unemployed," *Dudley Herald*, October 23, 1909, 11.
29. Joanne Bailey, "Masculinity and Fatherhood in England, c. 1760–1830," in *What Is Masculinity? Historical Dynamics from Antiquity to the Contemporary World*, ed. John Arnold and Sean Brady (London: Palgrave Macmillan, 2011), 168.
30. Andy Croll explores in detail the discourse surrounding hunger and the relief of women and children in this period in "Starving Strikers and the Limits of the 'Humanitarian Discovery of Hunger' in Late Victorian Britain," *International Review of Social History* 56, no. 1 (2011): 103–11.
31. "Distress at Dudley, Some Typical Cases," *Dudley Herald*, January 11, 1908, 3.
32. "Stourbridge Board of Guardians," *Dudley Herald*, May 2, 1908, 8.
33. "Dudley Town Council. Work for the Unemployed," *Dudley Herald*, January 9, 1909, 9.
34. "Dudley Distress Committee. How Work is Found for the Genuine Unemployed," *Dudley Herald*, October 23, 1909, 11.
35. *Report of the Royal Commission on the Poor Laws and Relief of Distress*, Cd. 4499 (1909), 365.
36. *Report of the Royal Commission on the Poor Laws*, 383.
37. The minority report of the commission emphasized structural causes of unemployment and recommended getting rid of the Poor Law entirely.
38. See, for example, Susan Kingsley Kent, *Making Peace: The Reconstruction of Gender in Interwar Britain* (Princeton, NJ: Princeton University Press, 1993).
39. Joanna Bourke, *Dismembering the Male: Men's Bodies, Britain and the Great War* (Chicago, IL: University of Chicago Press, 1996); and Alison Light, *Forever England: Femininity, Literature, and Conservatism between the Wars* (New York: Routledge, 1991). Martin Francis complicates this analysis in "The Domestication of the Male? Recent Research on Nineteenth- and Twentieth-Century British Masculinity," *Historical Journal* 45, no. 3 (2002): 637–52.
40. For more on these connections, see Marjorie Levine-Clark, "The Politics of Preference: Masculinity, Marital Status and Unemployment Relief in Post-First World War Britain," *Cultural and Social History* 7, no. 2 (2010): 233–52.
41. "Tipton Unemployed. Deputation to the Council," *Dudley Herald*, September 10, 1921, 8.
42. "Distress at Sedgley," *Dudley Herald*, September 24, 1921, 8.
43. "Stourbridge Guardians," *County Express*, January 22, 1921, 5, and "Stourbridge Guardians," *County Express*, July 23, 1921, 7. In a study of Depression-era Canadian work-relief schemes, Eric Strikwerda has found an even more blatant bias against single men, who were perceived to be a danger to the urban environment. See "'Married men should, I feel, be treated differently': Work, Relief, and Unemployed Men on the Urban Canadian Prairies, 1929–1932," *Left History* 12, no. 1 (2007): 46.
44. "The Local Coal Trade. Miners' Conference at Tipton," *Dudley Herald*, October 5, 1878, 4.
45. "Stourbridge Guardians," *County Express*, May 15, 1911, 4.
46. "Dudley Town Council. Deputation of Unemployed," *Dudley Herald*, September 17, 1921, 8.
47. "Tipton Unemployed. Deputation to the Council," *Dudley Herald*, September 10, 1921, 8.

48. "Unemployment. Brierley Hill Unemployed Organised," *Dudley Herald*, September 17, 1921, 7.
49. "Halesowen Unemployed," *Dudley Herald*, February 4, 1922, 8.
50. National Archives (NA), CAB 24/140/40, A Deputation from the Miners' Federation Received by the Prime Minister, December 2, 1922, 1–2.
51. NA, CAB 24/158/20, Deputation from the General Council of the Trades Union Congress to the Prime Minister, January 16, 1923, 10.
52. "Stourbridge Unemployed," *County Express*, January 14, 1922, 8.
53. "From the Stallage," *Dudley Herald*, April 16, 1921, 5.
54. "The First Complaint," *Dudley Herald*, February 25, 1922, 3.
55. "Brierley Hill Police Court. Quarry Bank Men Leniently Dealt With," *Dudley Herald*, March 24, 1923, 2.
56. "Theft by Dudley Coal Picker," *County Express*, June 19, 1926, 9.
57. "Obtaining Relief under False Pretences," *Dudley Herald*, July 1, 1922, 2.
58. "Obtaining Relief under False Pretences," *Dudley Herald*, July 1, 1922, 2.
59. "Wednesbury Police Court," *Dudley Herald*, September 3, 1921, 2.
60. "Important Unemployment Case," *Dudley Herald*, October 14, 1922, 5.
61. "Offence under the Unemployment Insurance Acts," *County Express*, January 6, 1923, 4.
62. Alice Kessler-Harris, *In Pursuit of Equity: Women, Men, and the Quest for Economic Citizenship in 20th-Century America* (New York: Oxford University Press, 2001).
63. SRO, D585/1/1/59, Board of Guardians Minutes, Stourbridge Union, June 9, 1921, 401.
64. SRO, D585/1/1/62, Board of Guardians Minutes, Stourbridge Union, November 6, 1925, 9.
65. Keith McClelland, "Masculinity and the 'Representative Artisan,'" 79.
66. Lees, *Solidarities*, 287.
67. On men's emotional responses to unemployment, see Sally Alexander, "Men's Fears and Women's Work: Responses to Unemployment in London between the Wars," *Gender and History* 12, no. 2 (2002): 401–25.
68. Matt Perry, *Bread and Work: The Experience of Unemployment 1918–39* (London: Pluto Press, 2000), 68.
69. "Suicide at Stourbridge. Unemployed Carter Hangs Himself," *County Express*, September 9, 1922, 9.
70. "Tragedy of Unemployment," *County Express*, October 21, 1922, 7.
71. "'Sick of Living': Woodside Man Who Was Worried to Death through Lack of Work," *Dudley Herald*, July 30, 1927, 12.
72. "Workless Man's Despair. Wordsley Forge-Roller Commits Suicide," *Dudley Herald*, August 2, 1924, 2. This case was also covered in the *County Express*, "Unemployment Tragedy. Wordsley Man Drowns Himself," August 2, 1924, 5.
73. "Christmas," *Dudley Herald*, December 21, 1878, 5.
74. "Workhouse Labour Yard. Many Unemployed Appeal to the Guardians," *County Express*, January 16, 1909, 5.
75. This approach to women's work has a long history. Historians have demonstrated that, especially in tight labor markets, working men attempted to demonize women's employment as undercutting men's wages and masculine responsibilities. For a good overview, see Katrina Honeyman and

Jordan Goodman, "Women's Work, Gender Conflict, and Labour Markets in Europe, 1500–1900," *Economic History Review* 44, no. 4 (1991): 608–28.
76. Morgan, *Women Workers*; and Blackburn, "Working-Class Attitudes."
77. Editorial, *The Advertiser*, April 4, 1891, 4.
78. "Correspondence," *The Advertiser*, April 11, 1891, 4.
79. Selina Todd offers an interesting analysis of young women's wage earning in the interwar period, showing that daughters earned both for their own spending money and to contribute to the family economy. "'You'd the Feeling You Wanted to Help': Young Women, Employment and the Family in Inter-War England," in *Women and Work Culture: Britain, c. 1850–1950*, ed. Krista Cowman and Louise A. Jackson (Burlington, VT: Ashgate, 2005), 123–40.
80. Clark, *Struggle for the Breeches*.
81. "The Strike in the Nail Trade," *The Advertiser*, August 29, 1891, 3.
82. "Women Displace Men. Stourbridge Labour Problem," *County Express*, May 23, 1919, 7.

4 "A reward for good citizenship": National Unemployment Benefits and the Genuine Search for Work

1. *Parliamentary Debates*, Commons, 5th ser., vol. 25 (1911), col. 707.
2. *Parliamentary Debates*, Commons, 5th ser., vol. 25 (1911), col. 708.
3. *Parliamentary Debates*, Commons, 5th ser., vol. 25 (1911), cols. 708–9.
4. Michael Hanagan, "Citizenship, Claim-Making, and the Right to Work: Britain, 1884–1911," *Theory and Society* 26, no. 4 (1997): 450. For overviews of the development of unemployment insurance, see, for example, Bentley B. Gilbert, *The Evolution of National Insurance in Great Britain: The Origins of the Welfare State* (London: Michael Joseph, 1966); José Harris, *Unemployment and Politics: A Study in English Social Policy, 1886–1914* (Oxford: Clarendon Press, 1972); and Roy Hay, *The Origins of the Liberal Welfare Reforms, 1906–1914* (London: Macmillan, 1975).
5. "Workhouse Labour Yard. Many Unemployed Appeal to the Guardians," *County Express*, January 16, 1909, 5.
6. "Dudley Notes. Local Government Board and the Unemployed," *Dudley Herald*, January 9, 1909, 6.
7. "Dudley Town Council. Work for the Unemployed," *Dudley Herald*, January 9, 1909, 9.
8. "Distress in Cradley," *County Express*, February 13, 1909, 3.
9. "Distress in Halesowen and Cradley. County Council's Appeal Futile," *County Express*, March 13, 1909, 8.
10. National Insurance Act, 1911, 1 & 2 Geo. 5, c. 55.
11. National Insurance Act, 1911.
12. *Parliamentary Debates*, Commons, 5th ser., vol. 25 (1911), col. 643.
13. Alan Deacon, *In Search of the Scrounger: The Administration of Unemployment Insurance in Britain, 1920–1931* (London: Bell [for the Social Administration Research Trust], 1976), 11.
14. *Parliamentary Debates*, Commons, 5th ser., vol. 21 (1911), col. 587.

15. *Parliamentary Debates*, Commons, 5th ser., vol. 21 (1911), col. 589.
16. *Parliamentary Debates*, Commons, 5th ser., vol. 21 (1911), col. 592.
17. *Parliamentary Debates*, Commons, 5th ser., vol. 21 (1911), col. 593.
18. *Parliamentary Debates*, Commons, 5th ser., vol. 21 (1911), col. 599.
19. *Parliamentary Debates*, Commons, 5th ser., vol. 21 (1911), col. 638.
20. *Parliamentary Debates*, Commons, 5th ser., vol. 21 (1911), col. 651.
21. John Burnett, *Idle Hands: The Experience of Unemployment, 1790–1990* (New York: Routledge, 1994), 196.
22. Lynn Hollen Lees, *The Solidarities of Strangers: The English Poor Laws and the People, 1700–1948* (New York: Cambridge University Press, 1998), 327.
23. Burnett, *Idle Hands*, 196.
24. For a discussion of benefits to ex-servicemen, see Chapter 6.
25. Deacon, *In Search of the Scrounger*, 13–14.
26. Ministry of Labour, Employment and Insurance Department, Memorandum L.E.C. 82/2, July 1923, reprinted as Appendix II in Ministry of Labour, *Unemployment Insurance: Directions to Local Employment Committees Regarding Grant of Uncovenanted Benefit* (London: HMSO, 1924), 4.
27. Deacon, *In Search of the Scrounger*, 15.
28. W.R. Garside, *British Unemployment, 1919–1939: A Study in Public Policy* (Cambridge: Cambridge University Press, 1990), 37–8, and Ministry of Labour, *Unemployment Insurance*, 4.
29. Garside, *British Unemployment*, 39.
30. Deacon, *In Search of the Scrounger*, 36, and Desmond S. King, *Actively Seeking Work? The Politics of Unemployment and Welfare Policy in the United States and Great Britain* (Chicago, IL: University of Chicago Press, 1995), 79n63. See also Garside, *British Unemployment*, 39, and Lydia Morris, *Dangerous Classes: The Underclass and Social Citizenship* (New York: Routledge, 1994), 39.
31. Deacon, *In Search of the Scrounger*, 37–8.
32. Deacon, *In Search of the Scrounger*, 33.
33. National Archives (NA), PIN 29/2076, Office of the Umpire, Appeal Records.
34. NA, PIN 29/2076, Office of the Umpire, Appeal Records.
35. Matt Perry, *Bread and Work: The Experience of Unemployment 1918–39* (London: Pluto Press, 2000), 43.
36. Deacon, *In Search of the Scrounger*, 10; National Industrial Conference Board, *Unemployment Insurance in Theory and Practice* (New York: The Century Co., 1922), 42–4.
37. NA, PIN 29/1–2, Umpire's Decision Books; PIN 29/3350–5, Umpire's Decisions.
38. These are non-sequential files in NA, PIN 29.
39. Quoted in Deacon, *In Search of the Scrounger*, Appendix I, 93–5.
40. See, for example, Deacon, *In Search of the Scrounger*; and Keith Laybourn, *Unemployment and Employment Policies Concerning Women in Britain, 1900–1951* (Lewiston, NY: Edwin Mellen Press, 2002).
41. NA, PIN 29/1, Umpire's Decision Book, 1925, Case No. 1683/25, 204.
42. NA, PIN 29/1960, Office of the Umpire, Appeal Records.
43. NA, PIN 29/2, Umpire's Decision Book, 1926, Case No. 4010/26, 245–6.
44. NA, PIN 29/3384, Umpire's Decisions, Decision No. 283/29, January 21, 1929.
45. Ministry of Labour, *Directions to Local Employment Committees*, Memorandum L.E.C. 82/2, July 1923, 12.
46. NA, PIN 29/3350, Umpire's Decisions, Decision No. 7164, March 10, 1924.

47. NA, PIN 29/3355, Umpire's Decisions, Decision No. 35/25, January 7, 1925.
48. NA, PIN 29/2, Umpire's Decision Book, 1926, Case No. 4792/26, 288–9.
49. NA, PIN 29/3355, Umpire's Decisions, Decision No. 9042, December 23, 1924.
50. NA, PIN 29/1, Umpire's Decision Book, 1925, Case No. 107/25, 16–17.
51. NA, PIN 29/2, Umpire's Decision Book, 1926, Case 1404/26, 175–8. The full decision is quoted in Deacon, *In Search of the Scrounger*, 93–9.
52. NA, PIN 29/3355, Umpire's Decisions, Decision No. 9/25, January 1, 1925.
53. NA, PIN 29/3350, Umpire's Decisions, Case No. 4543, March 15, 1924.
54. NA, PIN 29/3355, Umpire's Decision, Case No. 8643, October 23, 1924.
55. NA PIN 29/1200, Office of the Umpire, Appeal Records.
56. NA, PIN 29/3355, Umpire's Decisions, Decision No. 8766, November 7, 1924.
57. NA PIN 29/1200, Office of the Umpire, Appeal Records.
58. NA, PIN 29/3384, Umpire's Decisions, Decision No. 391/29, January 17, 1929.
59. On women's work and respectability, see Selina Todd, "'You'd the Feeling You Wanted to Help': Young Women, Employment and the Family in Inter-War England," in *Women and Work Culture: Britain, c. 1850–1950*, ed. Krista Cowman and Louise A. Jackson (Burlington, VT: Ashgate, 2005), 133–4.
60. Ministry of Labour, *Directions*, 18.
61. Ministry of Labour, *Directions*, 18.
62. Ministry of Labour, *Directions*, 10.
63. Ministry of Labour, *Directions*, 10.
64. NA, PIN 29/2, Umpire's Decision Book, 1925, Case No. 1067/26, 92–3.
65. NA, PIN 29/3350, Umpire's Decisions, Decision No. 7141, March 4, 1924. See also NA, PIN 29/3350, Umpire's Decisions, Decision No. 6981, February 7, 1924.
66. NA, PIN 29/3350, Umpire's Decisions, Decision No. 7228, March 21, 1924.
67. NA, PIN 29/3351, Umpire's Decisions, Decision No. 7367, April 11, 1924.
68. NA, PIN 29/1181, Office of the Umpire, Appeal Records.
69. NA, PIN 29/1, Umpire's Decision Book, 1925, Case No. 370/25, 66.
70. NA, PIN 29/1, Umpire's Decision Book, 1925, Case No.942/25, 124–5.
71. Deacon argues that from 1925, with the reintroduction of the means test assessing household incomes in deciding benefit cases, "women were primarily affected." Throughout much of the 1920s, "the proportion of women disallowed benefit was two and a half times that of men." Deacon, *In Search of the Scrounger*, 54–5.
72. NA, PIN 29/1, Umpire's Decision Book, 1925, Case No.942/25, 124–5.
73. NA, PIN 29/1, Umpire's Decision Book, 1925, Case No. 616/25, 97; NA, PIN 29/1183, Office of the Umpire, Appeal Records.
74. Keith Laybourn argues that this "discrimination" against women was explicitly codified with the Anomalies Act of 1931: "after the Anomalies Act was implemented in October 1931 married women were discriminated against because they were considered to be dependent upon their husband's earnings and not 'genuinely seeking work,' especially if there was none to be had in their district. In other words, married women with employed husbands, or husbands who were receiving unemployment benefit, were considered to be simply supplementing the family income at the expense of the state rather than intent upon seeking work. Unemployed married women were thus considered to be little better than scroungers needlessly and unfairly consuming the precious and limited resources of the state." Keith Laybourn, *Unemployment and Employment Policies*, 105.

75. NA, PIN 29/1, Umpire's Decision Book, 1925, Case No. 355/25, 64–5.
76. NA, PIN 29/1197, Office of the Umpire, Appeal Records.
77. NA, PIN 29/1197, Office of the Umpire, Appeal Records.
78. NA, PIN 29/3354, Umpire's Decisions, Decision No. 8613, October 14, 1924.
79. NA, PIN 29/3350, Umpire's Decisions, Decision No. 7123, March 3, 1924.
80. NA, PIN 29/3351, Umpire's Decisions, Decision No. 7733, June 12, 1924.
81. NA, PIN 29/3353, Umpire's Decisions, Decision No. 8080, August 18, 1924.
82. Julie-Marie Strange complicates this dichotomy in "Fatherhood, Providing, and Attachment in Late Victorian and Edwardian Working-Class Families," *Historical Journal* 55, no. 4 (2012): 1007–27.
83. See for example, NA, PIN 29/3350, Umpire's Decisions, Decision No. 7188, March 13, 1924.
84. NA, PIN 29/3354, Umpire's Decisions, Decision No. 8570, October 10, 1924.
85. NA, PIN 29/3350, Umpire's Decisions, Decision No. 7124, March 3, 1924.
86. NA, PIN 29/3350, Umpire's Decisions, Decision No. 6956, January 30, 1924.
87. NA, PIN 29/3352, Umpire's Decisions, Decision No. 7998, July 25, 1924.
88. NA, PIN 29/1188, Office of the Umpire, Appeal Records.
89. NA, PIN 29/3351, Umpire's Decisions, Decision No. 7593, May 17, 1924.
90. NA, PIN 29/1, Umpire's Decision Book, 1925, Case No. 885/25, 118–19.
91. Garside, *British Unemployment*, 49.

5 "Married men had greater responsibilities": The First World War, the Service Imperative, and the Sacrifice of Single Men

1. "Recruiting Rallies in Dudley and District," *Dudley Herald*, October 9, 1915, 5.
2. "Recruiting Rallies in Dudley and District," *Dudley Herald*, October 9, 1915, 5.
3. Nicoletta Gullace argues that much of the propaganda of the war focused on the dangers to British home life posed by the prospect of a German victory, in 'The Blood of Our Sons': Men, Women, and the Renegotiation of British Citizenship during the Great War (New York: Palgrave Macmillan, 2004).
4. P.E. Dewey, "Recruiting and the British Labour Force during the First World War," *Historical Journal* 27, no. 1 (1984): 199; and R.J.Q. Adams, "Asquith's Choice: The May Coalition and the Coming of Conscription, 1915–1916," *Journal of British Studies* 25, no. 3 (1986): 247.
5. Adams, "Asquith's Choice," 250.
6. For excellent introductions to the culture of the war and place of recruitment and the draft, see Adrian Gregory, *The Last Great War: British Society and the First World War* (New York: Cambridge University Press, 2008), and George Robb, *British Culture and the First World War* (New York: Palgrave, 2002).
7. See, for example, R.J.Q. Adams and Philip P. Poirier, *The Conscription Controversy in Great Britain, 1900–18* (Columbus, OH: Ohio State University Press, 1987); Keith Grieves, *The Politics of Manpower, 1914–18* (New York: St. Martin's Press, 1988); George Q. Flynn, *Conscription and Democracy: the Draft in France, Great Britain, and the United States* (Westport, CT: Greenwood Press, 2002); David Monger, *Patriotism and Propaganda in First World War Britain: The National War Aims Committee and Civilian Morale* (Liverpool: Liverpool University Press, 2012); Robb, *British Culture*; and Gullace, 'Blood of Our Sons.'

8. Gullace, *'Blood of Our Sons.'*
9. "Serious Disturbances at Dudley Port and Quarry Bank," *Dudley Herald,* August 15, 1914, 6.
10. "Dudley Board of Guardians," *Dudley Herald,* August 22, 1914, 8; and "Dudley Town Council," *Dudley Herald,* October 10, 1914, 3.
11. "Workmen's Collections," *Dudley Herald,* January 2, 1915, 7, and "Earl of Dudley's Workpeople Set an Excellent Example," *Dudley Herald,* February 13, 1915, 5.
12. G.C. Allen, *The Industrial Development of Birmingham and the Black Country, 1860–1927* (1929; repr., New York: A.M. Kelley, 1966), 375–6.
13. "Correspondence," *Dudley Herald,* April 17, 1915, 7.
14. "Munitions Workers," *Dudley Herald,* September 4, 1914, 6.
15. "Local Retrospect," *Dudley Herald,* January 1, 1916, 5.
16. National Archives (NA), LAB 2/169, Letter from Williams to Wolff, August 7, 1914, with accompanying list of exchanges.
17. NA, LAB 2/169, "Recruiting," August 31, 1914.
18. NA, LAB 2/169, "Recruiting," August 31, 1914.
19. "Munitions Workers," *Dudley Herald,* September 4, 1915, 6.
20. "Recruits Wanted for the Worcesters," *Dudley Herald,* February 27, 1915, 7.
21. "Recruiting Rallies in Dudley and District," *Dudley Herald,* October 9, 1915, 5.
22. "Patriotic Demonstration at Brierley Hill," *Dudley Herald,* August 7, 1915, 7.
23. "Workmen's Duty in Wartime," *Dudley Herald,* March 13, 1915, 11.
24. "Old Hill Police Court," *Dudley Herald,* September 4, 1915, 10.
25. "Halesowen Police Court," *Dudley Herald,* September 4, 1915, 11.
26. There is a large literature on women's war work, including Gail Braybon, *Women Workers in the First World War: The British Experience* (London: Croom Helm, 1981); Deborah Thom, *Nice Girls, Rude Girls: Women Workers in World War I* (New York: I.B. Tauris, 1998); and Angela Woollacott, *On Her Their Lives Depend: Munitions Workers in the Great War* (Berkeley, CA: University of California Press, 1994).
27. "Doings in Dudley," *County Express,* June 19, 1915, 6.
28. Susan Pedersen, "Gender, Welfare, and Citizenship in Britain during the Great War," *American Historical Review* 95, no. 4 (1990): 984–5.
29. Pedersen, "Gender, Welfare, and Citizenship," 985.
30. Lomas looks at the complicated bureaucratic and cultural machinery surrounding separation allowances and widows' pensions in "'Delicate Duties': Issues of Class and Respectability in Government Policy Towards the Wives and Widows of British Soldiers in the Era of the Great War," *Women's History Review* 9, no. 1 (2000): 123–47.
31. "To Single Men," *County Express,* July 24, 1915, 3.
32. "Hasbury Soldier's Appeal to Single Young Men," *County Express,* August 7, 1915, 5.
33. Gullace, *'Blood of Our Sons,'* 102.
34. Adams, "Asquith's Choice," 256–7.
35. Quoted in Roy Douglas, "Voluntary Enlistment in the First World War and the Work of the Parliamentary Recruiting Committee," *Journal of Modern History* 42, no. 4 (1970): 580.

36. Adams, "Asquith's Choice," 257–8.
37. *Parliamentary Debates*, Commons, 5th ser., vol. 77 (1915), cols. 213–437.
38. *Parliamentary Debates*, Commons, 5th ser., vol. 77 (1915), cols. 216–17.
39. *Parliamentary Debates*, Commons, 5th ser., vol. 77 (1915), col. 229.
40. *Parliamentary Debates*, Commons, 5th ser., vol. 77 (1915), col. 227.
41. *Parliamentary Debates*, Commons, 5th ser., vol. 77 (1915), col. 231.
42. *Parliamentary Debates*, Commons, 5th ser., vol. 77 (1915), col. 253.
43. *Parliamentary Debates*, Commons, 5th ser., vol. 77 (1915), col. 262.
44. *Parliamentary Debates*, Commons, 5th ser., vol. 77 (1915), col. 382.
45. *Parliamentary Debates*, Commons, 5th ser., vol. 77 (1915), col. 234.
46. *Parliamentary Debates*, Commons, 5th ser., vol. 77 (1915), col. 245.
47. *Parliamentary Debates*, Commons, 5th ser., vol. 77 (1915), col. 246.
48. William Henry Stoker, *The Military Service Acts Practice: Containing the Consolidated Acts, Proclamations, Regulations and Orders, with Notes of Cases and Tribunal Decisions* (London: Stevens and Sons, Ltd., 1918).
49. James McDermott, "Conscience and the Military Service Tribunals during the First World War: Experiences in Northamptonshire," *War in History* 17, no 1. (2010): 63.
50. Dewey, "Recruiting," 215.
51. Gerald E. Shenk, *'Work or Fight!' Race, Gender, and the Draft in World War One* (New York: Palgrave Macmillan, 2005), 6.
52. James McDermott, *British Military Service Tribunals, 1916–1918: 'A Very Much Abused Body of Men'* (Manchester: Manchester University Press, 2011).
53. McDermott, *British Military Service Tribunals*, 2–4. The National Archives website also notes the lack of records: "Looking for Records of Conscientious Objectors," National Archives, accessed January 9, 2012, http://www.national archives.gov.uk/records/research-guides/first-world-war-conscientious-objectors.htm
54. My discussion does include some reporting on tribunals beyond the first newspaper of the month.
55. "Amblecote Tribunal," *County Express*, January 15, 1916, 2.
56. "Brierley Hill Tribunal," *Dudley Herald*, March 18, 1916, 7.
57. "Tribunal Anomalies," *County Advertiser*, March 18, 1916, 2.
58. See, for example, McDermott, *British Military Service Tribunals*, Chapter 3, "The Matter of Conscience"; and Gullace, *'Blood of Our Sons,'* especially Chapter 5, "Conscription, Conscience, and the Travails of Male Citizenship."
59. One man had a ten-month exemption, and another had an exemption of a year, with both of these cases coming in 1916.
60. "Lye Tribunal. Forty More Cases," *County Express*, June 3, 1916, 5.
61. "Halesowen Tribunal. An Objection by the Military Representative," *County Advertiser*, March 4, 1916, 3.
62. "Local Tribunals. Dudley. The Rights of Married Men," *County Advertiser*, March 4, 1916, 5.
63. "Halesowen Tribunal," *County Express*, April 15, 1916, 4.
64. "The War. Halesowen Tribunal," *County Express*, April 29, 1916, 4.
65. "Halesowen Tribunal," *County Express*, April 1, 1916, 7. On shaming during the war, see Nicoletta Gullace, "White Feathers and Wounded Men: Female Patriotism and the Memory of the Great War," *Journal of British Studies* 36, no. 2 (1997): 178–206.

66. "Local Tribunals. Severe! Dudley Tribunal Criticised," *County Advertiser*, April 1, 1916, 5.
67. "Stourbridge Tribunal. The New Military Instructions. Fetching up the Single Men," *County Express*, April 8, 1916, 3.
68. "Local Tribunals. Halesowen. The Single Men Scandal," *County Advertiser*, August 5, 1916, 3.
69. "Kingswinford Tribunal. Married Man's Attestation," *County Express*, March 18, 1916, 5.
70. "Halesowen Tribunal. Many Interesting Cases," *County Express*, April 8, 1916, 7.
71. "Rowley Regis Tribunal. Giving Up His Badge," *County Express*, March 3, 1917, 5.
72. "Amblecote Tribunal," *County Express*, August 5, 1916, 3.
73. "Halesowen Tribunal. Many Interesting Cases," *County Express*, April 8, 1916, 7.
74. "Stourbridge Tribunal. Interesting Local Cases," *County Express*, March 25, 1916, 3.
75. "The War. Halesowen Tribunal," *County Express*, March 4, 1916, 4.
76. "Halesowen Tribunal. Single Men's Postponements and Married Men's Claims," *County Express*, March 11, 1916, 5.
77. "Kingswinford Tribunal. Cases from Many Trades. An Application for Unstarring," *County Express*, March 11, 1916, 7.
78. "The War. Halesowen Tribunal," *County Express*, April 29, 1916, 4.
79. "The Calling of Young Chain Strikers. Question Again Before Rowley Tribunal," *Dudley Herald*, March 3, 1917, 6.
80. "Rowley Regis Tribunal. Equality of Sacrifice," *County Express*, April 7, 1916, 2.
81. "Local Tribunals. Halesowen," *County Advertiser*, April 8, 1916, 3.
82. "Local Tribunals. Dudley. A Batch of Appeals Dismissed," *County Advertiser*, May 6, 1916, 3.
83. "Tipton Military Tribunal," *Dudley Herald*, August 17, 1918, 7.
84. "Rowley Regis Tribunal. Single Men Should Go First," *County Express*, June 2, 1917, 3.
85. "Halesowen Tribunal," *County Advertiser*, May 4, 1918, 3.
86. "The War. Halesowen Tribunal," *County Express*, March 4, 1916, 4.
87. "Rowley Regis Tribunal. Second Court," *County Express*, July 1, 1916, 5.
88. "Rowley Regis Tribunal," *Dudley Herald*, March 3, 1917, 5.
89. "The War. Stourbridge Tribunal," *County Express*, March 4, 1916, 2.
90. "Local Tribunals. Amblecote," *County Advertiser*, April 22, 1916, 7.
91. "Rowley Regis Tribunal," *Dudley Herald*, February 3, 1917, 2.
92. "Rowley Regis Tribunal," *Dudley Herald*, June 29, 1918, 2.
93. "Rowley Regis Tribunal," *Dudley Herald*, August 24, 1918, 2.

6 "The whole world had gone against them": Ex-Servicemen and the Politics of Relief

1. "British Legion Activity," *Dudley Herald*, February 2, 1924, 10.
2. "British Legion Activity," *Dudley Herald*, February 2, 1924, 10.
3. Deborah Cohen provides an excellent account in *The War Come Home: Disabled Veterans in Britain and Germany, 1914–1939* (Berkeley, CA: University of California Press, 2001).

4. Bentley Gilbert argues that this phrase itself has been misunderstood, "David Lloyd George: Land, the Budget, and Social Reform," *American Historical Review* 81, no. 5 (1976): 1066.

5. David Vincent, *Poor Citizens: The State and the Poor in Twentieth-Century Britain* (London: Longman, 1991), 54.

6. Studies of veterans of the First World War have focused on the emotional, psychological, and physical trauma that ex-servicemen brought home with them to Britain. See, for example, Cohen, *War Come Home*; Joanna Bourke, *Dismembering the Male: Men's Bodies, Britain, and the Great War* (Chicago, IL: University of Chicago Press, 1996); Jessica Meyer, *Men of War: Masculinity and the First World War in Britain* (Basingstoke: Palgrave Macmillan, 2009); Jessica Meyer, "'Not Septimus Now': Wives of Disabled Veterans and Cultural Memory of the First World War in Britain," *Women's History Review* 13, no. 1 (2004): 117–38; Peter Leese, *Shell Shock: Traumatic Neurosis and the British Soldiers of the First World War* (Basingstoke: Palgrave Macmillan, 2002); and Seth Koven, "Remembering and Dismemberment: Crippled Children, Wounded Soldiers, and the Great War in Britain," *American Historical Review* 99, no. 4 (1994): 1167–202.

7. Quoted in Niall Barr, *The Lion and the Poppy: British Veterans, Politics, and Society, 1921–1939* (Westport, CT: Praeger, 2005), 93.

8. Barr, *The Lion and the Poppy*, 93.

9. Cohen, *War Come Home*, 105–6.

10. National Archives (NA), T 161/41, Letter to the Minister of Labour from J.R. Griffin, General Secretary of the National Federation of Discharged and Demobilised Sailors and Soldiers, July 20, 1920.

11. NA, PIN 15/1100, "Broken in the Wars," *Daily Express* clipping, June 13, 1918.

12. NA, PIN 15/1100, "Ex-Soldiers in the Workhouse," *Daily Express* clipping, June 16, 1918.

13. NA, PIN 15/1100, Letter from the Clerk to the Guardians of Bath Union to the Secretary of the Local Government Board, June 17, 1918.

14. NA, PIN 15/1100, Memo to the Minister from John Collie, June 29, 1918.

15. NA, PIN 15/1100, Letter from Ministry of Pensions to the Assistant Secretary of the Local Government Board, August 23, 1918.

16. For example, Staffordshire Record Office (SRO), D585/1/1/59, Stourbridge Union Guardians' Minutes, March 4, 1921, 91.

17. NA, PIN 15/1100, Programme of a Mass Meeting held on Clapham Common on September 1, 1918. The National Federation of Discharged and Demobilised Sailors and Soldiers. Battersea and Wandsworth Branch.

18. "Ex-Soldiers' Meeting at Great Bridge," *Dudley Herald*, July 17, 1920, 2.

19. NA, PIN 15/1101, Minute Sheet, Disabled Men in Receipt of Poor Law Relief, September 23, 1922.

20. Cohen, *War Come Home*, 41–4.

21. NA, PIN 15/1101, Minute Sheet, from Hore to Secretary, March 3, 1924.

22. NA, PIN 15/1101, Copies of House of Commons, Questions and Answers on Ex-Servicemen in Workhouses, 1920–26.

23. NA, PIN 15/1101, House of Commons, Question and Answers, November 25, 1920.

24. NA, PIN 15/1101, Transcript, Questions and Answers, House of Commons, March 4, 1926. Questioned by Mr. Walter Baker, answered by Major G.C. Tryon.

25. NA, PIN 15/1101, Ex-Servicemen in Poor Law Institutions, December 23, 1918.
26. NA, PIN 15/1100, Letter from John Collie to Mr. Hore, January 13, 1919.
27. Robert Humphreys, *No Fixed Abode: A History of Responses to the Roofless and Rootless in Britain* (New York: St. Martin's Press, 1999), 125.
28. NA, PIN 15/1101, Ex-Servicemen in Poor Law Institutions, December 23, 1918.
29. NA, PIN 15/1101, Handwritten Note to Mr. Hore, January 13, 1919.
30. NA, PIN 15/1101, Handwritten Note to Mr. Hore from Mr. Mathew, April 26, 1919.
31. NA, PIN 15/1101, Ministry of Pensions to HB Simpson, January 26, 1919.
32. NA, PIN 15/1101, From Mr. Hore to Nicholson, June 10, 1919.
33. "British Legion Activity," *Dudley Herald*, February 2, 1924, 10.
34. Barr, *The Lion and the Poppy*, 95.
35. NA, PIN 15/1101, Note on Return from the Ministry of Health as to the Number of Ex-Service Men and their Dependants in Receipt of Poor Relief on 3rd May, 1924.
36. NA, PIN 15/1101, Note from Morrison to Hore, May 31, 1924.
37. Barr, *The Lion and the Poppy*, 94.
38. NA, T 161/46, Memorandum by the Minister of Labour on the Training of Fit Ex-Service Men, May 20, 1920.
39. Bourke, *Dismembering the Male*; Cohen, *War Come Home*.
40. NA, T 161/46, Memorandum by the Minister of Labour on the Training of Fit Ex-Service Men, May 20, 1920.
41. Cohen, *War Come Home*, 16.
42. NA, T 161/46, Memorandum by the Minister of Labour on the Training of Fit Ex-Service Men, May 20, 1920.
43. NA, T 161/46, Cabinet Draft Minutes on the Training of Fit Ex-Service Men, June 24, 1920.
44. NA, T 161/46, Cabinet Draft Minutes on the Training of Fit Ex-Service Men, June 24, 1920.
45. NA, T 161/41, Memorandum by the Minister of Labour, Cabinet Out of Work Donation, July 17, 1920.
46. W.R. Garside, *British Unemployment, 1919–1939: A Study in Public Policy* (Cambridge: Cambridge University Press, 1990), 35–6.
47. NA, T 161/41, "Report on the Enquiry Made to Ascertain what Classes of Ex-Service Men are Remaining on Donation for Long Periods and Why their Unemployment Continues," Prepared by Hugh McRae, October 15, 1919.
48. Susan Pedersen, *Family, Dependence, and the Origins of the Welfare State: Britain and France, 1914–1945* (New York: Cambridge University Press, 1993), 126–7.
49. NA, T 161/41, "Report on the Enquiry Made to Ascertain what Classes of Ex-Service Men are Remaining on Donation for Long Periods and Why their Unemployment Continues," Prepared by Hugh McRae, October 15, 1919.
50. NA, CAB 24/92, Memorandum by the Minister of Labour, "Out-of-Work-Donation," November 5, 1920.
51. NA, CAB 23/18, CC 4 (19), Cabinet Conclusions, November 7, 1919.
52. NA, CAB 23/22, CC 43 (20), Cabinet Conclusions, July 29, 1920.
53. NA, T 161/41, Memorandum by the Chancellor of the Exchequer, n.d. (July 1920).

54. NA, T 161/41, Memorandum by the Minister of Labour, July 17, 1920.
55. NA, CAB 23/22, CC 43 (20), Cabinet Conclusions, July 29, 1920.
56. NA, T 161/41, J.R. Griffin, the General Secretary of the National Federation of Discharged and Demobilised Sailors and Soldiers, July 20, 1920.
57. NA, T 161/41, Memorandum by the Minister of Labour, July 24, 1920. Underlining in original.
58. This was articulated even more clearly in a September 1920 Cabinet discussion, which stressed that "public opinion would not support the Government in referring [ex-servicemen] to the Poor Law." NA, CAB 23/22, CC 53 (20), Cabinet Conclusions, September 30, 1920.
59. NA, T 161/41, Draft Cabinet Minutes on Out-of-Work Donation Extension, July 29, 1920.
60. NA, T 161/41, Chancellor of the Exchequer on the Coal Strike and Out of Work Donation, May 14, 1920. My emphasis.
61. NA, LAB 2/856/15/ed5374, "Report of Proceedings between a Deputation from the British Legion and the Minister of Labour," October 17, 1921, 22–3.
62. For an excellent discussion of disabled ex-servicemen and employment, see Meyer, *Men of War*, 97–127.
63. Meaghan Kowalsky, "'This Honourable Obligation': The King's Roll National Scheme for Disabled Ex-Servicemen 1915–1944," *European Review of History* 14, no. 4 (2007): 567–84; Cohen, *War Come Home*, 39–40, 109–10.
64. Cohen, *War Come Home*, 39.
65. Bourke, *Dismembering the Male*, 56.
66. NA, PIN 15/485, Summary of Submissions to be Presented by the Deputation from the National Federation of Discharged and Demobilised Sailors and Soldiers, Waiting upon the Prime Minister on Friday, 6th February, 1920.
67. NA, LAB 2/855/ED5412/2/1921, Extracts from Minutes of Proceedings at a Deputation from the National Federation of Discharged and Demobilised Sailors and Soldiers to the Prime Minister, February 6, 1920.
68. NA, LAB 2/748, To the Minister from Phillips, May 7, 1920.
69. NA, LAB 2/748, Committee on the Re-Employment of Ex-Service Men. Recommendation Adopted on Thursday 6th [1920] May with regard to Training of Non-Disabled Ex-Service Men.
70. NA, LAB 2/748, From Phillips to Barlow, May 11, 1920.
71. On the Unemployment Grants Committee, see Garside, *British Unemployment*, 303–7. For discussion of the limitations of what could be accomplished by the Unemployment Grants Committee, see K.J. Hancock, "The Reduction of Unemployment as a Problem of Public Policy," *Economic History Review* 15, no. 2 (1962): 334–8.
72. NA, LAB 4/150, Unemployment Grants Committee (UGC), Preference to Ex-Service Men.
73. NA, LAB 4/150, UGC, Preference to Ex-Servicemen.
74. NA, LAB 4/150, UGC, Preference to Ex-Servicemen.
75. NA, LAB 4/150, UGC, Preference to Ex-Servicemen.
76. NA, MH 57/126, UGC, "Interim Report of Proceedings from 20th December, 1920 to 2nd March, 1922," 7.
77. NA, LAB 2/856/15/ed5374, "Report of Proceedings between a Deputation from the British Legion and the Minister of Labour," October 17, 1921, 28.

78. NA, LAB 4/150, Cabinet Unemployment Committee, Preference for Ex-Service Men on State Assisted Schemes in Relief of Unemployment, n.d. (January 1923?).
79. NA, LAB 4/150, Cabinet Unemployment Committee, Preference for Ex-Service Men on State Assisted Schemes in Relief of Unemployment, n.d. (January 1923?).
80. "Unemployment at Brierley Hill," and "Stourbridge District," *County Advertiser*, February 12, 1921, 5.
81. "Rowley Council. Unemployment in Cradley Heath," *County Advertiser*, March 5, 1921, 2.
82. "Unemployment in Brierley Hill. Relief Committee Formed," *County Express*, February 19, 1921, 7.
83. "Unemployment. Increase in Brierley Hill District. Relief Measures," *County Express*, February 26, 1921, 12.
84. "Unemployment Debates. Brierley Hill Scheme Criticized," *County Advertiser*, March 5, 1921, 3.
85. "Brierley Hill and Distress, How It Is Being Dealt With," *County Advertiser*, March 5, 1921, 5.
86. "District News. Brierley Hill. Ex-Service Men on the Defensive," *Dudley Chronicle*, March 12, 1921, 7.
87. "District News. Brierley Hill. Ex-Service Men on the Defensive," *Dudley Chronicle*, March 12, 1921, 7.
88. "Mr Bullus and Ex-Service Men," *Dudley Chronicle*, April 2, 1921, 2.
89. Gullace, *"Blood of Our Sons,"* demonstrates the powerful rhetoric driving soldiers to fight in order to protect the home.
90. See Cohen, *War Come Home*.

7 "No right to relieve a striker": Trade Disputes and the Politics of Work and Family in the 1920s

1. For an introduction to the 1920s strikes, see Margaret Morris, ed., *The General Strike* (Harmonsdworth: Penguin Books, 1976); Anne Perkins, *A Very British Strike: 3 May–12 May 1926* (London: Macmillan, 2006); G.A. Phillips, *The General Strike: The Politics of Industrial Conflict* (London: Weidenfeld and Nicholson, 1976); and Roy Church and Quentin Outram, *Strikes and Solidarity: Coalfield Conflict in Britain, 1889–1966* (New York: Cambridge University Press, 1998).
2. "Strikers and Out-Relief. Special Meeting of Stourbridge Guardians," *County Express*, May 15, 1926, 7.
3. Staffordshire Record Office (SRO), D585/1/1/62, Stourbridge Guardians Minutes, May 14, 1926, 156.
4. "Lye Relief Complaints. Deputation to the Board of Guardians," *County Express*, July 3, 1926, 9.
5. National Archives (NA), CAB 24/140/40, A Deputation from the Miners' Federation received by the Prime Minister, December 2, 1922.
6. "April Coal Strike?" *The Times*, March 28, 1921, 8.
7. "Out-of-Work Pay to Be Claimed," *The Times*, March 30, 1921, 10; and "'Wage Offers Mean Distress,'" *The Times*, April 4, 1921, 15.

8. This was originally to have been a strike against wage reductions by the Triple Alliance, but on Black Friday the railway and transport workers backed out, which became a potent symbol of betrayal in the mining industry. Bill Williamson, *Class, Culture, and Community: A Biographical Study of Social Change in Mining* (Boston: Routledge and Kegan Paul, 1982), 166.

9. There is an issue of language here, which I will discuss below: the Miners' Federation identified the dispute as a lock-out, arguing miners were perfectly willing to work under reasonable terms. I will continue to use the word "strike," although I am conscious of the tension around the word.

10. "Unemployment at Brierley Hill," *Dudley Chronicle*, February 12, 1921, 5.

11. "Unemployment and Distress," *Dudley Herald*, April 30, 1921, 4.

12. "Hitting the Glass Trade," *Dudley Herald*, April 30, 1921, 7.

13. "The Coal Strike," *Dudley Herald*, April 9, 1921, 8.

14. Dudley Archives and Local History Service (DALHS), G/Du/2/8/9, Dudley Board of Guardians, Minutes of the Finance Committee, January–March 1921.

15. DALHS, G/Du/2/8/9, Dudley Board of Guardians, Minutes of the Finance Committee, April–December 1921, January 1922.

16. Andy Croll, "Strikers and the Right to Relief in Late Victorian Britain: The Making of the *Merthyr Tydfil* Judgment of 1900," *Journal of British Studies* 52, no. 1 (2013): 128–52.

17. NA, MH 57/121, "Illegal Relief," [1923].

18. NA, MH 57/121, "Relief to Strikers," [1923].

19. NA, MH 57/121, "Relief to Strikers," [1923].

20. John Gennard, *Financing Strikers* (New York: Wiley, 1977), 19.

21. Patricia Ryan, "The Poor Law in 1926," in *The General Strike*, ed. Margaret Morris (Harmonsdworth: Penguin Books, 1976), 359.

22. "Distress among Miners," *The Times*, April 18, 1921, 12.

23. The most written about example of local government protesting harsh national relief policies is Poplar in London. See, for example, P.A. Ryan, "'Poplarism' 1894–1930," in *The Origins of British Social Policy*, ed. Pat Thane (London: Croom Helm, 1978), 56–83.

24. NA, MH 57/121, "Illegal Relief," [1923].

25. NA, MH 57/121, "Relief to Strikers," [1923].

26. NA, MH 57/121, "Illegal Relief," [1923].

27. NA, MH 57/121, "Relief to Strikers," [1923].

28. NA, MH 57/121, "Relief to Strikers," [1923].

29. DALHS, G/Du/1/42, Dudley Guardians Minutes, May 6, 1921, 103.

30. NA, MH 57/121, Poor Law Relief: Case for the Opinion of the Law Officers of the Crown, 1921, 1.

31. NA, MH 57/121, Poor Law Relief, 2.

32. NA, MH 57/121, "Relief to Strikers," [1923].

33. NA, MH 57/121, Poor Law Relief, 2.

34. NA, MH 57/121, Poor Law Relief, 3.

35. See Morris, ed., *The General Strike*.

36. NA, MH 57/115, Ministry of Health Circular to Boards of Guardians, May 5, 1926.

37. SRO, D585/1/1/62, Stourbridge Guardians Minutes, May 7, 1926, 152.

38. DALHS, G/Du/2/1/3, Dudley Union Committee Minutes, May 6, 1926, 117–18.
39. "Stourbridge Guardians. The Large Increase in Out Relief," *County Express*, June 19, 1926, 9.
40. "Lye Relief Complaints. Deputation to the Board of Guardians," *County Express*, July 3, 1926, 9.
41. NA, MH 57/118, Coal Dispute, 1926. Memorandum Summarizing the Reports of General Inspectors on the Effect of the Coal Dispute on the Administration of Relief in Certain Unions, February 1927, Section 4.
42. "Out Relief," *Dudley Herald*, July 9, 1921, 7.
43. NA, MH 57/116, Deputation from National Association of Relieving Officers, July 26, 1926.
44. NA, MH 57/116, Deputation of Relieving Officers, July 1926.
45. NA, MH 57/118, Coal Dispute, 1926. Memorandum Summarizing the Reports of General Inspectors on the Effect of the Coal Dispute on the Administration of Relief in Certain Unions, February 1927.
46. NA, MH 57/118, Coal Dispute, 1926, Section 1.
47. NA, MH 57/118, Coal Dispute, 1926, Section 4.
48. "'Wage Offers Mean Distress,'" *The Times*, April 4, 1921, 15.
49. "Mr. Cook's Reply," *The Times*, May 22, 1926, 12.
50. "The Coal Trade Crisis. Another Momentous Friday," *Dudley Herald*, April 23, 1921, 7.
51. "The Coal Strike. Local Strike Pay," *Dudley Herald*, April 16, 1921, 8.
52. "Labour Appeal for Miners," *The Times*, May 4, 1921, 10.
53. "Owners on the Failure," *The Times*, April 13, 1921, 10.
54. "Mr. Churchill and Miners," *The Times*, August 23, 1926, 12.
55. "Distress at Old Hill," *Dudley Herald*, May 14, 1921, 2.
56. "Distress in the Black Country. Relief for Needy Miners Families," *County Advertiser*, June 25, 1921, 3.
57. "Distress at Old Hill," *Dudley Herald*, May 14, 1921, 2.
58. NA, MH 57/115, Mr. Francis to Mr. Forber, May 18, 1926.
59. NA, MH 57/116, Strike Cases, Twelfth List, June 10, 1926.
60. NA, MH 57/116, Deputation of Relieving Officers, July 1926.
61. NA, MH 57/115, Letter from Salford Union to the Prime Minister, July 3, 1926, and Copy Resolution Passed at a Meeting of the Guardians of the Wortley Union Held July, 15, 1926.
62. NA, MH 57/115, Letter from the Birmingham Trades Council to the Prime Minister, September 9, 1926.
63. House of Commons, "A Bill to Amend the Law in Respect of Insurance against Unemployment," *Sessional Papers* (27), 1920, vol. 5.
64. NA, PIN 29/2, Umpire's Decision Book, 1926, Case 2453/26, August 17, 1926, 189.
65. NA, PIN 29/1429, Office of the Umpire, Appeal Records.
66. NA, PIN 29/1474, Office of the Umpire, Appeal Records.
67. NA, PIN 29/2, Umpire's Decision Book, 1926, Case 1939/26, July 27, 1926, 173–4.
68. NA, PIN 29/1419, Office of Umpire, Appeal Records.
69. NA, PIN 29/2, Umpire's Decision Book, 1926, Case 2096/26, August 5, 1926, 180–1.

70. NA, PIN 29/1434, Office of the Umpire, Appeal Records.
71. NA, PIN 29/1429, Office of the Umpire, Appeal Records.
72. NA, PIN 29/1478, Office of the Umpire, Appeal Records.
73. NA, PIN 29/1442, Office of the Umpire, Appeal Records.
74. NA, PIN 29/1449, Office of the Umpire, Appeal Records.
75. NA, PIN 29/1452, Office of the Umpire, Appeal Records.
76. NA, PIN 29/1483, Office of the Umpire, Appeal Records.
77. "Brierley Hill Trades Council," *Dudley Herald*, August 13, 1921, 9.
78. "Brierley Hill Trades Council," *County Express*, August 13, 1921, 7.
79. "End of the Coal Trade Dispute. Local Miners and Unemployment Benefit," *County Express*, December 4, 1921, 9.
80. NA, LAB 8/53, Unemployment Insurance Acts, 1920–1926. Decision Given by the Umpire, November 1926.
81. NA, LAB 8/53, "Unemployment Benefit – Trade Dispute Disqualification as Affecting Benefit Claims of Miners Who Remain Unemployed After District Settlements," nd.
82. NA, LAB 8/53, To Price from Bircham, November 8, 1926.
83. NA, LAB 8/53, Extract from Discussion between Cabinet Coal Committee and Miners' Federation, November 11–12, 1926.
84. NA, LAB 8/53, Note by the Minister of Labour, December 15, 1926, 1.
85. NA, LAB 8/53, Deputation from Executive of Miners' Federation to the Minster of Labour, Montagu House, 4 p.m., Wednesday, December 15, 1926.
86. NA, LAB 8/53, Miners' Deputation, December 1926.
87. NA, LAB 8/53, Miners' Deputation, December 1926.

8   "Younger men are given the preference": Older Men's Welfare and Intergenerational Responsibilities

1. National Archives (NA), PIN 29/1176, Office of the Umpire, Appeal Records.
2. See, for example, Pat Thane, *Old Age in English History: Past Experiences, Present Issues* (New York: Oxford University Press, 2000); Pat Thane, "Old People and Their Families in the English Past," in *Charity, Self-Interest and Welfare in the English Past*, ed. Martin Daunton (New York: Routledge, 1996), 113–38; M.A. Crowther, "Family Responsibility and State Responsibility in Britain before the Welfare State," *Historical Journal* 25, no. 1 (1982): 131–45; Margaret Pelling and Richard M. Smith, eds, *Life, Death, and the Elderly: Historical Perspectives* (New York: Routledge, 1991); L.A. Botelho, *Old Age and the English Poor Law, 1500–1700* (Rochester, NY: Boydell Press, 2004); and Susannah R. Ottaway, *The Decline of Life: Old Age in Eighteenth-Century England* (New York: Cambridge University Press, 2004).
3. Thane, *Old Age*, 168–9.
4. Richard Wall, "Relationships between the Generations in British Families, Past and Present," in *Families and Households: Divisions and Change*, ed. Catherine Marsh and Sara Arber (Basingstoke: Macmillan, 1992), 70, 76–84.
5. Crowther, "Family Responsibility," 132. See also, for example, Thane, *Old Age*, 170; and Wall, "Relationships between the Generations," 80–1.

6. S.G. and E.O.A. Checkland, eds., *The Poor Law Report of 1834* (New York: Penguin, 1974), 115. For discussion of the legal aspects of family liability, see Crowther, "Family Responsibility."

7. Ann Orloff, *The Politics of Pensions: A Comparative Analysis of Britain, Canada, and the United States, 1880–1940* (Madison, WI: University of Wisconsin Press, 1993), 131.

8. Thane, *Old Age*, 167.

9. Crowther, "Family Responsibility," 145.

10. See Orloff, *Politics of Pensions*, 121–51.

11. Staffordshire Record Office (SRO); from the Halesowen District, D585/1/5/27, D585/1/5/29, D585/1/5/32, and D585/1/5/35; from the Stourbridge District, D585/1/5/47 and D585/1/5/50; and from the Kingswinford District, D585/1/5/68, D585/1/5/70, D585/1/5/73, and D585/1/5/76.

12. See, for example, Lynn Hollen Lees, *The Solidarities of Strangers: The English Poor Laws and the People, 1700–1948* (New York: Cambridge University Press, 1998), 275–86.

13. SRO, D585/1/1/137, Cases of Individual Paupers, Stourbridge Union, Parts 1, 3, and 5.

14. For studies of intergenerational care, see, for example, David Thomson, "'I Am Not My Father's Keeper': Families and the Elderly in Nineteenth-Century England," *Law and History Review* 2, no. 2 (1984): 265–86; Wall, "Relationships between the Generations," 63–85; and Richard Wall, "Elderly Persons and Members of Their Households in England and Wales from Preindustrial Times to the Present," in *Ageing in the Past: Demography, Society, and Old Age*, ed. D. Kertzner and P. Laslett (Berkeley, CA: University of California Press, 1995).

15. SRO, D585/1/5/29, Application and Report Book, Cakemore Parish, Halesowen District, Stourbridge Union, April 2, 1891.

16. SRO, D585/1/5/76, Application and Report Book, Kingswinford Parish, Kingswinford District, Stourbridge Union, June 15, 1911.

17. SRO, D585/1/5/29, Application and Report Book, Cradley Parish, Halesowen District, Stourbridge Union, May 7, 1891.

18. Thane, "Old People and Their Families," 120.

19. SRO, D585/1/29, Application and Report Book, Cradley Parish, Halesowen District, April 2, 1891.

20. SRO, D585/1/29, Application and Report Book, Cradley Parish, Halesowen District, April 2, 1891.

21. SRO, D585/1/76, Application and Report Book, Kingswinford Parish, Kingswinford District, Stourbridge Union, March 30, 1911.

22. SRO, D585/1/5/48, Application and Report Book, Stourbridge Parish, Stourbridge District, Stourbridge Union, April 6, 1871.

23. "A Son Summoned for the Support of His Father," *Dudley Herald*, February 12, 1876, 4.

24. "Sons and Their Father's Support," *County Express*, September 8, 1906, 6.

25. "Sons and Their Father's Support," *County Express*, September 8, 1906, 6.

26. SRO, D585/1/1/137, Stourbridge Union, Cases of Individual Paupers, Part 5, Case 3427.

27. SRO, D585/1/1/50, Stourbridge Guardians Minutes, June 26, 1908, 177–8.

28. "Stourbridge Police Court. Guardians' Cases," *County Express*, December 7, 1929, 13.

29. SRO, D585/1/1/28, Stourbridge Guardians Minutes, July, 11, 1879, 344.
30. "Guardians' Prosecutions at Tipton," *Dudley Herald*, September 26, 1908, 8.
31. SRO, D585/1/1/137, Cases of Individual Paupers, Part 5, Case 4047.
32. Paul H. Douglas and Aaron Director, *The Problem of Unemployment* (1931; repr., New York: Arno Press, 1976), 415.
33. "Dudley Trades Council. Successful Annual Meeting," *Dudley Herald*, February 4, 1922, 5.
34. For general discussions of gender and what counts as work, see, for example, Joanna Bourke, "Housewifery in Working-Class England, 1860–1914," in *Women's Work: The English Experience, 1650–1914*, ed. Pamela Sharpe (New York: Arnold, 1998), 332–58; Deborah Simonton, *A History of European Women's Work 1700 to the Present* (New York: Routledge, 1998); and Andrew August, *Poor Women's Lives: Gender, Work, and Poverty in Late Victorian London* (Madison, NJ: Fairleigh Dickinson University Press, 1999).
35. For discussion of gender, types of assistance in intergenerational relationships, and the invisibility of women's help, see Gill Jones, "Short-Term Reciprocity in Parent-Child Economic Exchanges," in *Families and Households: Divisions and Change*, ed. Catherine Marsh and Sara Arber (Basingstoke: Macmillan, 1992), 26–44; Emily Abel, *Who Cares for the Elderly? Public Policy and the Experiences of Adult Daughters* (Philadelphia, PA: Temple University Press, 1992); and Thane, "Old People and Their Families," 129. Thane specifically mentions how the records themselves make any form of non-residential support invisible.
36. Edward Higgs, "Women, Occupations and Work in the Nineteenth Century," *History Workshop Journal* 23, no. 1 (1987): 59–80; and Edward Higgs, "Household and Work in the Nineteenth-Century Censuses of England and Wales," *Journal of the Society of Archivists* 11, no. 3 (1990): 73–7.
37. SRO, D585/1/5/32, Application and Report Book, Cradley Parish, Halesowen District, Stourbridge Union, June 27, 1901.
38. In 1871, the difference was about 600,000; by 1901, this had grown to more than a million. Chris Cook and Brendon Keith, *British Historical Facts, 1830–1900* (New York: St. Martin's Press, 1975), 232.
39. SRO, D585/1/5/73, Application and Report Book, Kingswinford Parish, Kingswinford District, Stourbridge Union, March 27, 1891.
40. SRO, D585/1/5/73, Application and Report Book, Kingswinford Parish, Kingswinford District, Stourbridge Union, March 27, 1891.
41. Ancestry.co.uk, accessed October 10, 2013. Sarah does not appear in the 1891 census.
42. SRO, D585/1/1/37-38, Board of Guardians Minutes, Stourbridge Union, 1890–2.
43. SRO, D585/1/1/80, House Committee Book, Stourbridge Union, 1910–13.
44. For a discussion of elderly women's residence patterns over time, see Richard Wall, "The Residence Patterns of Elderly English Women in Comparative Perspective," in *Women and Ageing in British Society since 1500*, ed. Lynn Botelho and Pat Thane (New York: Pearson Education, 2001), 139–65.
45. SRO, D585/1/5/29, Application and Report Book, Cradley Parish, Halesowen District, Stourbridge Union, April 2, 1891.
46. SRO, D585/1/5/32, Application and Report Book, Cakemore Parish, Halesowen District, Stourbridge Union, June 13, 1901.

47. Pat Thane, "Women and the Poor Law in Victorian and Edwardian England," *History Workshop Journal* 6 (Autumn 1978): 38. See also Lees, *Solidarities*, 264–8.

48. Since I have little information about the wages and occupations of younger women who were actually contributing to their parents' maintenance, I am using the broader category of all adult women under 55 in the study whose earnings were recorded as a way to assess regional wages for women.

49. SRO, D585/1/5/29, Application and Report Book, Cradley Parish, Halesowen District, Stourbridge Union, April 9, 1891.

50. SRO, D585/1/5/32, Application and Report Book, Cradley Parish, Halesowen District, Stourbridge Union, July 25, 1901.

51. On contributions to the family economy, see Selina Todd, "'You'd the Feeling You Wanted to Help': Young Women, Employment and the Family in Inter-War England," in *Women and Work Culture: Britain, c. 1850–1950*, ed. Krista Cowman and Louise A. Jackson (Burlington, VT: Ashgate, 2005), 123–40.

52. SRO, D585/1/1/137, Cases of Individual Paupers, Part 3, Case 7550, 3.

53. SRO, D585/1/1/137, Cases of Individual Paupers, Part 3, Case 7562, 3.

54. Orloff, *Politics of Pensions*, 208.

55. SRO, D585/1/1/24, Stourbridge Guardians Minutes, October 24, 1873, 387.

56. SRO, D585/1/1/45, Stourbridge Guardians Minutes, January 3, 1902, 45.

57. SRO, D585/1/1/137, Cases of Individual Paupers, Part 1, case 1063, 3.

58. SRO, D585/1/1/137, Cases of Individual Paupers, Part 1, case 10xx [page torn], 3.

59. SRO, D585/1/1/137, Cases of Individual Paupers, Part 3, case 7035, 3.

60. *Report of the Royal Commission on the Aged Poor*, C. 7684, 1895; and House of Commons, "Report from the Select Committee on the Aged Deserving Poor," *Sessional Papers* (296), 1899.

61. House of Commons, "Aged Pensioners. A Bill to Provide Pensions to the Aged Deserving Poor," *Sessional Papers* (114), 1901, vol. 1, 2.

62. House of Commons, "Aged Pensioners. A Bill to Provide Pensions to the Aged Deserving Poor," *Sessional Papers* (114), 1901, vol. 1, a.

63. House of Commons, "Aged Pensioners (no. 2). A Bill to Provide Pensions for the Aged Deserving Poor." *Sessional Papers* (15), 1902, vol. 1.

64. House of Commons, "Old Age Pensions (no. 3). A Bill to Provide Pensions for the Aged Deserving Poor," *Sessional Papers* (146), 1906, vol. 4, a.

65. Orloff discusses the passage of this Act in a wider context, *Politics of Pensions*, 211–14.

66. The aged poor who were too young to qualify for OAP also continued to prove deservedness based on work histories to poor law authorities. William W., for example, 62 years old, began receiving a regular poor law pension in March 1912, when a "doctor says he has finished work." SRO, D585/1/1/137, Cases of Individual Paupers, Part 1, case 1064, 3.

67. See, for example, Ramsay MacDonald, *Parliamentary Debates*, 4th ser., vol. 191 (1908), cols. 406–8; and Mr. Soares, *Parliamentary Debates*, 4th ser., vol. 191 (1908), col. 412.

68. *Parliamentary Debates*, 4th ser., vol. 191 (1908), col. 433.

69. *Parliamentary Debates*, 4th ser., vol. 191 (1908), col. 431. Samantha Williams makes this point about the fluidity between paupers and ratepayers under the Old Poor Law in *Poverty, Gender, and Life-Cycle under the English Poor Law, 1760–1834* (Woodbridge: Boydell & Brewer Press, 2011).

70. *Parliamentary Debates*, 4th ser., vol. 191 (1908), col. 388.
71. *Parliamentary Debates*, 4th ser., vol. 191 (1908), col. 406.
72. *Parliamentary Debates*, 4th ser., vol. 191 (1908), col. 413.
73. *Parliamentary Debates*, 4th ser., vol. 191 (1908), col. 414.
74. *Parliamentary Debates*, 4th ser., vol. 191 (1908), col. 420.
75. *Parliamentary Debates*, 4th ser., vol. 191 (1908), col. 1562.
76. *Parliamentary Debates*, 4th ser., vol. 191 (1908), cols. 1562–3.
77. *Parliamentary Debates*, 4th ser., vol. 191 (1908), col. 1573.
78. *Parliamentary Debates*, 4th ser., vol. 191 (1908), col. 436.
79. *Parliamentary Debates*, 4th ser., vol. 192 (1908), col. 147.
80. William A. Casson, ed., *The Old Age Pensions Act, 1908, together with the Text of the Regulations* . . . 3rd ed. (London: Chas. Knight and Co., 1908), 1–30.
81. "Doings in Dudley," *County Express*, January 21, 1911, 5.
82. Bernard Harris, "Gender and Social Citizenship in Historical Perspective: The Development of Welfare Policy in England and Wales from the Poor Law to Beveridge," in *Gender and Well-Being: The Role of Institutions*, ed. Elisabetta Addis, Paloma de Villota, Florence Degavre, and John Eriksen (Burlington, VT: Ashgate Publishing, 2011), 38.
83. Dudley Archives and Local History Service, G/Du/2/1/3, Dudley Guardians' Committee Book, Unemployment Committee, April 22, 1926, 115.

9   "He did not realise his responsibilities": Giving Up the Privileges of Honest Poverty

1. Stourbridge Record Office (SRO), D585/1/1/137, Cases of Individual Paupers, Part 5, case 4070, 1.
2. "Stourbridge Police Court. A Wife's Maintenance," *County Express*, September 24, 1921, 7.
3. SRO, D585/1/1/137, Cases of Individual Paupers, Part 5, case 4070, 1.
4. "Dudley Police Court. An Ex-Service Man," *Dudley Herald*, July 3, 1920, 8.
5. "Dudley Police Court. Maintenance Arrears," *Dudley Herald*, July 31, 1920, 5.
6. "Wife Maintenance," *Dudley Herald*, September 24, 1921, 7.
7. "Committed for Two Months," *Dudley Herald*, November 26, 1921, 4.
8. "Dudley Police Court. Order Reduced," *Dudley Herald*, April 15, 1922, 7.
9. Ellen Ross, *Love and Toil: Motherhood in Outcast London, 1870–1918* (New York: Oxford University Press, 1993), 72.
10. Anna R. Igra offers a close analysis of welfare politics related to the desertion of Jewish women in New York City in *Wives Without Husbands: Marriage, Desertion, and Welfare in New York, 1900–1935* (Chapel Hill, NC: University of North Carolina Press, 2006).
11. See, for example, Pat Thane, "Women and the Poor Law in Victorian and Edwardian England," *History Workshop* 6 (1978): 32. The Poor Law's punitive attitude toward unmarried mothers and their children eased over the course of the century.
12. Jane Humphries, "Female-Headed Households in Early Industrial Britain: the Vanguard of the Proletariat?" *Labour History Review* 63, no. 1 (1998): 49; see also Lynn Hollen Lees, *The Solidarities of Strangers: The English Poor Laws and*

the People, 1700–1948 (New York: Cambridge University Press, 1998); and Thane, "Women and the Poor Law."

13. Thane, "Women and the Poor Law," 39.
14. "Out-Door Relief," *Dudley Herald*, July 14, 1883, 4.
15. Lees, *Solidarities*, 335.
16. SRO, D585/1/5/48, Application and Report Book, Stourbridge Parish, Stourbridge District, Stourbridge Union, September 22, 1871.
17. SRO, D585/1/1/137, Cases of Individual Paupers, Part 3, case 7023, 3.
18. SRO, D585/1/1/137, Cases of Individual Paupers, Part 1, case 3409, 2.
19. "Guardians Loan Relief," *Dudley Herald*, April 9, 1921, 2; Iris Minor, "Working-Class Women and Matrimonial Law Reform, 1890–1914," in *Ideology and the Labour Movement*, ed. David E. Martin and David Rubenstein (London: Croom Helm, 1979), 105; and Herbert Davey, *Maintenance and Desertion under the Poor Law and under the Summary Jurisdiction (Married Women) Act, 1895* (London: Law and Local Government Publications, 1931), 14–15.
20. George Behlmer, "Summary Justice and Working-Class Marriage in England, 1870–1940," *Law and History Review* 12, no. 2 (1994): 229.
21. As Jennifer Davis has noted in her study of the London Police Courts, "The press was . . . crucial for transmitting the lessons of the police court to a wider audience." Jennifer Davis, "A Poor Man's System of Justice: The London Police Courts in the Second Half of the Nineteenth Century," *Historical Journal* 27, no. 2 (1984): 317.
22. Davis, "Poor Man's System," 322.
23. I will discuss below cases that demonstrate this point.
24. Temple Chevallier Martin and George Temple Martin, *The Law of Maintenance and Desertion and Affiliation, 3rd edition* (London: Stevens and Haynes, 1910), 2.
25. Sydney Davey, *Maintenance and Desertion under the Poor law and under the Summary Jurisdiction (Married Women) Act, 1895* (London: Law and Local Government Publications, 1925), 17.
26. S. Davey, *Maintenance and Desertion*, 5–6; Martin and Martin, *Law of Maintenance and Desertion*, 13. I have very few references pointing to wives' maintenance of their husbands, all of which are in the Stourbridge Board of Guardians' Minutes. On February 28, 1873, the board "ordered that proceedings against Agnes McVee for the maintenance of her husband be stayed, upon her undertaking to repay 3/6 per week during the time he remains chargeable," SRO, D585/1/1/24, Stourbridge Guardians Minutes, 210. On October 27, 1876, "Jemima Mullett to pay 1/week toward maintenance of husband in workhouse," SRO, D585/1/1/26, Stourbridge Guardians Minutes, 381.
27. O.R. McGregor, Louis Jacques Blom-Cooper, and Colin S. Gibson, *Separated Spouses: A Study of the Matrimonial Jurisdiction of Magistrates' Courts* (London: Duckworth, 1970), 12.
28. Behlmer, "Summary Justice," 241–2.
29. By the early twentieth century, there were concerns about the inability of the poor to formally end their marriage ties. Efforts to assist poor petitioners with legal counsel (the Poor Person's Procedure 1914) and through the decentralization of the divorce court proceedings from the 1910s did increase the numbers of poor people applying for divorce. See Lawrence Stone, *Road to Divorce, England 1530–1987* (New York: Oxford University Press, 1990);

Colin S. Gibson, *Dissolving Wedlock* (New York: Routledge, 1994), 86–7; and Griselda Rowntree and Norman H. Carter, "The Resort to Divorce in England and Wales, 1858–1957," *Population Studies* 11, no. 3 (1958): 192–4.

30. McGregor, Blom-Cooper, and Gibson, *Separated Spouses*, 16.
31. "Stourbridge. Board of Guardians. Deserted Wives," *County Express*, April 10, 1886, 5.
32. McGregor, Blom-Cooper, and Gibson, *Separated Spouses*, 14–15.
33. S. Davey, *Maintenance and Desertion*, 54. Ellipses in original. A maintenance order was actually broader than alimony, which referred specifically to payments from husband to wife in the event of divorce or separation. See H.C. Gutteridge, "The International Enforcement of Maintenance Orders," *International Law Quarterly* 2, no. 2 (1948): 155.
34. See, for example, Stone, *Road to Divorce*.
35. McGregor, Blom-Cooper, and Gibson, *Separated Spouses*, 14. Men did not have the same ability to take their wives to court for maintenance orders, and they could only sue for separation based on habitual drunkenness, as determined by the Act of 1902.
36. Gail Savage, "The Operation of the 1857 Divorce Act, 1860–1910: A Research Note," *Journal of Social History* 16, no. 4 (1983): 104.
37. Olive Anderson, "State, Civil Society and Separation in Victorian Marriage," *Past and Present* 163, no. 1 (1999): 171; McGregor, Blom-Cooper, and Gibson, *Separated Spouses*, 22. Applications for maintenance orders were 9,553 and 16,545, respectively. Behlmer notes, "Prior to the First World War, more than nine out of ten matrimonial complaints received summary treatment. During the inter-war years between twelve and seventeen thousand formal petitions for judicial separation were heard annually in police courts." Behlmer, "Summary Justice," 238.
38. Tanya Evans, "The Other Woman and Her Child: Extra-Marital Affairs and Illegitimacy in Twentieth-Century Britain," *Women's History Review* 20, no. 1 (2011): 50.
39. McGregor, Blom-Cooper, and Gibson, *Separated Spouses*, 22.
40. S. Davey, *Maintenance and Desertion*, 17–18; Martin and Martin, *Law of Maintenance and Desertion*, 26.
41. "Wednesbury. A Painful Case," *Dudley Herald*, June 10, 1871, 3.
42. "District Intelligence. Sedgley," *County Express*, March 11, 1876, 3.
43. "Halesowen Police Court," *County Express*, July 24, 1886, 3.
44. "Brierley Hill Police Court. Young Quarry Bank Couple Separated," *Dudley Herald*, January 29, 1921, 4.
45. Joanna Bourke, *Working-Class Cultures in Britain, 1890–1960* (New York: Routledge, 1994), 62.
46. Bourke, *Working-Class Cultures*, Chapter 3, "Home: Domestic Spaces," 62–97.
47. "A Lamentable Tale of Married Life," *Dudley Herald*, March 5, 1921, 5.
48. "Dudley Police Court. A Wife's Choice," *Dudley Herald*, November 12, 1921, 8.
49. A. James Hammerton, *Cruelty and Companionship: Conflict in Nineteenth-Century Married Life* (New York: Routledge, 1992), 39.
50. "Desertion," *County Advertiser*, April 23, 1921, 8.

51. For studies of working-class marriages that contextualize domestic violence, see, for example, Hammerton, *Cruelty and Companionship*; and Ross, *Love and Toil*.
52. See, for example, Nancy F. Cott, *Public Vows: A History of Marriage and the Nation* (Cambridge, MA: Harvard University Press, 2000) and John Gillis, *For Better, For Worse: British Marriages, 1600 to the Present* (New York: Oxford University Press, 1985).
53. Hammerton, *Cruelty and Companionship*, 56.
54. For the economics of working-class marriage, see Gillis, *For Better, for Worse*, 231–84; and Humphrey Southall and David Gilbert, "A Good Time to Wed? Marriage and Economic Distress in England and Wales, 1839–1914," *Economic History Review* 49, no. 1 (1996): 35–57.
55. "Old Hill Police Court. Marriage A Failure," *County Express*, November 17, 1894, 8.
56. Minor, "Working-Class Women and Matrimonial Law Reform," 118; Ernest James Lidbetter, *Maintenance and Desertion* (London: Law and Local Government Publications, 1934), 84; and H. Davey, *Maintenance and Desertion*, 98.
57. Minor, "Working-Class Women and Matrimonial Law Reform," 118.
58. Anderson, "State, Civil Society and Separation," 171. Judicial Separation through the High Court was a very different matter from separation and maintenance through the Magistrate's Courts.
59. "Old Hill. Neglecting to Maintain His Wife," *County Express*, May 20, 1871, 6.
60. "To Pay or Go Down," *Dudley Herald*, December 10, 1921, 2.
61. "Wednesbury Police Court. Alleged Wife Desertion," *Dudley Herald*, September 24, 1921, 2.
62. "Brierley Hill Police Court. Unmanly Conduct of a Husband," *County Express*, March 30, 1901, 2.
63. "Matrimonial Case," *County Express*, March 29, 1919, 7.
64. "Pensnett. Absconding Husband Sent to Prison," *County Advertiser*, February 21, 1920, 7.
65. "Dudley Police Court. The Everlasting Matrimonial Troubles," *Dudley Herald*, February 11, 1922, 8.
66. Ross, *Love and Toil*, 73.
67. "Guardians' Prosecution," *Dudley Herald*, August 18, 1883, 6.
68. "What Constitutes Desertion?" *Dudley Herald*, November 26, 1921, 8.
69. "Tramps," *Dudley Herald*, January 20, 1894, 5.
70. Local Government Board, *Eighth Annual Report*, 1878–9, xix.
71. "A Caution to the Guardians," *County Express*, June 12, 1886, 5.
72. "The Strike and Judgment Summonses," *Dudley Herald*, May 7, 1921, 7.
73. "Dudley Police Court," *Dudley Herald*, May 14, 1921, 8.
74. "Out-of-Work Husbands. The Problem of Wife Maintenance," *County Express*, January 21, 1922, 7.
75. "Brierley Hill Police Court. Maintenance Arrears," *County Express*, November 26, 1921, 11.
76. "Brierley Hill Police Court. An Unemployed Husband," *County Express*, May 28, 1921, 7.
77. "Desertion of Family," *Dudley Herald*, November 11, 1871, 3.
78. "Deserting His Wife," *County Express*, October 12, 1901, 2.

79. Royal Commission on Divorce and Matrimonial Causes, *Minutes of Evidence Taken Before the Royal Commission on Divorce and Matrimonial Causes*, vol. XVIII, Cd. 6479 (1912), 294.
80. Royal Commission on Divorce, *Minutes of Evidence*, 296.
81. Daniel Gorman argues that the imperial citizen in this period was one who "demonstrated commitment to the socio-political community." *Imperial Citizenship: Empire and the Question of Belonging* (New York: Manchester University Press, 2006), 6.
82. Miriam Cohen and Michael Hanagan, "Politics, Industrialization and Citizenship: Unemployment Policy in England, France and the United States, 1890–1950," *International Review of Social History* 40, Supplement 3 (1995): 91–129; Dudley Baines, *Migration in a Mature Economy: Emigration and Internal Migration in England and Wales, 1861–1900* (Cambridge: Cambridge University Press, 1985); and, for earlier in the century, Robin F. Haines, *Emigration and the Labouring Poor: Australian Recruitment in Britain and Ireland, 1831–1860* (New York: St. Martin's Press, 1997).
83. See, for example, Steven Constantine, "British Emigration to the Empire-Commonwealth since 1880: From Overseas Settlement to Diaspora?" *Journal of Imperial and Commonwealth History* 31, no. 2 (2003): 20, 22–3; and Carl Bridge and Kent Fedorowich, "Mapping the BritishWorld," *Journal of Imperial and Commonwealth History* 31, no. 2 (2003): 4–5.
84. Gary B. Magee and Andrew S. Thompson, "The Global and the Local: Explaining Migrant Remittance Flows in the English-Speaking World, 1880–1914," *Journal of Economic History* 66, no. 1 (2006): 178.
85. Gary B. Magee and Andrew S. Thompson, "'Lines of Credit, Debts of Obligation': Migrant Remittances to Britain, c.1875–1913," *Economic History Review* 59, no. 3 (2006): 567.
86. SRO, D585/1/5/48, Application and Report Book, Lye Parish, Stourbridge District, Stourbridge Union, March 27, 1891.
87. SRO, D585/1/1/137, Cases of Individual Paupers, Part 1, Case 3424, 3.
88. SRO, D585/1/1/137, Cases of Individual Paupers, Part 3, Case 7030, 3.
89. SRO, D585/1/1/137, Cases of Individual Paupers, Part 3, case 7036, 3.
90. I explore this more fully in "From 'Relief' to 'Justice and Protection': The Maintenance of Deserted Wives, British Masculinity and Imperial Citizenship, 1870–1920," *Gender & History* 22, no.2 (2010): 302–21.
91. National Archives (NA), MH 57/182b, January 21, 1908 reference to Dudley 11171/62. It is unclear to what the Dudley reference points except as a previous case where poor law authorities had expressed concern about overseas desertion.
92. NA, MH 57/182b, Letter from Colonial Secretary Lord Elgin to High Commissioner for South Africa, July 1907.
93. NA, MH 57/182b, Letter from Colonial Secretary Lord Elgin to High Commissioner for South Africa, July 1907.
94. Imperial Conference, *Minutes of Proceedings of the Imperial Conference, Dominions No. 7*, Cd. 5745 (1911), 206.
95. "Imperial Conference," *The Times*, June 10, 1911, 11.
96. Imperial Conference, *Minutes*, 208–9.
97. Imperial Conference, *Minutes*, 211.
98. Imperial Conference, *Minutes*, 211.

99. See, for example, Ian Christopher Fletcher, Laura E. Nym Mayhall, and Philippa Levine, eds, *Women's Suffrage in the British Empire: Citizenship, Nation, and Race* (New York: Routledge, 2000).
100. Imperial Conference, *Minutes*, 208.
101. Imperial Conference, *Papers*, Memorandum by the Local Government Board, Scotland (1911), 227.
102. Imperial Conference, *Papers*, 228.
103. NA, MH 57/182b, Correspondence from C.P. Lucas, Undersecretary of State for the Colonies, to the Local Government Board, August 2, 1911.
104. NA, MH 57/182b, Draft of a Bill to Facilitate the enforcement in the United Kingdom of Maintenance Orders made in other parts of His Majesty's Dominions and vice versa.
105. *Parliamentary Debates*, Lords, 5th ser., vol. 39 (1920), col. 513. On Lord Birkenhead and marriage law reform, see Stephen Cretney, *Family Law in the Twentieth Century* (New York: Oxford University Press, 2007), 780.
106. *Parliamentary Debates*, Lords, 5th ser., vol. 39 (1920), cols. 513–14.
107. *Parliamentary Debates*, Lords, 5th ser., vol. 39 (1920), col. 514. On Lord Buckmaster, see Cretney, *Family Law*, 781–2, 216–23.
108. For an extended discussion of the uses of gender and sexuality to restore "normalcy" in postwar Britain, see Susan Kingsley Kent, *Making Peace: The Reconstruction of Gender in Interwar Britain* (Princeton, NJ: Princeton University Press, 1993).
109. *Parliamentary Debates*, Commons, 5th ser., vol. 133 (1920), col. 71.
110. By 1925, there were about 50 territories in the British Empire participating in reciprocal arrangements. Davey, *Maintenance and Desertion*, 36–7.
111. NA, MH 57/182b, Minutes of Interdepartmental Conference, March 20, 1912, 4.
112. NA, MH 57/182b, Minutes of Interdepartmental Conference, March 20, 1912, 5.
113. Lord Buckmaster, for example, had pushed to include affiliation orders when the Bill was introduced in the House of Lords. *Parliamentary Debates*, Lords, 5th ser., vol. 39 (1920), col. 514.
114. *Parliamentary Debates*, Commons, 5th ser., vol. 132 (1920), col. 2160.
115. *Parliamentary Debates*, Commons, 5th ser., vol. 132 (1920), col. 2161.

Conclusions

1. Iain Duncan Smith, "Speech: Reforming Welfare, Transforming Lives," October 25, 2012, Cambridge University, accessed April 21, 2014, https://www.gov.uk/government/speeches/reforming-welfare-transforming-lives
2. Iain Duncan Smith, "Speech: Jobs and Welfare Reform: Getting Britain Working," April 7, 2014, Business for Britain at Pimlico Plumbers, London, accessed July 25, 2014, https://www.gov.uk/government/speeches/jobs-and-welfare-reform-getting-britain-working
3. Morgan Whitaker, "Paul Ryan Blames Poverty on Lack of Work Ethic in Inner Cities," MSNBC.com, March 12, 2014, updated March 14, 2014, accessed April 21, 2014, http://www.msnbc.com/politicsnation/ryan-generations-men-not-working

4. This is different than the discourse about "welfare queens" who rely on benefits other than those specifically connected to being out of work.
5. David Cameron's 2011 Father's Day essay in the *Telegraph* clearly articulates these assumptions. "David Cameron: Dad's Gift to Me Was His Optimism," *The Telegraph*, June 11, 2011, accessed April 21, 2014, http://www.telegraph.co.uk/news/politics/david-cameron/8584238/David-Cameron-Dads-gift-to-me-was-his-optimism.html
6. Duncan Smith, "Reforming Welfare."
7. Patrick Butler, "Benefit Cap is Failing to Achieve Its Aims, Study Concludes," *The Guardian*, October 22, 2013, accessed April 21, 2014, http://www.theguardian.com/society/2013/oct/23/benefit-cap-failing-achieve-aims
8. "Benefit Cap," gov.uk, accessed April 21, 2014, https://www.gov.uk/benefit-cap
9. Anthony Brundage, *The English Poor Laws, 1700–1930* (New York: Palgrave, 2002), 151.
10. Brundage, *Poor Laws*, 152.
11. W.R. Garside, *British Unemployment, 1919–1939: A Study in Public Policy* (Cambridge: Cambridge University Press, 1990), 49; Frederick M. Miller, "The Unemployment Policy of the National Government, 1931–1936," *Historical Journal* 19, no. 2 (1976): 460.
12. Ann Orloff, *The Politics of Pensions: A Comparative Analysis of Britain, Canada, and the United States, 1880–1940* (Madison, WI: University of Wisconsin Press, 1993), 10.
13. "Transcript: President Obama's Jan. 7 Remarks on Unemployment Insurance Extension," *Washington Post*, January 7, 2014, accessed April 21, 2014, http://www.washingtonpost.com/politics/transcript-president-obamas-jan-7-remarks-on-unemployment/2014/01/07/79c65704-77bc-11e3-b1c5-739e63e9c9a7_story.html

Bibliography

Archival Sources

<u>Dudley Archives and Local History Service</u>
G/Du Records of the Dudley Poor Law Union
  Dudley Guardians' Minutes Books
  Dudley Guardians' Committee Books

<u>National Archives</u>
CAB Records of the Cabinet Office
HLG Records of the Ministry of Housing and Local Government
LAB Records of the Ministry of Labour
  LAB 2 Records of the Military Recruitment Department
  LAB 4 Unemployment Grants Committee and Cabinet Unemployment Committee
  LAB 8 Unemployment Insurance
MH Records of the Ministry of Health
  MH 30 Poor Law Records
  MH 32 Poor Law Correspondence
  MH 57 Local Government Board and Ministry of Health
PIN Records of the Ministry of Pensions and National Insurance
  PIN 15 War Pensions Records
  PIN 29 Office of the Umpire
T Records of the Treasury
  T 161 Records of Supply Divisions

<u>Staffordshire Record Office</u>
D585 Records of the Stourbridge Poor Law Union
  Relieving Officers' Application and Report Books
  Cases of Individual Paupers
  Stourbridge Guardians' Minute Books
  Stourbridge Union Committee Books

<u>Worcestershire Record Office</u>
Records for Powick Asylum

Periodicals

County Advertiser
County Express
Dudley Chronicle
Dudley Herald
Labour Gazette
London Times
Staffordshire Advertiser

Official Publications

Act for the Relief of the Poor, 1601, 43 Eliz. 1, c. 2.

House of Commons. "A Bill to Amend the Law in Respect of Insurance against Unemployment." *Sessional Papers* (27), 1920, vol. 5.

House of Commons. "Aged Pensioners. A Bill to Provide Pensions to the Aged Deserving Poor." *Sessional Papers* (114), 1901, vol. 1.

House of Commons. "Aged Pensioners (no. 2). A Bill to Provide Pensions for the Aged Deserving Poor." *Sessional Papers* (15), 1902, vol. 1.

House of Commons. "Old Age Pensions (no. 3). A Bill to Provide Pensions for the Aged Deserving Poor." *Sessional Papers* (146), 1906, vol. 4.

House of Commons. "Report from the Select Committee on the Aged Deserving Poor." *Sessional Papers* (296), 1899.

House of Commons. "Report of the Select Committee on Distress from Want of Employment." *Sessional Papers* (321), 1896, vol. 9.

House of Commons. "Second Report of the Select Committee on Distress from Want of Employment." *Sessional Papers* (253), 1895, vol. 8.

Imperial Conference. *Minutes of Proceedings of the Imperial Conference, Dominions No. 7.* Cd. 5745. 1911.

Local Government Board. Annual Reports, 1871–1911.

Ministry of Labour. Employment and Insurance Department, Memorandum L.E.C. 82/2, July 1923. In *Unemployment Insurance: Directions to Local Employment Committees regarding Grant of Uncovenanted Benefit* by Ministry of Labour. London: HMSO, 1924.

National Insurance Act, 1911, 1 & 2 Geo. 5, c. 55.

Parliamentary Debates, 1871–1929.

Poor Law Commission. "General Out-Door Labour Test Order." In *Eighth Annual Report of the Commission*, 1842 (389), 103–4.

Report of the Royal Commission on the Aged Poor. C. 7684, 1895.

Report of the Royal Commission on the Poor Laws and Relief of Distress. Cd. 4499. 1909.

Royal Commission on Divorce and Matrimonial Causes. *Minutes of Evidence Taken Before the Royal Commission on Divorce and Matrimonial Causes.* Vol. XVIII, Cd. 6479. 1912.

UK Census. Ancestry.co.uk. http://www.ancestry.co.uk/.

Vagrancy Act, 1824, 5 Geo. 4, c. 83.

Printed Primary Texts

Beveridge, William. *Unemployment: A Problem of Industry.* London: Longmans, Green, and Co., 1909.

Booth, Charles. *Life and Labour of the People in London.* London: Macmillan and Co., 1892.

Casson, William A., ed. *The Old Age Pensions Act, 1908, together with the Text of the Regulations . . .* 3rd ed. London: Chas. Knight and Co., 1908.

Davey, Herbert. *Maintenance and Desertion under the Poor Law and under the Summary Jurisdiction (Married Women) Act, 1895.* London: Law and Local Government Publications, 1931.

Davey, Sydney. *Maintenance and Desertion under the Poor law and under the Summary Jurisdiction (Married Women) Act, 1895*. London: Law and Local Government Publications, 1925.

Douglas, Paul H., and Aaron Director. *The Problem of Unemployment*. 1931. Reprint, New York: Arno Press, 1976.

Hannington, Wal. "Unemployment and the Labour Government." *Labour Monthly*, December 1929.

Lidbetter, Ernest James. *Maintenance and Desertion*. London: Law and Local Government Publications, 1934.

Martin, Temple Chevallier, and George Temple Martin. *The Law of Maintenance and Desertion and Affiliation*. 3rd ed. London: Stevens and Haynes, 1910.

National Industrial Conference Board. *Unemployment Insurance in Theory and Practice*. New York: The Century Co., 1922.

Rowntree, Seebohm. *Poverty: A Study of Town Life*. London: Macmillan, 1901.

Stoker, William Henry. *The Military Service Acts Practice: Containing the Consolidated Acts, Proclamations, Regulations and Orders, with Notes of Cases and Tribunal Decisions*. London: Stevens and Sons, Ltd., 1918.

Select Secondary Sources

Adams, R.J.Q. "Asquith's Choice: The May Coalition and the Coming of Conscription, 1915–1916." *Journal of British Studies* 25, no. 3 (1986): 243–63.

Adams, R.J.Q., and Philip P. Poirier. *The Conscription Controversy in Great Britain, 1900–18*. Columbus: Ohio State University Press, 1987.

Alexander, Sally. "Men's Fears and Women's Work: Responses to Unemployment in London Between the Wars." *Gender and History* 12, no. 2 (2002): 401–25.

Allen, G.C. *The Industrial Development of Birmingham and the Black Country, 1860–1927*. New York: A.M. Kelley, 1966.

Anderson, Olive. "State, Civil Society and Separation in Victorian Marriage." *Past and Present* 163, no. 1 (1999): 161–201.

August, Andrew. *Poor Women's Lives: Gender, Work, and Poverty in Late Victorian London*. Madison, NJ: Fairleigh Dickinson University Press, 1999.

Bailey, Joanne. "Masculinity and Fatherhood in England, c. 1760–1830." In *What Is Masculinity? Historical Dynamics from Antiquity to the Contemporary World*, edited by John Arnold and Sean Brady, 167–86. London: Palgrave Macmillan, 2011.

Baines, Dudley. *Migration in a Mature Economy: Emigration and Internal Migration in England and Wales, 1861–1900*. Cambridge: Cambridge University Press, 1985.

Barnsby, George. *Social Conditions in the Black Country, 1800–1900*. Wolverhampton, UK: Integrated Publishing Services, 1980.

Barnsby, George. "The Standard of Living in the Black Country during the Nineteenth Century." *Economic History Review* 2nd series 24 (1971): 220–39.

Barr, Niall. *The Lion and the Poppy: British Veterans, Politics, and Society, 1921–1939*. Westport, CT: Praeger, 2005.

Behlmer, George. "Summary Justice and Working-Class Marriage in England, 1870–1940." *Law and History Review* 12, no. 2 (1994): 229–75.

Blackburn, Sheila. "Working-Class Attitudes to Social Reform: Black Country Chainmakers and Anti-Sweating Legislation, 1880–1930." *International Review of Social History* 33, no. 1 (1988): 42–69.

Blewett, Neal. "The Franchise in the United Kingdom 1885–1918." *Past and Present* 32, no. 1 (1965): 27–56.

Bock, Gisela, and Susan James, eds. *Beyond Equality and Difference: Citizenship, Feminist Politics, and Female Subjectivity.* New York: Routledge, 1992.

Botelho, L.A. *Old Age and the English Poor Law, 1500–1700.* Rochester, NY: Boydell Press, 2004.

Bourdieu, Pierre. *Outline of a Theory of Practice.* New York: Cambridge University Press, 1977.

Bourke, Joanna. *Dismembering the Male: Men's Bodies, Britain and the Great War.* London: Reaktion Books, 1996.

——. "Housewifery in Working-Class England, 1860–1914." In *Women's Work: The English Experience, 1650–1914,* edited by Pamela Sharpe, 332–58. New York: Arnold, 1998.

——. *Working-Class Cultures in Britain, 1890–1960.* New York: Routledge, 1994.

Boyer, George R. "Poor Relief, Informal Assistance, and Short Time during the Lancashire Cotton Famine." *Explorations in Economic History* 34, no. 1 (1997): 56–76.

Brady, Sean. *Masculinity and Male Homosexuality in Britain, 1861–1913.* New York: Palgrave Macmillan, 2005.

Braybon, Gail. *Women Workers in the First World War: The British Experience.* London: Croom Helm, 1981.

Bridge, Carl, and Kent Fedorowich. "Mapping the BritishWorld." *Journal of Imperial and Commonwealth History* 31, no. 2 (2003): 1–15.

Briggs, Eric. "The Myth of Pauper Disqualification." *Social Policy and Administration* 13, no. 2 (1979): 138–41.

Brundage, Anthony. *The English Poor Laws, 1700–1930.* New York: Palgrave Macmillan, 2001.

Burnett, John. *Idle Hands: The Experience of Unemployment, 1790–1990.* New York: Routledge, 1994.

Butler, Judith. *Gender Trouble: Feminism and the Subversion of Identity.* New York: Routledge, 1990.

Canaday, Margot. *The Straight State: Sexuality and Citizenship in Twentieth-Century America.* Princeton, NJ: Princeton University Press, 2009.

Canning, Kathleen. *Gender History in Practice: Historical Perspectives on Bodies, Class, and Citizenship.* Ithaca, NY: Cornell University Press, 2006.

Canning, Kathleen, and Sonya Rose, eds. *Gender, Citizenships, and Subjectivities.* Oxford: Blackwell Publishing, 2002.

Checkland, S.G., and E.O.A. Checkland, eds. *The Poor Law Report of 1834.* New York: Penguin, 1974.

Church, Roy, and Quentin Outram. *Strikes and Solidarity: Coalfield Conflict in Britain, 1889–1966.* New York: Cambridge University Press, 1998.

Clark, Anna. "The New Poor Law and the Breadwinner Wage: Contrasting Assumptions." *Journal of Social History* 34, no. 2 (Winter 2000): 261–81.

——. *The Struggle for the Breeches: Gender and the Making of the British Working Class.* Berkeley: University of California Press, 1997.

Cohen, Deborah. *The War Come Home: Disabled Veterans in Britain and Germany, 1914–1939.* Berkeley: University of California Press, 2001.

Cohen, Miriam, and Michael Hanagan. "Politics, Industrialization and Citizenship: Unemployment Policy in England, France and the United States, 1890–1950." *International Review of Social History* 40, Supplement 3 (1995): 91–129.

Connell, R.W. *Masculinities*. 2nd ed. Berkeley: University of California Press, 2005.

Constantine, Steven. "British Emigration to the Empire-Commonwealth since 1880: From Overseas Settlement to Diaspora?" *Journal of Imperial and Commonwealth History* 31, no. 2 (2003): 16–35.

Cott, Nancy. *Public Vows: A History of Marriage and the Nation*. Cambridge, MA: Harvard University Press, 2000.

Cretney, Stephen. *Family Law in the Twentieth Century: A History*. New York: Oxford University Press, 2005.

Critchlow, Donald T., and Charles H. Parker, eds. *With Us Always: A History of Private Charity and Public Welfare*. Lanham, MD: Rowman and Littlefield, 1998.

Croll, Andy. "Strikers and the Right to Relief in Late Victorian Britain: The Making of the *Merthyr Tydfil* Judgment of 1900." *Journal of British Studies* 52, no. 1 (2013): 128–52.

———. "Starving Strikers and the Limits of the 'Humanitarian Discovery of Hunger' in Late Victorian Britain." *International Review of Social History* 56, no. 1 (2011): 103–31.

Crowther, M.A. "Family Responsibility and State Responsibility in Britain before the Welfare State." *Historical Journal* 25, no. 1 (1982): 131–45.

———. *The Workhouse System, 1834–1929: The History of an English Social Institution*. Athens, GA: University of Georgia Press, 1982.

Daly, Mary. *The Gender Division of Welfare: The Impact of the British and German Welfare States*. New York: Cambridge University Press, 2000.

Davis, Jennifer. "A Poor Man's System of Justice: The London Police Courts in the Second Half of the Nineteenth Century." *Historical Journal* 27, no. 2 (1984): 309–35.

Daunton, Martin, ed. *Charity, Self-Interest and Welfare in the English Past*. London: UCL Press, 1996.

Deacon, Alan. *In Search of the Scrounger: The Administration of Unemployment Insurance in Britain, 1920–1931*. London: Bell [for the Social Administration Research Trust], 1976.

Denman, James, and Paul McDonald. "Unemployment Statistics from 1881 to the Present Day." *Labour Market Trends* (January 1996): 5–18.

Dewey, P.E. "Military Recruiting and the British Labour Force during the First World War." *Historical Journal* 27, no. 1 (1984): 199–223.

Douglas, Roy. "Voluntary Enlistment in the First World War and the Work of the Parliamentary Recruiting Committee." *Journal of Modern History* 42, no. 4 (1970): 564–85.

Driver, Felix. *Power and Pauperism: The Workhouse System, 1834–1884*. New York: Cambridge University Press, 1993.

Evans, Tanya. "The Other Woman and Her Child: Extra-Marital Affairs and Illegitimacy in Twentieth-Century Britain." *Women's History Review* 20, no. 1 (2011): 47–65.

Finlayson, Geoffrey. *Citizen, State, and Social Welfare in Britain, 1830–1990*. New York: Oxford University Press, 1994.

Flynn, George Q. *Conscription and Democracy: The Draft in France, Great Britain, and the United States.* Westport, CT: Greenwood Press, 2002.

Foucault, Michel. *The History of Sexuality. Volume I: An Introduction.* New York: Vintage Books, 1990.

———. *Discipline and Punish: The Birth of the Prison.* New York: Vintage Books, 1995.

Frader, Laura Levine. *Breadwinners and Citizens: Gender in the Making of the French Social Model.* Durham, NC: Duke University Press, 2008.

Francis, Martin. "The Domestication of the Male? Recent Research on Nineteenth- and Twentieth-Century British Masculinity." *Historical Journal* 45, no. 3 (2002): 637–52.

Garside, W.R. *British Unemployment, 1919–1939: A Study in Public Policy.* Cambridge: Cambridge University Press, 1990.

Gennard, John. *Financing Strikers.* New York: Wiley, 1977.

Gibson, Colin S. *Dissolving Wedlock.* New York: Routledge, 1994.

Gilbert, Bentley B. "David Lloyd George: Land, the Budget, and Social Reform." *American Historical Review* 81, no. 5 (1976): 1058–66.

———. *British Social Policy, 1914–1939.* Ithaca, NY: Cornell University Press, 1970.

———. *The Evolution of National Insurance in Great Britain: The Origins of the Welfare State.* London: Michael Joseph, 1966.

Gillis, John R. *For Better, For Worse: British Marriages, 1600 to the Present.* New York: Oxford University Press, 1988.

Glynn, Sean. "Employment, Unemployment and the Labour Market." In *British Social Welfare in the Twentieth Century*, edited by Robert M. Page and Richard Silburn, 180–98. New York: St. Martin's Press, 1999.

Gordon, Linda. *Pitied But Not Entitled: Single Mothers and the History of Welfare.* New York: Free Press, 1994.

———. "The New Feminist Scholarship on the Welfare State." In *Women, the State, and Welfare*, edited by Linda Gordon, 9–35. Madison: University of Wisconsin Press, 1990.

Gorman, Daniel. *Imperial Citizenship: Empire and the Question of Belonging.* New York: Manchester University Press, 2006.

Gosden, P.H.G.H. *The Friendly Societies in England, 1815–1875.* New York: Barnes and Noble, 1961.

Gregory, Adrian. *The Last Great War: British Society and the First World War.* New York: Cambridge University Press, 2008.

Grieves, Keith. *The Politics of Manpower, 1914–18.* New York: St. Martin's Press, 1988.

Gullace, Nicoletta. *'The Blood of Our Sons': Men, Women, and the Renegotiation of British Citizenship during the Great War.* New York: Palgrave Macmillan, 2004.

———. "White Feathers and Wounded Men: Female Patriotism and the Memory of the Great War." *Journal of British Studies* 36, no. 2 (1997): 178–206.

Gutteridge, H.C. "The International Enforcement of Maintenance Orders." *International Law Quarterly* 2, no. 2 (1948): 155–72.

Haines, Robin F. *Emigration and the Labouring Poor: Australian Recruitment in Britain and Ireland, 1831–1960.* New York: St. Martin's Press, 1997.

Hammerton, A. James. *Cruelty and Companionship: Conflict in Nineteenth-Century Married Life.* New York: Routledge, 1992.

Hanagan, Michael. "Citizenship, Claim-Making, and the Right to Work: Britain, 1884–1911." *Theory and Society* 26, no. 4 (1997): 449–74.

Hancock, K.J. "The Reduction of Unemployment as a Problem of Public Policy, 1920–29." *Economic History Review* 15, no. 2 (1962): 328–43.

Hannington, Wal. *Unemployed Struggles, 1919–1936; My Life and Struggles Amongst the Unemployed.* New York: Barnes & Noble Books, 1973.

Harris, Bernard. "Gender and Social Citizenship in Historical Perspective: The Development of Welfare Policy in England and Wales from the Poor Law to Beveridge." In *Gender and Well-Being: The Role of Institutions,* edited by Elisabetta Addis, Paloma de Villota, Florence Degavre, and John Eriksen, 29–62. Burlington, VT: Ashgate Publishing, 2011.

———. *The Origins of the British Welfare State: Social Welfare in England and Wales, 1800–1945.* New York: Palgrave Macmillan, 2004.

Harris, José. *Unemployment and Politics: A Study in English Social Policy, 1886–1914.* Oxford: Clarendon Press, 1972.

Hay, Roy. *The Origins of the Liberal Welfare Reforms, 1906–1914.* London: Macmillan, 1975.

Hennon, Charles B., Suzanne Loker, and Rosemary Walker, eds. *Gender and Home-Based Employment.* Westport, CT: Auburn House, 2000.

Higgs, Edward. "Women, Occupations and Work in the Nineteenth Century." *History Workshop Journal* 23, no. 1 (1987): 59–80.

———. "Household and Work in the Nineteenth-Century Censuses of England and Wales." *Journal of the Society of Archivists* 11, no. 3 (1990): 73–7.

Honeyman, Katrina, and Jordan Goodman. "Women's Work, Gender Conflict, and Labour Markets in Europe, 1500–1900." *Economic History Review* 44, no. 4 (1991): 608–28.

Horne, John. "Masculinity in Politics and War in the Age of Nation-States and World Wars, 1850–1950." In *Masculinities in Politics and War: Gendering Modern History,* edited by Stefan Dudink, Karen Hagemann, and John Tosh, 22–40. Manchester: Manchester University Press, 2004.

Horrell, Sara, and Jane Humphries. "The Origins and Expansion of the Male Breadwinner Family: The Case of Nineteenth Century Britain." *International Review of Social History* 42, Supplement S5 (1997): 25–64.

Humphreys, Robert. *No Fixed Abode: A History of Responses to the Roofless and Rootless in Britain.* New York: St. Martin's Press, 1999.

Humphries, Jane. "Female-Headed Households in Early Industrial Britain: the Vanguard of the Proletariat?" *Labour History Review* 63, no. 1 (1998): 31–65.

Hurren, Elizabeth. *Protesting About Pauperism: Poverty, Politics, and Poor Relief in Late-Victorian England, c. 1870–1914.* Rochester, NY: Boydell and Brewer, 2007.

Igra, Anna R. *Wives without Husbands: Marriage, Desertion, and Welfare in New York, 1900–1935.* Chapel Hill: University of North Carolina Press, 2006.

Ingraham, Chrys, ed. *Thinking Straight: The Power, the Promise, and the Paradox of Heterosexuality.* New York: Routledge, 2005.

Jackson, Stevi. "Gender, Sexuality, and Heterosexuality: The Complexity (and Limits) of Heteronormativity." *Feminist Theory* 7, no. 1 (2006): 105–21.

Janssens, Angelique. "The Rise and Decline of the Male Breadwinner Family? An Overview of the Debate." *International Review of Social History* 42, Supplement S5 (1997): 1–23.

Jones, Gill. "Short-Term Reciprocity in Parent-Child Economic Exchanges." In *Families and Households: Divisions and Change,* edited by Catherine Marsh and Sara Arber, 26–44. Basingstoke, UK: Macmillan, 1992.

Kent, Susan Kingsley. *Making Peace: The Reconstruction of Gender in Interwar Britain.* Princeton, NJ: Princeton University Press, 1993.

Kerber, Linda K. *No Constitutional Right to be Ladies: Women and the Obligations of Citizenship.* New York: Hill and Wang, 1998.

Kessler-Harris, Alice. *In Pursuit of Equity: Women, Men, and the Quest for Economic Citizenship in 20th-Century America.* New York: Oxford University Press, 2001.

King, Desmond S. *Actively Seeking Work? The Politics of Unemployment and Welfare Policy in the United States and Great Britain.* Chicago: University of Chicago Press, 1995.

King, Steven, and Alannah Tomkins, eds. *The Poor in England, 1700–1850: An Economy of Makeshifts.* New York: Palgrave, 2003.

Koven, Seth. "Remembering and Dismemberment: Crippled Children, Wounded Soldiers, and the Great War in Britain." *American Historical Review* 99, no. 4 (1994): 1167–202.

Koven, Seth, and Sonya Michel. "Womanly Duties: Maternalist Politics and the Origins of Welfare States in France, Germany, Great Britain, and the United States." *American Historical Review* 95, no. 4 (October 1990): 1076–108.

Kowalsky, Meaghan. "'This Honourable Obligation': The King's Roll National Scheme for Disabled Ex-Servicemen 1915–1944." *European Review of History* 14, no. 4 (2007): 567–84.

Laybourn, Keith. *Unemployment and Employment Policies Concerning Women in Britain, 1900–1951.* Lewiston, NY: Edwin Mellen Press, 2002.

Lees, Lynn Hollen. *The Solidarities of Strangers: The English Poor Laws and the People, 1700–1948.* New York: Cambridge University Press, 1998.

Leese, Peter. *Shell Shock: Traumatic Neurosis and the British Soldiers of the First World War.* Basingstoke, UK: Palgrave Macmillan, 2002.

Levine-Clark, Marjorie. *Beyond the Reproductive Body: The Politics of Women's Health and Work in Early Victorian England.* Columbus: Ohio State University Press, 2004.

———. "Engendering Relief: Women, Ablebodiedness, and the New Poor Law in Early Victorian England." *Journal of Women's History* 11, no. 4 (2000): 107–30.

———. "The Politics of Preference: Masculinity, Marital Status and Unemployment Relief in Post-First World War Britain." *Cultural and Social History* 7, no. 2 (2010): 233–52.

———. "From 'Relief' to 'Justice and Protection': The Maintenance of Deserted Wives, British Masculinity and Imperial Citizenship, 1870–1920." *Gender and History* 22, no. 2 (2010): 302–21.

Levitan, Kathrin. "Redundancy, the 'Surplus Woman' Problem, and the British Census, 1851–1861." *Women's History Review* 17, no. 3 (2008): 359–76.

Lewis, Jane. "Gender and the Development of Welfare Regimes." *Journal of European Policy* 2, no. 3 (1992): 159–73.

———. "Gender and Welfare in Modern Europe." *Past and Present* 1, Supplement (2006): 39–54.

———. *The Voluntary Sector, the State & Social Work in Britain: The Charity Organization Society/Family Welfare Association since 1869.* Aldershot, UK: Edward Elgar, 1995.

———. *Women and Social Policies in Europe: Work, Family and the State*. Brookfield, VT: Edward Elgar, 1993.

Light, Alison. *Forever England: Femininity, Literature, and Conservatism between the Wars*. New York: Routledge, 1991.

Lister, Ruth. *Citizenship: Feminist Perspectives*. New York: NYU Press, 2003.

Lomas, Janis. "'Delicate Duties': Issues of Class and Respectability in Government Policy Towards the Wives and Widows of British Soldiers in the Era of the Great War." *Women's History Review 9*, no. 1 (2000): 123–47.

MacKinnon, Mary. "English Poor Law Policy and the Crusade against Outrelief." *Journal of Economic History 47*, no. 3 (1987): 603–25.

Magee, Gary B., and Andrew S. Thompson. "The Global and the Local: Explaining Migrant Remittance Flows in the English-Speaking World, 1880–1914." *Journal of Economic History 66*, no. 1 (2006): 177–202.

Magee, Gary B., and Andrew S. Thompson. "'Lines of Credit, Debts of Obligation': Migrant Remittances to Britain, c.1875–1913." *Economic History Review 59*, no. 3 (2006): 539–77.

Marshall, T.H. "Citizenship and Social Class." In *Inequality and Society*, edited by Jeff Manza and Michael Sauder, 148–54. New York: W.W. Norton and Co., 2009.

McLaren, Angus. *The Trials of Masculinity: Policing Sexual Boundaries, 1870–1930*. Chicago: University of Chicago Press, 1997.

McClelland, Keith. "'England's Greatness, the Working Man'." In *Defining the Victorian Nation: Class, Race, Gender and the Reform Act of 1867*, edited by Catherine Hall, Keith McClelland, and Jane Rendall, 71–118. New York: Cambridge University Press, 2000.

———. "Masculinity and the 'Representative Artisan' in Britain, 1850–80." In *Manful Assertions: Masculinities in Britain since 1800*, edited by Michael Roper and John Tosh, 44–73. New York: Routledge, 1991.

McDermott, James. *British Military Service Tribunals, 1916–1918: 'A Very Much Abused Body of Men'*. Manchester: Manchester University Press, 2011.

———. "Conscience and the Military Service Tribunals during the First World War: Experiences in Northamptonshire." *War in History 17*, no. 1 (2010): 60–85.

McGregor, O.R., Louis Jacques Blom-Cooper, and Colin S. Gibson. *Separated Spouses: A Study of the Matrimonial Jurisdiction of Magistrates' Courts*. London: Duckworth, 1970.

Meyer, Jessica. *Men of War: Masculinity and the First World War in Britain*. New York: Palgrave Macmillan, 2009.

Mink, Gwendolyn. "Aren't Poor Single Mothers Women? Feminists, Welfare Reform, and Welfare Justice." In *Whose Welfare?* edited by Gwendolyn Mink, 171–88. Ithaca, NY: Cornell University Press, 1999.

Minor, Iris. "Working-Class Women and Matrimonial Law Reform, 1890–1914." In *Ideology and the Labour Movement*, edited by David E. Martin and David Rubenstein, 103–24. London: Croom Helm, 1979.

Monger, David. *Patriotism and Propaganda in First World War Britain: the National War Aims Committee and Civilian Morale*. Liverpool: Liverpool University Press, 2012.

Morgan, Carol. *Women Workers and Gender Identities, 1835–1913: the Cotton and Metal Industries in England*. New York: Routledge, 2001.

Morris, Lydia. *Dangerous Classes: The Underclass and Social Citizenship*. New York: Routledge, 1994.

Morris, Margaret. *The General Strike*. Harmondsworth, UK: Penguin Books, 1976.

Orloff, Ann. "Gender in the Welfare State." *Annual Review of Sociology* 22 (1996): 51–78.

Orloff, Ann Shola. "Gendering the Comparative Analysis of Welfare States: An Unfinished Agenda." *Sociological Theory* 27, no. 3 (2009): 317–43.

————. *The Politics of Pensions: A Comparative Analysis of Britain, Canada, and the United States, 1880–1940*. Madison: University of Wisconsin Press, 1993.

Ottaway, Susannah R. *The Decline of Life: Old Age in Eighteenth-Century England*. New York: Cambridge University Press, 2004.

Palliser, D.M. *The Staffordshire Landscape*. London: Hodder and Stoughton, 1976.

Parsons, Harold. *Portrait of the Black Country*. London: R. Hale, 1986.

Pateman, Carol. *The Sexual Contract*. Stanford, CA: Stanford University Press, 1988.

Peden, G.C. "The 'Treasury View' on Public Works and Employment in the Interwar Period." *Economic History Review* 37, no. 2 (1984): 167–81.

Pedersen, Susan. *Family, Dependence, and the Origins of the Welfare State in Britain and France, 1914–1945*. New York: Cambridge University Press, 1993.

Pedersen, Susan. "Gender, Welfare, and Citizenship in Britain during the Great War." *American Historical Review* 95, no. 4 (1990): 983–1006.

Perkins, Anne. *A Very British Strike: 3 May – 12 May 1926*. London: Macmillan, 2006.

Perry, Matt. *Bread and Work: The Experience of Unemployment 1918–39*. London: Pluto Press, 2000.

Phillips, G.A. *The General Strike: The Politics of Industrial Conflict*. London: Weidenfeld and Nicholson, 1976.

Pinker, Robert. "New Liberalism and the Middle Way." In *British Social Welfare in the Twentieth Century*, edited by Robert M. Page and Richard Silburn, 80–104. New York: St. Martin's Press, 1999.

Popay, Jennie, Jeff Hearn, and Jeanette Edwards, eds. *Men, Gender Divisions, and Welfare*. New York: Routledge, 1998.

Riley, Denise. *'Am I That Name': Feminism and the Category of Women in History*. Minneapolis: University of Minnesota Press, 1987.

Riley, James C. *Sick, Not Dead: The Health of British Workingmen during the Mortality Decline*. Baltimore: Johns Hopkins, 1997.

Robb, George. *British Culture and the First World War*. New York: Palgrave, 2002.

Rose, Sonya O. *Limited Livelihoods: Gender and Class in Nineteenth-Century England*. Berkeley: University of California Press, 1992.

————. "Respectable Men, Disorderly Others: The Language of Gender and the Lancashire Weavers' Strike of 1878 in Britain." *Gender and History* 5, no. 3 (1993): 382–97.

Rosenheil, Sasha, ed. *Beyond Citizenship: Feminism and the Transformation of Belonging*. New York: Palgrave Macmillan, 2013.

Ross, Ellen. *Love and Toil: Motherhood in Outcast London, 1870–1918*. New York: Oxford University Press, 1993.

Rowntree, Griselda, and Norman H. Carter. "The Resort to Divorce in England and Wales, 1858–1957." *Population Studies* 11, no. 3 (1958): 188–233.

Ryan, P.A. "'Poplarism' 1894–1930." In *The Origins of British Social Policy*, edited by Pat Thane, 56–83. London: Croom Helm, 1978.

Ryan, Patricia. "The Poor Law in 1926." In *The General Strike*, edited by Margaret Morris, 358–78. Harmondsworth: Penguin Books, 1976.

Savage, Mike. "Class and Labour History." In *Class and Other Identities: Gender, Religion, and Ethnicity in the Writing of European Labour History*, edited by Lex Heerma van Voss and Marcel van der Linden, 55–71. New York: Berghahn Books, 2002.

Savage, Gail. "The Operation of the 1857 Divorce Act, 1860–1910: A Research Note." *Journal of Social History* 16, no. 4 (1983): 103–10.

Schilt, Kristen, and Laurel Westbrook. "Doing Gender, Doing Heteronormativity: 'Gender Normals,' Transgender People, and the Social Maintenance of Heterosexuality." *Gender and Society* 23, no. 4 (2009): 440–64.

Scott, James C. *Seeing Like a State: How Certain Schemes to Improve the Human Condition Have Failed*. New Haven, CT: Yale University Press, 1998.

Scott, Joan W. "Gender: A Useful Category of Historical Analysis." *American Historical Review* 91, no. 5 (1986): 1053–75.

Seccombe, Wally. "Patriarchy Stabilized: The Construction of the Male Breadwinner Norm in Nineteenth Century Britain." *Social History* 11, no. 1 (1986): 53–76.

Shah, Nayan. *Stranger Intimacy: Contesting Race, Sexuality, and the Law in the North American West*. Berkeley: University of California Press, 2011.

Shenk, Gerald E. *'Work or Fight!' Race, Gender, and the Draft in World War One*. New York: Palgrave Macmillan, 2005.

Silva, Elizabeth Bortolaia. "Introduction." In *Good Enough Mothering? Feminist Perspectives on Lone Motherhood*, edited by Elizabeth Bortolaia Silva, 1–9. New York: Routledge, 1996.

Simonton, Deborah. *A History of European Women's Work: 1700 to the Present*. New York: Routledge, 1998.

Snell, K.D.M., and J. Millar. "Lone-Parent Families and the Welfare State: Past and Present." *Continuity and Change* 2, no. 3 (1987): 387–422.

Solinger, Rickie. *Wake Up Little Susie*. New York: Routledge, 2000.

———. *Beggars and Choosers: How the Politics of Choice Shapes Adoption, Abortion, and Welfare in the United States*. New York: Hill and Wang, 2001.

Southall, Humphrey, and David Gilbert. "A Good Time to Wed? Marriage and Economic Distress in England and Wales, 1839–1914." *Economic History Review* 49, no. 1 (1996): 35–57.

Stedman Jones, Gareth. *Outcast London: A Study in the Relationship between Classes in Victorian Society*. New York: Oxford University Press, 1971.

Stone, Lawrence. *Road to Divorce, England 1530–1987*. New York: Oxford University Press, 1990.

Strange, Julie-Marie. "Fatherhood, Providing, and Attachment in Late Victorian and Edwardian Working-Class Families." *Historical Journal* 55, no. 4 (2012): 1007–27.

Strikwerda, Eric. "'Married men should, I feel, be treated differently': Work, Relief, and Unemployed Men on the Urban Canadian Prairies, 1929–1932." *Left History* 12, no. 1 (2007): 30–51.

Thane, Pat. *Old Age in English History: Past Experiences, Present Issues*. New York: Oxford University Press, 2000.

———. "Old People and Their Families in the English Past." In *Charity, Self-Interest and Welfare in the English Past*, edited by Martin Daunton, 113–38. New York: Routledge, 1996.

———. "Women and the Poor Law in Victorian and Edwardian England." *History Workshop Journal* 6 (Autumn 1978): 29–51.

Thom, Deborah. *Nice Girls, Rude Girls: Women Workers in World War I*. New York: I.B. Tauris, 1998.

Todd, Selina. "'You'd the Feeling You Wanted to Help': Young Women, Employment and the Family in Inter-War England." In *Women and Work Culture: Britain, c. 1850–1950*, edited by Krista Cowman and Louise A. Jackson, 123–140. Burlington, VT: Ashgate, 2005.

Tosh, John. *Manliness and Masculinities in Nineteenth-Century Britain: Essays on Gender, Family, and Empire*. New York: Pearson Longman, 2005.

Trainor, Richard H. *Black Country Elites: The Exercise of Authority in an Industrial Area, 1830–1900*. New York: Oxford University Press, 1993.

Valenze, Deborah. *The First Industrial Woman*. New York: Oxford University Press, 1995.

Vincent, David. *Poor Citizens: The State and the Poor in Twentieth-Century Britain*. London: Longman, 1991.

Wall, Richard. "Relationships between the Generations in British Families, Past and Present." In *Families and Households: Divisions and Change*, edited by Catherine Marsh and Sara Arber, 63–85. Basingstoke, UK: Macmillan, 1992.

Whiteside, Noel. "Constructing Unemployment: Britain and France in Historical Perspective." *Social Policy and Administration* 48, no. 1 (2014): 67–85.

Williams, Karel. *From Pauperism to Poverty*. London: Routledge and Kegan Paul, 1981.

Williams, Samantha. *Poverty, Gender, and the Life-Cycle under the English Poor Law, 1760–1834*. Rochester, NY: Boydell and Brewer, 2011.

Williamson, Bill. *Class, Culture, and Community: A Biographical Study of Social Change in Mining*. Boston: Routledge and Kegan Paul, 1982.

Woollacott, Angela. *On Her Their Lives Depend: Munitions Workers in the Great War*. Berkeley: University of California Press, 1994.

Index

and masculinity, 2, 3, 5, 6, 8–9, 87, 96, 233, 238
and old age pensions, 197
and poor law relief, 36–7
and suicide, 75, 76–7
and unemployment, 34, 75, 232–3
and welfare, 232–3
Derby, Lord (Edward George Villiers Stanley), 119, 120
Derby Scheme, 118–20, 121
and marital status, 118–20
Desertion, *see* wives (abandoned)
Deservedness, 8, 30, 36–8, 40, 41, 46, 49, 51, 52, 66, 83, 84, 89, 93–4, 96
of abandoned wives, 209, 210
of aged poor, 183–4, 197–8, 204
and citizenship, 37–8
of elderly men, 183–4
and family liability, 66, 67, 69–70
and fatherhood, 64–5
and honest poverty, 17, 50–1, 70, 235, 237
and marital status, 50–2, 62–3, 64, 66, 233
and military service, 136
and old age pensions, 199, 200–1
and Poor Law, 36–7, 45–6, 62, 63–4
of single mothers, 229–30
of strikers, 159, 162
and strikes, 159–60, 175–8, 179–80
and task work, 44–5
and unemployment benefit, 83, 86, 93, 105
of veterans, 139–41, 142–6, 147–52, 154–5, 158
and welfare, 233, 237
and work imperative, 34–5, 66, 106, 233, 234
and work relief, 35, 66
Dewey, P.E., 125
Disabled veterans, 140–1, 142–4, 147, 153
employment of, 262n62
and Poor Law, 140–3
preferences for, 147, 152, 153, *see also* preferential hiring of veterans
unemployment of, 139, 153

Divorce, 213–14
and Poor Person's Procedure (1914), 271n29
Dole, *see* unemployment benefit
Domestic duties
and women's deservedness, 215–16
Domestic service
and genuinely seeking work test, 100, 103
for married women, 100, 103
and unemployment benefit, 97–8, 100, 103
and women's work, 97–8, 103
Domestic violence, 212, 273n51
and maintenance orders, 212–13, 215, 217
Draft (military), *see* conscription
Dudley Board of Guardians, 29–32, 43, 44, 45, 46, 63–4, 72, 161, 165, 167
Dudley Poor Law Union, 11–15, 29, 35–6, 84, 161
see also Black Country; Black Country industries
Duncan Smith, Iain, 232–3

Elderly, *see* aged poor
Emigration, 223–4
and maintenance of wives and children, 224
Employment, *see* seeking work; unemployment; women's work; work
Enfranchisement, *see* voting
Ex-servicemen, *see* veterans

Family economies
and marital separation, 216–17
and women's work, 7, 73–4, 79, 193–7, 201, 204–5, 220, 236–7, 268n35, 269n51
Family liability, 2, 66, 67, 70, 80–1, 83, 91, 93, 98, 216, 237, 267n6
for abandoned wives, 211
and aged poor, 183, 197–8, 204
across the British Empire, 225–7
as cause of suicide, 75–7
as cause of theft, 70–2
as cause of welfare fraud, 72–3

and masculinity, 109–10, 111, 114, 115, 118, 120–4, 130, 136
and single men, 109–10, 117–21, 123–4, 136–7
as solution to unemployment, 112–13
and unskilled workers, 122–3
and voluntarism, 110–11, 118
versus war work, 115–16, 123, 136
and work imperative, 111, 114, 122–3, 136
see also service imperative; veterans
Military service exemptions, 124–36
dataset, 125–6
and family liability, 128–30, 135–6
and marital status, 126, 128–36
public opinion about, 126
and separation allowances, 135–6
and skill, 132
tribunals, 124–6, 130–1
and war work, 132–4
Military service organizations, *see* British Legion; National Federation for Discharged and Demobilised Sailors and Soldiers
Miners' Federation, 160–1, 178–9
Miners' strikes (1921 and 1926), 160–1, 166–70, 171, 172, 180, 222, 264n8
in the Black Country, 161
see also General Strike (1926); Merthyr Tydfil Decision; strikers; strikes
Ministry of Health, 4
and relief to strikers, 162, 164–8, 172
Minor, Iris, 218
Mond, Alfred, 164, 165, 166
Motherhood
and genuinely seeking work test, 103
see also single mothers

National Federation for Discharged and Demobilised Sailors and Soldiers (NFDDSS), 140, 142, 150, 152, 153, 157
National identity
and masculinity, 87
and military service, 115–16, 121

and work imperative, 46
see also citizenship, imperial
National Insurance Act of 1911, 41–2, 85, 87, 234–5
National Unemployed Workers Movement, 47
New Liberalism, 6, 38–9
New Poor Law, *see* Poor Law
Not genuinely seeking work, *see* genuinely seeking work test

Obama, Barack, 239
Old age pensions (OAPs), 184, 187, 197–204
Act of 1908, 197, 200, 202, 269n65
and citizenship, 199–201, 202
and dependency, 197
and deservedness, 199, 200–1
and gender, 197, 199, 201, 204
and honest poverty, 197, 199–200, 202–4
and maintenance of parents, 201–2
and Poor Law, 199–200
and poor law relief, 199, 200–1, 202, 204
and women, 201, 202, 204
and work imperative, 199, 202, 204
Orloff, Ann, 6
Out-of-Work Donation (OWD), 88, 139, 148–9, 150, 152
and marital status, 148–9
and single men, 149, 150–2
and veterans, 138–9, 148–52
and women, 148–9
Outrelief, 5, 28, 29, 33, 43, 44, 63, 233, 235
changing attitudes toward, 200–1
see also poor law relief

Palliser, D.M., 17
Parliamentary debates, 85–7, 120–4, 143–4, 200–2
Patriotism
and marital status, 118–20, 121–2
and war work, 116
Paupers and pauperism, 5, 9, 26, 33, 42, 46, 233–4, 243n36
versus unemployed men, 33, 34, 35, 36–7, 46

Pedersen, Susan, 117, 148
Perry, Matt, 5, 43, 75
Poor Law, 4–5, 10–11, 21, 27–8, 41,
    82–3, 166, 238, 241n6
  and ablebodiedness, 4, 28, 33
  and aged poor, 184–5, 199
  and citizenship, 5, 43–4, 83
  and deservedness, 36–7, 45–6, 62,
    63–4
  and family liability, 62, 63–4
  and honest poverty, 36–7, 64,
    233–4
  and loafers, 28, 33, 36–7, 45–6
  and masculinity, 4–5, 26–7, 27–8,
    41, 83, 233–4
  and old age pensions, 199–200
  and single mothers, 55, 209,
    270n11
  stigma of, 5, 26–7, 34, 36–7, 45,
    143, 245n5
  and task work, *see* Labour Test
  and unemployment, 4–6, 10, 17,
    25–7, 36–7
  and veterans, 139, 140–6
  and voting, 5, 11, 28–9, 31–2, 42,
    234
  and work imperative, 36–7, 45–6,
    144
  see also applicants for poor law
    relief; Labour Test; outrelief; poor
    law relief
Poor Law Amendment Act of 1834,
    see Poor Law
Poor law relief
  for abandoned wives, 208, 209–11
  to aged poor, 185, 187–8, 191,
    197–9, 204, 269n66
  applications for, *see* applicants for
    poor law relief
  and citizenship, 33, 37–8, 233–4,
    238–9
  and General Strike (1926), 159
  and honest poverty, 30–1, 33,
    233–4, 235, 238–9
  and maintenance of parents, 184–8,
    189–92, 193–4, 195–6, 204
  and maintenance of wives, 208,
    210–12, 213, 216–18, 220–1,
    222–3, 224–7, 230

  and maintenance orders, 210–11
  and marital status, 62–4
  for neglected women, 196, 209,
    217–18
  and old age pensions, 199, 200–1,
    202, 204
  to strikers, 167–8, 172
  and strikes, 159–60, 161–9, 179–80
  to unemployed men, 3–6, 9, 26–9,
    34, 36–8, 39–40, 41, 43–4, 45–8
  and unemployment, 29–30, 31–2,
    36, 245n5
  and vagrancy, 221
  and veterans, 140–1, 142–6, 150–1
  and voting, 5, 33
  work relief as alternative to, 34–5,
    36, 48–9, 234
  see also applicants for poor law
    relief; Labour Test; outrelief
Poplarism, 264n23
Poverty, *see* applicants for poor law
    relief; honest poverty; paupers
    and pauperism; Poor Law; poor
    law relief; unemployment; welfare
Preferential hiring of veterans, 152–7,
    158
  and disabled veterans, 147, 152,
    153
  and marital status, 154–5, 157
  and masculinity, 153
  trade union resistance to, 153,
    154–5, 156–7
  by Unemployment Grants
    Committee, 154–5
  and work imperative, 153
  and work relief, 154–5
  see also veterans, preferences for
Public works, *see* work relief

Relieving Officers
  Application and Report Books, 20, 52
  National Association of, 168
Representation of the People Act of
    1918, 38, 42, 139, 234
Residuum, *see* loafers; paupers and
    pauperism
Respectability, 2, 9, 96
  and applicants for poor law relief,
    209